BEN-GURION

MICHAEL BAR-ZOHAR

BEN-GURION

A Biography

WITHDRAWI

The centennial edition

Translated by
PERETZ KIDRON

ADAMA BOOKS, NEW YORK

Library of Congress Cataloging-in-Publication Data
Bar-Zohar, Michael, 1938–
Ben-Gurion.

Abridged translation of: Ben-Gurion.
Includes index.
1. Ben-Gurion, David, 1886–1973.   2. Prime ministers – Israel –
Biography.   3. Zionists – Palestine – Biography.
I. Title.

DS125.3.B37B28213   1986   956.94′05′0924 [B]   86-10741
ISBN 0-915361-59-0
ISBN 0-915361-60-4 (PBK.)

Adama Books, 306 West 38 Street, New York, N.Y. 10018
Printed in Israel

Contents

List of Illustrations

Acknowledgements

The author and publishers would like to thank the following for kind permission to reproduce the photographs: Yad Ben-Gurion, the Ben-Gurion Foundation, 1, 2, 3, 4, 5. 9, 11, 15, 21, 24, 28; Archive and Museum of the Jewish Labor Movement, 6; Jabotinsky House, 7; Jewish Agency Archive, 8; Israel Government Press Office, 12, 13, 14, 16, 17, 18, 19, 20, 23, 25, 26, 27, 29, 30; Mrs Sarah Stein, 22.

The two maps of Israel were drawn by John Payne.

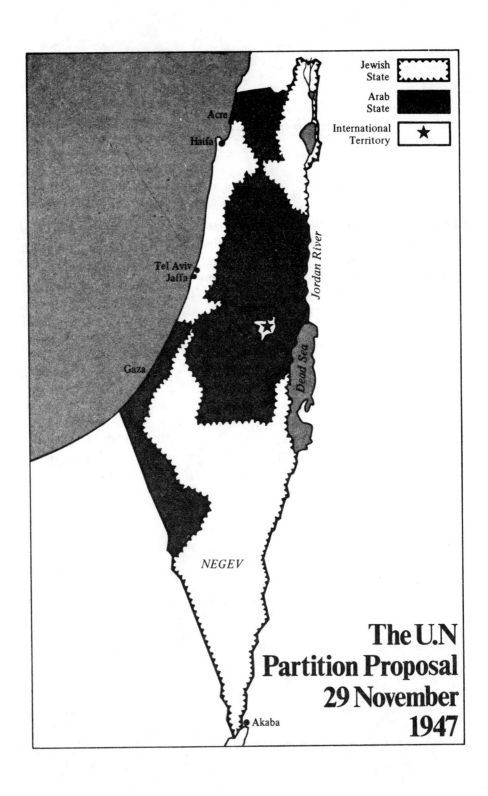

The U.N
Partition Proposal
29 November
1947

Safed •

Tiberias •

Nazareth •

Sejera •

Kfar Vitkin •

Rosh Ha'ayin •
Petah Tikvah •

Rishon-le-Zion •

Ramleh •

Rehovot •
Latrun

Etzion
bloc •

Hebron •

Gaza Strip

Dimona •

• Sdeh Boker

Eilat •

The 1949
Armistice Lines

Preface

In April 1964 I published my first book, *Suez Ultra-Secret*, which dealt with the extraordinary alliance between France and Israel during the Suez War. The book was based on my Ph.D. thesis, recently approved by the Paris University. *Suez Ultra-Secret* came out simultaneously in Paris and Tel Aviv, and I sent a dedicated copy to David Ben-Gurion, who had retired from power barely ten months earlier. A few days later I received a warm letter of thanks from him.

I had never met "the Old Man" before, but encouraged by the friendly tone of his letter, I asked his secretary to convey two questions to him: would he agree to my writing his biography? And would he allow me free use of his archives? I had no illusions and didn't really expect that he would seriously consider my approach. Many distinguished writers, scholars and university dons had vainly tried to obtain Ben-Gurion's co-operation and the use of his documents, but the Old Man had agreed only to be interviewed by two writers, who never caught a glimpse of his files; the biographies they produced were mostly anecdotical and inaccurate.

How big was my surprise when a few weeks later Ben-Gurion's secretary phoned me, to give me the short answer: "The Old Man agrees." I didn't believe that he really meant it. I assumed that Ben-Gurion had agreed only to meet me and hear my request. I went back to France, where my French publisher assured me that he would gladly commission me to write Ben-Gurion's biography. I then prepared a detailed aide-memoire in which I explained at length why I thought I was able to undertake this considerable challenge. I went to see Ben-Gurion on 23 November 1964, carrying with me the bulky aide-memoire.

"So you are Bar-Zohar," he said when I entered his study. We exchanged a few comments on my Suez book, and then he abruptly asked me: "Well, what are the questions?"

I was taken aback. "I brought you this aide-memoire," I started.

"No, no," Ben-Gurion impatiently said. "You are going to write my biography, aren't you? So what are your questions? How do you want to work? What material do you need?"

It became clear to me that he had already made up his mind. I never found out why he had decided to trust me, open his archives to me and confide in me, a twenty-six-year-old stranger. Years later, I found in his diary of the same day the following entry:

Michael Bar-Zohar came to me this afternoon. He wrote in French a book about the Sinai and Suez war ... He received a Ph.D. degree for that research. He was born in Bulgaria ... He wants to write the history of my life and work for a publishing house and asks for my help. He wants to talk to me from time to time on different subjects, in order to learn my opinions on Judaism and on world problems. I told him that in a week I shall return to [my kibbutz] Sdeh Boker, and I shall be ready to put my archives at his disposal, on condition that he doesn't publish state secrets.

That is how I started working on Ben-Gurion's biography. The Old Man indeed gave me access to his diaries, archives, letters and documents. He also agreed to my presence beside him during his current work, at his houses in Tel Aviv and Sdeh Boker, as well as while he was traveling around the country. From 1964 to 1966 I spent a great deal of my time at his side. I used to sit, almost daily, in a corner in his study following his conversations with his visitors – statesmen, party-leaders, newspapermen, senior army officers and intellectuals. I was present at closed private councils and at huge public rallies; at times the latter were warm encounters with enthusiastic throngs of supporters – and at other times they turned into tumultuous confrontations between Ben-Gurion and his angry political foes. I used every free hour in his agenda to interview him on various subjects connected with his life and achievements. When I was not with him, I studied his archives, went through a large variety of published material – books, articles, research papers – and interviewed his major followers and rivals. I was soon to realize that there was an astounding abundance of source material. Many hundreds of books, directly or indirectly connected with Ben-Gurion and the various fields where his activities have left their impact, have been published in Israel and abroad; the articles in newspapers, magazines, periodicals and scientific publications all over the world are virtually innumerable; the last count of the documents in Ben-Gurion's private archives approaches half a million.

The interviews that my research assistants and myself carried out were also a source of great importance, but had to be carefully checked and verified. The most important contributions in this field were made by leading Israeli figures such as Shimon Peres, Itzhak Navon, Moshe Dayan, Teddy Kollek, Yigael Yadin, Israel Galili, Igal Alon, Itzhak Rabin, Moshe

Sharett, Rachel Yanait Ben-Zvi, Ariel Sharon, Dov Joseph, Ze'ev Shareff, Pinhas Sapir, Abba Eban, Isser Harel and others. The interviews also yielded a by-product of documents, letters, notes and other written material. The members of Ben-Gurion's family and his close friends from the days of his youth also co-operated with me willingly.

In 1967 I published a first biography of Ben-Gurion, *The Armed Prophet* (Arthur Barker, London, 1967, Prentice-Hall, New Jersey, 1968). The book was translated into several languages, but I had the feeling that my work wasn't over yet. I decided to enlarge the scope of my research, even if it took me a few more years. I started this new stage as a part-time occupation during the years 1968–70, and from 1970 it became my main work.

During this second stage of my research I discovered new, unpublished material of decided importance. The Weizmann archives yielded hundreds of letters, documents and stenographic accounts, describing in detail the bitter strife between Weizmann and Ben-Gurion during the Second World War. Meyer Weisgal, Weizmann's devoted companion, let me see the chapter on the strained relations between Ben-Gurion and Weizmann, which had been eliminated from the latter's memoirs, *Trial and Error*, on Weisgal's insistence. In Ben-Gurion's archives, which had been reorganized, I also found a variety of documents: his correspondence with the British foreign ministers, Herbert Morrison and Anthony Eden, while he tried to negotiate an alliance with England, and with Prime Minister Harold Macmillan during the 1958 Middle East crisis; his dramatic exchange of messages with Presidents Kennedy and de Gaulle a few days before his final resignation in 1963; detailed accounts of the major crisis between Israel and the U.S.A. in the early sixties concerning the building of an atomic reactor in the Negev; the full diary of his closest aide, the late Nhemia Argov; the personal letters exchanged between Ben-Gurion and Miss Doris May, that cast a new light on Ben-Gurion's private life. Several of Ben-Gurion's diaries of the crucial fifties and early sixties which he had thought lost turned up at Sdeh Boker and supplied me with Ben-Gurion's minute-by-minute account of the Sevres conference, in October 1956, where the Suez War was decided, and details of the top-secret alliance he concluded with Turkey during a clandestine night flight to Ankara in 1958. Ben-Gurion's diaries of later years revealed his objection to the decision of the Israeli government to go to war in June 1967, and his personal tragedy when the outcome of the Six Day War made him realize that his political career was definitely over. Meanwhile, the veil of secrecy had been lifted on several subjects, previously considered as state secrets, and I was able to include them in my book, I also gained access to the private diaries of some of Ben-Gurion's closest collaborators.

I also found much help in recently published material like Sharett's private diaries, Dayan's autobiography, and quite a few documents, among which was the account of Ben-Gurion's attempts to negotiate with Egypt's President Nasser in 1956, by the intermediary Robert Anderson, President Eisenhower's special envoy. This negotiation, had it succeeded, could have prevented the Suez War. In the files of the Public Record Office in London, and in the Middle East Library at St Anthony's College in Oxford, I found fascinating material about the attitude of various branches of British Intelligence and government toward Ben-Gurion during and after the Second World War.

Only an infinitesimal part of the huge quantity of material about Ben-Gurion could be used in this book. Ben-Gurion was a man of phenomenal activity: since the age of fourteen and virtually until his death at eighty-seven, he conducted an intensive public life, wrote innumerable articles, speeches, letters, kept amazingly detailed diaries, was deeply involved in the fields of politics, syndicalism, Zionism, diplomacy, security, ventured into the intellectual world, and played a crucial part in every major event in the history of the Jewish settlement of Palestine and later of the State of Israel. The task of selecting the material and the subjects fit to be described and quoted in the book was not easy, and I can only hope that I have been objective.

I was deeply preoccupied with the choice of style I had to adopt when writing this biography. I reached the conclusion that I must try to achieve a synthesis between describing the statesman Ben-Gurion and revealing the man behind the legend; between the presentation of the fateful decisions, the deeds and the errors, and the exposure of the heart-searching agony, the reasoning, the secret hopes and dreams of the man who was alone at the top. Perhaps the most difficult task was to peel off the layers of myth and idealization that had been cast on the charismatic figure of Ben-Gurion by worshipping followers as well as by bitter foes.

Ben-Gurion and his wife, Paula, died before the present biography was written and published. I must admit that it was, therefore, easier for me to treat freely several aspects of Ben-Gurion's private life which I wouldn't have tackled while he and his wife were alive.

This book, as I stressed earlier, is based mainly on unpublished sources. The published material – books, articles, etc. – has been of only marginal importance. Most of it being in Hebrew, I don't believe that a bibliography could be of any use to the scholar who doesn't read that language. Therefore there will be no bibliography included in the translations of this book. I suggest that Hebrew readers refer to the Hebrew original of this biography, which is much more extensive, and whose three volumes include a reference-and-footnote apparatus, as well as a detailed biblio-graphy of all sources, published and unpublished.

I gratefully acknowledge the help of all those who assisted me in my research: the persons who agreed to be interviewed by me time and again; the staff of the various archives who gave me access to their documents and files: the Army archives, the Zionist archives, the Labor archives, the Labor Party archives, the Jabotinsky Institute, the Weizmann archives (all of them in Israel), the Public Record Office in London, and many other private archives, public libraries and institutions, in Israel and abroad. I would also like to express my gratitude to my assistants Yehuda Kave, Dalia Zidon and Hanna Eshkar. I am especially indebted to my main re-search assistant, Nilly Ovnat, to Mr Haim Israeli, Ben-Gurion's faithful secretary, who helped me devotedly over eleven years, and to Ina Friedman, for her skilful and efficient editing of the English version of this book. Professor Yehuda Slutzki, of the Tel Aviv University, Mr Ahuvia Malkin and Mr Gershon Rivlin spent many months in reading the manuscript and gave me invaluable advice and precious guidance to first-rate sources.

I cannot conclude this preface, however, without stressing the utmost importance of Ben-Gurion's own contribution to this book. I don't simply mean his contribution in agreeing to be interviewed by me over and over again, or in allowing me to read and quote his papers and diaries. We know how interviews can be inaccurate, and how even documents and letters may be misleading, representing, as they do, only limited fractions of the whole image. Diaries as biographical sources, as we all know, may be even more dangerous if not thoroughly analyzed, compared and contrasted with other sources. In talking of Ben-Gurion's contribution I refer to the chance that was given to me to follow closely over a long period of time his daily activity. Seeing Ben-Gurion at work, studying his way of thinking and speaking, observing his behavior, feeling almost physically the crushing weight of his personality in private meetings as well as in public rallies, allowed me, I believe, to grasp the magnetism he exuded and to witness the exertions of those indefinable qualities of authority, inspiration and leader-ship that turned men into his devout followers and enabled him to guide his nation through its most perilous struggles for independence and survival.

I

David Gruen

David was barely eleven, a pale Jewish boy wearing a long black gown in the Plonsk synagogue, when he first heard that the Messiah had arrived. He was a handsome man, they said, with proud, burning eyes and a black beard. His name was Theodor Herzl, and he would lead the people of Israel back to the land of their forefathers. With the innocence of childhood, David believed the story and, instantly became a fervent follower of the Zionism which was sweeping the Jewish world. The seeds of that Zionist faith had already been sown on his early childhood, when he sat on his grandfather's knee and learned the Hebrew language, word by word, from Zvi Aryeh Gruen; when he listened to his father, Avigdor Gruen, one of the local leaders of the Hovevei Zion ("Lovers of Zion"), a forerunner of the nascent Zionist movement. While still a child, David Gruen decided that one day he would make his home in the Land of Israel.

The faith that David imbibed at home was fostered by the unique atmosphere of Plonsk. There was something special about the town. It was neither large, nor famous, nor even prosperous. In fact it was no more than a small provincial township in Polish Russia that had grown up around a castle built by a Polish prince during the Middle Ages. More than it was Russian or Polish, Plonsk was Jewish. In 1881, five years before David was born, there were 4,500 Jews among its 7,824 inhabitants, most of them poverty-stricken traders and craftsmen.

Yet the town boasted the Kochari school, run by a group of scholars who, under the name of Kohol Koton ("Small Congregation"), attained widespread renown for their learning. After some time, another Kohol Koton society was formed in Plonsk, though of a different nature: its purpose was to "descend to the people" by advancing the study of the Bible and Hebrew grammar among the poor and uneducated. Headed by the local intellectuals, the society was considerably successful, and in 1865 all the leading intellectuals in the town established The Society of Friends of Learning and the Torah, proclaiming: "We shall endeavor to combine

Torah with learning . . . To exalt our holy language and Hebrew literature, which, to our regret, our present-day intellectuals . . . disperse as the wind . . . old and outworn they call it." Among the leaders of the society was a prosperous merchant who had once taught Hebrew at the renowned Kochari school. Zvi Aryeh Gruen, "a handsome, tall Jew", was a pious man who never went to bed before reading five chapters of the Bible. He was also well-educated, having mastered Hebrew, German and Polish (to which he added Russian in his old age), and his well-endowed library included works by Spinoza, Plato, and Kant. But first place in his affections was reserved for the Hebrew language.

Gruen had four sons. The third, Avigdor – deeply attached to Zvi Aryeh and to his beliefs – regarded himself as his father's spiritual heir. Like his father, Avigdor was well educated, a fervent Hebraist, and an active member of The Society of Friends of Learning and the Torah. He also took over the pursuit which his father followed in his old age, legal representation. Avigdor also became "one of the two Jewish 'advocates' in the town". In practice, Avigdor was a writer of petitions, but he was also authorized to engage in legal counseling. In the course of his work, he established close ties with the town's Russian and Polish authorities and acquired a respected position among the Jews.

Avigdor was tall and elegant, and his elongated face bore a moustache and an imperial beard. He was also particular about his appearance, being the first citizen of Plonsk to discard the traditional Jewish garb and replace it with a black tail-coat, hard collar, starched waistcoat, and a bow tie. While still young, he married Sheindel Friedman, a distant cousin, and the only daughter of a landowner, who gave the young couple two wooden houses at the end of Goats' Street and the large garden between them. Sheindel was "of small stature, with prominent features". It appears that she was frail, and six of the eleven children she bore died shortly after their birth.

The Gruen family enjoyed a comfortable life. The upper floor of their home was occupied by the family that tended the cows and other livestock, cleaned the house, and cooked the meals. Avigdor Gruen and his family lived on the lower floor. On occasion Avigdor's affairs would take him to Warsaw, forty miles away. But for the most part his life flowed along peacefully and quietly. He occupied a prominent position in the local Jewish community and worshipped at the "New Synagogue", which was reserved for the town's wealthiest and more respected citizens.

It may seem surprising, then, that this pillar of society should be infected by the insanity known by the name of "Love of Zion". Yet Avigdor's vulnerability to the disease dated back to his early youth, when he already held a warm affection for the Land of Israel. Upon the establishment of the Hovevei Zion movement in 1884, he became one of its first adherents and his home became a center for the Plonsk society's activities and meetings. It was there that the Lovers of Zion wove naive dreams of the Return to Zion, delivered enthusiastic Zionist orations, recited edifying verse, collected donations, and swore their allegiance to their ancestral homeland. And it was there, two years after the foundation of Hovevei Zion, that Sheindel Gruen gave birth to the fourth of her surviving children: David Yosef Gruen.

David was a sickly child, short and thin like his mother. He did not make friends with children of his own age and rarely went out to enjoy a run in the back yard. His head was disproportionately large, and the worried Avigdor took his son to the neighboring town of Plotsk to consult a specialist, who ran his fingers over the boy's head and assured Avigdor that his son would be a great man. Sheindel, a pious Jewess, concluded proudly that her "Duvcheh" would grow to become a great rabbi, learned in the Torah.

Sheindel had a special relationship with her taciturn son and favored him over his brothers, as much because of her pride in his intelligence as her awareness of his need. His health was poor, he was susceptible to illnesses, and he suffered occasional fainting spells. In concern for his health, she left the other children to take him to a village for the summer. David, who was distant from his brothers and sisters, was devoted to his mother, and her death in childbirth, when David was eleven, came as a great shock to him. It was a long time before he could reconcile himself to the bitter truth. "Every night, I saw Mother in my dreams," he later wrote. "I would talk to her and ask 'Why don't we see you at home?' For many years, the pain did not subside."

After Sheindel's death, the solitary, silent boy withdrew even more. His sisters were no substitute for his mother, and his father's second wife did not engage David's affections. On the contrary, he ignored her and maintained his aloofness right up to her death. But David was attached to his father. "It was from my father that I inherited my love for the Land of Israel . . . and for the Hebrew language." Indeed, his father filled David's heart with the spirit of Zionism in its most authentic form. But it was his grandfather, Zvi Aryeh, who actually taught him Hebrew. Every day, when David came to his office, the old man would lay aside his work, seat the boy on his knees, and patiently teach him Hebrew words. In this fashion, Hebrew became David's second mother tongue; he spoke and read it fluently.

"Duvcheh" acquired his formal education in the Jewish religious school known as the *heder*. Beginning at the age of five, he studied at a traditional *heder*; at seven he went on to study with a "modern" teacher, a hunchback who taught Hebrew grammar and Bible. The teacher would read out a passage from a German Bible and have the pupils repeat the German words without comprehending their meaning, whereupon he translated the verses. Later, David went on to a "reformed *heder*", where he learned Bible and Hebrew. In addition to his Jewish education, the curly headed, inquisitive boy also attended a Russian state school, where he acquired the rudiments of the Russian language and was exposed to the great Russian authors, who had a profound effect on his outlook.

Three books left their imprint on David's view of the world. *The Love of Zion*, by Avraham Mapu,

... breathed life into the pages of the Bible ... and enhanced my longings for the Land of Israel. Harriet Beecher Stowe's *Uncle Tom's Cabin* inspired me with a sense of horror at slavery, subjugation, and dependency ... After reading *The Resurrection* by Tolstoy, I became a vegetarian; however, on leaving my father's house, I could not prepare food in accordance with my wishes, and I reverted to eating meat.

But David's view of life was molded by more than reading and formal study. Every day, when he returned home from school, he would fling himself into the world of Hovevei Zion, which became an integral part of him. There was also a deep understanding between David and his father. Avigdor loved to seat the boy next to him on the bed and spend entire evenings lecturing to him on geography and history. Once only did Avigdor strike his son. "When it became known to my father that I was not following the ritual of putting on phylacteries, he slapped my face, for the only time in my life." However, the boy did not give in, stubbornly refusing to obey the religious precepts and resume his prayers. His taut lips and aggressively jutting jaw testified to his forceful and obstinate character. Avigdor Gruen retreated.

Avigdor was proud of David. Too authoritarian a character to reveal his thoughts to his son, he was nevertheless convinced that David stood head and shoulders above his peers. Accordingly, he decided that the boy should have the best education possible, and he was deeply concerned about the obstacles that Russian schools placed in the path of young Jews. In 1896, with Theodor Herzl's entrance on the Jewish scene, Avigdor had become a fervent Zionist. Deeply concerned over David's future, he decided to approach his spiritual mentor. David was fifteen when, without his knowledge, his father wrote about him to Herzl, the president of the Zionist Organization:

Plonsk, November 1, 1901

Leader of our people, spokesman of the nation, Dr Herzl, who stands before kings!

I have resolved that I shall pour out my heart to his highness . . . [Though I am] the youngest of the thousands of Israel, God has blessed me with a superior son, diligent in his studies. Still in the prime of his youthful years, about fifteen, his belly is [already] filled with learning, and in addition to our tongue, the Hebrew language, he also knows the language of the state, the lore of mathematics, and more, and his soul yearns for study. But every school is sealed before him, for he is a Jew. I have resolved to send him abroad, to study science, and several people have advised me to send him to Vienna, where there is also a center for Jewish learning, a college for rabbis. Thus I have resolved to bring this account before my lord, that he may commend my son and [also that I may] enjoy the benefit of my lord's advice and sagacity. For who is a mentor like unto him, and who, if not he, can advise me what to do? For I am powerless to maintain my son, whom I love like the apple of my eye.

My obseisances,
   Avigdor Gruen

The letter was never answered, and until the day of his death Avigdor did not tell his son of the approach to the president of the Zionist Organization.

When David was fourteen, he followed the example set by his father and his elder brother Avraham by flinging himself into Zionist activity. Together with his best friends, David helped to found the Ezra Society, whose purpose was to foster spoken Hebrew. Even though few of the boys could express themselves in the language, they began to address one another exclusively in Hebrew and found Hebrew words to replace the familiar Russian, Polish, or Yiddish terms. After long and exhaustive discussions with suspicious parents, conservative teachers, and tough employers of child labor, the members of Ezra succeeded in mustering about 150 children, many of them orphans and apprentices, whom they taught Bible and Hebrew – reading, writing, and speech. Within a half year, their efforts bore fruit: their tribe of ragged urchins roamed the garbage-strewn alleyways of Plonsk's slums prattling in Hebrew.

More than a mere provincial boys' club, Ezra was a very unique group of intimate friends headed by three leaders: Shmuel Fuchs, the oldest, tall and sturdy and a gifted organizer; Shlomo Zemach, two years younger, a scion of one of the town's wealthiest and most distinguished families; and David Gruen, the youngest. For his first lecture to the Ezra Society, David chose the topic "Zionism and Culture". He also made his first attempts at writing. Together with Shlomo Zemach and Shmuel Fuchs, he decided to publish a journal for young people under the auspices of the Ezra Society.

It contained David's earliest creative writing – poetry – but after a few issues the journal failed.

Shlomo and Shmuel were again at David's side when, at the age of seventeen, he made the most important decision of his life. On a hot August morning, the trio went out for a swim where the Plonka River flowed slowly past the town, forming a quiet shady lake. Naked, wet, and in high spirits, they squatted on the river bank with the daily paper and read a report of the Sixth Zionist Congress at Basel, where Herzl had presented his "Uganda Program" for the establishment of a Jewish state in Africa as a temporary haven for the Jews plagued by repeated outbursts of pogroms. Deeply disappointed by the plan, the three young men gave vent to rebellious thoughts. For them, the Land of Israel was the sole homeland of the Jewish people, and they began an earnest discussion on how best to combat the misfortune they called "Ugandism". There and then, they reached their decision: "We concluded that the most effective way to combat 'Ugandism' was by settling in the Land of Israel."

The decision was more than a plan of action; it was the crystallization of an ideology. Their dream of gaining possession of the Land of Israel could only be realized by deeds, not by words; their decision implied a commitment to the path of personal action and a total opposition to "verbal" Zionism. That hot summer morning witnessed the first expression of the ideology that was to become David Gruen's hallmark. From then on he would forego no opportunity to prove his preference for deeds over words. "In my eyes," he later wrote to his father, "settling the land is the only true Zionism, and all the rest is self-deception, empty talk, and a sheer waste of time."

With equal earnestness, the trio decided on the timetable of their departure for Palestine. Shlomo was to be the first to go; he would tour the land and then return to Plonsk. There was also a romantic reason behind this decision: young Shlomo Zemach was in love with Shmuel's beautiful sister and hoped to take her with him to Palestine. It was therefore decided that, having prepared the ground for her arrival, he would return to Plonsk. Then, with the aid of Shmuel and David, he would elope with her, and all four would set off together for Palestine.

David was to be the last to go. In any case, he was in no particular hurry. Palestine needed builders, he told his friends, so he would take up technical studies, and as soon as he acquired his engineer's diploma, he would set off. First, however, he decided to set out for Warsaw and prepare for his entrance examination to the technical college. David's departure for Warsaw was scheduled for that summer. Yet the autumn passed, and the winter too, and still he put it off. His friends' queries elicited evasive replies, which concealed his true reason for the delay: he was madly in love.

He refused to confide in anyone, but when Zemach and Fuchs heard the poems in which David lyricized about "the source of life, my hope and faith, the well of my life and the soul of my soul", they understood that he was in love. Apparently he admitted as much, but he refused to reveal the name of the girl or admit the depth of his passion. It was only a year later that he opened up, in a letter to Shmuel Fuchs:

I have always desired to pour out my heart to another person, but some mysterious force prevented me, sealing my lips . . . Yes, I loved – that you know – but you do not know how much . . . like the eruption of a burning volcano, the fire of my love raged in my heart. All the poems I wrote were no more than its smoky shadow . . . Suddenly, I began to cast doubt upon my love . . . did I really love? The question gave me no rest at night. At the same time, there were other moments when I was unable to believe that my soul could find room for such a foolish question . . . my love was yet so strong. However, gradually I became aware that I did not love her . . . in my heart I continued to feel a strong sense of love, but not for her. (To this day, I do not know whether I ceased loving her, or whether I never loved her at all . . .) It was the middle of the winter. Until then, I had been happy beyond bounds; afterwards, I was miserable . . . my heart grieved me so, my regrets so troubled me, until there were times when I sat in my bed all night and wept . . . I could no longer live in Plonsk. That was one of the reasons which impelled me to travel to Warsaw that summer – just as at the beginning of the winter, love was my reason for remaining in Plonsk. But all that belongs to the past . . . Even now, at times, love flashes within my heart like lightning; an ember will flare up – particularly when I am alone and I recall forgotten matters . . . But a moment later, it passed by . . . Has my heart hardened, turned to stone? Who can read the riddles of the soul? . . .

Such was David Gruen at the age of seventeen, a sensitive boy in love, crying at night from his first heartbreak; a boy who wrote poems about his beloved and repeatedly postponed the realization of his dreams to remain near her. Later in the same letter, he attempted to shrug off his candid confession: "'The morning is wiser than the evening,' says the Russian proverb – and with justice. Recalling what I wrote last night, I laugh at myself. What an absurdly sentimental style – I even thought of beginning the whole letter anew, but I am too lazy for that, and time does not permit it."

With a broken heart (though he later forgot the name of his first love), David left Plonsk and set off for Warsaw. But the year and a half he spent in the Polish capital seems to have consisted of a series of severe ordeals. He felt isolated and depressed in the big city. On top of that, the group of

friends he had left behind in Plonsk broke up and went their separate ways.
Contrary to their plan, Samuel Fuchs was the first to leave, and his departure – for England – was a severe blow to David, who was very attached to
Fuchs and regarded him as an "older brother". Their parting left David
with a sense of great sorrow.

In Warsaw, David lodged with relatives. But it soon became apparent
that they were undergoing financial difficulties, which also affected him.
Moreover, his father's financial position also deteriorated at this time, and
David did not want to ask him for money. Fortunately David succeeded in
finding part-time employment as a teacher, and matters improved for a
time. He rented a room together with a friend; but he nevertheless failed
to find peace of mind and was often depressed. To make things worse,
David's personal plans ran into obstacles. He had come to Warsaw to
study, but it was very difficult for a Jew to gain admittance to a Russian
high school because of the severe restrictions imposed by the czarist
government. So he decided to study at the technical school for young Jews
founded by a Jewish philanthropist named Vavelberg. To prepare for the
entrance examinations, he began taking private lessons in Russian, physics,
and mathematics. But in 1904, admittance to the Vavelberg school was
restricted to high-school graduates, and David's dream was shattered.

The young man was still groping for his way when bitter news arrived:
Theodor Herzl was dead. At first David succumbed to despair and his
confidence gave way: "Sad and bitter thoughts sometimes arise in my heart
concerning the future of Zionism and of our people," he wrote to a friend.
"Doubts and uncertainties suck my blood and poison my strength, and
there are times when they implant despair – cold and terrible as death – in
the soul . . . Can you possible restore my pure and powerful faith, unblem-
ished by any shadow of doubt or thoughts of despair!" He seemed to have
no one to turn to for moral support and encouragement. But just then
Shlomo Zemach, the dreamy young man from Plonsk, arose to lead the
way, and his example was followed by many others, including David
Gruen.

On 25 November 1904, David returned to Plonsk for a two-day visit.
That same day he held a secret meeting with Shlomo and the two decided
that Shlomo would leave for Palestine at the first opportunity. On 12
December, Shlomo's father sent the young man to the bank to cash a
check for 580 roubles. Overcoming his conscience, the young man reached
his decision: he took the money and made for Warsaw, where his friend
David was awaiting him.

It took a single day for Shlomo to complete his preparations for the
journey to Palestine. Afraid that his father would follow him and drag

him back home, he hid in a friend's house. That evening, the elder Zemach appeared in David's room. "I found him sitting in our room," David wrote to Fuchs the next day. "He spoke to me calmly, without any hint of emotion. You can imagine the conversation. I assured him that Shlomo had already left. I don't know whether he believed me or not, but he did not come back again and has probably returned to Plonsk."

Shlomo set off on 13 December, and a few weeks later he was in Palestine. Trembling with excitement, Shlomo Lavi, a friend of David's, came bursting into the seminary in Plonsk to read out the postcard he had just received from Shlomo Zemach: "My friends, Shalom! I am in Rishon le-Zion.* Before me now, as I write to you, lie the first two bishliks I earned with my own two hands . . . so it is possible to earn a living in our land. For breakfast and lunch, I eat bread and olives . . . Don't worry, come, and you will find work."

Shlomo Zemach's move had a profound impact on the young people of Plonsk. Overnight, the young man became a symbol of revolt against convention, against life in the Diaspora, against parents who forcibly prevented their sons from going to the Land of Israel. David Gruen's personal decision was considerably influenced by Zemach. He put off his own departure for more than a year, but all his activities in the course of that period were directed toward one goal: to prepare himself – and his friends – for their life in Palestine. He was no longer the same earnest young man who had set off for Warsaw in an elegant suit, dark waistcoat, and silk tie. David returned to Plonsk wearing a Russian blouse (*rubashka*), and this signified more than a mere change in fashion. While in Warsaw, he had witnessed first hand the first upheavals of the 1905 Russian Revolution and the violent social ferment that swept the Polish capital at that time. He had seen the strikers and the demonstrators, the orators calling for freedom and justice, and the Russian soldiers and policemen firing into the crowd. Although his description of these events was restrained, there is no doubt that his views were strongly influenced by these scenes, and even more so during the second stage of the revolution.

Then came another challenge to give David Gruen's life a new content: the emergence of the Bund (the non-Zionist Jewish Socialist Party), which threatened to replace Zionism in many hearts. David declared unrelenting war against the Bund, and in the ideological battle that ensued, his friends were startled to discover that he was a brilliant orator and a fierce debater with great powers of persuasion. His campaign against the Bund was not the first time that David had mounted the speaker's rostrum. In May 1904, at an assembly of Ezra, he had delivered a speech on Spinoza's view of the

* One of the early Jewish agricultural settlements established in Palestine.

Choice of Israel by the Almighty, and a few months later, when he delivered a eulogy to Herzl in the synagogue, "he reduced many people to tears". But his debut as an orator and a leader of stature came about during his "polemic war" against the Bund.

Again and again, Bund headquarters in Warsaw, seeing Plonsk as a hard nut to crack, sent its finest orators there; again and again, "Duvcheh" Gruen, short and sturdy in his Russian *rubashka*, would mount the synagogue rostrum and rout them with his sharp tongue. In the course of this confrontation, David emerged not only as an articulate orator with great analytical powers, but also as the bearer of a clearly defined political ideology. From the middle of 1905, he was among the active members of a new Jewish workers' movement – Poalei Zion ("Workers of Zion").

Poalei Zion arose as a synthesis of two movements that were stirring the Jewish people: Zionism and Russian socialism. It viewed Zionism as the aim of the Jews and socialism as the ideal framework for the just society that would emerge in the Jewish homeland. David founded a branch of Poalei Zion in Plonsk. He also organized the town's first strikes of tailors and rope-makers for decent working conditions. In the shadow of the 1905 Russian Revolution, the debate between the socialist Zionists and the socialist Bundists was conducted in a fittingly "revolutionary" atmosphere. The Bund representative would arrive at the Plonsk synagogue with a pistol on his hip and an escort of two bodyguards. David, likewise armed and guarded, would mount the rostrum to confront him. As a tense, dramatic silence descended upon the synagogue, the two men measured one another and the verbal battle commenced. It was not long before David Gruen could chalk up his first victory: halting the Bund offensive in Plonsk, he made Poalei Zion into the leading movement among the town's young people.

David's influence was soon felt far beyond the bounds of Plonsk. The Poalei Zion leadership in Warsaw, quick to recognize his talents, began to send him on various missions to the neighboring provinces, where despite his youthful appearance he was equally successful. His boyish face was beginning to mature, and he grew his first moustache and let his hair grow long. In fact, his long curly mane, Russian blouse, and peaked cap (in vogue among the revolutionaries) were sufficient reason for the Warsaw police to arrest him for subversive activity. His horrified relatives in Plonsk were certain that the "dangerous revolutionary" faced death by hanging. However, through the intervention of his father, who rushed up from Plonsk, David was quickly released.

Imprisonment was a painful experience for David. For the first time in his life, he encountered Jewish pimps. "I also heard language that horrified me. The trade in women was exclusively in Jewish hands. I never imagined before that such people existed." Yet it was not long before he was arrested again (on his way to an arbitration in a nearby township), and this time he was carrying incriminating documents relating to his political activity. His father again saved the day with a "contribution" of 1,000 roubles to help the police officer forget David's offense. Upon his release, he returned to his illegal activities.

In the summer of 1905, Shlomo Zemach returned from Palestine for a few months, as he had promised. He had not forgotten his original plan, and with David's help he tried to convince Shmuel Fuchs's sister to elope with him to Palestine. In the end she refused, and when the group of pioneers began to plan their departure for Palestine early in the summer of 1906, she was not with them. But Rachel Nelkin was.

Rachel was the step-daughter of Simcha Eizik, the leader of Hovevei Zion in Plonsk. She was a tall, beautiful girl with black eyes and dark hair braided around her head. The Gruen and Eizik families were close friends, and David knew Rachel from childhood. When he returned to Plonsk, he suddenly realized that she had turned into a beautiful young woman. With all the passion of youth, he fell in love with her; and this time he made no attempt to conceal his feelings from friends and family.

Rachel was also deeply attached to David and went so far as to commit an act that resulted in several families forbidding their daughters to befriend her: she appeared with him in the street unescorted! "People in Plonsk were very conservative," he recalled many years later. "A young man and a young woman just did not walk in the street together. So when I walked out with her, there was a terrible uproar in Plonsk: What is this? How dare he?"

Their romance almost ended in tragedy. David was not alone in his feelings for Rachel. Among the many others who longed for her was Shlomo Lavi, but he was too shy even to speak to her. Shlomo was madly jealous of David, who visited Rachel so frequently and even strolled the streets with her. One day, in a fit of envy, Shlomo drew a knife and hurled himself at his rival. David ran for his life, with Lavi pursuing him down the length and breadth of Plonsk until he was exhausted and the "Shakespearean drama" came to an end. In time, however, the two young men were reconciled and established a firm friendship.

At the end of that summer, a group of "pioneers" – the largest to date – left Plonsk for Palestine. They included Shlomo Zemach, David Gruen, Rachel Nelkin, and her mother. Rachel and David were together on the long journey to Odessa, and together they boarded the ramshackle Russian ship that was to carry them to Palestine. But they were emphatically not together when the time came to find a place to sleep on the hard floor of the fourth class. Rachel's mother, apprehensive about the passionate young man, decided to safeguard propriety by spreading her bedding between that of David and Rachel. Throughout the voyage, she lay between them like a rampart.

For most of the young pioneers of David's generation, the fulfillment of Zionism by settling in the Land of Israel was a painful revolt against their parents, ghetto life, and the ossification of Jewish tradition. Not so for David. He became a Zionist neither as an escape nor as a means of revolt. He grew up in a Zionist home, and was familiar with Hebrew from childhood. In fact, by the time he left for Palestine, he spoke the language fluently. On the eve of David's departure, a proud Avigdor Gruen even posed for a photograph with his son, standing beside the Poalei Zion banner.

Perhaps these were the reasons why David was so calm and confident in choosing his path. Years later, when referring to the Diaspora, he spoke of "the life imbued with poverty and suffering" of the Jewish masses. But David himself never tasted the humiliation of poverty or the bitterness of the pogroms that played such a large part in the decision of hundreds of young Jews to go to Palestine. The waves of pogroms that swept through czarist Russia never reached Plonsk. For the young people of Plonsk, that trip to Palestine was not a flight; it was undertaken for its own sake.

The voyage in the dilapidated Russian ship across the seemingly endless sea was a source of unending wonder and amazement for David. When the boat anchored in Smyrna, he encountered the colors of the exotic East for the first time, staring in fascination at the Blacks, Gypsies, Turks, and Arabs. He walked the narrow winding streets, stepping aside to make room for a caravan of overburdened camels with bells around their necks. The Arab passengers on the ship made "a very good impression" on him, appearing like "overgrown children, good-hearted and friendly". On the last night of the voyage, David did not close his eyes until, from out of the mists of dawn, the coast of Palestine appeared. "Morning light – and our ship gradually neared the Jaffa coast . . . a fresh breeze blew in our faces, and the sound of a bird – the first we had heard on our voyage – reached our ears . . . silent and speechless, I stood and gazed at Jaffa, and my heart was beating wildly . . . I had arrived."

2

The Beautiful Years

It all began – so they say – back in 1878 with that third-generation Jerusalemite lunatic, Yoel Moshe Salomon. Salomon was a tempestuous man, always at loggerheads with convention. Not content with breaking out of the narrow confines of Jerusalem's Old City and founding the Nahalat Ha'Shiva quarter outside its walls, he decided to lead the Jews of Palestine back to the soil. At that time, the Jewish community numbered several thousand people in Jerusalem, Jaffa, Safed, Hebron, and Tiberias, a good proportion of them living off charity from the Diaspora and devoting their lives to the study of Jewish scriptures. But two immigrants recently arrived from Hungary – Yehoshua Stampfer and David Gutmann – were taken by Salomon's fantasies and rode off with him to the banks of the Yarkon River, near the Arab village of Mulabbis, where a swampy area was up for sale.

The trio surveyed the malaria-afflicted Arabs, the carcasses of horses and cows flung by the riverside, the diseased, treacherous soil, and all the other indications of epidemics and ailments. The Greek doctor who had accompanied them promptly turned his horse around and galloped back to Jaffa, after pronouncing the air to be poisonous and declaring that death awaited every living thing that approached this spot. Salomon stared at his companions and said: "All the same!" Stampfer replied: "Let's try!" And they did: in that valley of death, they established the settlement of Petah Tikvah. It was followed by Rishon le-Zion, Zichron Ya'akov, and Rehovot. Each one followed its own path, strewn with graves, setbacks, and despair. Each had its heroes – a handful of pioneers in Russian blouses and boots, their eyes aflame and their hearts firm in the resolve to strike roots in the Land of Israel. The local Arabs would stare at them and shake their heads at the crazy Jews who had come to pitch their tents at the edge of the swamps in the land forsaken by God and man.

When the first immigrants from the Russian Zionist societies – the Hovevei Zion and the B.I.L.U. – came, it was no land flowing with milk and honey that greeted them. Centuries of war, neglect, and destruction had left ugly scars on the land once so lavishly praised by biblical scribes.

The coastal plain and other lowlands were filled with swamps. A combination of blazing sun and heavy rains had eroded the hillsides, long since stripped of their soil and thick woodlands. The Arab villagers tilled their soil in precisely the same manner that their ancestors had for generations. The steaming towns were ruled by imperious Turkish officials who merged arrogance and apathy with venality. Alongside the mosques and colorful marketplaces, colonies had been established by bizarre sects of Christian zealots – Germans, French, Americans, Swedes. The Holy Land attracted pilgrims from all over the world. Some were wealthy Westerners, but the majority consisted of troops of ragged Russian peasants clutching banners and icons and chanting doleful hymns as they trudged toward the Jordan River.

Nevertheless, for millions of Jews this was the land of their dreams, the place where their hopes and prayers centered. It was also the destination of a thin trickle of young pioneers, most of whom lacked bodily strength, were unaccustomed to physical labor, and had no experience in farming. All they possessed was a naïve faith and a fanatical, self-sacrificial resolve. The hard labor, malaria, and hunger claimed many victims. Of those who survived, many decided to leave that accursed land on the first available ship. Later, Ben-Gurion was to contend that of every ten immigrants who arrived with the Second Aliyah,* nine later left the country. The legendary "Return to the Soil" was not the work of thousands of pioneers. The "accounts" of professional Zionists notwithstanding, the pioneers were no more than a few hundred – at times, no more than a few score – ragged, underfed, and ailing young men. The description of an entire people returning to the soil is no more than a myth, an attempt to cover the reality that was far more modest and, consequently, all the more heroic.

On that hot, damp morning of 7 September 1906, a few pioneers welcomed David Gruen on the wharf of Jaffa harbor as, delighted and enraptured, he set foot on the soil of the Land of Israel. Once past the harbor gates, David stared about him. "This is even worse than Plonsk!" he thought. He found Jaffa a nightmare; its houses with their peeling façades, filthy alleyways, and noisy throngs of ragged idlers who drifted by aimlessly were repulsive. "Fat Arabs squatted next to their carts, and in between them was some miserable Jew's shop," was the way he described the scene. "I did not want to stay there." His friends led him to a hotel in the Jewish quarter of the town, but he refused: "I will not stay in Jaffa, not for a single night. This isn't the Land of Israel! Before the day is out, I'm going on to Petah Tikvah!"

That afternoon, fourteen young people, including Rachel Nelkin and

* Wave of Jewish immigration to Palestine, generally dated 1904-14.

Shlomo Zemach, set out for Petah Tikvah on foot. "We walked because there were no more carriages at that hour. There were orange groves all around, and one of the young men pranced and danced the whole way," Rachel Nelkin related. It was a wonderful moonlit night when they reached Petah Tikvah. Young Gruen was fascinated and "full of intoxication". New experiences followed one another in a rush. Hearing a strange sound from one of the courtyards, he was told that it was a donkey braying. "Never have I seen a donkey, nor did I know what 'braying' meant." In the distance, he heard a dreadful howling and was told, "That's the little foxes, spoiling the vineyards." To the ears of the enchanted dreamer, the wails were "like the sounds of a symphony". That whole night, David Gruen did not close his eyes. Every now and then he would walk out into the night and gaze about him. The first part of his dream had come true.

The following day, David and Shlomo Zemach rented a room together. By sunrise, David was already at work in the orange groves of Petah Tikvah, carting manure to drop into the holes freshly dug for new trees. "It's not easy work," he wrote to his father, "and it calls for great patience and devotion for those who have never worked before – which is the case of most of the workers – to withstand the summer heat and hoe the red clay . . . The sweat pours down, our hands are covered with callouses and sores, and our limbs seem about to fall apart . . . At the same time, the proprietor or his overseer stand nearby, calling *Yalla*! ['Hurry up'] . . ."

David Gruen was determined to till the soil, for this was the principal calling of Zionism. Hebrew labor on Hebrew soil – that was the only way for the Jewish people to regain its rights to the Land of Israel. "Conquest of labor" was the watchword of the young pioneers. "Only two kinds of workers will succeed in sticking it out in the country," David wrote, "those with tremendous will power and those who are capable, namely strong young men who have grown accustomed to hard work." David stood up to the challenge of labor. But where physical demands failed, malaria succeeded; and a few weeks after his arrival, David collapsed. Thereafter, malaria was to incapacitate him at regular intervals. Dr Stein, the Jewish physician called in to treat him, gave up all hope. "Nothing can be of any help here," he pronounced. "You cannot stay here. Leave the country!" But David stayed.

After experiencing malaria, he also savored the taste of hunger. "I spent less time working than suffering from fever and hunger. All three – work, malaria, and hunger – were new to me, and full of interest. After all, this was why I had come to the Land of Israel." If he had managed to save up a few coins, he would buy one *pitta* (a flat Arab loaf) every day and keep it until the afternoon; then he would chew it slowly to outwit his gnawing

hunger. But there were days when he did not even have that one *pitta*.
"It wasn't so bad during the day – I would talk to friends or try to concentrate on other matters. But nighttime was awful. From the moment I closed
my eyes, my fantasy would conjure up pots full of meat, fried chicken,
platters laden with food. I was afraid that I was taking leave of my senses.
In the morning, when I woke up worn out and exhausted, I would lift
my hand to my head and clumps of hair fell out and stuck to my fingers."
Rumors about the state of affairs in Palestine made their way back to
Plonsk. A concerned Avigdor Gruen sent his son a letter containing ten
roubles. He received the banknote back with David's reply: "Money is of
absolutely no use to me."

David was not alone in his pride or his need. In fact, it was precisely
because of their economic distress that the Jewish workers' groups lived
communally. Thus, almost inadvertently, they established the first communes in Palestine. The scant wages they earned were spent on food,
though occasionally a parcel or a money order would arrive from their
families. In the evenings they would congregate in the settlement's workers'
kitchen, singing and dancing late into the night. But there were also nights
and days of deprivation, of despair, and of fury.

"I was a day laborer," David Gruen was to relate in the Knesset many
years later, and his words still carried a taste of bitterness from the times
when he had to face daily humiliation at the hands of tough employers who
impassively selected workers for the day's chores. The employers themselves were Jews, farmers from the towns of Judea. Twenty years earlier,
they themselves had been idealistic dreamers. On first arriving from Russia,
their hearts were filled with Zionist fervor. But within a few years, they
had become unrecognizable.

The change was brought about by the gold of "the Benefactor", Baron
Edmond de Rothschild. The Baron was a "practical visionary". He bought
land, established agricultural settlements, and sent experts and advisers
to help the settlers who made their homes in "his" colonies – Petah Tikvah,
Rishon le-Zion, Zichron Ya'akov. But the more the Baron showered on the
settlers, the further their Zionist fervor declined. They gave up working
the land themselves and hired Arab laborers for pittance wages. When the
pioneers of the Second Aliyah began to arrive, they found the settlements
full of profit-hungry farmers who had drifted far away from the Zionist
ideal and were openly suspicious of the barefoot young newcomers. The
starry-eyed pioneers were required to present themselves at the center of
the settlement every morning, alongside the Arab workers who poured in
from near-by villages. The farmers and their overseers would walk among
them and look each one over while weighing up who would be hired and

who passed over. Yet even when a worker was hired, his troubles were not over: he knew he would have to spend the day in fierce competition with the Arab laborers, and the outcome would seal his fate in the days to come. After all, the Arabs were accustomed to the climate, used to working in the fields, and physically strong. This was the first ordeal the immigrants had to face upon arrival in the country. It gave the slogan "Conquest of Labor" a gloomy coloring.

Having personally experienced the humiliation of the day laborer, young Gruen was moved to revolt. The class-consciousness he had brought with him from Russia now merged with his Zionist ideals to set him into conflict with the Jewish farmers of Judea. Some contend that David Gruen's path was molded by two revolts: the first against Jewish life in the Diaspora, which brought him to Palestine; the second against the plantation farmers in the Judean lowlands, which heightened his socialist awareness. It was only natural that David now stepped up his political work in Poalei Zion.

Poalei Zion and Hapoel Hatzair ("Young Worker") were then the only Zionist Labor parties in Palestine. The fanatical enmity between the two struck David Gruen the moment he set foot on the soil of Palestine. While still in Jaffa harbor, he was accosted by a Jewish worker who launched into an unrelenting interrogation to find out whether he was for or against historical materialism. Helplessly, David stared at him in wide-eyed amazement. "It was my first day in the country, and I was ecstatic; but he overwhelmed me with his attacks on historical materialism and similar nonsense. 'What do you want of my life?' I demanded, but he wouldn't leave me alone."

The two parties were divided by a deep chasm, a fact that David Gruen found very odd, especially as he knew that of the nine "founding fathers" of Hapoel Hatzair in Palestine, four were from Plonsk. David was convinced there was no justification for two separate parties in the country. On the eve of his departure for Palestine, Shlomo Zemach told him about the establishment of Hapoel Hatzair, and David responded: "I am a member of Poalei Zion. There are no differences between the two of us: we are both struggling for the Hebrew language and are both in favor of Jewish labor." The two agreed that upon arriving in Palestine they would set about unifying the parties. But "right after our arrival in Palestine – influenced either by his friends or by the change in climate – Shlomo Zemach withdrew his support for the idea of unification. I didn't."

It was no mere change of climate that foiled the unification scheme, for there was a profound ideological difference between Hapoel Hatzair and Poalei Zion. Poalei Zion was on the way to becoming a Marxist party, decisively influenced by Russian revolutionary ideas and gradually shunting its Zionist program aside. On first arriving in Palestine, therefore, the pioneers from Plonsk – genuine Zionists, Hebrew-speaking, with deep traditional roots – turned their backs on the party. The establishment of Hapoel Hatzair was largely in reaction to Poalei Zion. Its members were not Marxists, and they advocated the Hebrew language, the Return to Zion, and practical fulfillment of their Zionist ideals.

In many ways, David Gruen was closer to Hapoel Hatzair than to the Poalei Zion he encountered on arriving in Palestine. After all, he was a devout Zionist and a fanatical Hebraist, and the Return to Zion was more important to him than any social or political ideology. At the same time, by his own testimony, he possessed a highly developed class consciousness and admired the spirit of the Russian revolution. He also believed in socialist principles; but his socialism was pragmatic, flexible, and – above all – harnessed to the service of his national and Zionist objectives. For David Gruen, Zionism and socialism fused into a single, central ideal: the working class is the spearhead of the Jewish renaissance, and national rebirth would be achieved only by practical work in the Land of Israel. The subjugation of socialist and party ideology to national and political objectives was to characterize David Ben-Gurion all along his political path.

In 1906, Poalei Zion held its first conference in Palestine and elected a five-man Central Committee, which included Gruen. In a secret ballot, he was also voted onto the ten-man committee charged with drawing up the party's program. True to the traditions of secrecy and conspiracy, which were an integral feature of the underground socialist parties in Russia, the ten men convened clandestinely in a tiny, unlit cubbyhole of an ancient Arab caravanserai. For two days and three nights, the ten committee members sprawled on the stone floor and rush mats and argued heatedly until they succeeded in producing the long-awaited document: "The Ramleh Program" (named after the town in which it was composed).

The program may have been written in Ramleh, but it bore a remarkable likeness to the Communist Manifesto, with some modest Zionist modifications. It was a prime example of its authors' ignorance of conditions in Palestine and their alienation from Zionism; in fact, the word "Zionism" was not even mentioned! It was only at the second session of the Poalei Zion conference that the Zionists gained their first victory, when the delegates adopted a resolution that expressly stated: "The party aspires to political independence of the Jewish people in this country."

For the first time, Poalei Zion had set itself an objective: the establishment of a Jewish state. It was, indeed, the beginning of a revolution – but no more than a beginning. For a number of years, David was to remain in the minority in Poalei Zion, and he failed in his attempt to introduce the

Hebrew language into the party's proceedings and publications. As a result, perhaps, Gruen did not take a particularly active role in party activity. Although he was a member of the Central Committee and at the beginning of 1907 he spent some time in Jaffa, at the party's request, he did not seem particularly attracted to party work. He preferred instead to till the soil.

The winter of 1906–7 was a hard one. Palestine had not experienced such cold for decades. Gruen spent the winter first in Jaffa and then in Petah Tikvah. He did not own warm clothing, and the boots sent by his father were too small for him. But he was employed in picking oranges, a job he found wonderfully easy. In the spring David moved to Kfar Saba, a newly founded settlement two hours' walk from Petah Tikvah. After a few weeks there, he set off for Rishon le-Zion to work in the wine cellars. Wearing a long apron, with his pants rolled up to the knees, he trod grapes barefoot in the wine cellar. On one occasion, he made a bet with a companion about who could tread grapes longer. David trod without stop for three days and three nights and won. For years afterwards, he could not stand the taste of wine.

David did not settle down in Rishon le-Zion either. After spending some time in the near-by settlement of Rehovot, he considered buying some land and becoming a farmer, so that he could bring his family to the country. But that way of life was not what had brought him to Palestine. He was looking for something different, more authentic, giving full expression to the ideal of the "Return to the Soil". Once again, it was his friend Shlomo Zemach who had the courage to step forward and blaze the trail. A few weeks after returning to Palestine with David, Shlomo set off for Galilee. At the time, David wrote to his father: "In Galilee things are quite different. There is plenty of milk, butter, and cheese. There are no day laborers . . . instead, there are annually employed workers who receive all their requirements and a monthly wage on top of that. Work there is also different . . . mainly, it's simple field cultivation."

That was not the real difference between Judea and Galilee, however. Galilee was remote frontier country, a region without Jaffa, without the Baron's settlements, without landowning farmers, without the remnants of Diaspora life. Galilee was full of hostile Arab villages and tribes. The settlements were few, inhabited by no more than several dozen farmers, and there were less than forty Jewish farm laborers. Going to Galilee was a Zionist act of profound significance. It meant leaving behind the existing structures brought in by the Turkish rulers, the Russian immigrants, or the French Baron and fulfilling the ideals of pioneering Zionism by creating settlements in a province cut off from the outside world.

One year after arriving in Palestine, David Gruen struck out for Galilee, thereby concluding one chapter of his life and opening another. This break related not only to his role as pioneer but to his intimate affairs as well. David's decision to leave Judea was undoubtedly motivated by more than ideology. However, even today, seventy years later, the precise influence of an episode in his personal life remains largely undisclosed. It was David's love for Rachel Nelkin.

The immigrants from Plonsk had made a name for themselves throughout Judea as an unusually determined and hard-working group. But Rachel was the exception. Dismissed from her first job in the orange groves of Petah Tikvah, the delicate young woman was shamed by her inability to find work, but she was even more offended upon learning that her young comrades from Plonsk were angry with her for tarnishing their reputation as excellent workers and pioneers. When the chorus of disapproval rose, David's voice was not raised in her defense; on the contrary, he supported her critics.

Apparently this was the source of the rift between them. Despite his love for her, David condemned Rachel for failing in what he considered as the main task: the conquest of labor in the Land of Israel.

Apparently love and ideology were mutually exclusive realms. David's feelings for Rachel were probably the most profound love he was ever to experience. Nevertheless, he did not marry her. Years later, when asked why not, Rachel hesitated for a moment and then replied: "David concerned himself with public matters, not with his own personal affairs." David himself said: "Get married? . . . Who thought of marriage then? We avoided it . . . because we didn't want to bring children into the world too soon. The country was wild and backward. We couldn't guarantee the children an appropriate Hebrew education. Only some time later . . . did we learn that despite everything, it was feasible to raise children in the Land of Israel."

"Aside from that," he added, "Rachel met someone, fell in love with someone . . ." He left the sentence dangling, frozen in mid-air.

Indeed, at this point, Yehezkel Bet-Halachmi appeared in Rachel's life. He was a delicate, quiet young man who had first met Rachel in Plonsk on his way to Palestine. Like all his peers, Yehezkel fell in love with her. She, too, noticed him, and remembered him when she arrived in Palestine and met him again on the pier in Jaffa. She encountered him a third time when she returned to work in the Petah Tikvah orange groves, still shame-faced and remorseful for having stained the reputation of the Plonsk pioneers. "But Yehezkel, kind-hearted and sensitive, was always encouraging, implanting faith and hope."

Thus the destinies of these young people worked themselves out. In many ways, Yehezkel was the opposite of David, and possessed those very traits that Rachel sought in David in vain. In time she grew increasingly indignant at David for "almost never being at home" (in Petah Tikvah) and not finding time for her. She also sensed that her standing had declined because of her failure to keep up at work and believed that a matter of admitted importance from a national viewpoint had become something of a personal affair for David. Eventually the two fell out totally. It was then that David left Petah Tikvah. He was deeply in love with Rachel and would continue to be for many years. A year after David's departure for Galilee, Rachel Nelkin married Yehezkel Bet-Halachmi. It would be many years before David's pain subsided.

David's destination in Galilee was Sejera, two long rows of red-roofed, stone buildings sloping down the hillside near the Tiberias road. The settlement, which housed several dozen farmers, was totally isolated, and the neighboring Arab villagers were not friendly. When David reached the bottom of that hillside one autumn day, he stopped in amazement. When he walked into the village and met its inhabitants, his wonder grew even more. Sejera was the only settlement in the country where all the work was done by Jews. "It was here I found the Land of Israel I had dreamed about. No more storekeepers or agents, no more outside workers, no idlers living on the labor of others. All the members of the settlement work and enjoy the fruits of their own labor."

David was hired to work on the farm at the top of the hill. For some time he also worked in the settlement itself, employed by a harness-maker from Russia who had decided to become a farmer in Palestine. In Petah Tikvah, David had dreamed of "hearing the song of the plowman"; now he himself had become a plowman. He described the scene to his father:

The plow handle in my left hand, the goad in my right, I walk behind the plow and watch the black clods turning over and breaking up, while the oxen advance slowly with measured pace, like important men of affairs. There is time to think and dream – and how would it be possible not to think when you strike along, plowing up the soil of the Land of Israel, and all about you see Jews plowing their soil in their land? This soil that stands revealed in all its magic, and in the splendor of its hues, is it not itself a dream?

Here in the fields of Sejera, David Gruen spent his finest years in Palestine.

David's picturesque descriptions and romantic imagery highlight a character possessing great powers of expression, blessed with the gifts of persuasion, full of fervor and Zionist faith. It might appear that as a young man David stood out among his peers. But such an impression would be inaccurate. David Gruen possessed all these traits, without any doubt. Yet they were hidden behind layers of shyness and an inclination toward solitude. Every now and then, his fervor would burst forth – in a speech delivered at a party conference, in a Hebrew lecture before the farmers of Sejera, or in the regional conference of the Jewish workers' society in Galilee, where his views were much admired. But most of the time he kept to himself, and for a long time he even slept alone in one of the storehouses. His companions had no idea what he did during the long winter evenings. In fact, his comrades at Sejera did not even know whether or not he liked agricultural work. David did not particularly distinguish himself as a laborer. Many stories made the rounds among the workers about his passion for reading. It was said that on one occasion he walked after the oxen totally immersed in a newspaper. When he finished reading and raised his eyes, he found himself in the field, but there was no trace of his oxen. They had made off halfway through the plot for the near-by pasture, and David hadn't even noticed. Instinctively, the other workers sensed that, unlike themselves, he did not aspire to remain a farmer all his life. Instead, with his unusual character and his exceptional gifts, he "felt that he could do something more important than walking behind mules". But David never shared such thoughts with any of them.

His isolation – both enforced and self-inflicted – seemed to have intensified in Sejera. The girl he loved was far away; his close friends were not at his side. David's remaining close friend, Shlomo Zemach, left Sejera soon after his arrival. His letters reflected an astounding longing for intimate friends and yet he remained completely alone. During those years, David experienced the first taste of the loneliness that was to be his lot, like that of all great leaders. But it was hard to bear, and the need for someone close erupted in his passionately nostalgic letters to his father and family.

On several occasions, I have walked alone, my eyes on the stars and my heart with you . . . Here is my land, a magic land, before me – so close, it stirs my heart – and all the same, my heart is crushed by yearnings for that alien land, the land of the shadow of death . . . like a convict released to freedom who has left all his friends and companions behind him in jail – and he walks about, free, but nevertheless, drawn back toward those closed walls . . .

Circumstances gave young Gruen an opportunity to pay a visit to the "jail". In the middle of 1908, his time came to report for duty in the Russian army. To save his father the heavy fine of 300 roubles if he failed to report for service, David decided to return to Plonsk. His father sent him thirty-five roubles for his fare and another forty to pay off his many debts. Early in the autumn, Gruen set sail from Jaffa. The journey went off smoothly, and he met his family and reported for military service. Being pronounced fit, and having sworn his loyalty to the Czar, he promptly slipped out of the camp and crossed the border into Germany on forged papers. At the end of December, he was back in Palestine.

For a number of weeks, David worked on the shore of the Sea of Galilee in the settlement of Kinneret, which had been founded during his absence. From there he turned south to the settlement of Menahamiya, where he also worked for a few weeks. But he was soon overcome by his nostalgia for Sejera, which he regarded as his home. Of all the Jewish settlements, Sejera was the first in its "Conquest of Labor"; it was also the first to "conquer" its own defense requirements. When David Gruen came to Sejera, the defense of both the settlement and the farm at the top of the hill was entrusted to Circassian guards. Their reputation as courageous warriors was enough to keep the settlement safe from the local Arab marauders. But no less than "Jewish labor", "Jewish defense" was a part of the young pioneers' dream.

One day the employees of the Sejera farm confronted its manager, Krause, and demanded to take over the watchman's job. Since their pathos-filled speeches about Zionist vision and the homeland got them nowhere, the young workers decided to adopt a ruse. They knew that the Circassian never kept a close watch on the farm at night, preferring to stay in the nearby Arab village. One night a few of the workers stole the manager's pedigree horse, hid it far from the farm, and rushed to tell Krause of the theft. The manager blew his whistle and shouted for the guard, but the Circassian was asleep in the neighboring village. Krause was left with no alternative: the following day he ordered one of the Jewish employees to take over guard duty.

That winter, the farm's employees triumphed again: the settlement's guard, caught stealing the property he was supposed to be protecting, was discharged, and the defense of the settlement, like that of the farm, was thereafter entrusted to Jewish watchmen. David Gruen claimed that for some time he was the settlement's first guard.

By this time the farm management and the settlement's farmers had abandoned their attitude of derision or disapproval of the pioneers. When the youngsters again asked Krause to supply arms to all the employees, he sent a carriage to Haifa for rifles. As the workers laid their hands on the weapons, they were as excited as children. David wrote:

The large hall of the caravanserai, where most of the workers lodged, suddenly took on the appearance of a bandits' nest. A visitor entering during the evening would see a score of young men sitting on their beds, each holding a rifle: one cleaning the barrel, another loading and unloading, another filling his cartridge pouch. The rifles were compared and the faults and virtues of each one listed; they were hung up on the wall and taken down again, shouldered and removed, until it was time to go to sleep.

During the celebration of Passover, 1909, the first test came. From out of the darkness surrounding the main hall came the sounds of shouting. A young Jew appeared in the doorway, panting heavily. He had been on his way from Haifa to Sejera with two companions when they were attacked by three armed Arabs, who tried to steal the donkey that carried their belongings and beat its Arab driver. In the tussle that followed, one of the Jews pulled out a revolver and fired at the attackers, wounding one of them. A group of young men left the festivities and headed for the scene of the incident. The place was deserted, but they found traces of blood at the roadside. When the inhabitants of Sejera heard the report, a cloud of despondency descended on them. They were acquainted with the tradition of the blood feud; if the wounded Arab should die, the members of his tribe would set out to redeem his blood. "From that moment on, we knew that one of us was going to be murdered," said David Gruen. "The only question was who."

The anxiety in Sejera grew two days later, when the wounded Arab died in a Nazareth hospital. Members of his tribe immediately attacked Sejera's herds and reaped the barley from the settlement's fields. Then, on the last day of Passover, the farm's field guard, Israel Korngold, set off early to take up his post. Noticing two Arabs on the hillside, he approached them, accompanied by an Arabic-speaking farmer. Suddenly shots rang out. The workers snatched up their rifles and rushed to the scene. They found the body of Korngold, who had been shot through the heart. His assailants had stolen his weapons and fled. As the farm bell sounded the alarm, several groups of workers ran to the near-by gullies to seek the killers. Three Arabs suddenly appeared from out of nowhere. Two Jews pursued them, while three others – David Gruen among them – tried to block their path. The three did not notice that they were running straight into a trap. As they passed by a row of cactus, David heard the man next to him shout: "I've been shot!" Gruen halted, stooping over his companion, and saw that the man was dead.

The murders at Sejera had a profound effect on David Gruen's views and on his future course. His notions on acquiring weapons and on an autonomous armed force were influenced by the deep shock he experienced at the murder of his friends. At the time, however, the incident was the end of the first chapter in Gruen's military career. The Hashomer Society of guards refused his application for membership, even though he was actively employed in guard duty. Later the members of the society were to contend that they rejected him because he seemed too absent-minded and dreamy, adrift in other worlds.

Six months later David Gruen left Sejera, following a strike that failed to achieve any tangible gains. He packed his few belongings, stuffed his pistol into his pocket, and went off to work in the settlement of Yavniel, where he remained for a few weeks, and then drifted on to Zichron Ya'akov, which he found very congenial. There he began to learn a little French and Arabic, consciously and systematically preparing for the tasks he had set out for himself. These had been formulated in his mind during the long days spent alone with his oxen in the fields of Sejera. Following the Young Turks' uprising, which led to ethnic minorities gaining representation in the Turkish parliament, David began to consider a political future for himself, beginning with law studies in Constantinople. Later he hoped to be elected to the Turkish parliament as the representative of the Jewish workers of Palestine and perhaps even become a cabinet minister. In Zichron Ya'akov, he began to formulate this idea more clearly:

In future I shall either remain a tiller of the soil, or become a lawyer. I consider myself suited to either, and I incline toward both . . . Whether as a worker or as a lawyer, I have but one single aim: to serve the Jewish worker in the Land of Israel. That is the content of my life; to this I shall devote myself wherever I may be. This task is sacred to me; I shall find my happiness in fulfilling it.

With the same earnestness that had earlier brought him to Palestine and then to Galilee, David now applied himself to this new plan. To become a lawyer, he required an extensive education; to be accepted at a university, he had to pass entrance examinations and learn foreign languages. While continuing his work as an agricultural laborer, he now devoted a good portion of his nights to study.

In fact, long before his arrival in Zichron Ya'akov, David Gruen had already begun to extend his knowledge. Beginning in Warsaw six years earlier, he had made efforts to acquire a broad education. In addition to taking mathematics lessons from a private teacher, he had read Goethe, Shakespeare, and Tolstoy. In Sejera he kept to his studious habits. As housing was scarce, he found a grain store beyond the settlement's fence, set out a couch in the corner, and on evenings when he did not teach Hebrew to his fellow-workers, he would withdraw at an early hour. By the end of the winter, there were rumors among the other workers that David knew Arabic and was even reading the Koran. The rumor was of doubtful accuracy, and it was certainly exaggerated. But it highlights David Gruen's thirst for enlightenment and education and his efforts to acquire them, whatever the circumstances.

In the middle of 1910, David was notified by Yitzhak Ben-Zvi that he had been chosen to serve on the editorial board of *Ahdut* ("Unity"), the official journal of the Poalei Zion Party. Rachel Yanait and Yitzhak Ben-Zvi had pressed the Poalei Zion conference held in the spring of 1910 to coopt David to the *Ahdut* editorial board. Gruen was surprised to hear of his appointment and reluctant to take it up. "What shall I write?" he would ask his friends. "I don't know how to write; I've never written." In the end, however, he packed his belongings and moved to Jerusalem. Later on there would be occasional opportunities for him to spend a few weeks working in one of the settlements. But by going to Jerusalem four years after having arrived in Palestine, David Gruen concluded a further chapter of his life. The practical implication of the Zionist ideal – and personal fulfilment of its precepts – had now become a matter of the past. From now on he was to occupy himself with public affairs: writing, organization, and party work. In the course of time, his memories of work in the fields would take on a magic halo of bliss. The days and nights in the Galilee and Zichron Ya'akov would remain in his thoughts as a life of integrity, and he would look back on that time with longing and nostalgia for the rest of his life.

3
Exile

The first winds of autumn were whistling through the alleyways of the Old City when David Gruen started working in Jerusalem. He was twenty-four years old, a thin, curly-headed young man, with dark, burning eyes, a pale face, and a small, carefully tended moustache. He used to wear a dark Russian *rubashka* and faded trousers, or a thick flannel suit and boots. He did not own an overcoat, and when the chill breezes swept over the Judean Hills, he would wrap himself in a thin black cape he had brought from Russia. The cape served as both overcoat and blanket, but it could not protect him from the freezing Jerusalem nights.

Gruen rented a dreary room in the slum known as "the Floyd Courtyard". It was actually a windowless cellar – damp, musty, and enveloped in permanent gloom. He hung up a kerosene lamp and brought in boxes and boards to improvise a table, chairs, and a bed.

Gruen's new quarters presented him with a knotty problem: his monthly salary barely paid his rent and his lunch. "During his time at *Ahdut*," Rachel Yanait recalled, "Ben-Gurion . . . actually went around hungry." Yet he was not as lonely as he had been in the settlements. For the first time since his separation from Shlomo Zemach, David Gruen had companions with whom he established ties of the deepest friendship. Both were members of his party and of the *Ahdut* editorial board. One was Yitzhak Ben-Zvi, tall, thin, with a pale face adorned by a moustache and a small beard. Two years older than Gruen, he was one of the founders of Poalei Zion and a veteran of intensive underground activity in Russia. The other was Rachel Yanait, a dreamy young woman who had come to Palestine alone and without a penny but was filled with a fervent Zionist vision and was in love with Jerusalem.

The trio became a familiar sight in the streets of Jerusalem. When darkness fell, they would head to an Arab café in the Old City that boasted the latest in modern technology: a gramophone that poured forth a stream of Oriental melodies. The three would take over one of the corner tables, order a tiny cup of Turkish coffee, and launch into heated discussions about

Zionism. These arguments did not end in the café. For hours on end, at times until dawn, the threesome would roam the alleys of Jerusalem and debate the future of the country. With unconcealed excitement they spoke of a *evreyskoye gosudarstvo* – a Jewish state.

In the course of these heated debates, David began to formulate and express the social and political views that had crystallized during his four years behind the plow. He was still bashful and withdrawn, and when he was asked to address a party meeting, he would beg Rachel or Yitzhak to take his place. But when he finally stood up to deliver his speech, his sentences were clear and fluent, and he exhibited total self-assurance.

At first, he also hesitated to write. "I told my companions that I had never written for a newspaper, and I didn't know whether I was capable of doing so . . . But a week before the publication of the first issue, something happened that shocked me into writing two articles. On that occasion, I did not sign them." Only in the second issue of *Ahdut*, which appeared a month later, did he summon up the courage to sign his name. It was a new name, a Hebrew name: Ben-Gurion. He appears to have adopted it from Yosef Ben-Gurion, who headed the independent Jewish government during the revolt against the Romans and was noted for his courage, honesty, love for his people, and fanatical battle for freedom.

Ben-Gurion remained in Jerusalem for a year, publishing articles in *Ahdut*. By then it was already clear to the young man that the Jewish people would acquire Palestine in only one way – not by words, but by deeds. He knew that such practical tasks could only be undertaken by the workers. Therefore they must be united and organized, irrespective of party, in one single framework, making them into the vanguard that would lead the entire people toward realization of the Zionist goal. At a time of fierce inter-party rivalry and hostility, such views were extremely unusual. At the same time Ben-Gurion supported another principle, which was to serve as his banner: neither the world Poalei Zion movement nor the world Zionist bodies would dictate the actions of the Palestinian workers. Those at work in Palestine would decide on their own path. If Jews in the Diaspora wished to influence developments in Palestine, they should settle there.

Years later, Ben-Gurion was to refer to his work for *Ahdut* as "a period of political training". For the first time, writing and political organization became his principal occupation. At the beginning of August 1911, the apprentice party official passed his first test when, together with Ben-Zvi, he set out to Vienna to represent Palestinian Poalei Zion at the third congress of the World Union of Poalei Zion. As far as the two Palestinian delegates were concerned, the proceedings began in a somewhat unfortunate manner. The other delegates were furious at the "separatist" resolutions of the Palestinian Poalei Zion, which had laid down the principle that the practical policies of the workers' bodies in Palestine would be determined not by the world conference, but by the Palestinian workers themselves. There was further indignation over a declaration by Ben-Zvi and Ben-Gurion, that Zionism would be realized by the workers living in Palestine, and not by the Zionists in the Diaspora. Finally, when the two delegates stressed that the unity of the Palestinian workers, irrespective of party differences, was more important than their links to the party in the Diaspora, there was an uproar. The conference adopted a resolution accusing the Palestinian delegates of "separatism".

This condemnation, and the isolation of the two Palestinian delegates in the face of a united front of their Diaspora comrades, brought home to Ben-Gurion the divergence of views between the pioneers in Palestine and the Diaspora Zionists. It showed him that if he wished to achieve his aims, he would have to act alone, even from a position of inferiority. At some time in the future, he would take over Diaspora Zionism and harness it to his own purposes.

Since his days in Sejera, Ben-Gurion had been developing the idea of "Ottomanization", namely, that the Jews of Palestine should renounce their foreign citizenship and become subjects of the Ottoman Empire. This would enable them to work towards the realization of their aims within legal and governmental channels. Accordingly, it was essential to establish a leadership that spoke Turkish and knew Ottoman law, and Ben-Gurion decided that the next step in his life must be the study of law and of the Turkish language. Within two months, two of Ben-Gurion's closest friends, Israel Shochat and Yitzhak Ben-Zvi, also decided to study in Constantinople. David himself reached a final decision after his father agreed to send him thirty roubles a month to pay for his studies.

On 7 November 1911, Ben-Gurion disembarked in the harbor of Salonika, the capital of the Ottoman province of Macedonia. Before registering at the Constantinople law faculty, he intended to study the Turkish language. He chose to study in Salonika because the cost of living there was far lower than in Constantinople and, in his own description, because "Salonika was a purely Jewish city. In those days, the only Jewish city in the world." The Jews of Salonika were an unusual community, and they amazed Ben-Gurion, primarily because of their occupations: most of them engaged in hard physical labor as stevedores in the port. "In their hearts, many people doubted whether the Jewish people – cut off from the soil and from labor for hundreds of years – was capable of bringing forth a working class. In [Salonika] I found an answer to that question."

The educated Jews of Salonika spoke French, but Ben-Gurion had come to learn Turkish. His tutor was a young Jew from the law faculty. Under his guidance David did wonders in his studies. By the end of December he was already reading Turkish newspapers. Despite his progress, however, Ben-Gurion's mood was downcast. The money he received from his father scarcely sufficed for his livelihood. His year in Salonika was a period of voluntary asceticism and enforced isolation. He was utterly alone, without a single friend to share his thoughts and feelings. Cut off from the Jews of the city by a spiritual and lingual barrier, he would sit in his room surrounded by dictionaries, papers and journals, studying from morning to night.

The bizarre personality of the stocky, ailing young man who had come from Palestine to learn Turkish evoked interest among the Jews of Salonika. A German Jew who published a book of his impressions of Salonika, did not overlook Ben-Gurion.

It seems there are persons to whom speech is not essential. With us here, for example, is Mr Gruen, who has just pulled seven different Hebrew journals from his pocket, and will, doubtless, only return to the world of reality after having consumed them from A to Z . . . Mr Gruen reads on and on . . . Soon, he will get up and walk away without taking his leave. But no one is surprised thereby, for, after all, this is Mr Gruen, and everyone knows his habits.

With the onset of spring, "Mr Gruen" began to prepare for the university examinations. He lacked a number of documents required for his registration, the most important of which was a matriculation certificate. But with the help of his good friend Ben-Zvi – and his father's money – he succeeded in obtaining a forged matriculation certificate from a Russian high school. In June 1912 he sat for the entrance examinations and passed them all successfully. Two months later, Ben-Gurion arrived in Constantinople and was admitted to the university, which bore the elaborate oriental title "The House of Wisdom".

Cannon fire and battle cries served as fearsome background music to the studies of the young men in Constantinople. Only a few months had passed since the armed clash between Turkey and Italy reached its peak with the Italian bombardment of the Dardanelles. Two months after Ben-Gurion's arrival in Turkey, the Balkan War broke out, destroying the Turkish foothold in Europe and bringing the battle to the very outskirts of the capital. On the horizon, the storm clouds were gathering for the world war, while the Young Turk government groped its way uncertainly. The mighty Ottoman Empire, rotten within and undermined from without, was disintegrating.

Ben-Gurion and his companions still did not grasp that they were living through the last days of a dying empire and clung to the idea of "Otto-manization". They persisted in their efforts to acquire Turkish citizenship and even adopted the latest Turkish fashions. Ben-Gurion took to wearing a flattened *tarboush*, clipped his moustache in the Turkish style and had a new suit made in the fashion of the *effendis* – a black tailcoat and buttoned waistcoat whose pocket held a watch on a glittering chain. But the affectation was short-lived. When the Balkan War broke out, hundreds of students were sent to the front and the university was closed. Ben-Gurion and Ben-Zvi decided to return to Palestine until it reopened. No sooner had Ben-Gurion disembarked in Jaffa than he reverted to the party activist, organizer and orator.

Upon returning to Constantinople four months later, Ben-Gurion fell sick several times. He had long been suffering from malnutrition; now he was also afflicted with scurvy, brought on by a severe vitamin deficiency. His financial situation deteriorated in Constantinople, since the allowance sent by his father was inadequate and did not arrive regularly. He often remained hungry, and he sometimes teetered on the verge of desperation. Most of his letters to his father repeated the same refrain: When would the money arrive? Avigdor, who at that time was marrying off a son and a daughter, found it difficult to finance David as well. In a moment of weakness, he backed a proposal suggested by David's eldest sister, Rivka, that David leave Constantinople, give up Palestine, and return to Russia to build his future there. "The objective I have set myself is a question of life for me," David erupted in his dramatic style. "There is only one single thing that can prevent me from attaining it – that is death!" It was hard to stand up to such fervor.

Hungry and ailing though he was, David did well in his studies. He received the highest grades on examinations and took great pride in reporting the fact to his family and relatives. But at the end of December 1913, in the middle of his second year of study, he fell ill again and was hospitalized in Constantinople for an extensive period. This time his family came to his assistance. When he left the hospital, they sent him the fare and he came to Russia for two months. He could not visit Plonsk, for he was considered a deserter from the army, but he travelled to Warsaw, Lodz, and Odessa, and stayed with his sister Rivka, who pampered and thoroughly fed him. During his absence, loyal friends signed his name on the attendance rolls at the university lectures.

In the middle of spring, he returned to Constantinople and sat for his examinations, with considerable success. On 28 July he and Ben-Zvi set sail for a vacation in Palestine. Three days later, while still at sea, they learned of the outbreak of the world war when two German warships engaged in pursuing the ramshackle Russian vessel that was carrying them. After an exhausting tour of the ports of the Mediterranean, they finally disembarked at Jaffa.

In Palestine they encountered a scene of despair and disintegration. After two months of hesitation, Turkey joined the war at the side of Imperial Germany, while confusion, fear, and hardship spread throughout the Jewish community. Some fled as the suspicious Turks constantly imposed the severest restrictions on the Jewish community, confiscated arms, levied heavy imports, and began to deport those Jews who were foreign nationals. The whole settlement project was in danger of destruction. In London and Cairo, Zionist leaders called upon Palestinian Jews to take the side of the Entente Powers. Ben-Gurion and Ben-Zvi were furiously opposed to these appeals. Above all, they feared that the Turks would wreak their vengeance upon the Jews of Palestine by deporting them *en masse*.

Ben-Gurion and Ben-Zvi quickly joined the Ottomanization Committee established in Jerusalem and obtained permission to recruit a Jewish militia to defend Palestine. But the militia met its end with the arrival of the Turkish vizier for the navy, Jemal Pasha, who had been appointed to command the Fourth Army on the Egyptian front. On his way south Jemal Pasha suppressed any manifestations of nationalism. First, he struck at the Arab national movement, hanging a number of its leaders in Beirut. Then came the turn of the Zionist movement in Palestine: the volunteer militia was disbanded and *Ahdut* was closed down. Jemal Pasha decreed that anyone found bearing a Zionist document would be put to death. Then came the arrests. Ben-Gurion and Ben-Zvi were interrogated at length about their contacts with the Zionist movement. Shortly afterwards orders were issued for their deportation from the Ottoman Empire. Manacled, they were taken aboard a boat in Jaffa harbor. On the deportation order, the Turkish governor had written: "To be banished forever from the Turkish Empire."

Neither Ben-Gurion nor Ben-Zvi believed it for a moment. On the contrary, in a spirit of enterprise and optimism they set sail for America on a dilapidated Greek boat named the *Patrus*. It was a rough, month-long voyage, and conditions in the third class were appalling. But in between storms, and even during them Ben-Gurion did not waste his time. He read several chapters of Hegel's works and jotted down notes for political activity in America. Above all, he studied English with his characteristic earnestness and diligence. At long last, from the deck of his ship, Ben-Gurion saw the coast of the New World. His first impressions were not very enthusiastic: "Here is the proud Statue of Liberty, towering from the sea at the entrance to the New World. And here are the famous 'sky scrapers' – buildings of thirty stories. Strange – despite their height they do not appear great. For some reason, they are absurd; they resemble cages."

Shabbily dressed, Ben-Gurion and Ben-Zvi underwent the immigration procedures and disembarked in New York harbor. Members of Poalei Zion came to welcome them, and the first thing they did was to remove the red Turkish *tarboushes* from the heads of the new arrivals. It was not considered politic for the two Zionist leaders from Palestine to walk the streets of New York dressed like Turks. The *tarboushes* found a more effective use in Poalei Zion's store of fancy-dress costumes used for the party's annual "Oriental Ball". It was a fitting ending to the Ottoman period in Ben-Gurion's life.

"The two Bens", as Ben-Gurion and Ben-Zvi were referred to by their comrades, did not waste time on meetings or tours. They were impatient to begin carrying out the plan they had brought from Palestine. "We immediately explained that we had come to organize . . . members into groups of Hehalutz (The Pioneer) with the aim of emigrating to Palestine and working there," Ben-Zvi later related. "Accordingly, we demanded that the Poalei Zion leadership organize a 'tour' of America for us, so that we could found Hehalutz groups everywhere . . ." "We did not know when we would return to Palestine," Ben-Gurion recalled, "but we hoped to be accompanied on our return by a whole army of pioneers."

Ben-Gurion and Ben-Zvi bought a large map of the United States, divided the country up between them, and began traveling from city to city to address young people and convince them to join the new organization. But the outcome of their campaign was disappointing. Only a few young people volunteered to join Hehalutz. Ben-Gurion spent long months traveling from town to town, speaking in halls that were three-quarters empty, and collecting small contributions for the weekly that the party was about to issue. Here and there, he recruited a few pioneers. One of the few who was won over by his ardor was a young woman from Milwaukee by the name of Goldie Mabovitch, later to be known as Golda Meir.

During the war years, there were a number of schemes competing with the notion of a "labor army" to conquer Palestine. The center of the Zionist movement was for all practical purposes in London, and the general mood there was that the Land of Israel would be awarded to the Jews by the victorious Entente armies as part of a postwar political settlement. At the same time, a young Zionist leader named Vladimir Jabotinsky was active in promoting the notion of a Jewish Legion to conquer Palestine from the Turkish army and claim it for the Jewish people. The latter idea drew little enthusiasm in the United States, which had not yet entered the war, and the former called for little activity on the part of the Jewish masses. Yet Ben-Gurion opposed both ideas on principle. In September he wrote:

There are various ways of conquering a country. It can be seized by force of arms; it can be acquired by political ruses or diplomatic guiles; it can even be bought with money . . . All these methods have but one aim – to enslave and exploit the native population. We, however, are seeking something very different in Palestine – a homeland. A homeland is not given or received as a gift; it is not possessed by gold or conquered by the power of the fist; it is built by the sweat of the brow. We shall receive our land not from a peace conference . . . but from the Jewish workers who shall come to strike roots in the country, revive it, and live in it. The Land of Israel shall be ours when a majority of its workers and guardsmen shall be of our people.

Two months later Ben-Gurion expounded his views in a long address before the Cleveland Conference of Poalei Zion. His speech evoked some support and agreement within the movement; but as Ben-Gurion himself said, "the Zionist movement as a whole was far from this view". In truth, so were the members of the American Poalei Zion (resolutions of support notwithstanding) for when Ben-Gurion and Ben-Zvi assessed the outcome of their efforts, they discovered that they had succeeded in recruiting no more than 150 pioneers throughout the United States and Canada.

In order to propagate their views, "the two Bens" published two books. *Yizkor* ("Commemoration"), written with two other Zionists, depicted the perilous lives and heroic deaths of the early watchmen in Palestine and made such a wide impact that they decided to write a second book, *Eretz Israel*, in which they would describe the Land of Israel to the Jewish masses in the United States. To carry out the research, Ben-Gurion devoted thirteen hours a day to research in the New York Public Library. He also travelled to the Library of Congress in Washington, and to other documentation centers. The party's central committee allocated him ten dollars a week until he completed the book.

Eretz Israel was published only in the spring of 1918, by which time events of enormous significance in the Jewish world were to have profound impact on the political path of "the two Bens". In the meanwhile, Ben-Gurion's "political apprenticeship", begun in Jerusalem, was resumed in New York. He wrote, lectured, collected money, plodded around the branches of his party all over the country and argued and debated fiercely at congresses, conferences, and meetings. At times he found himself in the minority, and at least once, he was forced to resign from one of his posts. He met, and worked alongside, several of the foremost leaders of his party – indeed, of the Zionist movement as a whole – and even though he remained a leader of secondary rank, his name began to get around. There are even those who claim that he was systematically preparing himself for the role of a political leader. Ben-Gurion's neighbor at the table in the New York Public Library was a Jewish socialist from Russia named Lev Deutsch. According to one story, Deutsch once asked a friend of Ben-Gurion's, "Who is that young man?" The friend replied, "One of the leaders of the workers' movement in Palestine." Deutsch was astonished. "Almost every day the man sits next to me and reads. Naturally, I am curious to know what he is reading. And I see that the books are extraordinary treatises: histories of the American parties, practical guides in the technique of conquest of the masses, practical books about the administrative apparatus, and so on."

For all the frenetic activity, a familiar pattern in Ben-Gurion's life repeated itself in America. He remained withdrawn and introverted, and his isolation grew. It was only in his letters to his father that he revealed his innermost thoughts, but he stopped writing to Avigdor when postal links were broken off after Poland's conquest by the Germans. He did not have any really close friends, with the exception of Ben-Zvi, and he was living in a land that he found enormous and strange. During those years in America, he sensed a renewed yearning for his beautiful childhood sweetheart, Rachel Nelkin. The letters he wrote to her from the United States were astonishing, considering the conventions of those times: David begged her to leave everything and to come to him in America! But Rachel was married, and it was impossible to turn the clock back.

Ben-Gurion was thirty, a pale earnest man who always dressed in the same shabby old suit, when he met Paulina ("Paula") Monbaz at the house of a mutual acquaintance. Short, bespectacled, with a broad face, Paula was not beautiful, but she was peppy, full of life and extremely outspoken. In contrast to the introverted young man, she was open, free, and fond of company and fun. She had been born in Minsk to a respected family; but when her father died, her family was impoverished, and she had to break off her medical studies and go to work as a nurse in a hospital operating theater. She was not a Zionist. The Land of Israel, the Return to Zion, Jewish state – none of these meant anything to her. She lived in a different world, and for some time, she was even captivated by anarchist ideas. She admired Trotsky, who was then residing in New York, and sat in the front row at his lectures, imagining that he had observed her presence and that in the midst of his fiery addresses he flung longing glances in her direction.

Paula had been going out with a doctor for several years, and they were thinking of getting married. Nevertheless, she was charmed by the young pioneer from Plonsk. "You should have seen his appearance!" she recollected later. "Bleary-eyed and shabby. But as soon as he opened his mouth,

I saw that this was a great man." Upon hearing of his literary work, she asked if she could be of help. "If you wish to, yes, please," he replied. She began to join him at the public library in the evenings and copied out long passages for him. The two began to go out together, and since both of them were earning little, they agreed to share the cost. Gradually, they fell in love. Over a year elapsed from the day they met until Ben-Gurion proposed. But he accompanied his proposal with a warning: if she agreed to marry him, she would have to leave America and to set out for "a small, impoverished land, where there is no electricity or gas, or electric trolleys".

Paula agreed. On the morning of 5 December 1917, she walked out of the operating theater, took off her gown, and rushed to New York's City Hall, where Ben-Gurion was waiting for her. The pair walked into the marriage registration bureau, paid two dollars, and the official there married Paula Monbaz to David Ben-Gurion. After the ceremony, the bride hurried back to the hospital, where an urgent operation awaited her, and Ben-Gurion set off for a meeting of the Poalei Zion Executive. "I arrived a quarter of an hour late, and the comrades were surprised at my tardiness. I explained that I was late because I had just gotten married. Of course, they all congratulated me, astounded that I had gotten married without telling a soul beforehand. And I was not married by a rabbi."

That evening Paula returned to the apartment she shared with her girl friends, while Ben-Gurion went back to the room he had taken with Ben-Zvi. It was only on the following weekend that the couple met and went out to hunt for an apartment. They found one at 631 Bedford Avenue in Brooklyn. But they did not remain together for long. Five months after their marriage, they were separated for eighteen months as a result of the great event that had occurred on 2 November 1917 – the Balfour Declaration.

The unexpected statement – which came in the form of a letter from Arthur Balfour to Lord Rothschild – exceeded the wildest dreams of even the most optimistic Zionists. It declared that "His Majesty's Government view with favour the establishment in Palestine of a national home for the Jewish People, and will use their best endeavours to facilitate the achievement of this object . . ." Credit for achieving the declaration is usually given to Dr Chaim Weizmann, who now became the unchallenged leader of the Zionist movement. In 1916, while directing a chemical laboratory in Manchester, Weizmann presented the First Lord of the Admiralty, Winston Churchill, with a brilliant solution for the problem of ammunition production: the formula for the manufacture of synthetic acetone. A few months later – according to one legend – the new British prime minister, Lloyd George, asked Weizmann how could he be repaid for his

contribution to the war effort. "Do something for my people," said
Weizmann – and asked for Palestine.

It is highly doubtful if that is the way matters really occurred, and it is
doubly doubtful whether the British would have fulfilled that request if
it had come up for sober consideration during peacetime. They had already offered Palestine to the French, as well as promising it to the Arabs.
At the same time, the British appear to have been eager to win the support
of the world's Jews for their struggle against the Central Powers. Their
leaders were especially interested in the Jews of Russia and the United
States and concerned over the sympathy which many Jews displayed for
Germany because of its war against Russia – the land of oppression and
pogroms. From the Continent came rumors that Germany would soon
publish a pro-Zionist proclamation and exert its influence on Turkey to
grant rights of immigration and settlement to the Jews. The five million
Jews of Russia, and those of Hungary, Austria, and Germany as well, were
a political factor that could not be overlooked. It was a trick of fate that
five days after the publication of the Balfour Declaration, Kerensky's
government was overthrown by the Bolshevik Revolution. Some scholars
believe that, had the revolution taken place a week earlier, the Balfour
Declaration would have been shelved.

Such analyses have the advantage of sixty years of hindsight. At the
time, Jews all over the world hailed the Balfour Declaration in a frenzy of
enthusiasm. Perhaps the only note of dissonance in the chorus of delight
was Ben-Gurion's familiar refrain:

Britain has not given Palestine back to us. Even if the whole country were
conquered by the British, it would not become ours through Great Britain giving
her consent and other countries agreeing ... Britain has made a magnificent
gesture; she has recognized our existence as a nation and has acknowledged our
right to the country. But only the Hebrew people can transform this right into
tangible fact; only they, with body and soul, with their strength and capital,
must build their National Home and bring about their national redemption.

His dogged stance was not meant to belittle the political value of the Balfour
Declaration. But in those weeks of heady celebration, it seemed to many
that the Messiah had come dressed in the garb of a British lord, and the
password of the day was that the Jewish people were on the brink of
Redemption. Ben-Gurion simply wanted to place matters in their proper
perspective.

The Balfour Declaration did change Ben-Gurion's views on one matter.
With the United States' entry into the war, the scales were now clearly
tilting in favor of the Entente Powers, and at the end of the summer of

1917, when the British army stood poised at the gates of Palestine, it was clear that Turkish rule there was coming to an end. The question of the Jewish Legion now arose again, and this time Ben-Gurion believed it was important that Jewish soldiers be among those risking their lives for the liberation of Palestine. The Balfour Declaration had naturally provided a boost for the establishment of the Jewish Legion, and Ben-Gurion placed himself at the vanguard of those demanding the formation of a Jewish battalion. He traveled to Washington to raise the idea before Supreme Court Justice Louis Brandeis, one of the prominent personalities of American Zionism, who brought it to President Wilson. But Wilson rejected the proposal, and a solution was found only when, at the instigation of Vladimir Jabotinsky, Jewish battalions were established within the British army. The 150 members of Hehalutz now volunteered for the Jewish Legion and, together with 200 Palestinian exiles in America, they became the nucleus of the American battalion that was to be named the 39th Battalion of the Royal Fusiliers.

On 26 April 1918, Ben-Gurion came to the little apartment in Brooklyn and informed his wife that he had signed up for the Jewish Legion. Paula broke into bitter tears. Four months pregnant, she was afraid of being separated from her husband. It was futile to remind her that before their marriage he had warned her of his intentions and she had agreed. She begged him not to leave, but he only promised her that after she gave birth he would immediately bring her and the baby to Palestine. On 28 May, Ben-Gurion swore his oath of allegiance in the offices of the British consul in New York, and the next day he set out for the battalion's training camp in Windsor, Canada. It was springtime in America, and wherever the train stopped, it was met by throngs of enthusiastic Jews, who cheered the heroes on their way to redeem Palestine. At Windsor Ben-Gurion was met by a bronzed soldier in British army uniform. He was Yitzhak Ben-Zvi who had arrived a week earlier.

Ben-Gurion was thirty-two, not exactly a youngster, but he was happy with his life in the camp. But Private Ben-Gurion was not an ordinary soldier. He was an experienced political activist, a gifted orator, and his name was well known among the soldiers of the Legion. According to his own testimony, even wild characters and criminals obeyed him. The officers noticed Ben-Gurion's special status and hastened to place a military seal upon it. "This morning, I was summoned by our company sergeant-major, Wilson, to accept the post of lance-corporal; however I got out of it gracefully, explaining that I would be more useful as an ordinary soldier than by bearing rank."

Ben-Gurion's private mutiny soon came to an end. At tent inspection, the sergeant-major reported to the camp commander that "this is the best man in the Jewish battalion", and told him that Ben-Gurion had declined the rank of corporal. The officer summoned Ben-Gurion and made it plain that "overseas there would be no committees and military men will be in charge, so I should therefore accept the stripe". The rebel surrendered to his fate, and within less than a month, he was promoted to full corporal.

On 11 July, the Legionaries set sail for England and Palestine in a convoy of some twenty ships. On 22 July, Ben-Gurion's company disembarked at Tilbury, England, and was conveyed to the camp at Hounslow. Ben-Gurion received a few days' leave, which he spent touring London and meeting with Zionist leaders. He was bitterly disappointed to learn that the forward units of the Jewish Legion were deliberately being held up in Egypt because General Allenby and his officers were opposed to the Balfour Declaration and not at all inclined to permit the Jews even the smallest role in liberating the country. On 14 August, however, the whole of the 39th Battalion of the Royal Fusiliers set sail for Egypt. Two weeks later they disembarked at Port Said.

Ben-Gurion was very excited about the prospect of meeting again his old friends who had remained in Palestine during the war. Many of them now volunteered for the Palestinian Jewish battalion. After a week in Egypt, he left his camp and traveled to Cairo, where the Palestinian battalion was encamped. That same day he fell ill with a severe attack of dysentery and was rushed to hospital, where he lay for several weeks. It was there that he received a telegram from Paula informing him of the birth of their daughter, Ge'ula. As usual, his personal joy took on a national dimension. "The birth of our child," he wrote to Paula, "occurs at the happy moment when our land is being redeemed, and the glory of this moment will light her entire life."

His national impulse and intimate personal feelings are also intertwined as a central motif in Ben-Gurion's correspondence with Paula during his service in the Legion. Prior to his arrival in Egypt, he wrote to Paula almost every day. He overwhelmed her with expressions of burning love, but he could not – nor did he wish to – separate his personal happiness from his national dream. "I know what price you are paying, with your youth and your happiness, for me and my ideals," he wrote her from Windsor. "The price is terribly high, and I do not know if I can repay you properly. But that is the cruelty of great love. If I were to stay with you now, I would not be worthy that you should bear my child, and our whole lives would be petty and pointless . . ."

From her letters, he learned that it was hard for her to bear the separation and that she found no comfort in his ideals. To strengthen her morale, he frequently described the rosy future awaiting them, combining the style of a revolutionary pamphlet with sentimental outpourings of love:

I know you well enough to have confidence that you will bear this heavy burden and climb, tearful and suffering, up the high mountain from which you will see a new world, a world of light and joy, glistening in the light of an ideal eternally fresh; another world is there, a world of supreme happiness, a wonderful universe, a world which few will have the privilege of entering, for only rich souls and profound hearts will be permitted access, and I know that your soul is rich and your heart is sufficiently large for the fine world and the fine life I wish to prepare for you.

And there were letters in which Ben-Gurion gave himself over completely to his longing and passion for his wife:

Again, like a youngster, a silly young man, I feel as though I am in love with you for the first time, and I seek your lips, your arms, and I want to press you to me, to embrace you with burning arms, to stand beside your bed, to bend over you, to cling to you and sink into your arms, oblivious to everything except you; like then, to be happy in your intimate love – together, arm in arm, lips to lips, heart to heart, in your maiden bed which was so sacred to me.

But their correspondence shows that this "revolutionary passion" – the combination of love for a woman and love for a homeland – was one-sided. Paula loved Ben-Gurion deeply. But despite all his efforts, and her own, she could not transcend the problems of an infatuated woman, lonely and abandoned. Nor did she manage to acquire the spirit of fighting for that "great ideal" which he depicted to her. The deep gap between their views prevented the "spiritual fusion" that Ben-Gurion so desired. Paula was embittered, frequently quarrelsome, burdened by the thousands of problems posed by everyday life in New York, and consumed by yearning for her husband. Alone, she had to give birth, raise her baby, and overcome her financial straits. She would detail her pains and her troubles in gloomy letters; accuse him of not loving her enough; suspect that he was already tired of writing to her whenever his letter arrived late. It is possible to understand her. Paula was not a Zionist, and her husband's ideology was no source of comfort to her. She loved Ben-Gurion and dedicated her life to him. But their love could not bridge the gap, between them.

Ben-Gurion did not undergo a baptism of fire. Before his battalion reached the front, the Turkish armies collapsed and Palestine was occupied by the British. Only on 6 November 1918, after a three-day journey, did he arrive in Tel Aviv on leave. Over three years earlier, he had been "banished forever". Now he was back among his friends, proud and happy in a uniform that bore the Shield of David on the sleeve. His exile had ended, and a new chapter was opening in his life.

4

Membership Card No. 3

While Ben-Gurion lay in the military hospital in Cairo, he received the journal *Ba'Avodah* (At Work), published by the Agricultural Union in Palestine. The outstanding item in that issue was a long, programmatic article by Berl Katznelson entitled "Toward the Forthcoming Days". It was a kind of credo, written at the onset of a new era in the history of Zionism; and its central theme was that Palestine would be built up by the Jewish agricultural worker. Katznelson stressed that the workers – the true vanguard of Zionism – should determine the path to be taken by the World Zionist movement.

Ben-Gurion read the article with great interest and saw that "in fact, we are of the same mind". When he rose from his sick-bed, he set out for the camp occupied by the Palestinian battalion in search of Berl Katznelson, the stocky, curly-haired mentor of the penniless socialist pioneers who had spent years roaming around Palestine from one job to another. When he found Katznelson in the camp and proposed the union of the two Labor parties in Palestine – Poalei Zion and Hapoel Hatzair – Berl said, "without enthusiasm: 'All right, let's go to the Hapoel Hatzair people.' They all lived in the same tent," which indicates how small the Jewish pioneer groups were at the time, "and the Hapoel Hatzair people agreed to the idea of unification."

Less than two weeks later, Ben-Gurion's battalion at long last departed for Palestine. A day after their arrival, he left the camp without a pass and made his way around Jaffa seeking converts for the idea of unification. His political activities put an end to the military career of Corporal David Ben-Gurion. On his return to camp after a four-day absence, he was caught, tried, and sentenced to be demoted to the rank of private, fined three days' pay, and transferred to another company. But Ben-Gurion was not too upset over the verdict, because a few days later he received a month's leave and returned to his political activities.

He met his first challenge when he presented the unification proposal to his own party, Poalei Zion, at a conference in February 1919. His task was not easy, for he was still a minor leader and anti-dogmatic in his socialist views. However, he possessed the gift of hurling himself into the fray with all his fiery temperament. The conference decided, by a majority vote, to support the unification proposal; but a Hapoel Hatzair conference convened at the same time now opposed the idea. Refusing to accept that verdict, Berl Katznelson and Ben-Gurion now convened a "general conference of all the workers of the Land of Israel". The eighty-one delegates adopted the unification plan formulated by Berl and decided on a name for their new organization: Ahdut ha-Avodah ("Labor Unity"). One of the important resolutions adopted at the conference demanded "international guarantees for the establishment of a free Jewish state in the Land of Israel that would strive for the creation of a Jewish majority in the country under the auspices of a representative of the League of Nations".

The establishment of Ahdut ha-Avodah was only a partial victory, or a step on the way to victory. At that time, the Zionist labor movements were a minority within the world Zionist movement, and the Palestinian workers were only a minority within that minority. Berl Katznelson and Ben-Gurion nurtured far-reaching aspirations: they wanted to unite the Palestinian workers into a cohesive body that would direct Zionist activity in Palestine, as well as determine the policies of the world Zionist movement. For this purpose, it was essential to unite all the workers in Palestine into a single organization. Ahdut ha-Avodah had the potential to become such a body. But when it became clear that the members of Hapoel Hatzair were not joining the new union, it was necessary to try and establish yet another general organization – above parties – that would unite all the workers in the country. By December 1920 that had been accomplished with the founding of the General Federation of the Hebrew Workers in the Land of Israel, known to this day as the Histadrut. Ben-Gurion, however, did not enjoy the good fortune of being among those who formulated the federation's basic principles. At that time, he was abroad again, and it was from afar that he followed the establishment of the workers' organization that was of such importance to him.

Yet the intervening months in Palestine held other joys for him. On Saturday 15 November 1919, Private David Ben-Gurion stood overcome with emotion on the pier of Jaffa harbor as he embraced his wife and his fourteen-month-old daughter, Ge'ula, whom he was seeing for the first time. He lodged his family in a hotel and took care of all their needs with exceptional devotion, as befits a family man. It was not in jest that he promised Paula before her departure: "I will supply eggs and milk, not only for drinking but for bathing our baby, if you so desire . . . I promise you, my Paula, that Ge'ula will have all the comforts that exist in Brooklyn and the Bronx, at least until she wants to go to the Metropolitan Opera House." When, at long last, he saw his daughter, his excitement knew no bounds: "Without any father's prejudices, I may say that she is one of the nicest, most attractive, charming, beautiful, and bright little girls I have ever seen."

Shortly after their arrival, Ben-Gurion was discharged from the army. For several months, he occupied himself with affairs of Ahdut ha-Avodah. At the end of spring, however, Ahdut ha-Avodah decided to send him to London to establish contact with the British Labour Party and direct the office of the Poalei Zion World Federation. At the beginning of June 1920, the family set off. Paula was pregnant and expecting at the end of summer.

The beginning of that year in Europe was tempestuous and dramatic: its continuation was dull and burdensome. Shortly after their arrival in London, Ben-Gurion left Paula and Ge'ula and set off for the Poalei Zion World Federation conference in Vienna. The mood of the conference was bellicose; and before it was over the World Federation had split between the left wing, which advocated adherence to the Third International and the severing of links with the World Zionist Congress, and the right wing, which followed the Zionist–Socialist principles of Ahdut ha-Avodah. Ben-Gurion was under great strain, both because of the forthcoming split and because he was waiting for a telegram notifying him that Paula was about to give birth. While the debate was at its peak, the telegram arrived and Ben-Gurion rushed back to London. A week after his return, Paula gave birth to a son. Ben-Gurion named the child Amos.

After the initial excitement, the Ben-Gurion family settled down in a tiny flat in Maida Vale. Every morning Ben-Gurion made his way by Underground to the Poalei Zion offices and personally experienced the frustrating life of a Diaspora Zionist leader. The routine and his remoteness from Palestine where things were really happening, left him depressed. In an unusual letter to Rachel Yanait, he revealed his gloomy feelings: "In London, my dear, you always live in a cold and monotonous fog, even though, to tell the truth, I have yet to see a fog proper . . . When, my dear Rachel, will offices be banished from this world?"

At that time, Ben-Gurion renewed regular contacts with his father and family in Poland and Russia, but there was a far-reaching change in their relationship. Now Ben-Gurion took upon himself the role of head of the family, helping to support his father and imposing his will upon his relatives – not infrequently to their indignation.

His father and sisters begged him to help them emigrate to Palestine, but Ben-Gurion adamantly refused, telling his father that "this question depends a great deal on my future. I definitely do not yet know how I will manage." On arriving in England, David attempted to appease his father's displeasure by proposing that he come to live with them in London. At first, he proposed that he come "together with the Aunt" (Avigdor Gruen's second wife), but then he withdrew this offer and limited it to Avigdor alone, claiming that he lacked the money to pay for "the Aunt's" fare.

No less strange was Ben-Gurion's attitude towards his sister Rivka. She begged him to help her come to Palestine, declaring that she was prepared to do any kind of work there. David flatly refused. "I do not believe that she will be able to work, or to find work she is fitted for." He was only prepared to help her immigrate on condition that she brought a sum of money large enough for her to subsist on the interest! The author of fiery articles and memoranda advocating mass immigration behaved like an anti-Zionist burgher when his own family was concerned. He even encouraged his sister to adopt a way of life that every apprentice socialist would have rejected as parasitic.

Relations between Ben-Gurion and his father deteriorated further as a result of Paula's visit to Plonsk. Originally planned for a few weeks, it ultimately lasted over a year. In March 1921, Ben-Gurion went to Vienna for a few months and sent Paula and the children to Plonsk to get to know his father. Soon, however, friction erupted between Avigdor Gruen and Paula. She complained bitterly about "the musty room" in which she was lodged; the drinking water, which she considered dirty; and the sanitary conditions. She also asked to have a servant hired for her. The elderly couple were indignant over what they considered to be Paula's capricious and ostentatious behavior. When Ben-Gurion visited Plonsk in May, he did not succeed in dispelling the accumulated bitterness between his father and his wife. Nevertheless, he did not take Paula and the children back with him – not even when relations between Avigdor and Paula reached crisis point, which made his father furious with him. Ben-Gurion did not initially intend to send his family away for an extended period – certainly not for a year. However, in May 1921, bloody rioting broke out in Jaffa, and Ben-Gurion rushed back to Palestine. It was more than a year before Paula and the children followed him.

When Ben-Gurion arrived back in Palestine late in the summer of 1921, the shock of the Jaffa disturbances had yet to wear off. The Palestinian Arabs were concerned over the express intentions of the Jews, who had come from afar to make Palestine their own country and set up a Jewish government with British assistance. A few weeks before the opening of the 1920 San Remo Conference, which was to deal with the British Mandate over Palestine, tensions built up – not unintentionally. Influential Arab leaders believed that a wave of rioting would cause the world's leaders to have second thoughts about delegating Britain to implement the Balfour Declaration. "The land is our land, the Jews are our dogs!" roared the inflamed Arab mobs that attacked the Jews of Jerusalem, sensing that their attacks were not entirely unwelcomed by the British authorities. Indeed, the high command of the British army in Palestine was not sympathetic to the Zionist cause. The San Remo Conference nevertheless entrusted the Mandate over Palestine to Britain, and the country's 64,000 Jews welcomed the first high commissioner, Herbert Samuel, with wild enthusiasm. But the applause, the tears of joy, and the waving of hats that greeted the tall Jewish aristocrat could not conceal the profound apprehension that had taken root among Palestine's Jews. The initial enthusiasm, touched off by the Balfour Declaration, was gradually wearing off.

The fact is that before the ink dried on the Balfour Declaration, Britain found itself entangled in a hair-raising predicament stemming from its mutually contradictory promises to the Arabs, the Jews, and its own allies. The French had been promised a mandate over Palestine; Hussein, sharif of Mecca, was given to understand that an Arab homeland would be created as far as the Mediterranean; and the Jews were to have their "national home" – all on the same territory. An embarrassed Britain frantically began to refashion the Middle East in an attempt to accommodate all, drawing new borders through the deserts, squabbling with the French over Palestine's northern boundary, and trying to appease the anger of the Arabs. When Samuel arrived to take up his post, the country's military governor did hand over – as was recorded in his official receipt – "one Palestine, complete". But it didn't remain complete for long. Within nine months His Majesty's colonial secretary, Winston Churchill, would decide to detach Palestine from Transjordan in order to establish an independent realm for the Hashemite Emir Abdulla.

In May 1921 there was a renewed outbreak of Arab violence in Palestine, and at the end of a week of rioting there were forty-seven Jewish dead. From the Arab viewpoint, the riots were fruitful. Sir Herbert Samuel temporarily halted Jewish immigration, and within a year Churchill had effected the partition of the country in a White Paper that restricted the meaning of the term "national home" and linked the rate of Jewish immigration to the country's "economic absorptive capacity", a concept sufficiently vague to serve Britain's political needs at any time.

These acts and proclamations were not "perfidy" or "betrayal" of the Balfour Declaration, as Zionist leaders alleged at the time. They were without doubt a departure from the Zionist aim that Balfour had envisioned. But they were Britain's attempt to cope with a reality that the Zionists refused to see. The disturbances of 1920 and 1921 shocked many Zionist leaders. Whatever became of the slogan: "A people without a land returns to a land without a people"? The simple truth was that Palestine was not an empty land, and the Jews were only a small minority of its population. In the days of empire building, the Western powers had dismissed "natives" as an inconsequential factor in determining whether or not to settle a territory with immigrants. Even after the world war, the concept of "self-determination", which the United States inscribed on its banner when it came to the aid of the Entente Powers, was still reserved exclusively for the "developed" peoples. Yet now the Middle East was in the throes of a revolution that would ultimately defeat the lingering exclusivist philosophy of the Victorian era; and the Zionist movement was suffering the bruises of the painful transition from one age to another.

The strains left their mark on the world Zionist Organization by precipitating internal conflict. The American Zionists were the most reluctant to come face to face with the new reality. They clashed with Chaim Weizmann over his stress on the need for immigration and the establishment of pioneering settlements as the necessary means for realizing the Zionist vision. Having achieved the Balfour Declaration, they believed, one merely had to lay the economic groundwork for the development of Palestine, and the "national home" would follow as a matter of course. In principle, Weizmann's views approximated those of the Palestinian workers, but he was never one of them and he never succeeded in becoming their leader.

When Weizmann arrived in Palestine for a visit in the spring of 1918, he entered the country in all his glory, wearing a fashionable white suit and surrounded by a delegation of Jewish and Zionist representatives from England, France, and Italy. The delegation was housed at General Allenby's headquarters, dined at the tables of distinguished generals, and toured the country in a special car placed at its disposal by the army. In contrast to the distinguished delegation stood a handful of ragged, emaciated pioneers decimated by four years of war. It is doubtful whether the British generals had even heard of their obstinate struggles, their dreams, or their projects. Weizmann himself hardly mentions them in his memoirs. But the gap between the Palestinian workers and the Zionist movement abroad was expressed in more than mere dress and behavior.

In July 1919 the pioneers grit their teeth when they read the latest circular sent out by the Zionist Organization: "Let no one venture to liquidate his house and business before knowing clearly whether he can settle in Palestine." The problem, as the Diaspora leaders saw it, was a lack of funds; and the fury of the Palestinians reached its peak in 1921, when the Zionist Executive reported to the Twelfth Zionist Congress:

In light of the economic conditions reigning in Palestine, and the Zionist Organization's financial straits, the Executive considered sending penniless pioneers to Palestine undesirable and accordingly dispatched to all the principal migration offices telegraphic instructions to refrain from sending emigrants to Palestine for the time being.

The Palestinian workers sensed, more and more, that they alone would have to bear the burden of implementing Zionism. For this, they would need power and instruments for action. The establishment of the Histadrut gave the workers the tool for carrying out their projects, and in 1921 that instrument was entrusted into the hands of David Ben-Gurion.

Ben-Gurion was thirty-five when he returned to Palestine and joined the Histadrut secretariat. In the members of the Histadrut, he saw the "army of labor" that would redeem the country. The characterization may seem a little high-flown. At its foundation in 1920, the Histadrut's membership was a total of 4,433 poor and downtrodden workers, out of a total population of 65,000 Jews in Palestine. There was unemployment in many sectors, and the postwar pioneers who had begun arriving from Eastern Europe hungered for bread. The Histadrut's coffers were empty. The organization was unknown abroad and did not have the backing of friends or contributors. The Zionist Congress looked down upon it, and the mandatory government had never even heard the names of the young men who headed it. But the leadership dreamed of establishing the "national home" by turning 4,000 workers into the kernel of the dominant force in Palestine and world Zionism.

That was the central aim Ben-Gurion set himself when he disembarked at Jaffa harbor, late in the summer of 1921. When he was elected to the Histadrut secretariat, he held the organization's membership card no. 3. He was not the sole secretary, but one after another the other secretaries dropped out, leaving affairs in his hands. Ben-Gurion's first twelve years as head of the Histadrut were the lean years of his career, a time of unequalled difficulty, humiliating poverty, hard work, and dire crises that often made the Zionist objective appear unattainable. However, during those same bitter years, the Jewish community in Palestine built up its power of resistance and struck roots in the soil. These were also the years when Ben-Gurion was forged into a national leader.

After convincing his colleagues to move the Histadrut headquarters from Tel Aviv to Jerusalem, for "national reasons", Ben-Gurion and another of the secretaries rented a room with a single bed in one of the city's poorer neighborhoods and took turns sleeping on the floor. He again went back to living in poverty. His salary as Histadrut secretary was tiny, and he sent a large portion to Paula and the children (who were still living with his

father in Plonsk) in addition to the small sum sent to his father. Every day
he would diligently record his expenses in his notebook. Often left penniless, he was obliged to beg a pound from a friend to get through the month.
Yet in addition to the usual food, kerosene, cigarettes, and newspapers,
Ben-Gurion had added another secret item to his expenditures. He had
begun buying books like a man possessed. Several times a week, Ben-
Gurion would record in his diary the list of books he had purchased. In
January 1922, he flung himself at books on Judaism; he asked a friend to
buy him Springer's history of art and a number of German books on questions of state; from a Jerusalem shop he ordered books on the geography
of Palestine, a biography of Jesus, books of Latin and Armenian grammar;
from Germany he received books on Christianity, Palestinian archaeology,
and the history and geography of the Middle East. During his first attack
of book-buying, in the spring of 1922, he concentrated systematically on a
number of subjects: Judaism, Christianity, the history of the ancient
civilization of the Middle East, the origins of Zionism, the writings of the
great socialists, the history of the Arabs, and textbooks on political problems. On 20 March, he counted his books, and recorded proudly: "The
number of my books is: German – 219; English – 340; Arabic – 13;
French – 29; Hebrew – 140; Latin – 7; Greek – 2; Russian – 7; Turkish –
2; dictionaries of various languages – 15. Total – 775 volumes."

Books by the score and by the hundreds piled up in his little room, and
Ben-Gurion read and studied them with astonishing diligence. Entertainment and parties were not to his taste. Aside from three or four people he
had almost no friends. In the evenings and at night, he would write articles
for labor journals. But he devoted most of his spare time to reading and
study – in an almost conspiratorial fashion. To read Plato in the original,
he began to study Greek. He was also to learn Spanish for a better understanding of Cervantes. Working alongside him, his colleagues could not, at
first, notice the profound but unobtrusive change which was taking place
in the young secretary of the Histadrut, whose brash, practical exterior did
not seem suited to study and research. Yet gradually, behind the party
politician, a different Ben-Gurion emerged – a man of broad horizons with
an unquenchable thirst for knowledge; a leader who was stepping ahead of
his comrades with giant strides. At first, they mocked him for his preten-
tiousness; but in the end he evoked their admiration for his spiritual
strength, persistence, and his eagerness to teach and enlighten himself in
preparation for new tasks and a new status.

In the spring of 1922, Ben-Gurion brought his wife and children back
from Plonsk. Although he neither said it nor wrote it, it appears that he
wanted to avoid the daily concerns of family life. Of his previous flowing

expressions of love, no remnant was left in his letters to Paula. He devoted almost no time to his family, and the burden of bringing up their children and maintaining their home fell entirely upon his wife. Not only was Ben-Gurion busy day and night with Histadrut affairs, but he also continued his trips abroad to congresses and conferences. "We grew up at home as though we had no father," was Ge'ula's comment on her childhood. Even when Ben-Gurion was in Palestine, he had almost no time to look after domestic matters, to say nothing of giving Paula a little of the entertainment and recreation to which she had been accustomed in the United States. During the years 1922 and 1923, Ben-Gurion's diary mentions only one single evening spent out together for entertainment.

Those were exhausting times for Ben-Gurion and his colleagues. Everything had to be built up from the foundations: Histadrut organizations, trade unions, agricultural and industrial cooperatives. Ben-Gurion chased all over the country looking after the affairs of workers employed in laying roads, draining swamps, and digging channels for the mandatory government. He trudged from conference to conference, was called upon to settle disputes, or to deal with difficult strikes, delivered long speeches at workers' meetings, and argued with junior officials of the mandatory government. Deprivation was in evidence everywhere. In some of the villages, the workers were paid starvation wages. The road gangs were dressed in rags and worn-out shoes, and those who managed to get hold of a board to serve as a bed were considered fortunate. The labor leaders were often overcome with despair when they realized that they had nowhere to turn for help.

At one stage, Ben-Gurion pinned his hopes on financial assistance from the Jewish workers in America. He sent their leaders a detailed memorandum about the Histadrut and its projects, inviting them to send a delegation to Palestine. "I consider the participation of the labor movement in America to be a more important act than the diplomatic victory of the Balfour Declaration," he wrote. But his major efforts, thoughts, and hopes focussed primarily in a different direction – the formation of a new type of Jewish society.

At that time, Ben-Gurion regarded his socialist concepts as being completely identical with Soviet Communism. He was, indeed, a "Bolshevik" – but conditionally. The Zionist cause was far more important to him than the Communist ideal, and whenever he had to choose between the two, he did not hesitate for a moment. He was also disturbed by the totalitarian character of the Soviet regime, and the dictatorship Moscow tried to impose on world socialists. With all his criticism of Moscow, however, 1919–23 were the "red years" in Ben-Gurion's ideological development; they could be called "the Soviet period" of his life.

On his return to Palestine after the riots of 1921, he brought with him the revolutionary idea of turning his party, Ahdut ha-Avodah, into a country-wide, disciplined, and well organized commune that would function as a single entity to impose its influence upon the Histadrut. His far-reaching plan was rejected by the party's Central Committee, and the disappointed revolutionary leader resigned all his posts in the party's executive.

That was not his only setback during those years. In fact, Ben-Gurion frequently found himself in the minority. This was principally because of his volcanic behavior and militant extremism. On many issues of political and ideological importance, he was to the left of the mainstream – often in opposition to the views of Berl Katznelson, Ben-Zvi and other colleagues. In the early 1920s, Ben-Gurion advanced a revolutionary proposal: to convert the Histadrut into a workers corporation, ". . . an egalitarian commune of all the workers of Palestine under military discipline . . . [that would] take over all the farms and urban cooperatives, the wholesale supplies of the entire working community, and the direction and conduct of all public works in the country".

In face of the fiercely critical reaction and the accusations of "Bolshevik" and "dogmatic" tendencies, Ben-Gurion was obliged to withdraw the proposal. He submitted a new plan that omitted such concepts as "military discipline", but this, too, was rejected by some of the Histadrut leaders. Finally he presented the Histadrut with a third plan that was far more moderate and prudent. It called for the establishment of a legal entity to be called the Worker's Corporation, to which every member of the Histadrut would automatically belong and to which the Histadrut would entrust the administration of all its financial and cooperative enterprises to "direct its activities toward the needs of all the workers". This was a new – and totally different – proposal, free of all the previous "Bolshevik" elements: the all-embracing commune, military discipline, central control of Histadrut leaders on the masses. On the basis of this proposal, the Histadrut founded its Workers' Corporation (Hevrat Ovdim), which developed into an open, pragmatic concern, quite unlike the frighteningly authoritarian organization Ben-Gurion had envisaged. It exists to this day and is justly proud of its immense achievements. However, in its various metamorphoses, Ben-Gurion's plan illustrated the extent to which its author was influenced by the ideals of the Soviet revolution.

Ben-Gurion's romance with Bolshevism and the Soviet Union ended in the 1920s. Ironically enough, his ardor began to cool as a result of his trip to Soviet Russia. He went to Moscow at the end of the summer of 1923 to represent the Palestinian workers at the International Agricultural Exhibition. His diary entries and letters during that trip reflect the many contradictory feelings he experienced during his three-month stay. He was not oblivious to the poverty and hunger he saw everywhere; but all his questions appear to have been directed at finding out whether Communist Russia would provide the answer to the Zionist challenges in Palestine. The success of the Palestinian pavilion drew him into weaving grandiose plans for strengthening contacts with Russia; he even planned to establish a branch of the Histadrut's Workers' Bank in Moscow! He admitted to the unfavorable Soviet attitude toward Zionism, but believed that the Russian regime could be won over to an increased understanding for the Jewish national cause. And while he was well aware of the latent anti-Semitism in the country, he sincerely believed that the Communist regime was the best guarantee of Jewish survival.

Only when he was alone and far from Moscow, on board a ship bound for Palestine, did he record his true opinion of the Soviet Union:

... We discovered Russia. Russia, floundering in the fire of rebellion and revolutionary tyranny. The land of deep conflicts and contradictions, which calls for a world-wide civil war to give power to the proletariat and denies its workers all rights as men, citizens, or class; which proclaims communism and abolition of private property, and divides out soil for the peasants for private farms ... The land of dazzling light and impenetrable darkness; the noblest aspirations for liberation and justice, amidst an ugly and poverty-stricken reality; the land of revolution and speculation, Communism and the NEP, holy suffering and vile corruption, revolt, and bribery, ideals and material rewards, changed values and age-long tyranny, the cult of labor and golden idols ... great and powerful is the urge to rebel – the holy rebellion against all the falsehood, lies, and trickery of the old world, worn-out and disintegrating from its sins, and the fraud, wickedness, and rule of material gain ... great and mighty are the obstacles on the way toward the new world and the new society. Who will overcome whom?

Despite his harsh words on the Soviet Union, however, Ben-Gurion continued to idolize Lenin. No other foreign, non-Jewish leader was ever granted similar praises by Ben-Gurion. "The prophet of the Russian revolution" was how Lenin was described in his diary:

He is great, this man. His glance is piercing, and he sees reality through a clear mirror, unobscured by any formula, saying, rhetoric or dogma ... He has a sharp far-seeing eye, cutting and penetrating through the thickets of life and its mysteries and dredges up from out of the depths of reality the dominant forces of the future ... There is integrity in his soul, he disdains any inhibitions, he is faithful to his aim, he knows neither concessions nor lenience, he is the most extreme of the extreme, he will crawl on his belly through the mire pit to attain his objective ... He will not spare the lives of children and innocents for the sake of the revolution ... a perfect tactical genius who knows how to withdraw

his lines of battle in preparation for a renewed onslaught, he does not hesitate
to oppose today what he favored yesterday . . . nor will he be snared by dogmas:
naked reality, cruel truth, and the real balance of forces are what he sees . . .

It seems to have been Ben-Gurion's greatest desire during these years to
emulate Lenin and learn from him, and in many ways he did. He even
adopted the dress of the Soviet leaders – a quasi-military uniform of rough
wool – during the 1920s.

Yet in the spring of 1924, a few months after Ben-Gurion's return to
Palestine, the course of events were to put his fantasies of Bolshevism to rest
forever. At the beginning of the year, the Polish government had issued
economic decrees directed against the Jews, and in response thousands
began to liquidate their holdings, gather up their savings, and emigrate.
With the United States closed to free immigration, large numbers of Jews
who had intended to set sail for the New World found themselves on ships
bound for Palestine. Most of the immigrants were of the middle class:
small traders, shopkeepers, agents, artisans, and tailors. They hadn't the
slightest training or inclination for agricultural work, and worst of all, most
of them showed no signs of strong Zionist motivation. Altogether, 65,000
immigrants arrived between 1924 and 1927, but only a minority of them
were pioneers willing to engage in hard physical labor.

Right from the start, Ben-Gurion and his colleagues were very suspicious
of this middle-class immigration. Palestine was crying out for pioneers;
instead the "landlords" came in masses. Tens of thousands settled in the
cities and tried to establish the kind of social and economic structures they
had left behind in the towns of Poland. They built factories, opened small
stores and workshops, and entered into real estate and land speculation.
Tel Aviv and the other towns altered their appearance. A wave of un-
planned building gave rise to new streets and neighborhoods; orange
groves were planted, and then sold and resold at rapidly increasing prices.
Suits, ties and soft hats appeared in the streets, and the *dernier cris* of
Warsaw and Lodz fashions conquered the pavements and cafés. The influx
of free enterprise and capital initially brought about economic prosperity.
The middle-class immigrants claimed that they, too, were capable of developing the country and realizing Zionist aims, not necessarily by means of
settlement on the land, workers' communes, or class struggle. Furthermore,
the emergence of this new political force evoked great satisfaction among a
considerable section of the leadership of the World Zionist Organization,
which was middle-class in character and highly suspicious of the Palestinian labor movement.

Far from weaving dreams of a country-wide workers' commune, the
Palestine labor movement was now fighting for its very existence. Middle-

class circles in the country, and abroad, launched a general offensive against the labor parties, which had for years been claiming exclusive possession of the formula for building and developing Palestine. The temporary prosperity gave new self-confidence to the centrist and right-wing Zionist parties. Vladimir Jabotinsky was one of the first to attack the labor movement; he was followed by Zionist federations and societies in Europe and America, as well as in Palestine. They were highly critical of the economic failure of the labor movement, proved that many of the new settlements were unviable, and pointed gleefully at the difficulties experienced by the Histadrut concerns. At the Fourteenth and Fifteenth Zionist Congresses, it was resolved to give priority to urban development over rural settlement and immigrants possessing means of their own over penniless pioneers. Palestine's economy was to be developed on a business-like, profit basis. In the light of the new trend, which the labor movement quickly dubbed "profit Zionism", the secretary of the Histadrut proclaimed:

... We have fought and we shall continue to fight against those who fall into the delusion that this great and difficult task – the realization of Zionism – can be accomplished solely by a profit-making joint-stock company; that it is feasible to do "good business" from bringing rootless masses into this small impoverished land ... If there is any fantasy that lacks foundation or charm, it is the empty notion that by means of the pursuit of profit, it will be possible to accomplish this unprofitable undertaking – to assemble a dispersed people, with no roots in labor, and to get it absorbed into a desolated, impoverished land.

Ben-Gurion's pessimistic predictions did not take long to materialize. After two years of prosperity, a severe economic crisis erupted in Palestine, striking first of all at the businesses of the new immigrants. In 1926 building stopped, many businesses went bankrupt, and there was severe unemployment throughout the country. The middle-class immigrants, who lacked strong Zionist motivation, began to leave Palestine *en masse*. In 1927, twice as many Jews left Palestine than immigrated to the country. "The middle class came – and failed," wrote Ben-Gurion. "It had to fail, because it wished to continue in Palestine the same means by which Jews gained their livelihood in the Diaspora; it did not comprehend that Palestine is not like Poland."

There was, however, a more pragmatic political conclusion to be drawn from this episode. Ben-Gurion was now convinced that the leaders of the Zionist movement "advocate the Zionist ideal but are remote from ... the realization of Zionism, except for donating money – more or less – without comprehending that money alone will not build a new land or a new state". In view of the "decay" affecting Zionism and the feelings of frustration and bitterness entertained by the leaders of the Palestine labor movement, Ben-Gurion thought up a new daring and ambitious plan: to instigate a revolution within the world Zionist movement and bring it into line with the pioneering path. For this purpose, it was essential for the Palestinian workers and their supporters in the Jewish world to gain the upper hand. With that, he set for himself the next objective: conquest of the Zionist movement.

Ben-Gurion did not believe that it would be possible to take over the leadership of the existing Zionist Organization, given the imbalance between the workers and the other groups within the Zionist establishment. Thus, it might be better to bypass the existing establishment and found a parallel Zionist Organization of a socialist nature. For the past four years, Ben-Gurion had, in fact, demanded the establishment of a new and independent world Zionist Organization, but most of his colleagues, including Berl Katznelson, opposed this notion. Moreover, for Ben-Gurion's comrades it was a most inappropriate moment to discuss, or even to dream, of taking over the world Zionist movement from within. Well-based in Berlin, Vienna, and London, it was respected and supported by hundreds of thousands of Congress voters in Jewish communities all over the world. Was it conceivable that the few pioneers in Palestine would succeed in conquering Jewish public opinion? It appeared to be an impossible task.

In this confrontation with his colleagues, Ben-Gurion's secret weapon was his naïve, almost childish faith in the united strength of the Palestinian workers, and in the justice of their cause. He was clearly prone to exaggeration and oversimplification, but those very traits made up the strength of the ambitious Histadrut secretary. Despite his comrades' opposition, he would not abandon his vision, even if he had to pursue it alone.

Ben-Gurion's systematic course of action in attempting to establish "a world organization" can be viewed in terms of five concentric circles, with the Palestinian Zionist labor movement at the center. The first and innermost circle was Ahdut ha-Avodah, his own party. The second, wider circle, consisted of the Zionist labor parties. Thus the unification of Hapoel Hatzair and Ahdut ha-Avodah into a single large labor party in Palestine and abroad was an essential prerequisite for the success of the plan. The third circle was the Histadrut, which Ben-Gurion saw as the new movement; the fourth embraced the Zionist labor movements, pioneering organizations, and the youth societies in various countries overseas, a reservoir of pioneers and the source of political and financial strength for the Histadrut and the labor movement. Finally, would come the fifth and outermost circle, an encompassing world-wide umbrella organization parallel to the Zionist Organization and united around the labor movement's Zionist–Socialist concepts.

Ben-Gurion did not encounter much opposition from his Ahdut ha-Avodah colleagues to the idea of a merger with the second largest labor party. But the leaders of Hapoel Hatzair were reserved and cautious. Long and exhaustive negotiations between the two parties went on for years, and in the mid-1920s, there was no sign of unification on the horizon. So Ben-Gurion advanced his sights and spent the 1920s directing most of his efforts to the key task of fortifying the Histadrut.

If Ben-Gurion's powers were inexhaustible, his physical strength was not. The constant travel all over the country and frequent missions to Europe, together with the tension and the burdens of his position, seriously undermined his health. In London, in 1921, he suffered blood poisoning and "fluttered between two worlds". Malaria continued to strike him at regular intervals. During his trips to Paris, he underwent examinations by specialists, and on one occasion he was obliged to lay aside all his business and spend a few days resting in a small town near the French capital. He often fell ill during congresses and conferences, and his psychological state appears to have affected his health; on occasion, great excitement or upset was often accompanied by high fever.

Gradually, his short, stocky figure became familiar and popular among the Palestinian workers. He spent most of his time among them, building up his personal authority. Usually he would wear uniform-style clothes, but occasionally he would appear in a black or white Russian blouse or in a light-colored summer suit he had bought on one of his trips. One day, he shaved his hair to the roots. It seems that his baldness was spreading rapidly, and he was trying to slow down the process. But during the course of the 1920s, he gradually went bald, and by the end of the decade his hair was silver and flapped in wings that dangled over his temples. The famous Ben-Gurion silhouette had received its final seal.

It was during this period that Ben-Gurion's diary became an inseparable part of his current occupation. He kept two journals: a notebook where he noted down brief details of meetings and important events; and a diary where he would write long and precisely detailed entries about his experiences. The events of a single day were capable of filling many pages. But the journal was selective: Ben-Gurion did not always note down everything that happened to him. Right from the start, a large proportion of the entries were for the benefit of his colleagues or for publication. Many years later, a young Yigal Allon sat in Ben-Gurion's room and gazed in wonder at the diligent old man bent over his journal and earnestly jotting down everything Allon was saying. Allon could not refrain from commenting: "Ben-Gurion, you write so much. Will you read it all as well?" Ben-Gurion snapped: "Others will read it."

The diaries reveal his preoccupation with accuracy and minute detail. There are hundreds of pages devoted to careful copies of documents, letters, statistical tables, census data, diagrams on immigration or population. Occasionally, some family event would occur which he found suitable for recording in his journal. Thus in between two dry census tables, one suddenly finds a number of personal comments; or a report of the sickness of one of his children, with a precise note of his temperature; or some words of wisdom uttered by one of his little geniuses. Trifles from his daily routine were recorded with the same earnestness as world-shaking events. Yet there were passages in his journal that were not intended for publication, where he expressed his feelings, his experiences, and his flaming emotions. At times, he wrote poems, lyrical descriptions of nature, emotional outpourings, thoughts he had formulated, quotations that had impressed him. These pages he concealed and preserved for himself.

During this period, two opposing traits stood out in David Ben-Gurion's character: on the one hand, a wealth of warmth and friendship; on the other, a hardness and a fierce, blunt manner of expressing himself. The same man who was capable of bursting into tears at a commemoration for Herzl was equally capable of offensive onslaughts on adversaries and friends alike. When "bourgeois" circles attacked the Histadrut workers, Ben-Gurion responded by calling the former "the free-enterprise parasites", "impotent", and "eunuchs of the will". But he did not reserve his sharp tongue for adversaries alone. Ben-Gurion was resolute, domineering, and imposed his will on his colleagues in the Histadrut. While he appreciated loyalty and confidence in his comrades, he did not go very far in encouraging them to show initiative.

Despite all the difficulties, the distressing poverty, and painful human problems, the Histadrut gradually acquired strength. In 1925 Ben-Gurion described it as "a kind of workers' state". By stages, that "workers' state" encompassed Hambashbir (a retail outlet), the Solel Boneh Construction Company, the Workers' Bank, and the Workers' Corporation. In June 1925 *Davar*, the workers' daily, appeared. In 1926, the workers' sport organization, Hapoel, was founded. The same year saw the establishment of Tnuva, a marketing network for agricultural produce, and of the insurance company Hasneh. Step by step, the Histadrut penetrated every sphere of life. "Members of the Histadrut," recorded a writer who visited Palestine years later, "grew food in their own settlements, marketed the produce collectively by their own marketing organization, invested their profits in their own banks, and went to their own doctors, ran their own schools ... In effect the Histadrut needs the bourgeois Zionist movement in only one single area and for one single purpose: money to balance its budget."

Completely immersed in Histadrut affairs, Ben-Gurion could not give sufficient attention to his family at home or in Plonsk. His letters to his father grew increasingly irregular and rare. With the sole exception of his widowed sister, Zipporah, and her children, he continued to resist the family's entreaties that he help bring them to Palestine claiming "my situation in this country is such that any public body here – is open to me and will gladly respond to a request to provide employment for anyone I propose. That is precisely the obstacle before me in using my influence on behalf of my relatives." However, Avigdor Gruen made it plain that he was determined to move to Palestine. He arrived in July 1925 and settled in Haifa, where he worked for many years as an accountant. Ben-Gurion also justly wrote: "I am unable to fulfill my duties towards my wife and children." Throughout the 1920s, his family life was a bizarre mixture of care and attention during the brief time he spent near his family and long months of absence from the country on Histadrut missions.

He seemed to spend half his time traveling, and each trip was an adventure in itself. Most of the time he was on his own, withdrawn into the solitude that had become his constant companion. During the lonely evenings abroad, he would write or reflect for hours at a time. In preparation for his arrival, he used to ask his comrades to rent him a room that should be "not expensive, but roomy so that I can walk about, and with a writing table". Most of Ben-Gurion's journeys were devoted to consolidating Jewish and international support for the Palestinian workers' movement. He took care to attend every international labor conference. But first and foremost, his purpose was to meet the Zionist–Socialist organizations that sympathized with the Palestinian labor movement. Stubbornly and persistently, he traveled from conference to conference, met "central committees" and "activist groups", gave interviews to provincial Jewish papers, solved the petty problems of some forsaken party branch, argued furiously against rivals, served as chairman of boring conferences, wrote hundreds of letters to humdrum politicians, and suffered countless bitter disappointments. His camp was growing in strength, the wheels were slowly beginning to turn, but this painful process was accompanied by friction, clashes, protests, arguments, storms, and crises.

But by the end of the 1920s, the Histadrut occupied a strong position among the Palestinian workers, and its authority was almost unchallenged. Even during the worst years of the economic crisis, with unemployment all over the country – the workers did not lose their faith in their leaders. Ben-Gurion's letters and speeches displayed a growing forcefulness and

self-confidence toward the end of the decade. He was now ready to undertake the final phase of his plan: establishing the world organization that
would serve as a counterweight to the Zionist Congress. However, a pre-
condition for this was unification of the Palestinian labor parties: Ahdut
ha-Avodah and Hapoel Hatzair.

Circumstances forced the two parties into one another's arms. The
"bourgeois offensive" against the Histadrut and the workers during the
mid-1920s built up the pressure toward unification. The leader of Hapoel
Hatzair remained unconvinced and was also on poor terms with Ben-
Gurion. But the desire of the rank-and-file for unification won the day.
After endless postponements, it was decided to hold talks during the
Histadrut Council in October 1927. In the course of seventeen successive
days, a war of attrition was fought between the leaders of the two parties,
who tried in vain to write a united program. In the end, the discussions
reached a dead end. Ben-Gurion was sick and tired. He left the meeting
and went home to sleep, bitterly disappointed by the feet-dragging and the
hair-splitting. But at five o'clock the next morning, the leader of Hapoel
Hatzair led a procession of jubilant workers to Ben-Gurion's house and,
overcoming the mighty obstacle known as Paula, woke Ben-Gurion with the
good news. After an all-night discussion, the leaders of the two parties had
succeeded in agreeing on a unified program. Overjoyed Ben-Gurion leaped
from his bed and the two men appeared, hand in hand, on the small
terrace. The crowd below greeted them with shouts of joy.

Although agreement had been achieved in principle, it took another two
years to work out a joint program in detail. In July 1929 the document
was presented to a referendum of members of both parties and was
overwhelmingly accepted, and a few months later the Land of Israel
Workers' Party (Mapai) was officially founded. But the high-spirited
mood of the Palestinian workers was short-lived. A month after the
unification was approved, the course of events in Palestine again took a
drastic turn.

Before dawn on the hot summer morning of 23 August 1929, riots broke
out. The focus of the rioting was Jerusalem, where a dispute had broken
out between the Jewish and Arab communities on procedures of worship
at the Western Wall. But if the Moslem masses were motivated largely by
religious zeal, their leaders were acting out of entirely different reasons.
Their call for a *jihad* ("holy war") against the Jews stemmed from their
anxiety in the face of increasing Jewish strength and the sight of Jews
striking roots in the country. The character of the Zionist movement was
likewise changing. In 1929, Dr Weizmann began to establish the "extended
Jewish Agency", consisting of an equal number of Zionists and non-

Zionists. His purpose was clear: to raise additional capital, increase immigration, purchase land, and extend Jewish settlement. In the eyes of the Arab leaders, the "extended" Agency resembled a kind of "Zionist government" whose aim was to force them out of the country. The establishment of the Agency was ratified at the Sixteenth Zionist Congress in August 1929, and the Arab leaders followed the Congress's deliberations closely. They were particularly concerned about Vladimir Jabotinsky's speech calling for the establishment of a Jewish state on both banks of the Jordan River. Thus when the ominous word *jihad* began to be whispered in the alleyways of Jerusalem, its significance was both religious and political.

The riots soon took on an unprecedented degree of cruelty and quickly spread through the coastal plain, the Jezreel Valley, and Galilee. Simultaneous attacks on dozens of settlements indicated that this was a coordinated action. Jews were evacuated from various settlements by British forces; in Jerusalem, Tel Aviv, Haifa and a number of other places, the Jewish defenders succeeded in halting the rioters and inflicting casualties upon them. Two days later, when the British army went into action on a full scale, the wave of riots began to subside. Official figures reported 133 Jews had been killed in various parts of the country, while 339 were injured; 104 Arabs were killed by the British and a further six died in a Jewish counterattack in the Tel Aviv area.

The political effect of the riots was ominous. The British government, concerned about its foothold in the Middle East, searched desperately for a solution to pacify the outraged Arabs. Ramsay MacDonald's Labour government hastily sent "objective" commissions of inquiry to Palestine, while in London, the anti-Zionist colonial secretary, Lord Passfield, was already planning a series of decrees to impose upon the Jews. Nineteen-thirty was a bitter year for the Zionist movement. In March the British commission of inquiry under Sir Walter Shaw published its findings, and they were a disastrous condemnation of the entire "national home" policy in Palestine. In its recommendations, the commission hinted that it was necessary to impose restrictions on the establishment of the Jewish national home and on Jewish immigration, it was also critical of land sales to the Jews. Sir John Hope-Simpson, a friend of Lord Passfield and an expert on population exchanges, was sent to Palestine and charged with the task of formulating practical proposals and presenting them to the British government.

The Zionist leaders entertained no illusions concerning the spirit and direction of these "proposals". When the Zionist leadership met in London in June 1930, it did not escape their attention that the present crisis might deal a fatal blow to Zionism. On 30 October 1930, Sir John Hope-Simpson

submitted his recommendations, and a few days later, Lord Passfield published a White Paper about future British policy in Palestine. It imposed
severe restrictions on Jewish immigration and land purchases, in accordance with the country's "economic absorptive capacity". Under the pretext of "a balance" between Jews and Arabs, the British government dissociated itself from further efforts for the national home.

Concern and anger overtook the Jewish world. Weizmann resigned from
the Jewish Agency, and with world Jewry enraged, the Labour government
found itself embarrassed and undecided. On the publication of the White
Paper, Ben-Gurion was so furious that he lost all sense of proportion and
flung out a furious call for rebellion against England. He presented an
apocalyptic vision of a bloody uprising, a desperate rebellion whose conclusion was likely to resemble the end of the Second Temple. But his impassioned words set most of Ben-Gurion's colleagues in Mapai against
him. They, too, were shocked by the White Paper, but the hysterical vision
of the Histadrut secretary shocked them no less. When he calmed down,
Ben-Gurion also dropped the idea of the "rebellion" and went so far as to
develop a new optimistic theory: "All our great creations were the fruit of
crises," he declared in a speech in December.

Aside from our very coming to Palestine, which was the fruit of the historical
crisis of an exiled people, the creation of the workers own economic enterprises
is the fruit of a crisis; the growth of Tel Aviv is the fruit of the 1921 riots;
workers housing in the towns and the return to the land is the fruit of unemployment in the towns. This new crisis should bear fruit in solidifying the
people's preparedness and doubling the Jewish community here in the near
future.

This was not merely empty talk. Ben-Gurion could testify from his own
experience that one of his greatest ambitions was realized amidst the severe
crisis that overtook the Zionist movement. In the course of that bitter year,
which began with the 1929 riots and ended with the publication of the
Passfield White Paper, Ben-Gurion took the decisive step toward implementing the plan that he had been nurturing for ten years: the establishment of the world Zionist–Socialist Organization to replace the existing
Zionist Organization. At the end of August 1930, the decision was adopted:
within one month, the World Congress for Labor Palestine would be held
in Berlin.

Right up to the last moment, the success of the conference hung by a
hair. Guided by his intention of establishing a movement in opposition to
the Zionist Organization, Ben-Gurion adopted a method which paralleled
that of the Zionist Congress: he sold "tickets" which approximated the
Zionist *shekel* (the voting certificate for elections to the Zionist Congress).

The Jewish response was considerable: some 240,000 tickets were sold in Poland, Palestine, America and Central and Eastern Europe. This was over and above Ben-Gurion's expectations. A second success was the respectable list of well-known personalities – Jews and non-Jews, Zionists, Socialists, labor leaders, scientists, and intellectuals – who promised to attend. The conference opened on 27 September 1930 and the hall was packed with 196 delegates from nineteen countries representing Zionist–Socialist organizations and parties all over the world. Ben-Gurion delivered the opening address, stating: "We have called this Congress now not because of the crisis, but in spite of it." He expressed his vision of the new organization's ideals: "A Jewish state, a laboring society, Jewish–Arab cooperation – these are the three aims encompassed in the deeds and aspirations of the Jewish worker in his homeland".

At its conclusion, the congress adopted a resolution to establish a World League for Labor Palestine, with the aim of "bringing to the Jewish public the truth about the workers of Palestine and about Palestine in general". The delegates undertook to raise at least £36,000 during the coming year to be placed at the disposal of the Histadrut. After singing the Hebrew workers' anthem and the Internationale, the delegates dispersed. Ben-Gurion was overjoyed. He wrote to his father: "The world-wide platform has been created from which the Jewish worker proclaimed his enterprise and his historical vision; the foundations were laid for a world-wide movement, focussed around the Palestine labor movement." That "world-wide movement" was his fondest wish.

Ben-Gurion could not have known that the League would soon sink into a prolonged hibernation and that the path of the labor movement would be completely unlike what he envisioned. His basic aim – conquest of the Zionist movement – remained, and he would continue to strive toward it with incredible obstinacy. But he changed his tactics radically following a series of dramatic developments in the Zionist movement that provided fertile ground for the growth of a labor leadership.

5

Conquest of the Zionist Movement

The change that made Ben-Gurion revise all his plans came about as a
result of the 1929 riots and the White Paper. Without these two developments, the dissolution and disintegration of the Zionist movement would
undoubtedly have continued, and the process might even have been
speeded up under the impact of the world economic crisis of 1929–30. But
in the middle of 1931, following on the riots and the White paper, two
decisive events forced Ben-Gurion to change his course.

The first event was the publication of a letter from Ramsay MacDonald
to Chaim Weizmann in February 1931. It was the fruit of a vigorous campaign conducted against the White Paper by the heads of the Conservative
opposition, liberal leaders, and even respected members of the Labour
Party. As a result of their pressure, Lord Passfield withdrew several of his
comments in the White Paper, and a joint committee, consisting of representatives of the British government and of the Jewish Agency, was hastily
established. On 13 February 1931, its work reached fruition in the personal
letter from the prime minister to Dr Weizmann, which – in its own elegant
way – implied the abrogation of the White Paper. Ramsay MacDonald
stressed the willingness of his government to implement the Mandate
faithfully; withdrew the decrees imposing restrictions on immigration,
settlement, and land purchases; and declared that regulation of immigration
"in accordance with the country's economic absorptive capacity" would be
dictated by clear economic, and not political, criteria. This "abrogation" of
the White Paper was followed, a few months later, by the appointment of a
new High Commissioner, Sir Arthur Wauchope, who proved to be sympathetic toward the Zionist ideal. In time, MacDonald's letter was to be
remembered as marking the beginning of the "Golden Age" of the
"National Home" period.

Although Chaim Weizmann had won that difficult battle, he did not
benefit personally from the victory. The letter simply did not succeed in
eradicating the shock which the Passfield White Paper had produced
within the Zionist movement. And the bitterness, disappointment, and

fury against "perfidious" England were also directed against the man who, for fourteen years, had appeared as the defender and the advocate of England and patron of Zionist cooperation with the Crown. Weizmann's position within the Zionist movement was seriously undermined, and insiders calculated that he would lose his majority at the Seventeenth Zionist Congress which would convene in Basel in July 1931. It seemed likely that there would be a fierce battle over the succession, which would also be a fight over the future policy of the Zionist movement.

The crystallization of the principal forces that would take part in that battle was the second decisive development in the period leading up to the Congress. The loosely bound centrist General Zionists, who had hitherto enjoyed an impressive majority and supported Weizmann, underwent a crisis and declined in power. In their place, the elections for the Seventeenth Congress brought to prominence two new power centers: the Labor faction became the largest in the Congress, with 29 per cent of the delegates; and the right-wing Revisionists, who first took part in Congress elections only six years earlier, became the third largest faction with 21 per cent of the delegates.

This was a change of far-reaching significance. Toward the center of the stage advanced the radical and revolutionary forces, each of which launched its onslaught against classical Zionism. The Revisionists had adopted a powerful and exhilarating slogan: "The aim of Zionism is gradually to convert the Land of Israel [including Transjordan] into a self-governing Jewish Commonwealth, resting on a permanent Jewish majority. Any other interpretation of Zionism, particularly the White Paper of 1922, is declared invalid." It must be admitted that this was the true and faithful slogan of Zionism. The other Zionist parties, including the Palestinian labor movement, favored quiet diplomacy toward the British and not arousing the anger of the Arabs prematurely. All the same, there is no doubt that the Revisionist slogan correctly expressed the feelings of Zionists all over the world and consequently gained many supporters.

Another trump card for the Revisionists was the personality of Vladimir Jabotinsky, who was lavishly endowed with the characteristics of a charismatic leader. Brilliant and original, he was a gifted writer, steeped in Western culture, and spoke and wrote in half a dozen European languages. Yet, his major drawback was his impractical approach and his inability to comprehend political situations. He obstinately refused to comprehend that the British were not prepared to play the role he had outlined for them. For many years he preached vehemently that Britain must be obliged to implement the Mandate literally and establish a Jewish state in Palestine at a time when Britain, consumed by regrets over the Balfour Declaration,

was searching for a way out of its commitments toward the Jews. In addition, an increasingly vitriolic conflict emerged between Jabotinsky and the
Palestinian labor movement. While Jabotinsky placed all his cards on the
Jewish state that the British would impose upon the country's Arab inhabitants, the labor movement put all its faith into practical construction work,
with or without British assistance.

These conflicting views over the implementation of Zionism were also
bound up with class differences: faced with the slogan that "the only force
building up the country are the workers", Jabotinsky progressively adopted
a position of open hostility. More and more, he turned to and received
support from the middle class. During the 1920s, he headed the attacks
on the labor movement's policies. Having been crowned "an enemy of
the working class", he decided to justify the title. "If there is a class which
bears the future, it is we, the bourgeoisie," he wrote in 1927. "Humanity is
not moving toward socialism; it is turning its back upon it."

To a large extent, Jabotinsky was the antithesis of David Ben-Gurion.
At the beginning of the 1930s, Ben-Gurion was only one out of a group of
leaders of the Palestinian labor movement, while Jabotinsky was the sole
leader of the Revisionists. Those who rebelled against him soon discovered
that they had little hope of overcoming his irresistible charm, his brilliant
rhetoric, his ability to draw the masses after him and impose his will decisively. His inclination towards the dramatic, his fascination with bombas-
tic slogans, theatrical effects, colorful pseudonyms, and extravagant
behavior was designed to impress his audience. Weizmann said of him: "He
was rather ugly, immensely attractive, well spoken, warm hearted, generous,
always ready to help a comrade in distress; all these qualities were, however, overlaid by a certain touch of rather theatrical chivalry, an odd and
irrelevant knightliness, which was not at all Jewish."

Jabotinsky's Revisionists and Ben-Gurion's workers – both fervent
supporters of revolutionary changes in the Zionist movement – had their
first confrontation at the Seventeenth Zionist Congress. In his speech to the
Congress, Ben-Gurion used every opportunity, every argument, and every
formulation to attack Jabotinsky and his supporters time and time again.
He called Jabotinsky and his men "little Churchills" and accused them of
giving young people "a chauvinistic education, imbibed with racial hatred
and hatred for workers". It seems that without being aware of it, Ben-
Gurion had launched the war of succession for the leadership of the Zionist
movement, for Weizmann's position as Congress president was desperate
and his fall appeared imminent.

The weakening of Weizmann's position was also obvious to the British
government, which was profoundly concerned. The British displayed great

trust in and respect for Weizmann and feared that following his departure, the leadership of the Zionist movement would fall into the hands of radical extremist elements. A few days before the convening of the Congress in Basel, Winston Churchill commented: "I don't believe the Jewish people will be so stupid as to let Weizmann go." But there was a different mood at the Zionist Congress. In the first contacts between leaders of the various factions, it became clear that Weizmann's principal support came from the labor movement's delegates – and even this was not given wholeheartedly. Thus, on 10 July 1931, Weizmann took a step of desperation, a last-minute attempt to regain the confidence of the Congress. For this purpose, he needed Ben-Gurion, even though the two were not particularly close. In greatest secrecy he summoned Ben-Gurion and informed him that he had just received a letter from Malcolm MacDonald, the son of the British prime minister, containing a hint that Ramsay MacDonald might agree to the establishment of a joint Arab–Jewish legislative assembly in Palestine on the basis of parity. (The principle of equal representation for Jews and Arabs approached the Zionist slogan, as contrasted with the concept of "proportional representation" adopted by the British and the Arabs.) Weizmann asked Ben-Gurion to fly to London in secret and meet the prime minister. Ben-Gurion was charged with reporting the outcome of his talks before the termination of the Congress.

The following day, Ben-Gurion flew to London, together with the secretary of the Political Department of the Zionist Executive, Professor Lewis Namier. The prime minister welcomed them at his country residence, Chequers, and they began a wide-ranging discussion of the situation within the Zionist movement, the Congress debates, MacDonald's letter to Weizmann, and the political scene in Palestine. When Ben-Gurion raised the subject of parity, demanding equal treatment for Jews and Arabs "in political as well as economic matters" and pointing out that in "our rights to Palestine, one should see not only the Jews already living in Palestine, but the Jewish people in the whole world . . .", MacDonald replied favorably. He even said that the mandatory authorities "ought to incline in favor of the Jews . . . That is the original intent of the Mandate, not to give the Jews in Palestine what the Arabs have, but more than that." Clearly, MacDonald was determined to do everything to ensure that Weizmann would retain his post.

Ben-Gurion returned to Basel bringing important tidings. But it was too late to turn the clock back. The Zionist Congress removed Weizmann from his post, electing Nahum Sokolov as president of the Zionist Organization by a majority of 118 to 98. At the same time, however, the labor delegates, together with their allies, succeeded in defeating the Revisionists. The policy adopted by the Congress was that supported by the Labor delegates – namely, a continuation of Weizmann's policy.

The Seventeenth Zionist Congress had an enormous influence on the course of the Zionist movement and its future policy. If Jabotinsky secretly entertained some hope of being elected president of the Zionist Organization, that hope was dashed. With two of its five seats, the labor delegates were the backbone of the new Zionist Executive, which was a coalition of all the parties excluding the Revisionists. Jabotinsky and his men left the Congress embittered and already harboring thoughts of splitting off from the Zionist movement. Moreover, the Zionist movement was left without a leader, having elected as president Dr Nahum Sokolov, a pale figure and not one of the race of giants.

Ben-Gurion may not have immediately grasped the significance of this new situation, but during that feverish July, his hand touched the levers of international power, and he experienced the intoxicating taste of influence on the fate of a nation. Gradually, it became clear to Ben-Gurion that because of the vacuum in the leadership of the Zionist movement and the growing strength of the labor movement, it would be possible to gain control of the Zionist Organization from within.

Shortly after the Zionist Congress, Ben-Gurion began to lose interest in the World League for Labor Palestine, to which he had devoted ten years of dreams and work. For a year he did not reveal his thoughts even to his closest colleagues. But to the astonishment of his colleagues at the Mapai Council, and the end of that period he set the labor movement an incomparably ambitious target: an immediate and general attack on the "official" Zionist movement with the aim of taking over its leadership.

Who dared to think in such terms in 1932? Ben-Gurion called for the formation of a popular plan of action "not only for pioneers, but also for all sections of the population, including private capital". He was determined to alter the image of the labor movement so that it would not automatically turn away those who were not workers. On the contrary, he wished to attract as members, or at least allies, from the middle class. His proposals were met by scepticism and disbelief.

At great length, he argued and debated with his Mapai comrades over the necessity to go over to the offensive, and it was with great difficulty that he persuaded them to try and aim for a majority in the Zionist Organization. However, at long last, on 31 March 1933, he set off for Eastern Europe, while several of his colleagues traveled to other countries, to win over the masses. This was to be the longest and most exhausting campaign of his life: four months of electioneering among the Jewish communities all over Eastern Europe. While his colleagues openly referred to him as "a lunatic", he was totally convinced that he would gain his objective of conquering the Zionist movement.

Europe in the 1930s witnessed the decline of democracy, the release of violent instincts, and the collapse of an entire system of values. The dark plague of Fascism and terror was accompanied by a surging wave of anti-Semitism, sweeping from Poland to Germany, from Russia to the Baltic shores. Anxiety overtook the Jews of Eastern Europe. Whether out of despair and the search for a radically new path, with a magic formula for redemption, or under the influence of the totalitarian winds that were howling through the continent, the Jewish masses rallied around personalities, slogans, and banners characterized by their Fascist coloring. The worship of fire and sword, of armed force, found its prophet and preacher in Vladimir Jabotinsky.

There was something sad and pathetic, almost tragic, about Jabotinsky. He was the prophet of action, of a dynamic Zionism, who reached for the conquest of Palestine. But his character lacked the patience to engage in humdrum everyday work; his stormy spirit could not take in the idea of settlement by stages, with monotonous physical toil. While the labor movement worked slowly but stubbornly and systematically over a period of years, Jabotinsky sought radical, dramatically swift solutions. And he was winning growing support in the Jewish towns and communities of Europe. His young followers in the Revisionist youth movement, Betar, marched in spangled uniforms; his speeches, full of slogans and magic formulas, set his listeners ablaze; his admirers regarded him as a unique heaven-sent leader. It is no wonder that Benito Mussolini referred to him as "the Jewish Fascist". Nor is it particularly odd that in 1930, Ben-Gurion called the Nazis "the German Revisionists", and, after reading an article by Hitler, noted: "I thought I was reading Jabotinsky – the same words, the same style, the same spirit." In the spring of 1933, when Ben-Gurion set out for Eastern Europe, the world's largest concentration of Jews and Zionists, he knew perfectly well that it would be the Revisionists who would be his principal opponents in the decisive election campaign. More than an election battle, this would be a personal duel between Jabotinsky and Ben-Gurion.

Three and a half months before the Congress elections, Ben-Gurion tore into the East European Jewish communities like a tornado. On 9 April 1933, he reached the railway station in Warsaw loaded down with pamphlets, articles, and plans of action. His notebooks were full of diagrams and data about the number of voters in the various European countries and the division of their votes between the Zionist parties in the past three Congress elections. From the moment he set foot in Warsaw, work went on at a feverish pace: mass rallies, discussions, trips; writing reports, slogans, leaflets, surveys, questionnaires, census reports; flooding the local press with articles and essays. Ben-Gurion's onslaught was unprecedented in its fiery energy and its persistence.

Ben-Gurion's strength scarcely sufficed for the enormous effort. As he traveled from Latvia to Estonia, from Lithuania to the various provinces of Poland, he often felt that he was on the verge of a breakdown. "I left Galicia in one piece. I must be made of cast iron," he wrote to Paula. Generous supporters gave him the money to pay for the election campaign, and he fired off one letter after another to Palestine demanding money and additional comrades for organization and propaganda work. But he succumbed to a deep depression when he realized that his colleagues in the party Central Committee still did not comprehend the importance of the campaign. His fear that "Jewish Fascism" would gain control of the Zionist movement would not subside, and he used any opportunity to settle his accounts with Jabotinsky – "Il Duce", as he called his rival.

At the first election meeting he attended, Ben-Gurion compared Jabotinsky to Hitler and termed the Revisionists "degenerates" who exploited "sensationalism" and engaged in "incitement" against the workers. Referring to the Soldiers' Union, which the Revisionists began to organize in Poland, Ben-Gurion wrote that they were "an illiterate mob, mostly unconnected to Zionism, with more than a few underworld elements – thieves and pimps". The Revisionists responded by publishing pamphlets attacking Ben-Gurion; they referred to him as "a British agent" and composed slogans denouncing the pact between Stalin, Hitler, and Ben-Gurion. The mutual attacks and personal slanders were eventually accompanied by growing violence. The disruption of rallies increased as the day of the elections approached, and Ben-Gurion was often pelted with stones and eggs. In "sensitive" places, he was surrounded by burly members of his party, who made way for him to reach his hotel or the assembly hall while exchanging blows with members of Betar or Communists. He was not very upset by all this and wrote calmly in his diary: "When I reached Jabotinsky in my speech, a Revisionist shouted: 'Down with the lies!' and there was a little uproar; blows were dealt and the hecklers were thrown out."

Despite the violence, Ben-Gurion's spirits rose. He sensed that the tide was slowly turning as growing crowds came to his meetings and greeting him with cheers. A dramatic event that occurred on 16 June 1933, also had a profound impact on the outcome of the elections. The labor leader Chaim Arlosoroff was murdered in Tel Aviv, and the crime was attributed to an extremist faction of the Revisionists. The tragedy deeply shocked Jewish voters all over the world, and when the elections were held in mid-July, Ben-Gurion's labor wing won an astounding victory: 44·6 per cent of the votes. The Revisionists were reduced to a mere 16 per cent. By the time Ben-Gurion left Poland for the Zionist Congress, he was certain that the Palestinian workers would form a coalition in the Zionist Executive and take the leadership of the movement into their own hands.

No one crowned the forty-eight-year-old labor leader in that stormy summer of 1933. But when he first mounted the orator's platform at the Eighteenth Zionist Congress in Prague, he was greeted with prolonged cheers. The reception surprised him. It seems he had not yet grasped that he had become "the unquestioned leader of the labor wing" of Zionism. Nor did he harbor any ambitions to be elected to a central position in the Zionist Executive. But matters unfolded otherwise. His reluctance to accept a post on the Zionist Executive was not a matter of modesty, but his election was inevitable. It was clear to all that he was now the senior political leader of the movement and was gifted with the most manifest traits and skills for the task. However, he agreed to join the Executive only conditionally: he would not undertake any portfolio and would not devote more than two days a week to the Executive's affairs; he would continue to serve as secretary of the Histadrut and live in Tel Aviv; and he would remain on the Executive no more than two years.

Despite the conditions, Ben-Gurion's joining the Zionist Executive brought about a revolutionary change in his life-style. His Tel Aviv home was enriched with what was then considered a symbol of luxury – a telephone. The Haganah (the Jewish Agency's underground military arm) provided him with a bodyguard, and the British police commander also offered him a permanent escort. Ben-Gurion was soon deeply involved in the affairs of the Zionist movement. His principal concern was with political matters, on which he worked together with Moshe Sharett.*

The first task that Ben-Gurion had outlined before the 1933 Congress was to step up immigration to Palestine. His anxiety over the fate of European Jewry gave him a sense of urgency, and he flung himself at the mandatory government with a fury for which the mild-mannered High Commissioner, Sir Arthur Wauchope, was totally unprepared. Faced with the aggressive tactics of the new Zionist leader, only a man without a heart, or a sworn foe of Zionism, could have stood firm – and Sir Arthur was neither. More than once he met Ben-Gurion halfway, accepted his contentions, and approved an intermediate "schedule" (the seasonal quota of immigration

---

* Sharett changed his name from Sherlok only upon the establishment of the State of Israel. In the interest of clarity, however, he is referred to here as Sharett throughout.

certificates) on top of the regular quota. Since the British issued immigration certificates according to the "economic absorptive capacity" of the country, Ben-Gurion became proficient in that subject. He was amazingly well-informed about the number of workers who could find employment in every orange grove, the size of the additional labor force required in every factory, the number of pioneers who could be absorbed in every kibbutz. He went into the minutest details, and conducted stubborn battles for every single certificate.

Ben-Gurion displayed the same thoroughness in mastering the details of Zionist diplomacy in London. He ignored Nahum Sokolov, the president of the Zionist Organization, without any pangs of conscience. Ben-Gurion knew that in this sphere, there was no one as good as Weizmann, and he attempted to bring him back into action. Still resentful about the terrible insult of his dismissal in 1931, Weizmann had not even bothered to attend the 1933 Congress. Although Ben-Gurion was a severe critic of Weizmann's moderation and hesitancy in political matters, he agreed that it was vital to maintain links with Britain while exerting pressure to ensure the British government's support in implementing the Mandate and speeding up the establishment of the national home. In general lines – though with a difference in emphasis – Ben-Gurion's policy resembled that of Weizmann. Immediately after the 1933 Congress, Ben-Gurion traveled to Merano, Italy, to visit Weizmann and lay the foundations for close cooperation during the next two years. He would also write to Weizmann at intervals, giving him detailed reports and addressing him with the deference of a junior approaching a senior. Whenever he came to London, to conduct negotiations on matters of immigration and settlement, he was well aware that Weizmann was the key man in relations with the British government.

At the same time, the labor movement felt insecure in its victory over the Revisionists, and the tension between the workers and the Revisionists in Palestine led to repeated flare-ups and violent clashes. The members of Betar became strike-breakers as a matter of principle, and tore up the red flags of the pioneering youth movement. In response groups of workers attacked Betar meetings and demonstrations in the spring of 1933 and early 1934, beat up the participants, and pelted them with stones. The heads of Mapai in Palestine were in a dilemma over how to deal with the violence of Betar. Many of them, whether for ideological or for tactical reasons, refused to be drawn into a vicious circle of violence, which would leave a stain on the labor movement.

Ben-Gurion was most resolute and extreme – both in his faith in the strength of the labor movement and in his views on the means to be adopted in order to overcome the Revisionists: "There is nothing more ridiculous, or more criminal, than to fight by constitutional means against force, which is entirely unconstitutional. In our fight against Betar, it is impossible to rest content with preaching: we must set up an organized force of our own against them." At the same time, unlike his colleagues in the Mapai leadership, Ben-Gurion did not believe that the Revisionists were capable of endangering the labor movement's hegemony. He overcame his urge to expel the Revisionists from the Zionist movement because he felt that the critical situation of Europe Jewry called for maximum unity. But continued violent conflict between workers and Revisionists, both in Palestine and in the Diaspora, was likely to cause untold harm to Zionist efforts, and a split in the Zionist movement would lead to severe consequences. All these considerations led Ben-Gurion to seek ways toward an understanding with the Revisionists.

Such an opportunity arose on 8 October 1934, when Ben-Gurion reached London. Pinhas Rutenberg, a close friend of Jabotinsky's, invited Ben-Gurion to a meeting with the Revisionist leader in his hotel room.

At first, the discussion was formal, cautious, and suspicious, but gradually the ice was broken. Jabotinsky addressed several "daring questions" to Ben-Gurion, whom he flattered by requesting that he reply "in the Ben-Gurion manner, without fear". Ben-Gurion expressed his willingness to discuss "everything, from labor relations to the final objective". To Ben-Gurion's surprise, Jabotinsky agreed with several of his views concerning the regime in Palestine and relations with Britain. As the atmosphere warmed up, both men sensed a growing surprise at their ability to sit together and agree on various topics. As Ben-Gurion described it:

Greatly aroused, [Jabotinsky] said, in the middle of our conversation: "If we reach a reconciliation between us, it will be a great Jewish achievement; but that achievement should be utilized for some grandiose project." I agreed. He asked me: "What project?" I said: "Some settlement project." He said: "I am not opposed to settlement on the land, but that is not a project. It is necessary to have a project in which all the people will participate. A giant mass project, with every Jew taking part." I asked: "Which?" He said: "A petition . . . You do not comprehend the value of a demonstration and a formulation. The word, the formula – they possess enormous strength." I sensed that, here, we had come to the fundamental conflict.

The meeting in Rutenberg's hotel room was the beginning of a series of intensive sessions. In the course of a month, Ben-Gurion and Jabotinsky met almost daily – either at Ben-Gurion's hotel, or at Jabotinsky's, or, increasingly less frequently, at Rutenberg's. The meetings were held in complete secrecy; Ben-Gurion did not even report them to his party colleagues in Palestine. In that clandestine atmosphere, the two men created a relationship of complete trust and confidence. They liked one another, and both were genuinely interested in reaching an agreement. At their meeting on 25 October, Jabotinsky even said that "he would join Mapai if it were to alter its name to Mabai ('Party of Builders of the Land of Israel'), for he did not support any ideological or class organization, only a general body". But arriving at an agreement was not easy, for on many matters their views were divergent or even diametrically opposed. On many occasions their discussions were fierce and nerve-racking. They were both sensitive men, the heads of two rival camps, and they had to make a supreme effort in order to bridge the chasm that lay between them.

On 26 October, after two weeks of negotiations, they again met at Rutenberg's hotel. This meeting lasted the whole night, but when they walked out into the cold, wet London streets at five o'clock in the morning, they bore the drafts of two agreements. The first aimed at eliminating violence from the relationships between the 60,000 members of Histadrut and the 7,000 members of the National Workers' Organization (the Revisionist trade union); the second, which was referred to as a "working agreement", regulated the question of organized labor and the division of labor between the two trade unions.

Both men were overjoyed. What remained now was to formulate a third agreement concerning the Zionist Organization. However, the agreements they had already reached inspired them with great confidence for the future. Ben-Gurion noted in his journal: "I do not know whether all the comrades in Palestine will welcome the agreement. As far as I am concerned, this matter is so important and fateful that I still find it hard to believe in its implementation. It is too good to be true [in English]." Jabotinsky proposed that they fly to Palestine immediately and convince their colleagues to adopt the agreement.

The following day, Ben-Gurion wrote Jabotinsky a warm letter: "I hope you will not be angry if I address you as a colleague and friend, without the ceremonial 'mister.' . . . Whatever happens, I grasp your hand in esteem." Jabotinsky replied in a similar tone: "My dear friend Ben-Gurion: I am moved to the depths of my being to hear, after so many years – and what years! – words like 'colleague and friend' coming from your lips . . . I grasp your hand in genuine friendship."

While the two men were giving expression to their feelings, however, their respective parties attacked them both furiously. On 28 October, the agreement was published in the Palestinian press, and at three o'clock, Berl Katznelson told Ben-Gurion over the phone that "the comrades take a negative view of the agreement". A short while later, a flood of telegrams descended on Ben-Gurion. A minority indicated support; the rest were highly critical. The Mapai Central Committee was angered by his action in signing the agreement without being authorized to do so and demanded his immediate return to Palestine.

The fierce opposition came as a sharp disappointment to Ben-Gurion. He immediately withdrew to his room and began to write a long letter to his colleagues containing a minutely detailed description of his negotiations with Jabotinsky. In the meantime, with opinion in Palestine up in arms, the flow of furious telegrams continued. The press – with the exception of the right-wing paper *Doar Hayom* – was also unfavorable in its comments. A few days later, Ben-Gurion began to receive letters of protests and reiterated demands that he refrain from signing a third agreement with Jabotinsky concerning cooperation in the Zionist Organization. Jabotinsky, being the sole leader of his movement, was not subject to such heavy pressure. Thus in spite of the protests and pressures, Ben-Gurion renewed the negotiations.

In complete secrecy, the two men began to weave "the great agreement", which was designed to bring about a complete reconciliation between the two movements. This time, however, pressures opposing the agreement were very strong in both camps. On 7 November, the Mapai Central Committee instructed Ben-Gurion "not to sign any Zionist agreement before the Central Committee discusses its full and final wording". The following day, Ben-Gurion also received insistent telegrams from Moshe Sharett and from his own close friend, Berl Katznelson. He was forced to give in and replied with a "reassuring" telegram: "Negotiations called off." Left with no choice, Ben-Gurion was forced to tell Jabotinsky that they could not reach an agreement in the Zionist sphere.

A few days later, Ben-Gurion was back in Palestine. In his usual fiery manner, he flung himself at his colleagues in an attempt to convince them to ratify the agreements he had already signed with Jabotinsky. The Mapai Central Committee decided to place the question before a national referendum of Histadrut members. Jabotinsky also encountered some difficulty in defending the agreement at the Revisionist World Conference in Cracow in January 1935. Among the other delegates who criticized the agreement, a young man named Menahem Begin addressed his grievance to his leader: "You may forget, sir, that Ben-Gurion called you Vladimir Hitler. But our memories are better." Jabotinsky replied: "I shall never forget that men like Ben-Gurion, Ben-Zvi . . . once wore the uniform of the Jewish Legion and fought together with me: and I am certain that should Zionism require it, they would not hesitate to put on their uniforms again and fight."

At the March 1935 Histadrut conference, the majority was opposed to the agreements. Ben-Gurion reminded his colleagues of the great historical compromises accepted by Lenin in signing the Brest-Litovsk peace treaty and in introducing the New Economic Policy. He attacked the Histadrut's factionalism and its claim to exclusive representation of the workers. Yet in a highly tense atmosphere, the referendum held on 24 March 1935, rejected the proposed agreements by 16,474 to 11,522. The vote was a blow to Ben-Gurion's prestige. His independent action aroused considerable anger and suspicion, and he failed to convince his colleagues of the innocuous contention that he had acted in London not as a representative of the party, but as "a member of the Zionist Executive" – in other words, that he had thrown off his workman's cap and replaced it with the top-hat of a Zionist leader. At the same time, the entire episode demonstrated how powerful Ben-Gurion actually was within Mapai. No one considered calling for his dismissal; no one called for a vote of no confidence, no one even proposed that he be reprimanded. Even though he had suffered a serious setback, it had not undermined his position as the rising leader of the labor movement.

The future was to prove the Jabotinsky–Ben-Gurion agreement to have been nothing more than an optical illusion. The opponents in both camps were shown to have been right. The paths of the two movements were in such sharp conflict that no friendly agreement could bridge the differences. The rejection of the agreements with Jabotinsky was undoubtedly the straw that broke the Revisionists' back. Only two weeks after the referendum, they decided to leave the Zionist Organization and found a Zionist movement of their own. Their secession freed the labor movement of its most dangerous rival in the struggle to "conquer the people". Once labor leaders strengthened their hold on the Zionist Executive, they lost their fear of the marching columns headed by Vladimir Jabotinsky.

For some time, Jabotinsky and Ben-Gurion retained their warm friendship. On 30 March, about a week after the Histadrut's rejection of the agreements, Jabotinsky wrote to Ben-Gurion:

Perhaps you will read these lines with altered eyes. I fear that I too have changed a little. For example, I must confess that, on receiving the news of the agreement's rejection, some internal weakness whispered: 'Bless be He who has released me . . .' and perhaps Ben-Gurion is offering up the same blessing at this moment . . . However, there is no change in the respect which I learned in London for Ben-Gurion the man and his ambitions.

Ben-Gurion replied to the letter . . . "Whatever happens, the London episode will never be erased from my heart . . . and if it is destined that we clash – remember that, among your 'enemies' there is a man who admires you and shares your pain. The hand . . . will be extended toward you even in the storm of battle."

Indeed? Within a short time, the relations between the workers and Revisionists would deteriorate again. Ben-Gurion would become the greatest enemy of the "dissidents" and fought them with all his strength. For some time, his relations with Jabotinsky were to remain correct; later the two men would again hurl accusations and insults at one another.

Jabotinsky seems to have despaired of his secession within a short time. His dramatic exit from the Zionist Congress, and the establishment of the new Zionist Organization, soon gave rise to disappointment, leaving him in a barren wilderness of exile. In July 1937, a few days before the Twentieth Zionist Congress, he came to see Ben-Gurion with a proposal for a Zionist National Assembly instead of the existing Congress. The Assembly would be chosen in world-wide general elections. "Your majority," said Jabotinsky, "does not reflect the true balance of forces." Ben-Gurion asked him: "And if, after all, you do not gain a majority? Will you make yourself subject to the National Assembly?" Jabotinsky replied openly: "I cannot be in the minority. I have nothing to do in the minority."

In 1940, Vladimir Jabotinsky died in the United States. Throughout his period of office as the prime minister of Israel, Ben-Gurion obstinately refused to fulfill the section in Jabotinsky's will in which he requested that a sovereign Jewish government bring his remains to be buried in Israel. Ben-Gurion offered varying pretexts for his opposition, but he did not give in. In a letter written in October 1956, he explained that there were two Jews worthy of being re-interred in Israel: Dr Herzl and Baron Edmond de Rothschild. What about Jabotinsky? "This country needs living Jews," wrote Ben-Gurion, "and not the bones of the dead." It was Ben-Gurion's successor, Levi Eshkol, who undertook this humanitarian gesture. To his dying day, Ben-Gurion could not arise above considerations of the political significance of the act.

6

The End of Political Zionism

Two leaders took over the helm of the Zionist movement in August 1935: Chaim Weizmann and David Ben-Gurion. Weizmann was again elected president of the World Zionist Organization, and Ben-Gurion was elected chairman of the Zionist Executive and the Jewish Agency Executive. In the previous two years, he had poured tremendous efforts into building up the labor movement's strength in Poland and the United States – the two principal centers of Jewish life. Indeed, the labor members to the Nineteenth Zionist Congress constituted 50 per cent of the delegates. When hundreds of Congress delegates convened at the charming lakeside resort of Lucerne, Ben-Gurion's colleagues swooped down on him, showering him with pleas. In the end, Ben-Gurion consented to advance his candidacy for the post of chairman of the Zionist Executive. He was voted in.

Weizmann was likewise undecided when he arrived in Lucerne. He had yet to recover from the painful humiliation of his dismissal four years earlier and was filled with bitterness. Moreover, his health was failing, and he wished to devote himself to scientific work at the Sieff Institute, which his friends had established in Rehovot. But his supporters, headed by the labor delegates and Ben-Gurion, gave him no rest. They knew that political activity centered on London, where effective action was impossible without Weizmann's great prestige. In the end, Weizmann was persuaded.

In the thirteen years that were to pass before the establishment of the Jewish state, these two men were to guide the movement. At times, they worked in full harmony; at other times, they were locked in a bitter personal conflict; and at times they clashed over opposing views on matters of principle. Their relationship was to dictate the course of affairs for the Zionist movement, and in time millions of Zionists divided into two camps: "Weizmannites" and "Ben-Gurionites".

The two men were different and at the same time very close. They represented two worlds, two ways of life, two schools of thought and action. Weizmann was a Jewish aristocrat, tall, dignified, elegantly dressed. He was a Jew through and through, who sensed the pain of his people's fate.

He was a proud Jew, who aroused deep respect in his collocutors – intellectuals, great scientists, generals, or powerful ministers. Weizmann knew how to address them as his equals – forcefully, authoritatively, and even sharply – though never appearing haughty or arrogant. Some claim that for several decades a considerable part of the English political world was under the sway of Weizmann's charm and moral authority.

Chaim Weizmann was a pronounced individualist – forceful, domineering, and hesitant to delegate authority. He was a lone wolf, capricious and arbitrary, fully aware of his own worth, and intolerant of the other leaders who surrounded him. He never joined any party (with the possible exception of his youthful activities in Berlin); and when Zionism was split by the great debate between supporters of "political Zionism" and Charterism on the one hand, and advocates of "practical Zionism", he settled for a synthesis of the two views and became one of the leaders of "synthetic Zionism" – a kind of "chemical" compound of the two schools. Settlement on the land was particularly dear to his heart. At the same time, Weizmann was in no hurry to settle in Palestine himself. He was infatuated with England's inhabitants, its customs, and its well-regulated society. For a long time, he regarded England as his home, and he remained true to it all his life. For many years, his links with Britain were the secret of his great power; but the day came when they brought about his downfall. As long as Britain kept its faith with the Declaration it had granted him and the Mandate as he understood it, Weizmann stood at the head of the Zionist movement. But when Britain changed its policy and betrayed its promises, he was to pay with his position.

Weizmann was blessed with prestige, fame, political and scientific success, a charming multi-faceted personality. But the very profusion of his gifts was also a drawback, for he lacked persistence, the ability to concentrate on a single task, the strength to march obstinately on along a humdrum road, the patience to go into minute details and to lay brick on brick in an effort whose objective was hidden beyond the horizon. He was impulsive and a brilliant improviser. When his imagination was aroused by some issue, he would tackle it with great enthusiasm; but when his interest waned, he directed his attention elsewhere.

Obstinacy and total dedication to a single objective were the most characteristic traits of David Ben-Gurion. He, too, was a gifted man, but in his path in life and in his traits, he was very unlike Weizmann. Instead of registering at Vienna University, he came to Palestine. He did not rest content with preaching practical Zionism – he put it into practice, daily, for years. He did not become a unique leader overnight, but climbed through the ranks slowly, and acquiring his posts by election. He was a self-taught genius, yet his want of a formal education was evident. He still found it difficult to speak foreign languages, even though he studied them independently with an iron self-discipline. He gradually learned the secrets of Western culture, but he was never at home in it. He did not possess the polish and the facile natural brilliance of Weizmann. In the thirties, Ben-Gurion was gruff, tough, lacking refinement and polish. He was a short, stocky man, his face tanned, his expression powerful, and energetic. His sense of humor was fairly poor, and his speeches and articles were wearisome and infinitely long. But he stood with both legs firmly planted in the realities of Palestine.

All those years, Weizmann regarded Palestine from his vantage point in Mayfair, London. Because of that – and perhaps also because of his affection for England – he may have been too moderate at times, not sensing the necessity of swift action. It was a long way from the salons of London to the life of want, hunger, strikes, and unemployment in the orange groves. There was a deep chasm between the practical Zionism of the Palestinian pioneers and that of Weizmann. Even when he did come to live in Palestine, in 1934, he built himself a comfortable home near his laboratories in Rehovot and remained cut off from the problems of day-to-day existence. The leaders of the labor movement – even those whose views approximated to his – did not all become his followers. At various times, some of them rallied around him in a group of fervent admirers. But there were those who did not spare him their wrath for his moderate and hesitant policy. They simply could not forgive him for allowing the middle-class Diaspora Zionists to retain their control of the Zionist movement during his term as president.

Ben-Gurion's attitude toward Weizmann fluctuated between profound admiration and merciless criticism. "You are now the king of Israel," Ben-Gurion was to write to Weizmann in 1937. "You do not possess an army or a navy, you were not crowned at Westminster, but the Jewish people sees the monarchial crown of Israel shining upon your head." In the same letter – a rare outpouring of emotion, Ben-Gurion went on to declare: "All my life I have loved you . . . I have loved you with all my heart and soul."

Yet in 1927, following the Fifteenth Zionist Congress, Ben-Gurion wrote forcefully in his journal: "This time saw the end of Weizmann's regime of personal fetishism. This was the last time Weizmann could repeat his saying '*C'est à prendre ou à laisser*' to the Congress. I hope that at the next Congress the majority will say it about Weizmann. And if Weizmann does not obey the majority, he will not remain in the Executive." He defined Weizmann's address to the Congress as "a speech of weakness and lack of faith". A year later, at a meeting of the Zionist Executive, Ben-Gurion was one of the chief critics of Weizmann and the Zionist leadership. In his journal, he defined Weizmann's speech as "Weizmann's usual lies", commenting that he was "ridiculous and wretched".

In subsequent years too, Ben-Gurion filled his journal with barbed comments about Weizmann. They indicate that he did not attach much importance to Weizmann's statements, his threats of resignation, or the dramatic ultimatums he presented to the Zionist leadership or the Executive. He viewed Weizmann's attitude toward the British government as "fatal", and following the report of the Shaw Commission (before publication of the 1930 White Paper), Ben-Gurion wrote: "I do not know who is more to blame – Passfield or Weizmann." During the Seventeenth Congress, in 1931, Ben-Gurion believed that Weizmann should resign. All the same, he did not express this view at the Congress itself, where he voted together with his colleagues for Weizmann to remain in his post.

In 1935, Ben-Gurion came to the conclusion that Weizmann was unequalled in directing the political affairs of the Zionist Organization and should therefore be restored to office in this sphere. However, he did not want Weizmann as a leader. He saw Weizmann as an instrument of the movement, a representative who could address the British on its behalf. When he notified several American Jewish leaders of his plan to restore Weizmann to the presidency, he added: "Weizmann will not be the ruler and leader, and he knows it. The Executive will lead, and he will be no more than its head, not its chief."

Ben-Gurion was well aware of his own deficiencies. During his tour of America, several Zionist leaders suggested to him that he should assume the presidency of the Zionist Organization, but he rejected the proposal outright. He knew that Weizmann was more effective on the British front and that Weizmann's prestige in the Jewish world was greater than his own. Thus, full of complaints and criticism of Weizmann, Ben-Gurion nonetheless came to London two months before the Nineteenth Congress and tried to persuade Weizmann to stand for the presidency.

At the plenary session of the Nineteenth Congress, Ben-Gurion proposed grandiose plans as the objectives of the Zionist movement: "To bring a million families, a million economic units, to strike root in the soil of our homeland." This was no mere slogan. After the record immigration figures of 1935, Ben-Gurion was convinced that the Zionist movement must now storm ahead with all its strength and bring in masses of Jewish emigrants (principally from Germany and Eastern Europe) settle them in Palestine, and find sources of livelihood for them. But to achieve this, he needed three instruments: a united and effective Zionist Organization;

American Jewry as a source of financial support; and the sympathy of Great Britain.

Toward these ends, he reorganized the Zionist Organization by transferring its Organizational Department to Jerusalem and reducing the number of members on the Zionist Executive to seven; making it into an efficient body and, incidentally, incurring the enmity of all those who failed to be elected to it. Calling up the support of American Jewry for the Zionist movement appeared to Ben-Gurion as a decisive and urgent task. "America," he wrote to an emissary of the labor movement there, "is a wide, gigantic sphere of activity . . . without a strong movement possessing ability and support in America, there will not be a world Zionist movement. There lie the masses, the power, the money. If we look ahead to a great future, we have no hope without America." He also devoted his efforts to cultivating sympathy in Britain. Slowly he built up his contacts with members of parliament, ministers, and influential statesmen and learned the ways and byways of British politics, though he deliberately placed himself in Weizmann's shadow.

Throughout the 1930s, Ben-Gurion also devoted his energies to reaching a reconciliation with the Arab nationalists. As far back as October 1921, Ben-Gurion had issued a warning against "the illusion that the Land of Israel is an empty country and that we can do whatever we wish without taking into account its inhabitants". For decades, large sections of the Zionist movement ignored the fact that there were Arabs living in Palestine. But Ben-Gurion did not overlook the Arab question. Nor did he pretend innocence on the subject. There is no doubt, however, that for a long time he was naïve. It was only at the beginning of the 1930s that he began the painful sobering-up process that led him to a realistic assessment of the situation.

From the moment that he began to consider the question of the Arabs of Palestine, Ben-Gurion reiterated endlessly that their right to the country was no less than that of the Jews. He was fiercely opposed to expropriating Arab property or driving Arabs off their lands. "Under no circumstances is it conceivable to drive out the country's present inhabitants. That is not the Zionist objective." Over and over again, he explained that most of the land in the country was untilled; there – and there alone – would the Jews settle. Land must not be purchased unless its owners were fully compensated; and the Arab share-croppers had to be left on their land. As a young man, Ben-Gurion was convinced that the *fellaheen* did not have any feeling for a homeland, in that they lacked a sense of nationality; but they did have "a feeling for the soil". He even went so far as to propose that the Jewish settlement organizations offer financial assistance to "the poor, exploited peasants", so that they could hold on to their land and not be obliged to sell it.

On returning to Palestine at the end of the First World War, Ben-Gurion adopted a new viewpoint. He now advanced the hard-line, rational, Marxist view that the Jewish and Arab workers belonged to the same class and they had to fight shoulder to shoulder against the rich *effendis* who exploited them and incited them against one another. These were the "Marxist–Bolshevik" years in Ben-Gurion's political development, and he proposed the unity of the Jewish and Arab working class.

The 1929 disturbances came as a severe blow to Ben-Gurion, and over-night his entire conception collapsed. At first he tried to place the blame on "gangs of pogromists . . . blood-thirsty agitators" and the British adminis-tration, stressing that the vast majority of Arab peasants had not taken part in the killings. He also traced the violence to religious agitation. Slowly, however, his views changed. In response to the riots, he demanded an immediate increase in immigration and 100 per cent Jewish labor in Jewish concerns. He also worked out a detailed "security plan": "It is impossible to survive long in a country that must be built under the protection of bayonets – and, moreover, of foreign bayonets," he declared. "It is essential to solve our defense problems by our own forces." He urged territorial continuity between the Jewish settlements, called for Jerusalem to be encompassed by Jewish suburbs and villages; and called for tens of thousands of pioneers to come to Palestine so that a Jewish defense force could be created.

For several months after the riots, Ben-Gurion remained undecided between various views and explanations. However, finally, his eyes were opened: for the first time, he used the term "Arab national movement" in its true significance – without blaming the British, without blaming the *effendis*, and without mention of classes. In a discussion that took place in November 1929, Ben-Gurion conceded that an Arab national movement did exist. "The Arab in the Land of Israel need not and cannot be a Zionist. He cannot want the Jews to become a majority. Herein lies the true conflict, the political conflict between us and the Arabs. [Both] we and they want to be the majority." This was an entirely new conception, a sober realism that would hereafter dominate his approach to the Arabs. Many years later, he was to admit that "the Arab national movement was born at almost the same time as political Zionism".

Despairing of a "humane" solution and a "Marxist" solution to the "Arab problem", Ben-Gurion saw no other path than the creation of "a Jewish majority" in Palestine and the continuation of the British Mandate until the Jewish community of Palestine was capable of standing up for

itself both politically and militarily. At the same time, he believed that it
was necessary to try and come to terms with the leaders of the Palestinian
Arabs and forge tolerance and understanding between the two peoples
living in Palestine.

In his efforts to find a common language with the Arabs of Palestine,
Ben-Gurion turned first to Musa Alami, a wealthy and respected landowner. Alami was known as an honest, intelligent man who was moderate
in his views and possessed great influence as the attorney-general of the
British mandatory administration. The two men first met at Moshe
Sharett's home in Jerusalem early in April 1934. They liked one another
and spoke frankly, but the positive first impression did not prevent Alami
from stating forthrightly: "I prefer the country to be poor and desolate,
even for another hundred years, until we Arabs are capable, alone, of
developing it and making it flourish." Alami expressed the bitterness of the
Palestinian Arabs at seeing their fertile land pass into Jewish hands; the
concessions for the large concerns in the country given to Jews; Jews taking
the places of Arabs in all the important posts. "Perhaps the Jews are obliged
to come here, but it is very bitter for the Arabs," he said.

Ben-Gurion immediately raised the question that occupied him most:
"Is there any possibility of reaching an understanding concerning the
establishment of a Jewish state in Palestine, including Transjordan?"
Alami replied with a question of his own: "Why should the Arabs agree to
such a thing?"

Ben-Gurion had an answer prepared. He proposed the establishment of
an Arab federation, which the newly founded Jewish state would join.
"Even if the Arabs of Palestine constitute a minority, they will not have a
minority status, because they will be linked to millions of Arabs in the
neighboring countries."

"That is a proposal that can be discussed," answered the Arab.

In mid-August, Ben-Gurion went to visit Alami at his country home
near Jerusalem and the two men began a series of meetings. Ben-Gurion
employed all his fervor in trying to arouse Alami's interest in his proposal
for an Arab–Jewish understanding. First he gave a short lecture on Zionism, to try and dispel the menace attached to terms such as "Jewish
labor", "a Jewish majority", "land purchases" and "free immigration".
He then went on to present Alami with a two-stage plan: Jewish and Arab
participation in a national government on a basis of parity, and, at a later
stage, a Jewish state on both banks of the Jordan as part of a regional
federation that would include Iraq. In return for Arab agreement to this
plan, Ben-Gurion was prepared to offer the Palestinian Arabs aid in
developing their agriculture and industry. In addition, he promised the

"political, moral, and financial influence" of world Jewry in helping the Arabs to develop their countries and to establish their unity.

Alami voiced apprehensions. In one of their talks, Ben-Gurion had to use all his powers of persuasion to reassure Alami that the Temple would not be rebuilt by the Jews on the site of the Mosque of Omar – in fact, it would not be rebuilt at all until the coming of the Messiah. His frank explanations and analyses inspired Alami's trust. For the first time, Arab and Jewish nationalists talked together without a wall of mutual suspicion dividing them. However, this only emphasized the depth of their dis-agreements. Musa Alami asked: Instead of the federation of Iraq, Trans-jordan, and Palestine, which you propose, why not join them into a single state? Ben-Gurion replied in the negative. Again Alami asked if it would be possible to restrict immigration during the coming decades, so that the number of Jews would not exceed one million? Again Ben-Gurion gave a firm negative answer. The only point on which Ben-Gurion was prepared to give way was the status of Transjordan *vis-à-vis* the Jewish state. "If we are guaranteed unrestricted immigration and settlement rights to the west of the Jordan, we will be prepared to discuss a special arrangement – temporary or permanent – for Transjordan."

Alami, well-versed in the art of bargaining and compromise, regarded Ben-Gurion's views as opening positions. Through the talks, he hoped – though it appears not wholeheartedly – to arrive at a compromise formula that would preclude both a Jewish state and free immigration. After a number of talks, Alami went to see the head of the Palestinian nationalist movement, Haj Amin el-Husseini (the mufti) to report on Ben-Gurion's proposals. At the end of August 1934, he told Ben-Gurion of the mufti's response. "The contents of our talks were a bombshell for the mufti. He never guessed that there are Jews who genuinely want understanding and agreement with the Arabs. As for himself, he is not opposed [to an under-standing] as long as it is possible to guarantee the religious, economic, and political rights of the Palestinian Arabs. Of course, he still has to consider the plan . . . For the time being, he cannot take any steps."

Ben-Gurion was pleased to hear the mufti's comments. On Alami's recommendation, he now traveled to Geneva to meet Ichsan Bey al-Jabri and Shakib Arslan, leaders of the Syrian–Palestinian Istiklal Party. He was full of great expectations when he reached the comfortable and ornate flat of Arslan, who was waiting together with his colleague Jabri. Arslan impressed Ben-Gurion as "a sluggish old man, but when he speaks, his courage and fervor are evident".

Indeed, fiery were the words of the old "lion" (Arslan is Turkish for a lion) as he launched a fanatical onslaught on Ben-Gurion. He dismissed the offers of Jewish aid in unifying the Arab states. "That unity," he said, "is certain in any case," and the Arabs were not in need of the Jews. As for Palestine, he stated plainly that "without a promise [by the Jews] that the Palestinian Arabs would remain in the majority, he was not prepared to negotiate on anything. The Arabs have no interest in creating a Jewish Palestine. Even if such a Palestine were established, [they] would never accept it. After all, Palestine is surrounded by tens of millions of Arabs." His conditions for an agreement: permanent minority status for the Jews in Palestine and a ban on settlement in Transjordan.

A month later, Ben-Gurion was astounded to find the contents of his confidential conversations with Arslan and Jabri printed in the December 1934 issue of the monthly *La Nation Arabe*. The two men wrote that they had agreed to meet Ben-Gurion after "receiving assurances of his serious character". In their conversation,

... he declared frankly that not only Palestine, but Transjordan too was the sub- ject of their claim ... He came to ask, with complete simplicity, what compensa- tion the Arabs would demand for agreeing to the establishment of a Jewish state in both countries, adding immediately that those Arabs who did not want to emigrate, were free to remain, and their land would not be taken from them.

Here the authors commented ironically: "We considered it our duty to ask him if what he was saying was in earnest, for we could not prevent our- selves from smiling on hearing such nonsense." They reiterated that his proposal contained

... absolutely nothing to induce one and a half million Arabs to despair and aban- don their homeland ... and to move to the desert. When someone has ideas that are so arrogant and presumptuous, he should not assume that he will receive his adversary's agreement. He would do better to go on, supported by British bayonets, and establish a Jewish state.

They termed his proposals "childish and irrational" and, accordingly, "we informed M. Ben-Gurion that there was no use in continuing this fantastic conversation".

From Ben-Gurion's point of view, this was the end of only one attempt to meet and talk with Arab leaders. He went on to hold discussions with Auni Bey Abd el-Hadi, the head of Istiklal in Palestine; Fuad Bey Hamza, director of foreign affairs in the government of King Ibn Saud of Saudi Arabia; St John Philby, a convert to Islam who served as an adviser to Ibn Saud; and Hafez Wahabah, a leader of the Palestinian Arabs. In meetings with the Christian Arab Antonious, Ben-Gurion proposed a five-point agreement, and both men agreed to present the proposals to the leaders of their respective communities. A few days later, however, Ben-Gurion discovered that Antonious had left the country for Turkey, and he never saw him again. In the end, nothing came of all these meetings, for in the interim, "facts on the ground" had overtaken Ben-Gurion's efforts to reach an understanding with the Arab nationalist movement.

In September 1935, the Third Reich adopted the Nuremberg race laws. For several years, Zionist leaders had been warning of the approaching catastrophe, and increased Zionist pressure on Great Britain, which came into effect following the change in the movement's leadership, began to show results. From year to year, there was an increase in the number of Jews permitted to enter the country, and in 1935, immigration reached an unprecedented record of 65,000. At the same time, the Palestinian Arab nationalists were influenced by two developments: the speed-up of Jewish expansion in Palestine; and the exciting events in the neighboring Arab countries, which gave rise to a new wave of nationalist feeling. In 1927 Transjordan was recognized as a constitutionally independent state (though still under a British mandate); Syria gained autonomy in 1932, as a stage on the way to national independence; and Iraq was about to sign a pact with Britain by which it would gain full independence. Only in Palestine did the Arabs remain a subjugated community. The nationalist leadership suggested that the Zionists were exploiting the rise of Nazism to establish a Jewish state at the expense of the Arabs; and they were seized with frustration on discovering that the wave of emancipation sweeping the East was passing by their own homeland. It seemed as though nothing could prevent a conflagration.

On the night of 15 April 1936, a group of Arabs halted a truck and fired on its Jewish occupants. One of them was killed, and two wounded (one of whom died of his wounds five days later). Members of Haganah's "Group B", which inclined to the right, struck back two days later and murdered two Arabs. That Saturday, Arabs were beaten up in Tel Aviv by angry Jews. The following day, an inflamed mob of Arabs poured into the streets of Jaffa, murdering every Jew they chanced upon. At the end of the day, sixteen Jewish fatalities were recorded. The Haganah took up positions to halt the rioters, evacuating the outlying neighborhoods, and, with great effort maintained the "self-restraint" policy proclaimed by the Jewish Agency Executive. This was the beginning of the 1936 disturbances.

The 1936 riots may have commenced spontaneously, but their continuation was far from haphazard. Within two or three days, National Committees were set up in Arab towns and villages throughout the country to launch a wild campaign of incitement. Six days after the massacre in Jaffa, the Supreme Arab Committee was established in Nablus, the stronghold of the Palestinian national movement. It was from there that instructions

were issued for the continuation of actions that historians were to dub "the
Arab Revolt". A few days after the Jaffa riots, the leaders of the Arab
Revolt decided to call a general strike throughout the country, while the
wave of terror was checked for a few weeks.

From the first moment, Ben-Gurion demanded that the Haganah
refrain from reprisals against Arab attacks and that the response to the
Arab general strike be expressed in two principal measures. First, everything must be done to prevent the strike from harming the Jewish community's economic interests and its normal way of life – by achieving 100
per cent Jewish labor in the Jewish economic sectors and creating a "Jewish
port" to overcome dependence upon the Arab port workers. Secondly, the
mandatory government must be arged to break the strike by force, for it
would be followed by disturbances and terrorism.

Ben-Gurion did not fear the Arabs as much as he did the British. He
reminded his colleagues that previous Arab riots – in 1921 and 1929 –
had been followed by detrimental political action by the British government. It was necessary to prepare for such an eventuality and take immediate steps against any plans to restrict immigration, limit Jewish rights, or
establish a Constituent Assembly – a proposal which had long given him
sleepless nights. He was deeply concerned about the possibility of a Royal
Commission of Inquiry being sent to Palestine, for he still remembered the
Shaw Commission's report, which had given rise to the 1930 Passfield
White Paper.

Above all, however, there was one basic assumption from which he did
not budge: the Jewish community must not come into conflict with Britain.
Britain was the only force that could break the strike and the wave of terror
that would come in its wake; it was also the only force capable of helping
the Jewish community by continuing the active implementation of the
"National Home" policy. Thus, it was incumbent upon the Jewish community to do everything in its power to preserve British sympathy.
Weizmann had been in London since March. He was now joined by Ben-
Gurion, and the two men launched a campaign of unprecedented intensity
to mobilize support for the Zionist view. They met Colonial Secretary
William Ormsby-Gore and the senior officials at the Colonial Office;
lectured to political and public bodies; conferred with Zionist sympathizers in Parliament; and briefed pro-Zionist journalists. Their efforts were
rewarded. Almost all the speakers in the debate on Palestine in the House
of Commons supported the Zionist view, and the press also adopted a
distinctly pro-Zionist line.

But the idyll did not last long. The situation in Palestine continued to
deteriorate, precisely because the Arab rebellion did not attain its objec-

tives. Although the Arab strike was complete, the country's economy was not paralyzed. The Jewish community succeeded in organizing to supply its own needs. The railways were not halted, nor did industry and the ports cease to function. One of the paradoxical outcomes of the strike was that it gave the Jews their opportunity to attain additional economic objectives. The mandatory government approved the construction of a wharf at Tel Aviv, and thousands of jobs left by Arab workers gave the Jews the opportunity to demand a sizeable "schedule" of immigration to fill them. In frustration, the Arabs decided to renew their terror campaign. At first they engaged in murder, killing solitary Jews in the large towns, in the fields, and on the highways. Then armed bands began to launch violent raids. The heads of the rebellion summoned a famous officer, Fawzi Kaukji, to come from Iraq and head a "private army".

The renewed violence caused alarm in official circles in Palestine and Britain. In the offices of the High Commissioner in Jerusalem and at the Colonial Office in London, frightened voices proposed a temporary halt to immigration. And suddenly Chaim Weizmann began to think aloud about the idea. Ben-Gurion was horrified. He tried to dissuade Weizmann, but he was too late. On 9 June 1936, the president of the Zionist Organization met with Nuri Said Pasha, the prime minister of Iraq, for a long discussion on a possible solution to the crisis in Palestine, and Weizmann agreed to Nuri's proposal of a temporary halt to immigration. Nuri Said seized the opportunity and reported to the British government. On 25 June, the colonial secretary sent a letter to Weizmann asking whether there was any truth in the report. Ben-Gurion was in despair. The following day, he attempted to persuade Weizmann to send letters to Ormsby-Gore and to Nuri Said denying that he had accepted the proposal. "It was a very painful conversation," Ben-Gurion noted. "It is hard to see a man in his downfall."

The incident poisoned their relationship. Ben-Gurion was again apprehensive when he accompanied Weizmann to a meeting with Ormsby-Gore. The colonial secretary asked: "What do you think about suspending immigration during the time the Royal Commission [of Inquiry] is in Palestine?" Weizmann replied that he "could not give an answer now". Ben-Gurion left the meeting "broken, dejected, and depressed, as I have never been before". "Chaim has already made us lose this round," he reported to his colleagues. "I did not just see the disaster that now awaits us because of this man. All the political failure of previous years also became clear to me."

For the most part, the Mapai leadership shared Ben-Gurion's view – although in a less extreme form – that Weizmann was a valuable asset to the Zionist movement but that he had to be "watched" to prevent him making unwise steps. Weizmann himself was also vividly aware of the unpleasant fact that everyone was attempting to "watch" him. In a conversation in London, he said bitterly: "They chose a leader, and they don't want to let him lead: instead they want to lead him."

Weizmann did not have a particularly high opinion of Ben-Gurion. In his memoirs, he was to mention Ben-Gurion's name only twice, incidentally, without granting him even a little of the status which Ben-Gurion deserved. (In publishing his memoirs, Weizmann removed several pages of severe criticism of Ben-Gurion from the manuscript.) It is possible that Weizmann's disregard for Ben-Gurion covered up his growing fear of the ambitious Palestinian leader who had become his rival in the Zionist leadership. Ben-Gurion, on the one hand, admired Weizmann's "charm", his brilliant powers of oratory, his proud appearance. Yet at the same time, Ben-Gurion was full of criticism of Weizmann. His journal and memoirs relating to 1936 are full of violent attacks on the president of the Zionist Organization.

During the summer, the number of violent incidents increased, and so did the bloodshed. Jews were murdered in Safad, Jaffa, and Jerusalem, and in the course of a single night, thirty-eight settlements were attacked or harassed. There were attacks on the highways; oil pipelines and railway tracks were damaged; and under the command of Kaukji, the revolt took on a pronounced anti-British character. At first, the Haganah obeyed the order of the Jewish Agency to exercise "self-restraint". Yet in view of the increasing number of murders during the summer, the Haganah was given permission to carry out reprisal actions. Moreover, the British approved an increase in the number of Jewish auxiliary police. Ben-Gurion regarded the establishment of this "Jewish army" as a great achievement, but he remained opposed to counter-terror actions by the Haganah for fear that the British would stop supplying the Jews with arms.

On 2 September, the British Cabinet convened for its decisive meeting on the Palestine crisis and resolved not to capitulate to the Arab demands by halting immigration. On the contrary, it was decided that the Arab Revolt should be crushed, by force if necessary. An entire British division was now stationed in Palestine, and Britain was capable of quelling the Arab uprising. Yet the government preferred not to send its units into action immediately, for the Revolt was gradually losing impetus. Behind the scenes, Arab leaders, headed by Nuri Said, negotiated with British representatives, and in the end, they reached a face-saving agreement. A group of Arab kings and rulers addressed an appeal to the Palestinian Arabs to restore calm and called on them "to put their trust in the good intentions of their friend, Britain, which has proclaimed that it will deal justly". On 11 November 1936, the Supreme Arab Committee announced the end of the strike and the revolt.

Once again, the victory and respite from frenetic activities was short-lived for the Zionist leadership. In November 1936, one of Ben-Gurion's growing fears was realized: a Royal Commission of Inquiry, headed by Lord Peel, appeared in Palestine. Memories of the Shaw Commission destroyed Ben-Gurion's peace of mind. Together with Moshe Sharett, Chaim Weizmann, and their close colleagues, Ben-Gurion took part in meetings to work out the principal outlines of the Jewish case and divide the burden of testimony. The rivalry between Weizmann and Ben-Gurion found its expression here as well. The moment it was decided that Weizmann would present the Zionist political case, Ben-Gurion decided that he himself would not appear before the commission, sensing that he would be put in the shade of Weizmann's natural authority, proud appearance, and rhetorical ability.

At first this seemed like a sensible decision. Weizmann gave his public testimony before the commission in a wonderfully brave and powerful speech, and Ben-Gurion was full of admiration. "Chaim has once more regained his position within the Jewish people," he wrote in his journal, "and there is no doubt that his words will unite the movement as it has not been united for many years." A few days later, however, Ben-Gurion again became fiercely critical. After his public appearance, Weizmann gave the rest of his testimony *in camera*. When the text of his statement reached Ben-Gurion, he was seized with anger. Weizmann had given dangerously vague answers to the question of immigration. At a closed consultation with a few of his colleagues, Ben-Gurion expressed the opinion that Weizmann "must not be permitted to testify *in camera*. He is very powerful when he attacks, and when he is the sole speaker. In an argument, he is helpless."

As Weizmann continued his testimony, Ben-Gurion fumed, "This testimony is, in my opinion, a political catastrophe." Indeed, when speaking of the dangers looming over six million European Jews, Weizmann pointed out that only two million could be rescued – one million would come to Palestine, and another million would emigrate to other countries. When asked how long it would take to bring a million Jews into Palestine and absorb them, Weizmann replied, "Twenty-five or thirty years, it's hard to say." He also hinted that the immigration of that million might satisfy the demands of the Zionist movement. He wanted the immigration plan to be carried out as quickly as possible, "but we must be aware that, if we go too fast, we may break our necks".

Ben-Gurion's fury was justified. In one blow, Weizmann had disavowed all the plans for a large-scale immigration and the creation of a Jewish majority. Instead, he had depicted Zionist objectives as nothing more than the immigration and absorption of one million Jews to reach western Palestine in the course of thirty years! Ben-Gurion sent Weizmann his resignation as head of the Jewish Agency's Political Department, stating, "After long and bitter reflection, it became clear to me that in questions of Zionist policy, my ideas do not coincide with yours . . ." The letter left a profound impact on Weizmann, and at the initiative of those close to him, a meeting was arranged with Ben-Gurion. The result was that Ben-Gurion withdrew his resignation, and a week later he also testified before the Royal Commission.

The Peel Commission heard dozens of testimonies – including those of Moshe Sharett, Vladimir Jabotinsky, and prominent Arab leaders – and at the end of January, it terminated its work in Palestine. A hint as to the way the scales were tilting reached Weizmann's ears. It transpired that Sir Stafford Cripps was preparing a proposal for the partition of the country into two states, one Jewish and the other Arab. Weizmann was first asked for his opinion on this proposal at a confidential meeting of the commission on 8 January 1937. When Ben-Gurion came to hear of it, the notion fired his enthusiasm. Who would have dared to dream that the British would propose an independent Jewish state! Ben-Gurion summoned the Mapai Central Committee to his home. "This plan might, at first sight, appear fantastic," he told his colleagues, "and, indeed, it may have been fantastic a year ago, and it may be fantastic in another year; but not at present for there are extenuating factors." His words did not arouse enthusiasm.

Decades later, after the horrors of the Holocaust in Europe, Ben-Gurion's colleagues were to concede that he had been right when he supported the idea of partition in February 1937. Chaim Weizmann, already detecting the impending catastrophe, adopted the idea with great enthusiasm at a time when it was nothing more than a vague intellectual exercise in the minds of two or three British leaders. Ben-Gurion understood the significance of the term "state" with what statesmen would one day define as his "prophetic sense". Thus two leaders of the Zionist movement were in accord regarding the objective for 1937. But many others opposed their views. "Zionism," Ben-Gurion wrote to Sharett, "is now walking, not on a tight-rope, but a hair. The opponents of partition are living in a fool's paradise." Ben-Gurion employed all his energy and his rhetorical ability to persuade his Central Committee colleagues of the importance of partition. "What we face now is not just 'the danger of partition', but also the establishment of a Jewish state." He confessed himself to be "moved to the depths of my heart and the chasm of my soul by the great and wonderful redeeming vision of a Jewish state, whose hour has pealed . . ."

The Peel Commission marked out the borders of its partition plan. The Jewish state would include Upper and Lower Galilee, the Jezreel Valley, and the coastal plain. This area – less than one quarter of the area of western Palestine – was the home of 258,000 Jews, as against 225,000 Arabs. The Arab state was allocated the remaining part of Palestine and Transjordan, with several Jewish footholds remaining within its boundaries. Britain would also retain an enclave in the country: a mandatory "protectorate" constituting a corridor from Jerusalem to the sea that would include Bethlehem, Jerusalem, Lod, and Ramleh. Nazareth, Acre, Safed, Tiberias, and Haifa were also to remain under British protection. The Jews would enjoy special arrangements for utilizing Haifa port until the completion of a joint Tel Aviv–Jaffa port, which would be managed by Jews and Arabs under British auspices. England would safeguard the Holy Places in the reduced mandatory areas and by means of agreement with the Arab and Jewish states.

These were the main points of the Peel report. When they became known, they aroused a storm that rocked and divided the Jewish world. Emotional debates erupted everywhere. The extreme left, brandishing its banner of a bi-national state, angrily rejected the plan; the religious partisans brandished the Bible; the Revisionists chanted their pretentious slogans; the moderate right-wing did not want to hear of any cession of territory. Within Ben-Gurion's own party and among his own dearest friends, there were also violent objections to the plan. But the greatest outcry against the partition plan did not undermine Ben-Gurion's belief that a revolutionary historical change was on the threshold. He was deeply impressed by Britain's willingness to carry out transfers of Arabs from the Jewish state to other areas; he was thrilled by the idea of a joint border with Lebanon, the only Christian state in the Middle East and, in his eyes, a future ally. With his dreams of the "conquest of the sea", he was pleased that such a long coastal strip had been allocated to the Jewish state.

Yet there was one crucial difference in the way Ben-Gurion and his colleagues assessed the Peel plan: Ben-Gurion saw beyond it. He never regarded the partition borders as the last word, but his vision was spelled out in only one document: a letter to his son, Amos:

A partial Jewish state is not the end, but only the beginning. . . . We shall bring into the state all the Jews it is possible to bring . . . we shall establish a multi-faceted Jewish economy – agricultural, industrial, and maritime. We shall organize a modern defense force, a select army . . . and then I am certain that we will not be prevented from settling in the other parts of the country, either by mutual agreement with our Arab neighbors *or by some other means.* Our ability to penetrate the country will increase if there is a state. Our strength *vis-à-vis* the Arabs will increase. I am not in favor of war . . . [but if] the Arabs behave in keeping with [their] barren nationalist feelings and say to us: Better that the Negev remain barren than that Jews settle there, *then we shall have to speak to them in a different language. But we shall only have another language if we have a state.*

The true litmus test of Jewish opinion, however, would be the Twentieth Zionist Congress, held in August 1937. The delegates arrived agitated and disturbed. They believed that it would be up to them to determine the fate of Zionism by deciding whether or not to establish the Jewish state. For the first time, the Zionist movement was called upon to decide the question of the "final objective" – not because it had at long last decided to touch upon a topic that had hitherto been taboo, but because the greatest of the world powers, with the means to establish a state for the Jewish people, was now asking that people to decide.

Overriding inter-party differences, a powerful coalition fought to prevent the partition of Palestine, and there was no chance of gaining massive support for the Peel program. On top of the debate within the labor movement, the right-wing, religious groups, and the Americans were all opposed to the plan. It appeared that forty years after its creation and twenty years after receiving the Balfour Declaration, the Zionist movement was not yet strong or mature enough to take this heavy responsibility upon itself. In the end, the Congress adopted the compromise formula advanced by those leaders who favored partition. According to the resolution, the leaders of the Zionist movement were authorized to enter into negotiations with the British government on the partition plan. However, the Congress did not say "yes" to partition; it did not unite as one man to fight all over the world and with all its strength, for the state it had been offered.

Ben-Gurion still believed in the prospects of the plan. He did not know that, at precisely the same time, the new developments in Europe and the Middle East had begun, surreptitiously, to erect a powerful barrier before Great Britain's Zionist sympathies or that the partition plan, so precious to him, would fall victim to a deep-seated change in British policy. Once again, the winds of war were blowing through a helpless, panic-stricken Europe, and the free world – intimidated or purposely shutting its eyes – once again bowed its head. America feverishly fortified its isolationism; the French Third Republic was in its death throes; and Neville Chamberlain's Britain bent its knees to appease the "brown plague" of Hitler and his accomplices. In Palestine the Arab revolt had broken out again, and in response to the partition plan, an inter-Arab conference issued an indignant call for the annulment of the Balfour Declaration, threatening that if

Britain did not alter the policy in Palestine, "we shall avail ourselves of the freedom to combine with other European Powers whose policy is hostile to that of Great Britain".

During 1937, the British government came to the conclusion that the "Jewish National Home" policy had been erroneous from the outset. It had led to a dangerous undermining of the Empire's relations with the Arab and Moslem world just at a time when Britain was more than ever in need of the friendship and loyalty of the Middle East's Arabs and India's Moslems. Britain tried to turn back the clock of history. Step by step, it turned its back on its irksome commitments to the Jews stemming from the Balfour Declaration. The government imposed drastic restrictions on immigration, letting in only 1,000 Jews a month; and the fair and tolerant High Commissioner, Sir Arthur Wauchope, who was identified with the government's pro-Zionist policy, was replaced by Sir Harold MacMichael, whom Ben-Gurion later described as "a terrible man; the worst of all the High Commissioners". In December 1937, the British government officially declared that it no longer considered itself bound to the partition plan.

Ben-Gurion's response was unambiguous: "If [the British] decree that we are to be abandoned to the mufti, only the Jewish community in Palestine can save us." It would be necessary, he concluded, to oppose such a decree "not with words, not with demonstrations, but by concrete deeds . . . The youth will arise – the young in age and the young in spirit; they will raise the banner of revolt and fight." These words, written early in the autumn of 1938, marked the profound change that had taken place in his own views. Until then he had contended that the Jewish community in Palestine must avoid clashing with the British. But Britain now was attempting to abrogate its commitments. In that case, "we, too, shall withdraw our support of Britain, and build up our own military strength, so that we can, if necessary, fight the British as well". Ben-Gurion was certain that Palestine was no more than a small and restricted sector in the world-wide front where the British Empire had drawn up its forces to defend its interests. Even though the Jewish community there numbered no more than 400,000, if it launched a vigorous and united uprising, it could withstand the limited forces that Britain could spare to put down the insurrection. Consequently, even a small people – if it showed determination – could ward off the great British Empire. In this spirit, Ben-Gurion wrote to his colleagues in Palestine that one of their present objectives must be "to build up our strength – in the police, the army, immigration as far as possible . . . it is possible that we will have to employ the little strength we have".

It appeared as though political Zionism was on the brink of collapse. Yet Ben-Gurion and his Zionist Organization colleagues participated in one further attempt to reconcile their differences with Britain and formulate a solution to the troubled situation in Palestine. At the end of 1938, the British government decided to convene the St James's Conference as a last attempt to reach an agreement with the Jews and the Arabs since the recommendations of the Peel and Woodhead Commissions had led to deadlock. The conference was a weird and dismal affair and was doomed to failure. There was no doubt in the minds of the Zionist leaders – and Ben-Gurion in particular – that the "agreement" desired by the British would be emphatically pro-Arab for Britain was not risking much by harming the Jewish cause: "Even if Britain makes trouble for us in Palestine," Ben-Gurion wrote, "it is inconceivable that the Jews will be on Hitler's side . . . Not so the Arabs. They have to be bought, because they can [afford to] be on Hitler's side."

The very atmosphere of the conference could not have been more incongruous with the sense of impending crisis. At 10.30 a.m. on 7 February 1939, a high-ranking Arab delegation walked through the Friars' Court gate into the Palace of St James. After clinking glasses in the Queen Anne Room, they were seated in the Portrait Room, whereupon in strode Neville Chamberlain dressed in formal attire, followed by a large retinue of aides. After a short opening ceremony, the delegation rose and left the palace through the same gate, where journalists and photographers were waiting. At 11.45 Chamberlain repeated his entrance into the Portrait Room to greet the Zionist delegation, headed by Dr Chaim Weizmann and Ben-Gurion. At the end of the short ceremony, these delegates left the palace by way of the Delegates' Gate, where they too were awaited by members of the press. At their arrival and departure, the Zionists did not encounter a single Arab representative. The British prime minister was forced to conduct the opening ceremony twice because the Arabs vigorously refused to sit in the same room as the Jews.

For five weeks, the heads of the British government held parallel meetings with the two hostile delegations, hurrying between one party and its rival. They transmitted the minutes of the meetings, held consultations among themselves, initiated informal talks, and threatened to impose their will if the two delegations failed to reach agreement. As the winds of war blew strong in Europe, a game of cat and mouse was in progress between a group of Arabs, who were sure of their bargaining power, and a Jewish delegation plunged into despair on discovering that it had been summoned to witness – and perhaps even assist – the destruction of the Jewish National Home. Everything was conducted with respectful decorum and was therefore ten times more cruel and revolting. A few weeks later, when Ben-Gurion fell ill, the Foreign Secretary Malcolm MacDonald sent him a huge bouquet of flowers, with wishes for a speedy recovery. Bitterly, Ben-Gurion commented: "You have to learn manners and etiquette from these dignitaries. Even when they lead you up to the scaffold, they maintain their courtesy and their smiles."

It was indeed a march to the scaffold, even if the backdrop was splendid and the ceremony festive. Malcolm MacDonald, who presided, explained calmly that Britain had to gain the goodwill of the Arab states in order to safeguard its bases and strategic routes, which would be vital if war should break out. Adopting many of the Arab contentions, MacDonald urged the Jews to be "realistic". Palestine was not an empty country and it was impossible to establish a Jewish state there. The Arabs were demanding self-government, and they were within their rights to do so. Immigration had to be restricted; a demographic "ceiling" of 35–40 per cent had to be accepted for the Jewish minority; and the sale of land to Jews had to be prohibited in large sections of the country. MacDonald and his colleagues rejected the arguments advanced by Weizmann and Ben-Gurion regarding the moral validity of the Balfour Declaration.

Ben-Gurion had his first clash with MacDonald when the British raised their practical proposals concerning drastic restrictions on immigration, which would be halted completely in a few years. Ben-Gurion commented sharply: "We have been told . . . that continued immigration requires the help of British bayonets. [Yet] it is impossible to prevent the immigration of Jews into the country . . . other than by force of British bayonets, British police, and the British Navy. And, of course, it is impossible to convert Palestine into an Arab state, over Jewish opposition, without the constant help of British bayonets!" In an informal talk with MacDonald, on 16 February, Ben-Gurion advanced three feasible options: (1) a Jewish state within an Arab–Jewish federation, which he considered "the ideal solution"; (2) partition along the lines of the Peel plan; or (3) postponement of the talks for another five years, in the course of which immigration would continue according to quotas to be agreed by all three parties.

Gradually, however, the members of the Jewish delegation comprehended that the British had not come to the conference to seek a way out of the crisis, but to place an official seal on a policy they had already adopted. On 26 February, Chaim Weizmann received an official letter from the British government. When he opened the envelope and studied its contents, he was horrified: it was the draft of a White Paper that was soon to be published. Its principal provisions were the establishment of an Arab state in Palestine within five years, during which time immigration would be restricted and subsequently made conditional upon Arab consent. "I could not believe my eyes," Weizmann wrote. It transpired that the draft had reached Weizmann in error, since it had been sent by the Colonial Office for the approval of the Arab delegation!

A few days later, the British succeeded in convincing the heads of the Arab states to come to a joint meeting with the Jewish delegation. The discussion was held at St James's Palace, during the evening of 7 March. It was an intimate meeting, held in a relaxed atmosphere. Four Englishmen, four Jews, and three Arabs met in a small room near a blazing fireplace. However, it soon became clear that this was a three-sided "dialogue of the deaf". Each side presented its contentions, calmly and with restraint, but without the faintest spark of understanding for the points made by its adversaries. The principal Arab spokesman, Ali Maher of Egypt, addressed Ben-Gurion pleasantly:

Don't you think that, first of all, peace should be restored to the Holy Land? Take your time. Halt immigration for a while, peace will be established, you will win Arab friends . . . [and] you can continue your activities later. You may even become a majority. But do not hurry . . . Let there first be peace, and if, for that purpose, you have to slow down – is peace not worth it?

Ben-Gurion sensed that all eyes were fixed upon himself and his colleagues. He began his reply by expressing his appreciation for the spirit of peace in Maher's words and stressed that it had not been the Jews who disturbed the peace in Palestine. As for the appeal to halt immigration, he replied with a parable:

The appeal to halt our work for some time resembles an appeal by happy families, blessed with many children and living in comfort, to a woman who, after many years of childlessness, is about to give birth. When she is overtaken by birth-pangs, the neighboring women rebuke her and shout: "Could you stop this noise and not hurry to give birth, so that we can sleep in peace!" The mother cannot stop. It is possible to kill the child, or to kill the mother; but it is impossible to expect her to cease giving birth.

These were impressive words. But the conciliatory tone adopted by Ali Maher had struck home at the weak point of the Jewish delegation – Chaim Weizmann. "I was glad to hear the words of Ali Maher," said the president of the Zionist Organization. "For the first time, after twenty years, I heard words of friendship and respect from a Moslem. In this spirit, we can talk. We are prepared for negotiations with the Palestinian Arabs . . . Palestine can absorb fifty or sixty thousand people a year. If they tell us: We will make an agreement, slow down – we will find a common ground."

Moshe Sharett was appalled by Weizmann's words: "I thought my hair was turning white. I sensed that a chasm was opening up at our feet." But Malcolm MacDonald immediately responded to the statement, which constituted a withdrawal from the official Zionist line. "This meeting has not been in vain," he said. "At long last, we have found a common language. It seems that there is common ground on a slowdown of immigration for a time."

Ben-Gurion broke in: "I am sorry to disrupt the rejoicing, but I do not yet see any 'common ground'. We do not agree to any slowdown. Dr Weizmann spoke of mutual concessions, and each one of us is prepared for negotiations on a give-and-take basis. But there can be no talk of a slowdown; that is a unilateral assumption."

Weizmann, having apparently grasped his grave error, remained silent. Reluctantly, Malcolm MacDonald said: "We shall continue the discussion tomorrow." But Ben-Gurion did not let up. "In the continuation of our discussion, will it be possible to consider a speed-up of immigration?"

"No!" said Malcolm MacDonald vigorously.

"Why not?" Ben-Gurion persisted.

"Because on the basis of a speed-up, there will be no agreement."

Ben-Gurion flung back the ball: "I am afraid that on the basis of a slowdown, there will also be no agreement."

The British were furious at Ben-Gurion for having pulled Weizmann into line, thereby closing any opening for the kind of settlement they desired. When the negotiations resumed, Ben-Gurion remained the most forceful member of the Jewish delegation. There was sharp tension between him and MacDonald, and Moshe Sharett wrote admiringly that Ben-Gurion "had saved the situation, even though he sacrificed himself to do so".

Ben-Gurion attended the last informal meeting with the British delegation, with the feeling that all was "over and done with". He saw clearly that the British would do whatever they wished, even at the price of a schism with the Jews. Britain's "perfidious plan", as Ben-Gurion termed it, was presented to the Jewish and Arab delegation on 15 March. Chaim Weizmann did not attend the meeting, and Ben-Gurion also refused to appear. Britain proposed the establishment of an independent Palestinian state, possibly federal in structure, but neither Jewish nor Arab. Its constitution would be determined by a constituent assembly, to be elected within two years. The state would be established within a period not exceeding ten years. In the course of the next five years, 75,000 Jews would immigrate; thereafter any further immigration would be subject to Arab consent, and vigorous measures would be taken against illegal immigration. Furthermore, severe restrictions would be imposed on the sale of land to Jews. One of the provisions hinted that the Jews could bring about the continuation of the Mandate if they did not agree to the establishment of an independent state.

These proposals satisfied a large part of the Arab demands but not all of them, for the establishment of an independent state was made subject to Jewish consent. Consequently, the Arabs rejected the proposals, though in a most moderate tone.

From the Zionist viewpoint, there was no doubt that the British plan spelled the end of the National Home, as defined in the Balfour Declaration. There was some symbolism in the date on which the proposals were published. On 15 March 1939, Hitler invaded what was left of Czechoslovakia. Many saw a similarity between the British abandonment of Czechoslovakia and their betrayal of the Jews.

Late in the evening of 15 March 1939, the Zionist delegation gathered in Ben-Gurion's hotel room to discuss what was to be done about the British proposals. On 17 March, Weizmann dispatched a brief letter to MacDonald: "The Jewish delegation, having given profound consideration to the proposals placed before it by His Majesty's Government on 15 March 1939, regrets that it is unable to accept them as a basis for agreement, and has therefore decided to disband." Thus terminated the St James's Conference. At first Ben-Gurion fell into a deep depression. Yet a few days later, he pulled himself together. In the midst of crisis he again felt a surging faith in the strength and future of the Jewish people. In a letter to the Executive members in Jerusalem, he analysed the situation without any attempts at adornment: "We emerged from the London conference beaten but not defeated . . . This time, we brought up a new contention, which did its work: our strength in Palestine. The English had never heard that argument before, and, before the talks in London, I imagine they did not take it into account. This appears to me to have been the principal – if not the sole – innovation in our talks with the English. The government has discovered that there is Jewish power in Palestine."

The following day, he disclosed his views on the objective of the Zionist struggle: "The sole objective to be aimed for and fought for is independence for the Jews of Palestine, in other words, a Jewish state . . . After the English have announced definitely [that there will be] no mandate, there is no way other than a Jewish state."

On 17 May 1939, the British government published its repressive decrees in a White Paper. In fact, Ben-Gurion had already initiated the period of "militant Zionism" many weeks before the White Paper was published. From the moment he returned to Palestine, he focused most of his activity on preparing the Haganah for the fight against the new British policy. He summoned the heads of the Haganah, and went into the most minute details concerning its manpower and weapons complements.

To his colleagues in the Zionist Executive, Ben-Gurion presented a detailed plan for civil disobedience and the preparations for a struggle against the White Paper. To his colleagues in Mapai, he proposed a campaign of terror (which they characteristically opposed). Within the Jewish community, there was growing confusion and calls for energetic action. Ben-Gurion's office was deluged with delegations from all over the country and all classes calling for resolute leadership and vigorous action against the British. Some brought detailed operational plans, and others even went so far as to urge the establishment of a dictatorship.

Early in June, Ben-Gurion gained the Jewish Agency Executive's approval to establish Special Actions Squads, a secret "underground within an underground" whose main function was to serve as an arm for anti-British operations. In addition, it also carried out reprisal actions against Arab terrorists and punitive actions against informers within the Jewish community. He also took action on the subject of illegal immigration. Ben-Gurion had previously been adamantly opposed to an organized effort to smuggle Jews into Palestine, fearing that it would harm official immigration (the mandatory authorities deducted the number of illegal immigrants known to them from the official quota of entry certificates). Now, however, with Britain denying Jewish immigration rights, he made illegal immigration into a symbol of the Zionist campaign. He also considered it to be a political weapon of the first order. He proposed a plan whereby a thousand immigrants would come every week, and that in every instance of immigrants being deported, demonstrations, protests and disorders would follow – events that had "news value" for the world press. He also initiated a scheme whereby boats filled with immigrants would be brought right up to the coast of Palestine by force, and the disembarking immigrants would be covered by armed Haganah men. He was not intimidated by the danger of armed clashes with the British. On the contrary, he believed that in this way the Jewish people would demonstrate its right to immigration and its readiness to fight for that right. Furthermore, the armed confrontation with the British would arouse tremendous reverberations throughout the world. While still in London at the end of the St James's Conference, Ben-Gurion asked a senior British politician: "What will happen if we use force to bring in immigrants? Will we be fired upon?" The Englishman replied: "A government that fires on Jewish refugees immigrating into Palestine would not survive one week."

Yet this time, Ben-Gurion had gone too far. Many of his colleagues had yet to adjust to the sharp change in Ben-Gurion's policy toward Britain.

After all, for twenty years they had supported cooperation with the British, and they were also reluctant to launch armed actions that were liable to lead to heavy loss of life. The disagreement in the Jewish Agency broke out with the approach of the *Colorado*, with 380 illegal immigrants on board. Ben-Gurion demanded that the ship be ordered into Tel Aviv, where the immigrants would be brought ashore with the help of the Haganah. The Jewish Agency Executive hesitated and objected to the plan. But Ben-Gurion did not give in. He raised the issue before the Mapai Political Committee, though there, too, a majority voted against him. Enraged, he promptly announced that if his proposal was not accepted, he would resign. In the meanwhile, the British intercepted the ship outside Palestinian territorial waters and brought it into Haifa. Ben-Gurion then suggested a forcible takeover of the port, to enable the immigrants to disembark. When this proposal was likewise rejected by the Zionist Executive, as well as by his party colleagues, he did not persist. The idea of executing illegal immigration by armed force was shelved.

At the end of August 1939, the Twenty-First Zionist Congress convened in Geneva in the shadow of the White Paper and of the rapidly deteriorating international crisis. While the Congress was voting on its resolutions, it received news of the Molotov–Ribbentrop pact between the Soviet Union and Nazi Germany. In a prophetic speech about the "darkness" descending upon the world, Weizmann took his leave of the Congress delegates. He did not know that he was seeing most of them for the last time.

As Ben-Gurion was on his way back to Palestine by ship, the news reached him that Germany had invaded Poland. It was 1 September 1939. The Second World War had broken out. Shortly after his return to Palestine, he summoned Yitzhak Sadeh, one of the senior commanders of the Haganah, and informed him of the disbandment of the Special Action Squads. The era of "militant Zionism" had, indeed, begun. But before it fought for its own state, the Jewish people had to fight for its existence. It was Ben-Gurion who coined the slogan that was to guide his people through six years of bitter suffering: "We must help the British in their war [against Hitler] as though there were no White Paper, and we must resist the White Paper as though there were no war!"

7

The War Years

On 3 September 1939, two days after Hitler's columns invaded Poland, Ben-Gurion's ship anchored in Jaffa harbor. When he summoned the Haganah commanders five days later, he was already prepared to outline his "war aims": "The world war of 1914–18 brought us the Balfour Declaration," he declared. "This time, we have to bring about a Jewish state." This led him to his second aim: "The establishment of a Jewish army, first and foremost in this country and for this country."

Ben-Gurion gradually realized that the contingencies of war would not lead to a shelving of the White Paper and a rapprochement between England and the Zionist movement, as he had hoped. The British were arresting Jews who possessed arms and imposing severe punishments on them. But Britain's hard hand was evident not only in matters of arms and self-defense. In the atmosphere of the "Phoney War" that prevailed in the winter of 1939–40, England went back to "business as usual". And that business included implementation of the sections of the White Paper directed against the apple of the Zionist movement's eye: settlement of the Land of Israel.

On 28 February, Britain published the drastic Land Regulations, which were a sentence of strangulation for Jewish settlement. They divided the country into three zones. In Zone A, which comprised 65 per cent of the country, land transactions were permitted between Arabs alone; in Zone B (30 per cent of the country), land purchases by Jews were prohibited, except in special cases. The "free zone" for Jewish land purchases was restricted to the Sharon Valley and the northern coastal plain and urban properties. Thirty-two years after the Balfour Declaration, the Jews' right to purchase land was restricted to a "Pale of Settlement" comprising 5 per cent of the land in western Palestine!

The Jewish community was up in arms, and once again Ben-Gurion emerged as the leader of "militant Zionism". The day after the publication of the Land Regulations, he handed in his resignation as a member of the Jewish Agency Executive. In doing so he intended to renounce his official responsibilities in order to devote himself to the armed struggle against the mandatory government. He also gained the Zionist Executive's consent to conduct a protest campaign in the form of militant demonstrations against the mandatory government. The campaign opened on 29 February with a general strike and mass demonstrations in the towns and settlements. Day after day, the violent demonstrations went on and the police used force to disperse them, injuring and arresting dozens of Haganah members. The campaign reached its peak on 5 March, when the Haganah command instigated a particularly aggressive demonstration against the British police. Haganah units prepared obstacles to block escape routes, collected nails and glass splinters to puncture the tires of the police vehicles, poles to smash street lamps, and clubs and knuckle-dusters for large-scale clashes. Select groups were issued with arms, in case the police should open fire. In addition, a special unit was to break into the police stations in the course of the night and burn the garages and vehicles.

The moderate elements in the Jewish community – particularly the middle class – were overcome with anxiety over the possible repercussions. The Tel Aviv command of the Haganah dispatched two emissaries to beg Ben-Gurion to halt the demonstrations, which were bringing "disaster" to the city. He received the emissaries standing up, and according to the testimony of an eye-witness,

> He stormed at them like a flood of lava, upbraiding them for their timidity and their misguided comprehension of the political situation. He boiled [with anger] and concluded [by declaring] that the Zionist Executive . . . alone was responsible for implementing political policy, and it was up to [the Haganah] to obey or resign . . . Discredited, the two [emissaries] left Ben-Gurion's room . . . [but] Ben-Gurion continued to storm.

At the same time, several prominent Tel Aviv citizens approached the Zionist authorities in Jerusalem and exerted heavy pressure for the demonstrations to be called off, lest they cause "hundreds of deaths and thousands of injuries". Under the pressure, the demonstrations were indeed suspended.

The policy of violent struggle led to a sharp polarization within the leadership of the Jewish community. Many feared the ramifications of a confrontation with England, but there were also some who honestly believed that "attacking England helps Hitler". Ben-Gurion found himself isolated within the Jewish Agency Executive. When it became clear that a majority in the Zionist executive bodies did not support the policy he had proposed, he decided to resign.

The Jewish Agency Executive rejected his resignation by a large majority, and Berl Katznelson urged him strongly to withdraw it. But Ben-Gurion did not give his colleagues a clear-cut answer and unexpectedly he decided to go to England and America. On 1 May, a seaplane brought him to England, and he was only to return to Palestine ten months later.

The day after his arrival in London, Ben-Gurion attended a meeting at the Zionist offices. Once again, he advanced his activist proposals; once again they were rejected. Yet world events intervened to settle the clash within the Zionist movement by causing Ben-Gurion to revise his stand. Hitler's armies, which had invaded Denmark and Norway a few weeks earlier, now attacked the Lowland countries. On 13 May, Germany began its Blitzkrieg into France, which collapsed like a house of cards. London suddenly became a front line. Italy joined the war, and the Middle East was also set ablaze. "War against Hitler as though there were no White Paper" now became the task of the first order. Ben-Gurion himself conceded that international events now placed "militant Zionism" at the bottom of the scale.

With the spread of the conflagration, the British government fell, and on 10 May King George VI summoned Winston Churchill to form a Cabinet. The establishment of the new government and the dramatic deterioration of the military situation finally persuaded Ben-Gurion to shelve his resignation. Churchill was noted for his profound sympathies for the Zionist ideal and his vigorous opposition to the 1939 White Paper. Within the government and the smaller War Cabinet, there were several other outspoken friends of the Zionist movement. Yet Ben-Gurion did not harbor very high hopes that England would improve its attitude toward Zionism. Nor did he believe that the White Paper would be abrogated. He understood that with the war at its height, Britain would attempt to maintain the unity of its empire and would not risk alienating tens of millions of Arabs and Moslems by annulling the White Paper.

The summer of 1940, which Ben-Gurion spent in London, was to remain etched deep in his memory. He witnessed the wonderful bearing of the British under the crushing aerial blows of the blitz, and his emotional involvement in the battle was tremendous. In later years, when Ben-Gurion led the nascent State of Israel during the War of Independence, he would repeatedly refer to the heroism of the British people during the blitz and draw encouragement from the example. "In Tel Aviv, in May 1948, while weighing up the risks and chances of a declaration of independence, I recalled the men and women of London during the blitz. And I told myself: 'I have seen what a people is capable of achieving in the hour of supreme trial. I have seen their spirit touched by nobility. ... This is what the Jewish people can do.' We did it."

It was also during his stay in London that Ben-Gurion first expressed his life-long admiration for Winston Churchill. "He was unique," Ben-Gurion wrote, adding:

What he did in 1940 was a rare feat in history; he lifted an entire nation out of the depths of humiliation and defeat, instilled in them the spiritual strength to hold fast against heavy cdds, and eventually roused them to efforts which ensured victory. He was able to do so by his unique combination of qualities – magnetic leadership, powerful eloquence, contagious courage . . . a deep sense of history and an unshakeable faith in the destiny of his people . . . I think . . . that if not for Churchill, England would have gone down . . . History would have been quite different if there had been no Churchill.

Ben-Gurion spent five months in embattled London and devoted most of his energies to the campaign for the establishment of a Jewish army. Early in September, Weizmann met Churchill and the then minister of war, Anthony Eden, and received specific assurances about the establishment of a Jewish military unit in Palestine. With that much accomplished, on 21 September Ben-Gurion left for America. He reached New York early in October 1940 only to find that the American Jewish leaders, headed by Supreme Court Justice Brandeis, were reluctant to adopt any position against the White Paper because of their sympathy with the British over their fateful struggle against Hitler. During his three-and-a-half-month stay in the United States, Ben-Gurion did not succeed in undermining this attitude, despite the supportive views of two Zionist leaders – Dr Nahum Goldmann and the vigorously militant Rabbi Abba Hillel Silver. In mid-January 1941, when Ben-Gurion left New York on his way back to Palestine, he revealed a little of his disappointment in a letter to Mrs Tamar de-Sola-Poole, the President of the Hadassah:

I shall not deny the distressing feeling which American Jewry has awakened in me. Even in Zionist circles, I did not find an adequate awareness of the seriousness of this desperate and tragic hour in the history of Israel. Does the fate of millions of their kin in Europe concern Jewry in America less than the fate of England affects the people of America? Is Palestine less dear to the five million Jews in the United States than Britain is to the 130 million people in America? . . . I fear that American Zionists have not yet fully grasped the tremendous and weighty responsibility which history has imposed upon them in the present fateful hour.

On that low note, Ben-Gurion began his journey to Palestine during the war-torn winter of 1941. The month-long trip turned into an exciting adventure, during which the fifty-five-year-old Zionist leader traveled over most of the globe. Because of the danger of submarines in the Atlantic, he traveled by a Clipper from east to west: San Francisco, Honolulu, New Zealand, Australia, Indonesia, Singapore, Siam, Calcutta, Karachi, Basra and the Sea of Galilee. On 13 February 1941, when the heavy plane touched down on the Sea of Galilee, Ben-Gurion appeared before his colleagues (who had not seen him for ten months) with a bold new political program. The program had essentially been formulated by him in May 1940, but it was summed up in brief in a letter he wrote before leaving America:

It is essential [to make] the maximum effort during the war and immediately after it [to find] a full and fundamental solution to the Jewish problem by trans- ferring millions of Jews to Palestine and establishing it as a Jewish Common- wealth, an equal member of the family of nations that will be established after the war.

Ben-Gurion's new idea was the fruit of many months of thought. He grasped the fact that the war created a revolutionary situation which would destroy one world order and establish another in its place, as had occurred after the First World War. From the viewpoint of the Jewish people, this reconstruction of the world had to lead to the establishment of a Jewish state. Thus Ben-Gurion supported the creation of a military force that would take an active part in the fighting and, at the end of the world war, would be capable, if necessary, of conquering Palestine. He also came to the conclusion that by the time the war was over, Britain would not be the same mighty power it had been before. Thus the Jewish people had to seek a new protectress. He believed, the focal point of power and leadership in the free world would soon shift from London to Washington, and America would emerge as the leading power in the postwar world. It was therefore vital to launch an extensive propaganda campaign in the nerve centers of the American administration. In addition, as European Jewry – Zionism's traditional reservoir and the stronghold of the pioneering youth movement – had been cut off and silenced by the Nazi occupation, the American Jewish community, which now appeared as the principal center of world Jewry, had to be activated in support of Zionism's goals.

With these two aims in mind, on 22 June 1941, Ben-Gurion again set out for America, flying first to London to make the acquaintance of the new colonial secretary, Lord Moyne. The meeting with Moyne was a bitter disappointment. Palestine could not provide a solution for the Jewish problem, he claimed, because it is a small country. "How many Jews can you settle in Palestine?"

"That depends on the kind of regime," replied Ben-Gurion. "If there arises a regime which desires Jewish settlement and immigration, it is possible to settle millions."

"Millions?" Moyne wondered. "How many millions?"

"It is possible, within a short time, to settle three million Jews."

"After the war, it won't be possible to wait many years," Moyne remarked. "Millions of Jews are being uprooted and ruined, and it will be essential to find a solution quickly, and on a large scale." Moyne's solution: "To establish a Jewish state in Western Europe. The Hitler regime must be destroyed, we shall drive the Germans out of East Prussia, settle the Jews, and establish a Jewish state there."

Ben-Gurion was astounded. "I believe in your victory," he said, "and you can do with the Germans whatever you wish. You can drive the Germans out of East Prussia with machine-guns – but even with machine-guns, you will not be able to bring masses of Jews to East Prussia. The Land of the Jews is Palestine."

A further disappointment was in store for the Zionist leaders regarding the Jewish division within the British army. Churchill's promise to Weizmann to establish such a division had been pending for the past year, and Anthony Eden, had even agreed that it should serve in the Middle East. In December 1940, a divisional commander was appointed and practical preparations were instituted. However, the plan aroused considerable opposition in the Colonial Office and among the British political and military establishment in the Middle East, who warned of extreme Arab reactions. When Lord Moyne and General Wavell joined the opponents, Churchill was forced to retreat. The plan was shelved, but Weizmann was told nothing. For several months, the British government misled the Zionist leaders with the pretext that formation of the division had been held up due to a shortage of equipment. Only on 15 October, after Weizmann increased his pressure on Lord Moyne, did the British government notify him officially that the plan had been abandoned. The following day, Ben-Gurion left London under a cloud of disappointment, and on 21 November he reached America.

If we were tempted to mark a precise date for the inauguration of the Ben-Gurion era in Zionism, it would be that autumn evening in 1941 when Ben-Gurion disembarked at New York harbor. The assault he now launched upon American Jewry bore a striking resemblance to his onslaught in East Europe in the 1933 election campaign. He arrived in America after his political program had gained the hesitant approval of his colleagues in Palestine; he had overcome the indifference of his colleagues in London, whose attention was focused on the political arena in England; and he had liberated himself from Weizmann's dominant image and his moderating patronage. It was all clear to him now: he had come to mobilize the world's greatest power – and, above all, the Jewish masses living there –

for a crusade whose central objective was the establishment of a Jewish state.

In New York, Ben-Gurion met with a joint committee of Zionists and non-Zionists to which he presented the first draft of his plan. The central point in the section dealing with "peacetime", was that on "Constituting Palestine as a Jewish Commonwealth, for the sake of the settlement in Palestine of all the Jews who will desire or need to emigrate after the war". One by one, he succeeded in mobilizing the support of the larger Zionist organizations. In defiance of the views of anxious Zionist leaders, Ben-Gurion began to canvass government officials. For some time he settled in Washington, where, with the assistance of Supreme Court Justice Felix Frankfurter, he attempted to organize a propaganda campaign among government circles.

With the arrival of spring, the picture was encouraging. Ben-Gurion's political program enjoyed the support of most of the Zionist organizations in America. Its adoption was facilitated by an article published by Weizmann in the January issue of *Foreign Affairs*, calling for the establishment of a Jewish Commonwealth in Palestine after the war. Weizmann himself reached New York in the middle of April. At that time, the American Zionist leaders, headed by Nahum Goldmann and Meyer Weisgal, were already organizing the first national conference of American Zionists. Ben-Gurion saw that conference as the long hoped-for platform from which he could present his political program.

Thus the Biltmore Hotel went down in Jewish history. Between 9 and 11 May 1942, 603 conference delegates convened in the old hotel at the corner of Madison Avenue and 43rd Street in New York. The importance of the resolution adopted by the conference outstripped that of the decisions adopted by any of the Zionist Congresses since Herzl founded the Zionist movement in Basel. Its three principal sections set down the Zionist demands after victory was attained:

(1) The gateway to Palestine shall be opened to Jewish immigration. (2) The Jewish Agency shall be authorized to manage immigration into Palestine and redeem its wilderness, including the development of unpopulated and uncultivated areas. (3) Palestine shall be constituted as a Jewish Commonwealth, as part of the structure of the new democratic world.

The Biltmore Conference broke the most sanctified taboo of political Zionism. For the first time, after decades of evasiveness, Zionism proclaimed its "final objective", a Jewish state in Palestine.

It is doubtful whether most of the conference delegates understood that with a few short sentences they had abandoned the traditional Zionist policy of moderation and replaced it with a militant, activist approach that implied an almost certain conflict with Britain. Nor did they comprehend that the resolution meant turning their backs on the policies of Dr Weizmann and adopting the perilous path proposed by Ben-Gurion. It is difficult to believe that the resolution would have been passed with such ease if the delegates – who supported it unanimously – had grasped its true meaning.

The adoption of the Biltmore Program also marked the beginning of the changeover in the Zionist leadership. Weizmann and Ben-Gurion saw the Biltmore Program in totally different ways. "I would like to say a word about the Biltmore Declaration, of which such a fuss had been made by Ben-Gurion," Weizmann wrote ironically a few months after the conference.

It has become . . . a new Decalogue, or certainly a new Basel programme . . . it is nothing of the kind. The Biltmore Declaration is just a resolution, like the hundred and one resolutions usually passed at great meetings in this country or any other country. It embodied, in somewhat solemn terms, the chief points as laid down in my article in *Foreign Affairs*. But, B.-G., after his stay here of eight or nine months, had absolutely nothing to show by way of achievement and so he stuck on the Biltmore resolution, more or less conveying the idea that it is the triumph of his policy, as against my moderate formulation of the same aims, and he injected into it all his own extreme views.

In contrast, Ben-Gurion wrote: "I had no doubt that this program would replace the one adopted in Basel forty-five years before, and would, after the war, become the objective of the Jewish people."

Their diverging attitude toward the Biltmore Program was symptomatic of the two men's long-smouldering disagreement on principles. The source of tension between them lay in Weizmann's failure to comprehend two crucial events that occurred in 1939 and his consequent resistance to altering his previous policy. The first event was Britain's withdrawal of support for Zionism. The second was the outbreak of the world war. In light of these two major developments, Ben-Gurion adopted far-reaching conclusions and a new policy. Yet even after the St James's Conference and the White Paper, the Land Regulations and the shelving of the plan for a Jewish army, Weizmann remained faithful to his policy of negotiations with Britain, and behind-the-scenes diplomacy. He was vigorously opposed to extreme measures, and Ben-Gurion's inclination to violent resistance aroused his fear and indignation. On various occasions, Weizmann proclaimed his support for the Biltmore Program, but he then hastened to prove that his view was entirely different. In April 1947, eight months before the U.N. voted to partition Palestine into a Jewish state and an

Arab state, he still wrote: "The Biltmore Program proclaimed with much trumpeting, was soon revealed to be a mirage . . ." Militant Zionism could not have had a greater foe than Weizmann.

Yet the ideological deep differences between Weizmann and Ben-Gurion are only part of the picture. The relationship between the two men cannot be fully comprehended without considering the sharp personal conflict that flared up between them a month after the Biltmore Conference. On 10 June 1942 Ben-Gurion notified Weizmann by phone "that he is no longer linked with him for any practical purpose". The following day, Ben-Gurion sent Weizmann a letter explaining his reasons for severing their relations.

Since you came here you acted entirely on your own, consulting and cooperating from time to time with people of your personal choice as one does in his private affairs. Frankly, I do not think that this is in the best interests of our movement . . . I wish I were convinced that you could conduct our political affairs and guide the movement alone. I am sorry to say that I am not; and that it seems to me some of the things you have said and done so far are not very helpful to our cause. . . . You know well, I hope, my high personal regard and deep friendship for you. You know, too, perhaps, that I don't care very much for formalities. But unless the executive and the emergency committee with your whole-hearted support can assure the necessary common and united action, I really don't see how our work can properly be done, or what use I can be here or how I can share in the responsibility.

In response, Weizmann called Ben-Gurion's letter an "astounding document", and vigorously rejected the allegations that he had failed to consult his colleagues: "If you, for reasons I am unable to comprehend, choose to absent yourself from some or most of these consultations, the fault is surely not mine . . . Contrary to your opinion, I am charged with the responsibility for conducting Zionist political affairs. I say it because it is a fact." Then Weizmann flung back a charge at Ben-Gurion: "Nor is it irrelevant . . . to inquire whether this inexplicable document, so completely at variance with all the facts, is not aimed by indirection to cover up the failure of a mission which was, I believe, rather nebulous in its nature and without set purpose." At the end of the letter, he "totally" rejected Ben-Gurion's conclusion and informed him that he was regarding "the whole incident as merely the result of a temporary mood, dictated not by calm judgement but rather by an imaginary grievance caused undoubtedly by the many heartbreaking disappointments which all of us must face at this crucial hour".

Ben-Gurion replied the following day: "You are not empowered to conduct Zionist policy *alone*, and it is also my considered opinion that it is

not to the benefit of Zionism and Palestine that you conduct affairs alone."
In response, Weizmann broke off relations with Ben-Gurion in a curt
letter, concluding with the words: "Today I am leaving for a trip in the
Middle West, and I do not think that any useful purpose will be served by
continuing the correspondence further."

In this fashion, the latent war between Ben-Gurion and Weizmann
flared up again with greater vehemence than ever before. Ben-Gurion felt
that the time had come to take decisive action, lest Weizmann gain the
upper hand. On 19 June 1942, after the breakdown of his correspondence
with Weizmann, he wrote Dr Stephan Wise, chairman of the American
Emergency Committee, repeating his charges against Weizmann and threatening that "unless this dangerous situation is rectified immediately, I will
be left with no choice other than to ask the Zionist Executive and the
Palestine Zionist Executive to demand Dr Weizmann's resignation".
Before undertaking such a drastic step, however, Ben-Gurion asked Wise
to convene an informal meeting with Weizmann and the American Zionist
leaders.

The meeting, which took place eight days later, was attended by nine
persons, including Dr Wise, Meyer Weisgal, Nahum Goldmann, Weizmann and Ben-Gurion. Ben-Gurion spoke first, reiterating his principal
contention about not being consulted and unabashedly revealing, in
Weizmann's presence, the true reason for his concern:

It is my view that while Dr Weizmann can render invaluable service in con-
certed action, he can do incalculable harm when he acts alone. He does not always
grasp realities when he is confronted with a new situation and may give an unexpected answer without realizing what it means. He wants always to seem reasonable and not only to be reasonable to an Englishman. ... When he hears
conversations, he hears more what he would like to hear than what he does hear.
On many occasions his reports are unduly optimistic. He identifies personal
position and personal courtesy with political courtesies.

For this reason I believe it is not in the interest of the movement that Dr
Weizmann should act alone. That is why this Executive acted on the principle
that when it was necessary for Dr Weizmann to act politically, somebody else
should be there. This system worked more or less until the war.

Ben-Gurion mentioned a number of incidents in which he considered
Weizmann to have failed, bringing examples from meetings about which he
had not consulted Ben-Gurion.

You can do the best work and fail ... I consider myself a devoted personal
friend of Dr Weizmann's, whatever he may think. I know it is disagreeable, but I
feel I prevented him from making certain mistakes ... If no way can be found

David Gruen (seated in center of first row) taking leave of his friends in Plonsk on the eve of his departure for Palestine. Rachel Nelkin is seated on his right

A barefoot David Gruen (center) with other young pioneers by a wine cellar in Rishon le-Zion

David Ben-Gurion expresses
his identification with
"Ottomanization" by wearing
the customary Turkish
tarboush

Paula and David Ben-Gurion
soon after their marriage

David Ben-Gurion in the uniform of the Jewish Legion

Ben-Gurion (center) with the Executive of the Histadrut. Berl Katznelson is seated beside him

OPPOSITE ABOVE Vladimir Jabotinsky, Ben-Gurion's friend and rival

OPPOSITE LEFT David Ben-Gurion seated between Dr Chaim Weizmann and Moshe Sharett (first row, far left), two men against whom he was to conduct bitter struggles in his political career

ABOVE Ben-Gurion reading out the Proclamation of Independence of the State of Israel on 14 May 1948

The ship *Altalena* burning off the coast of Tel Aviv

Prime Minister Ben-Gurion on a visit to the Israel Defense Forces during the newly constituted army's first major maneuvers

Defense Minister Ben-Gurion in full army uniform on a trip to Eilat

Ben-Gurion and Ambassador Abba Eban present President Truman with a candelabrum (the official symbol of the State of Israel) during Ben-Gurion's 1951 visit to the United States

The Prime Minister at work

out of the situation, I will have to say to the Executive that if Weizmann can do the work only in the way he is doing it, it is better that he should resign.

Weizmann replied with considerable heat. He conceded that Ben-Gurion's words had been stated "in the greatest sincerity and no personal pique", but accused him of "misinterpretation, misunderstanding, and, in a great many cases, misstatements". He vigorously rejected the allegation that he had acted on his own. "Whether one has always to run in couples is something [whose] wisdom must be decided; whether I need a *kashrut* supervisor I must leave to you or to the Congress or to whoever to decide."

One after another, Weizmann rejected Ben-Gurion's complaints and finally revealed how personally insulted he was by the confrontation:

. . . The whole construction of these charges, I am genuinely sorry to have to say, is painfully reminiscent of purges . . . I do not say I have not made mistakes – mistakes which would justify my being hanged from every lamp post of this city – but here are a whole host of imaginary charges culminating in an act of political assassination . . . I shall act as I did. I shall not swerve, because I think that is the right way. I shall be collegial. If in most cases I choose to see people alone, or sometimes go with another, that must be left to my discretion. But quite frankly I see here a desperate attempt to produce charges based on hot air in order to justify – quite honorably, for Brutus was an honorable man – an act of political assassination. The future corpse is not worried.

I did not know that another member of the Executive was always sent to England to watch that I should not make mistakes. Ben-Gurion . . . is worried. That is his usual state. I reported [on a meeting held in London]. Either the report is accepted or I am a liar, or I am incapable of giving an accurate statement. . . . I am invited to Secretary [of the Treasury Henry] Morgenthau's for lunch next week. Must I take [Louis] Lipsky or B.-G. along? That is what is at issue. I reject the offensive statements that I am a *Fuehrer*. I am not. I am a poor sinner.

The participants left the meeting stunned. According to Meyer Weisgal, Chaim Greenberg, leader of the Zionist labor faction in America, left with tears streaming down his cheeks, saying: "I never believed I'd live to see the day when a leader of the Palestinian labor movement said such terrible things." Indeed, Ben-Gurion's words were harsh. But Weizmann's reply was no less offensive. Even his faithful admirer, Dr Stephen Wise, was forced to request that the term "political assassination" be struck from the minutes. He dispatched a letter to Weizmann asking that he write to Ben-Gurion immediately and withdraw the term "untruths" and "delusions", which he had flung at him. Weizmann did not do so.

Although Weizmann's harsh reply to and insinuations about Ben-Gurion

caused some indignation, there is no doubt that the chairman of the
Agency Executive suffered a severe setback. Most of those participating in
the meeting accepted Weizmann's views and rejected Ben-Gurion's
allegations. After the meeting, Ben-Gurion remained silent, while Weizmann and his supporters showered him with abuse. "Ben-Gurion's
presence here has been an irritatant and a source of disruption almost from
the day of his arrival eight months ago," Weizmann wrote. "He is in a
constant state of jitters, nervous tension; which reduces every meeting –
either in the Emergency Committee or elsewhere, to the gyrations of an
insane asylum." "B.-G. has just gone off," Weizmann wrote to another
confidant. "The best solution of the problem would be to send him back to
Jerusalem. That is involved with great difficulties. I am trying to do my
best to get him transportation."

The difficulties were caused by the wartime shortage of planes, but
in the middle of September Weizmann finally succeeded in getting rid of
the troublesome Ben-Gurion. Frustrated and defeated, Ben-Gurion
returned to Palestine. He related the Weizmann episode to no more than a
few of his colleagues on the Jewish Agency Executive, which decided to
summon Weizmann to Palestine "as soon as possible for consultations and
clarification of current problems". But Weizmann, not wanting to confront
Ben-Gurion on his own home territory, turned down the invitation on the
grounds that the state of his health did not permit him to undertake such a
journey. Instead, Weizmann drafted a long letter to the Executive, reiterating his sharp criticism of Ben-Gurion.

I have watched Mr Ben-Gurion carefully during his stay here. His conduct and
deportment were painfully reminiscent of the petty dictator, a type one meets so
often in public life now. They are all shaped on a definite pattern: they are
humorless, thin-lipped, morally stunted, fanatical and stubborn, apparently
frustrated in some ambition, and nothing is more dangerous than a small man
nursing his grievances introspectively.

A short time later, Weizmann returned to London. That ended the first
round – an ugly and dismal round – in the struggle between the two giants
of the Zionist cause – for the leadership of the movement and for the power
to determine its policy. In America, it was Weizmann who won the round;
in Palestine, Ben-Gurion won a more important victory.

Ben-Gurion reached Palestine on 2 October 1942. He had been away for
fourteen months, and in his absence the Middle East had experienced
stormy ups and downs. When the Afrika Korps, Rommel's fearsome
armored desert army, thrust its way into Egypt early in June 1942, the
Jewish Agency in Palestine was terrified of an invasion by Hitler's armies,

while the Arabs in the Middle East, praying for a British downfall, rejoiced and cheered. Even then Britain maintained its refusal to set up a Jewish army. However, at the end of 1941, the mandatory authorities granted a kind of informal recognition to the Haganah's "storm companies" (the Palmach) and trained their men for special tasks. Rommel's offensive was halted at El Alamein, and two months after Ben-Gurion's return to Palestine, Montgomery launched a counterattack which defeated the Afrika Korps.

Calmly and dispassionately, the mandatory authorities continued to apply the White Paper decrees as though they had never heard of the world war. The gateway to the country remained bolted before the handful of refugees that succeeded in escaping from the Nazi terror and set sail in the Mediterranean in cockleshell boats. Several boats loaded down with human cargo failed to find a single port anywhere in the "free" world where Jews were permitted to set foot, and they were forced to turn round and head back to occupied Europe. Several boats went down at sea, and ships intercepted by the British were sent off to the remotest corners of the earth, where their passengers were imprisoned in detention camps.

In the autumn of 1942, the Jewish community in Palestine received the most terrible news of all: the German plan known as the "Final Solution" was being put into effect. Sixteen escapees from Poland told of ghettos and torture, humiliations and mass graves; of wholesale executions; and of places whose names had never before been heard – Auschwitz and Majdanek and Treblinka and Sobibor, where millions of Jews were being led to slaughter. The leaders of the Jewish community were filled with an intolerable feeling of horror and helplessness. Their despair was all the more extreme as the heads of the Great Powers ignored their appeals and the mandatory authorities pedantically fulfilled every provision of the White Paper while an entire people was being annihilated in Poland. The Jews of Palestine were torn in their attitude toward England. On the one hand, over 20,000 of them joined the British army to fight against Hitler; on the other, here was Britain providing daily proof that she was a sworn foe of Zionism. The feeling spread that sooner or later, it would be necessary to break away from Britain.

The atmosphere in Palestine was therefore especially tense when Ben-Gurion returned bearing the Biltmore Program. In his campaign on its behalf, he reached the pinnacle of his glory in presenting it as a response to the most powerful aspirations of the Jewish people. His plan for the mass immigration of two million Jews constituted a dramatic and essential solution for the refugees from the European Holocaust – and at the same time guaranteed a Jewish majority in Palestine. His call for political independence inspired the Jews of Palestine – and Europe – with hope, while at the same time holding out promise of a real solution for the Jewish problem. The Biltmore Program, as interpreted by Ben-Gurion, gradually became the new commandment of the Zionist movement. On 11 October, the Zionist Executive unanimously adopted it. On 10 November, the Inner Zionist Executive in Jerusalem voted overwhelmingly in favor of Ben-Gurion's maximalist interpretation of the program. Ben-Gurion had every right to feel proud of his triumph. He had become the incarnation of Zionism as he understood it. Weizmann was far away, and his path of moderation failed to express the spirit of rebellion against Britain that now spread among the Jews of Palestine. Ben-Gurion led his people into a stubborn resistance to every British government act undertaken in accordance with the White Paper regulations. Even those who were not his friends or admirers had to admit that the Jews of Palestine had found their leader and spokesman in Ben-Gurion. When Berl Locker, a Weizmann loyalist, reached London in 1943, he was forced to concede that "Ben-Gurion has gained in influence, he is the leader on the spot". But he was not yet the leader of the world movement.

From Washington, reports arrived of negotiations conducted by Weizmann and his men with the confidants of Ibn Saud; of Weizmann's entirely different interpretation of the Biltmore decisions; of meetings, acts, and statements out of keeping with the militant views of the Palestinian leaders. Ben-Gurion exploded in anger. He complained to the Mapai Political Committee that Weizmann was again behaving as though the business of the Executive were his own personal affair. He attacked Weizmann with extreme vehemence: "I do not know what to advise if Weizmann does not make political departure. Let him be a 'parade president', without touching political matters . . . or let him not be president . . . Weizmann's presence [causes] the greatest harm . . . Zionism is not a private matter." Hinting that he intended to resign, he added, "My days on the Executive are numbered."

A majority in the Political Committee backed Ben-Gurion and agreed that Weizmann had to be summoned to Palestine. This was the origin of the idea of holding a world Zionist convention in Palestine, and the Jewish Agency Executive extended its invitation to Weizmann. But the Zionist Organization president vigorously declined the invitation and no such world Zionist convention took place. In London, Weizmann told a confidant that Ben-Gurion has gone completely crazy in his aversion and distrust of him, adding that "he will never again sit with him on the same Executive again".

In October, the crisis erupted again. At the end of June 1943, Weizmann had returned to London and was informed by Leo Amery, a cabinet minister, that a governmental committee had been established to formulate a new Palestine policy and one of the feasible solutions was the partition of Palestine and the establishment of a Jewish state in areas other than Samaria. "Too little and too late," replied Weizmann. Ben-Gurion was again furious. Weizmann was in London conducting his policies and meeting British leaders while the Jewish Agency Executive in Jerusalem was shackled, receiving no more than occasional reports and quite unable to make its voice heard. A few days after Weizmann's meetings, Moshe Sharett and Berl Locker cabled him with an urgent request to come to Palestine. Weizmann again refused. He believed that London was again the center of Zionist activity, and also told his friends frankly that he "will not face Palestine empty-handed and will not sit at the same table with Ben-Gurion". On receipt of Weizmann's negative answer, Ben-Gurion rose at a meeting of the Zionist Executive in Jerusalem and announced his resignation.

His move caused a sensation, with the echoes reaching London. Weizmann continued to pretend ignorance of the reasons for Ben-Gurion's indignation. He invited a delegation to come from Palestine, adding "Let Ben-Gurion come. I shall not cooperate with him; I simply can't cooperate with him."

Over the course of two months, the Mapai Political Committee and its Central Committee held a long series of meetings at which Ben-Gurion's attacks on Weizmann reached their peak. For the first time, Ben-Gurion described the history of his unsettled relations with Weizmann and concluded, ". . . the best thing would be to remove him from political affairs, not from the Zionist [movement]". Even Moshe Sharett, who disagreed with Ben-Gurion's conclusions, had to admit that his description of Weizmann's errors was accurate. However, Ben-Gurion did not succeed in convincing his colleagues to accept the necessity of removing Weizmann from his powerful position. The weakness of his stance stemmed from its extremism. He obstinately refused to accept any compromise formula or any attempt to force Weizmann to collaborate with his colleagues. When Ben-Gurion maintained his opposition, Berl Katznelson's patience ran out. Once more, he undertook the task of curbing Ben-Gurion, and urged him to withdraw his resignation.

Ben-Gurion emerged strengthened, from the latest round in his struggle against Weizmann, for unlike the previous year, he was no longer isolated in his stand. Under pressure from his colleagues in London, Weizmann sent a cable to Ben-Gurion asking him to withdraw his resignation. Ben-Gurion did not succeed in undermining Weizmann's position, but this time there was a dramatic shift in the balance of power between the two men.

The conclusion of the latest outbreak in the conflict with Weizmann hardly gave Ben-Gurion any respite. Scarcely a week passed when he was faced by a bitter schism within his own party, Mapai. The breakaway group, Faction B, had officially been formed at the end of 1938 and was composed of a large section of the kibbutz movement, the cream of the labor party. Its political and military doctrine advocated an anti-British struggle and the creation of a Jewish self-defense force, which made the faction an ally of Ben-Gurion. Yet the point of strain arose over the question of partition, to which Faction B was vigorously opposed, advocating a vague plan for an international mandate over the whole of Palestine. It had rejected the Peel plan of 1937 and viewed the Biltmore Program as the thin end of the wedge that would eventually lead to partition. The final break came in March 1944 at a meeting of the Mapai General Council. Splitting off from Mapai after a tempestuous debate, Faction B adopted the old name of the party founded by Ben-Gurion, Berl Katznelson, and Yitzhak Tabenkin (the faction's present leader) – Ahdut ha-Avodah. Ben-Gurion had been abandoned by many of his allies – the vigorous activists, the kibbutz members, and the élite of the Haganah, the Palmach members, many of whom followed Tabenkin out of Mapai. Thus Ben-Gurion advanced from confrontation to confrontation: first Weizmann, then Tabenkin, and then, in the summer of 1944, the worst blow of all.

On the night of 15 August 1944, Ben-Gurion was awoken by David Hacohen, one of the prominent members of Mapai. As he stood in the doorway dressed in pajamas, looking sleepy and alarmed, he was ordered back to bed by Hacohen.

"Ben-Gurion, I have just been informed that Berl Katznelson has died," said Hacohen.

Ben-Gurion fell backwards. Then he sat up, staring ahead with a frozen glance. Suddenly, his face twisted into a terrible grimace, and he fell on the bed. David Hacohen was stunned.

He covered himself up with a sheet, wrapping it around his head, and uttered sighs and groans like a wounded beast . . . It was awful. I have never seen anyone so shaken. He rolled around, banging his head on the mattress. His mouth uttered incoherent words: "Berl, without Berl. How is it possible without Berl . . . Oh Berl, how will I live without you?"

At dawn Ben-Gurion reached Jerusalem and made for the flat where Katznelson's body lay. There were many people in the room when Ben-Gurion entered it. He stopped, looked into the faces of his friends, and fainted. When he came around, he asked to be left alone with Berl. As the others left the room, they heard Ben-Gurion's broken voice addressing the corpse. "How can you do this, Berl, how can you leave us?..." Then there was silence. For two hours he sat alone in the room with the dead man. When he emerged, he said to his son, Amos, "He was the only true friend I had."

Berl Katznelson's death was a cruel blow to David Ben-Gurion. He loved Berl with a rare devotion, and later he was to say that Berl was "the man who was closest to me in my life". Katznelson's passing also brought about the fundamental change in Ben-Gurion's status. Now that he was on his own, he became the principal, and almost the sole, leader of his party. In his future decisions, there would no longer be anyone at his side to curb his impulsive outbursts and his daring leaps.

Thus at the end of the war, Ben-Gurion was left more lonely than ever before, his shoulders stooping under the weight of his burden, while all around him the ranks of the great leaders were thinning out. Weizmann was ailing, a man of another generation, no longer capable of bringing Ben-Gurion under his control. Tabenkin had withdrawn into his fortress of sectarian fanaticism. Yitzhak Ben-Zvi and several other founding fathers of the labor movement were moving onto the sidelines. And now, Berl, Ben-Gurion's "compass", was gone. In this terrible solitude, without a close friend to understand him, Ben-Gurion rose to the task of leading the Palestinian Jewish community through fateful trials.

On top of all the other tribulations which Ben-Gurion experienced during the war years, he also had to cope with a severe family crisis. His relationship with Paula struck a reef, and she was on the verge of desperation. Ben-Gurion could scarcely be said to have lived a normal family life. During his stays in Palestine, he pursued his activities as a public personage with such intensity that he was not even aware of domestic problems, nor was he inclined to concern himself with them. On his trips, when he ordered dozens of books and asked that they be delivered to his home, it never even occurred to him that Paula would have to pay out ten of the seventeen pounds that constituted his monthly salary. Paula did everything in her power to free him of financial worries. She would cook and launder till late at night and often surreptitiously gave up a meal to leave enough for her husband and children. Later, medical experts were to discover that she suffered from chronic malnutrition. When Ge'ula got married, there was no money to sew her a wedding dress, or to buy her furniture. The Jewish Agency sent a money order, which Ben-Gurion – always a stickler on personal morals – angrily sent back.

In addition to her household cares, Paula was also responsible for the children's education. Ben-Gurion did not intervene; withdrawn into his study, he neither talked to his children nor played with them. They learned not to bother him. Only on one occasion was Amos summoned to his father's study, after an unsatisfactory school report. "When I am old," said Ben-Gurion sadly, "I shall be very angry with myself for not paying more attention to your studies. But Amos, I am busy! I cannot do it, even though I am sure that when I am old, it will grieve me."

Under the circumstances, it was only natural that Paula became bitter and nagging. But there was a deeper gap between her and her husband. Ben-Gurion was still full of a tremendous spirit of romance. (Renana, his younger daughter, remembers him as romantic and sensual.) But his wife failed to provide an outlet for his romantic yearnings, any more than she shared his political views. As a result, he felt isolated even in his own home. Paula would occasionally reveal her resentment to her husband. She accused him of not loving her enough and not giving her enough attention. One of these outbursts occurred a few days before a journey abroad. He replied in a soothing letter from Stockholm:

I love you more than you perhaps believe . . . The trouble is, darling, that you do not know me well, even though I know that you love me very much. But love alone is not sufficient. I want you to share the matters that engage my attention. I want you to display interest in my work and my battles. Then you will be happier, your life will be richer and more interesting.

Yet their relations did not improve. In 1937, responding to an embittered letter from her, he wrote to her frankly:

My life is very hard . . . I have never complained, and I am not complaining now . . . but I am very lonely, even though I have many friends and companions . . . and at times it's very, very hard for me. There are moments when . . . hard and bitter questions torture me, and I have no one to turn to. I stand alone, with a heavy burden upon me, at times an intolerable burden . . . Every sign of love and friendship from you are so precious to me . . . But there are times when, without wishing it, without knowing it, without evil intentions, you grieve me, and my sufferings increase, and my solitude grows worse.

Paula did not derive much enjoyment at Ben-Gurion's side. But her daily problems paled into insignificance compared with the crisis she faced during the war: she was convinced that there were other women in her husband's life.

At first sight, her suspicions may appear surprising. The notion of Ben-Gurion courting women hardly fits with his personal and public image. Yet in his youth, he was romantic and sensitive, and attracted to beautiful girls, so when he matured and occupied a leading position, it is far from necessary to assume that he was indifferent to feminine beauty. To this day, no woman has published a word about romantic attachments with Ben-Gurion. This may indicate the special attitude of the women who sought his company in attempting to safeguard his reputation. When Ben-Gurion was prime minister, his confidants and aides erected a screen of secrecy around his private life, and nothing was ever published about his relationships with women.

Some observers attempt to explain Ben-Gurion's love affairs as a corollary of his bitter disappointment in Paula, who did not fulfill his emotional needs. Whether or not that was so, Ben-Gurion believed that the love affairs of a public figure were no sin, nor do they harm a man's public image. Years later, he came to the defense of Moshe Dayan, when one of his love affairs became public knowledge. In responding to a letter from an irate husband who accused Dayan of seducing his wife, Ben-Gurion wrote:

I hope that you will not be angry with me, if I make a distinction between the intimate, personal aspect, and the public side . . . Not only in our times, but in previous generations and even in ancient times, a distinction was made – and such a distinction must be made – between the two planes . . . A man can be an ascete and a saint all his life and be unfitted to public tasks; and the opposite is also possible.

Citing King David and Admiral Nelson as two former personalities to prove his case, Ben-Gurion went on to conclude: ". . . It is impossible (in my opinion, impermissible) to examine the secret, intimate life of a person – man or woman – and thereby to determine their standing in society." When Ruth Dayan came to complain to him shortly afterwards, Ben-Gurion repeated his view: "You have to get used to it," he told Dayan's weeping wife. "Great men's private lives and public lives are often conducted on parallel planes that never meet . . ."

Ben-Gurion's words did not comfort Ruth Dayan, whose world had "collapsed". Paula Ben-Gurion seems to have felt the same way in the 1940s, when she concluded that her husband was unfaithful to her. Shocked and desperate, she hurried to close friends of Ben-Gurion in Jerusalem and poured out her heart, threatening to kill herself. With great effort, his friends succeeded in calming Paula. "We urged her to return to him and to take an interest in his activities and his work, and thus regain his love," a woman friend related, "and that's what happened. She forced herself to become involved in all his activities and his struggles: she attached herself closely to him, identifying completely with him, and thus conquered her place with him." Although Paula's suspicions did not evaporate, and on one occasion she upbraided her daughter for inviting home a friend "who was Father's mistress", after that crisis Ben-Gurion and Paula were reconciled, and their relations gradually restored.

Oddly enough, considering Paula's assessment of his powers, this was the period when people began to call Ben-Gurion "the Old Man". As far as he could remember, the custom began when he was in a restaurant with some friends. A little girl stood up at the neighboring table and asked aloud: "Who is that old man?" and the nickname stuck. Ben-Gurion was then in his late fifties, and his standing was high as the leader of the Palestinian Jews. His speeches, books, and pamphlets were sold, studied, and quoted in all earnestness and great enthusiasm. The heaven-sent gift of personal charisma began to appear about him like a halo. People were embarrassed in his presence and, either captivated by his charm or magnetized by his powerful personality, were afraid to argue with him.

Ben-Gurion did not indulge in small talk. He was never a party-goer, a back-slapper, or joke-swapper. He avoided gossip and polite pleasantries, and was excessively practical and to the point. A well-known writer once came to Berl Katznelson absolutely incensed. "I went to see Ben-Gurion," he muttered, "and he immediately asked: 'What do you want? What is the matter?' It is impossible simply to sit down and chat with him." The following day, Berl told the writer, "Ben-Gurion wishes to see you. Please go to his home this afternoon." The writer was surprised but did as he was told. On entering Ben-Gurion's study, he found him burrowing through the documents on his guest. The Old Man raised his head, said, "Sit down," and went back to his documents. Finally, he laid down his pen, bent forward, and stared curiously at his guest. "*Nu,*" he said. "Chat! Chat!" Seeing the expression of amazement on his guest's face, he explained innocently: "You said that it's impossible to chat with me, so let's try. Chat!"

Ben-Gurion was also by nature authoritarian and held strong views on the subject of leadership. He also believed that telling the truth was of great importance in political life. Later he was to define his views on what a leader must and must not do.

You must know what you want to achieve, be certain of your aims and have these goals constantly in mind. You must know when to fight your political opponents and when to mark time. You must never compromise on matters of principle . . . And since the world never stops for a moment, and the pattern of power changes its elements as like the movement of a kaleidoscope, you must constantly reassess chosen policies, toward the achievement of your aims.

Although this summary was written years later, it reflects the circumstances and need for flexibility during the war years. As the tide began to turn in favor of the Allies, directing the course of Zionist policy between the war against Hitler and the war on the White Paper became an increasingly sensitive process. On the one hand, the British government appeared to be making a gesture of conciliation toward the Jews of Palestine when Winston Churchill notified Dr Weizmann of the government's decision to establish a Jewish Brigade as part of the British army. The Brigade tasted no more than a few months of battle at the end of the Italian campaign. But the military training it received, the service in a regular military unit, its fighting spirit, and decisive role it played in organizing the Holocaust survivors and sending them off to Palestine as illegal immigrants, all made the Brigade into one of the most important factors in the impending struggle for the establishment of a Jewish state.

During the war, Churchill also resolved to implement the Balfour Declaration's promise by establishing a Jewish state in Palestine, and in 1943 he set up a ministerial committee that adopted a basic program for the partition of Palestine. But while Whitehall was considering partition, the mandatory government continued its faithful implementation of the White Paper. In view of the heavy hand the British were adopting in Palestine, who would have imagined that their prime minister was secretly preparing plans for a Jewish state? The pro-Revisionist circles decided to give vent to their frustration by launching a campaign of anti-British terror actions while the war was still in progress.

There was irony in this turnabout in Revisionist policy. At the outbreak of war, the Revisionists and their military arm, the Irgun Zvai Leumi (I.Z.L.), adopted Jabotinsky's line of cooperation with the British against Hitler. The I.Z.L. followed this policy so closely that they even boycotted the stormy demonstrations that Ben-Gurion organized against the Land Regulations! However, the extent of this cooperation angered some of the more fanatical elements of the I.Z.L., headed by Avraham Stern, who called for all-out war against Britain in the form of a large-scale terror campaign. These divergent views were irreconcilable, and after Jabotinsky's death the I.Z.L. split; Stern's faction emerged in time as the Lohamei Herut Israel (Lehi). The I.Z.L. entered a long period of confusion and doubts, torn by the conflicting urges to enlist in the British army or to go to war against the White Paper. Stern's organization was undecided on how to act against the British. Its extremist slogans did not call forth any public backing; and the bank robberies to finance its activities and attacks that resulted in the deaths of Jewish policemen made the Lehi the objects of general distaste. The organization suffered a severe blow when the British discovered Stern's hideout, forced their way in, and murdered him.

In 1944, however, the I.Z.L. ended its armistice with the British and went into action. Its renewed militancy was fanned by the arrival in Palestine of the former head of Betar in Poland, Menahem Begin, a bold and pugnacious man with unusual organizational and oratorical gifts. Taking over the leadership of the I.Z.L. Begin breathed new life into the weakened organization, leading its members to the bold and violent campaign against the British. I.Z.L. squads blew up British intelligence headquarters all over the country, attacked police stations, and assassinated British officers. Disguised as British soldiers or policemen, or as Arabs, they stole weapons from British camps and took hostages.

Many I.Z.L. members were killed or wounded in the raids, and a section of the Jewish community, especially its youth, were filled with admiration for the brave freedom fighters who risked their lives in the war against foreign rule. But the majority of the Jewish community was vigorously opposed to terrorism. The Jewish Agency leadership regarded violence as no more than a political weapon to be employed with certain political and moral restrictions. But the I.Z.L. overstepped these bounds. Its attacks on the British were accompanied by a sorry list of bank robberies and extortions to finance its operations, as well as the killing of "traitors" and "informers".

As the tension escalated in Palestine, there was increasing danger of confrontation between the "dissidents" – the I.Z.L. and Lehi – and the Haganah. In October 1944, Begin met Moshe Sneh, head of the Haganah's national headquarters and Ben-Gurion's confidant. According to Sneh's report, Begin reiterated that "after the death of Jatobinsky, we regard David Ben-Gurion as the only man who should lead the Zionist political struggle. We are prepared to place ourselves under his command. But [only] when Ben-Gurion stands at the head of a committee of national liberation, or at the head of a Jewish provisional government; when he begins the war against the [British] government." Begin spoke of struggle, while Sneh spoke of political ideas. He demanded that the I.Z.L. cease its acts of terror, even if only provisionally. But their conversation was a dialogue of the deaf, as was Begin's meeting with Eliyahu Golomb, the unofficial leader of the Haganah. Failing to persuade Begin to halt the terror, Golomb's sharp parting words made it quite plain that the Haganah would strike at the I.Z.L. with all the means at its disposal in order to put a stop to its terror campaign. According to Begin, Golomb said, "We'll go in and wipe you out!" At that time, a number of Haganah men were already preparing contingency plans against the I.Z.L. At the peak of this internal tension, came the assassination in Cairo.

In November 1944, Weizmann was about to come to Palestine after a five-year absence. Before leaving he met Churchill, who advised him to go to Cairo to meet Lord Moyne, the resident British minister in the Middle East. "He has changed and grown in the past two years," said Churchill. Whether or not Moyne had "changed and grown", Weizmann never found out. Two days later, Moyne was murdered by two members of the Lehi who were sent to Cairo especially for the assassination. Weizmann was horrified. In a letter to Churchill, he expressed his "deep moral indignation and horror" and declared that "political crimes of this kind are an especial abomination". Ben-Gurion did not send any letters of condolence, but he now resolved to strike out at the dissidents.

It is perhaps ironical that Ben-Gurion, the most militant of the labor leaders, should have headed the campaign against the dissidents. At the same time, his stand against them was characteristic. Ben-Gurion believed in a struggle that would focus around the implementation of fundamental Jewish rights, as laid down by the Balfour Declaration, with arms being used in self-defense against British attempts to deny those rights by force. But he looked upon anti-British terrorism in wartime as a stab in the back of an ally.

Thus began the operation that went under the unfortunate nam e of the "*saison*" (the hunting season). Amidst the heightened tension which followed the Moyne assassination, Ben-Gurion persuaded the Jewish Agency Executive to adopt a far-reaching resolution:

The Jewish community is called upon to spew forth all the members of this harmful, destructive gang, to deny them any shelter or haven, not to give in to their threats, and to extend to the authorities all the necessary assistance to prevent terror acts and to wipe out [the terror] organization, for this is a matter of life and death.

The resolution aroused widespread resentment, but Ben-Gurion did not retreat; he was resolved to cooperate with the British against the dissidents. "There are two choices facing us," he said in November 1944, "terrorism, or a Zionist political struggle; terrorist organizations or an organized Jewish community. If we want a Zionist political struggle . . . we must rise and take action against terrorism and terrorist organizations. It is necessary to act, not just to talk."

This statement marked the second phase of the "*saison*", in which I.Z.L. members all over the country were picked up, taken to lonely houses or kibbutzim, interrogated – and in some cases beaten and deprived of their financial resources. Lists of names were handed over to the British police for arrest, and in some cases Haganah members handed I.Z.L. men over directly to the British. The campaign might well have set off an internecine war, but the I.Z.L. decided to show restraint. "You shall not raise your hands, nor use weapons, against young Jews," Menahem Begin ordered the I.Z.L. leaders. "They are not to blame. They are our brothers. They are being deceived, misled . . . There shall not be a war of brothers." There was no war of brothers.

The "*saison*" went on for several months, up to March 1945. In the short run, the campaign achieved its aims: there were no further actions by the I.Z.L. until the end of the war (the Lehi halted its campaign after coming to an agreement with the Haganah, and its members were not harmed in the "*saison*"). However, the organizations were not smashed, and Menahem Begin managed to evade capture. For the present, Ben-Gurion had won his confrontation with the dissidents; but it was a dismal triumph. The internal struggle left open wounds and polarized opposing camps with a blinding hatred that would not quickly fade. The brief period of the "*saison*" left tensions that re-emerged to do harm at several decisive moments during the struggle for a Jewish state.

8

The Struggle for Statehood

On 8 May 1945, Ben-Gurion walked through the streets of war-torn London gazing at the excited crowds preparing to celebrate the downfall of Nazi Germany. He wrote only one line in his diary: "Victory day – sad, very sad." The defeat of Nazi Germany was no victory for the Jewish people. During six years of war, six million of its numbers had been massacred, and on victory day, Ben-Gurion sank into deep depression. He knew that the true test, the decisive battle, still lay ahead.

On arriving in London, Ben-Gurion learned of the encouraging talk between President Roosevelt and Dr Stephan Wise in Washington. Wise was told that the Big Three Summit Conference at Yalta had decided to give Palestine to the Jews and to permit further immigration. The president also held a four-hour talk with Ibn Saud, which disappointed him. Ben-Gurion took a very skeptical view of these reports. In fact, Roosevelt's attitude toward the Palestine question displayed an astounding degree of double-dealing. Together with his pro-Zionist statements to Jewish leaders, he was lavish with contradictory promises to Arab statesmen. On his way back from the Yalta Conference, he did indeed meet Ibn Saud but seems to have made him promises quite unlike those reported to Wise. On returning to Washington on 1 March, Roosevelt had declared: "I learned more about the Moslem problem and the Jewish problem by talking to Ibn Saud for five minutes than I would have learned about it by means of exchanging two or three dozen notes."

A few days later, Roosevelt sent a secret note to Ibn Saud in which he reiterated his promise that "I will not undertake, in my role as head of the executive branch in this administration, any action likely to be hostile to the Arab people." Roosevelt's pro-Zionism was unreliable. Later, most observers were of the opinion that if Roosevelt had completed his term of office, it is doubtful whether a Jewish state would have come into being. Churchill, on whom the Zionists placed great hopes, unexpectedly evaded a scheduled meeting with Weizmann. The president of the Zionist Organization could not have known that the partition plan secretly prepared by the British government had been shelved. During the last weeks of the war, Zionism was in a far from satisfactory state.

Ben-Gurion sensed that there was not much for him to do in England. Originally he had planned to spend no more than a short time there before going on to the United States, which was now the center of activity. But he was still in London when Weizmann received Churchill's disappointing letter postponing any discussion of the Palestine issue. Ben-Gurion reached the United States a week later. Churchill's letter had strengthened his feeling that a confrontation with England was inevitable. In his first lecture to the Zionist Emergency Committee, and in a press conference the next day, he spelled out the watchword: "There is a possibility of resistance in Palestine if, with American help, we fail to induce England to alter its policy." This sentence comprised the whole of Ben-Gurion's new strategy: one last attempt would be made to persuade Britain to rescind the White Paper and agree to the establishment of a Jewish state. If it did not agree – an armed struggle.

However, plans for the short-term struggle could not be permitted to obscure long-term objectives or the means to attain them. Ben-Gurion looked beyond the impending conflict with the British to their departure and the establishment of a Jewish state. When these objectives were attained, the young state could expect to come under attack by the neighboring Arab states. It was therefore vital to acquire enormous quantities of arms, and the means to manufacture them independently, so that when war came the Jews would be able to repel the invaders. This was Ben-Gurion's principal aim in going to America.

On arriving in New York, Ben-Gurion took up his quarters at the Hotel Fourteen on 60th Street, which served many of the Palestinian Jews who came to the city. He immediately summoned Meyer Weisgal and outlined his plan. Weisgal introduced Ben-Gurion to his friend Henry Montor, "who was gifted with a brilliant capacity for raising money and knew everyone worth knowing". Montor gave Ben-Gurion a list of seventeen men "of means, whose loyalty to the security of the Palestine Jewish community could be relied upon". Then Ben-Gurion met with his friend the millionaire Rudolph Sonnenborn and said that he "wished to meet with a number of friends in his home, for a vital purpose". After receiving Sonnenborn's consent, Ben-Gurion sent telegrams to each of the Jews on Montor's list summoning them to Sonnenborn's house at 9.30 in the morning of 1 July 1945, for a "vital" matter. On the appointed day, all seventeen appeared.

The secret meeting at the apartment on 57th Street deserves to be recorded in history. Until five o'clock in the afternoon, the participants showered Ben-Gurion with questions about his plans to acquire millions of dollars in arms to defend a state that had yet to be created. It was a stifling day, but no one left. At the end of the meeting, each of the eighteen millionaires undertook to do everything within his power for the project. This was the beginning of the Sonnenborn Institute. As a cover, Sonnenborn engaged in shipping equipment and medicines for hospitals, but secretly he collected the first million dollars to purchase arms. Later he would go on to collect further millions to buy arms and many ships to serve illegal immigration. After the meeting, a satisfied Ben-Gurion noted in his journal: "That was the best Zionist meeting I have ever had in the United States."

At the end of July, Ben-Gurion sailed for England on the *Queen Elizabeth*. On board with him were many of the prominent leaders of the American Zionist movement. They were on their way to London for the first international Zionist conference to be held since the outbreak of the war. The ship was still at sea when the results of the British general elections were published: Churchill and the Conservative Party had suffered a crushing defeat. The British people voted the Labour Party, under Clement Attlee, into office, and Ernest Bevin was appointed foreign secretary. Both the Zionist leaders on the ship and many in Palestine openly celebrated the Labour victory as an event of historic importance. They were now convinced that the Jewish state would soon arise.

Their confidence stemmed from the clearly pro-Zionist position long held by the Labour Party. Since 1939, the party had been vehemently opposed to the White Paper and its regulations. In 1940, in the midst of the war, it tabled a motion of no confidence over the issue of the Land Regulations. In December 1944, the party went further than even the official Zionist program. Its annual conference adopted the far-reaching proposal for Palestine to be constituted as a Jewish Commonwealth, for its borders to be extended, and for its Arab population to be transferred to the neighboring countries! The notion was so radical that even the Zionist leaders, including Ben-Gurion, had hastened to dissociate themselves from the "population transfer" idea in order not to provoke the Arabs.

Unlike his enthusiastic colleagues, however, Ben-Gurion remained skeptical about the future under Labour. At the Zionist conference held in August 1945, he thanked the Labour Party for its sympathetic attitude, but he also issued a grave warning to his colleagues:

Do not rely too much on this great change, and do not assume that the question of the White Paper has been solved thereby ... The assumption that a party in power resembles a party in opposition is unsubstantiated ... And we have no assurances that on gaining power the party will expect of itself what it did of others and fulfill those expectations ... And I wish to tell the British

Labour Party: if, for some reason or other, it maintains the White Paper regime for an unlimited period . . . we in Palestine will not fear, nor draw back in the face of England's great power, and we shall fight against her.

Ben-Gurion's words shocked the Weizmann camp – first and foremost Weizmann himself. Weizmann's speech did begin forcefully: "Palestine as a Jewish state should be one of the fruits of victory, and with God's help, it shall be!" But then he again expressed his doubts about the slogan of "a Jewish state immediately", repeating his view that the process could take five years and come about gradually. His words angered many of the delegates who supported the Biltmore Program and demanded that the policy be clearly and vigorously confirmed. Again Ben-Gurion entered into a sharp confrontation with Weizmann, this time over a fundamental difference of views.

Beginning March 1945, activism had increasingly become the bone of contention between Weizmann and Ben-Gurion. For Weizmann, nothing had changed in Zionism's aims or the mode of their implementation. He continued to adhere to the slogan "another goat and another acre", while "Ben-Gurion's sense of urgency was more in keeping with the pace of events and . . . the mood in the Zionist camp", as Nahum Goldmann described the confrontation. The pressure exerted by the activists at the London conference forced Weizmann to retreat. In the end, he relinquished his position and accepted the forceful resolution that reconfirmed the Biltmore Program and implicitly threatened the British government with "heightened tension in Palestine", should it evade a solution of the problem.

The touchstone of the Labour government's intentions regarding Palestine was the appeal from President Truman to permit the immediate immigration of 100,000 Jewish refugees into Palestine. At the height of the Potsdam Conference in the summer of 1945, Truman sent Churchill a memorandum expressing the hope that the immigration restrictions imposed by the White Paper would be abolished immediately. Three days later, however, Churchill's government was defeated, and his successor, Clement Attlee, sent Truman a non-committal answer. The president did not drop the issue, however. On returning to Washington, he told a press conference: "We want to send to Palestine as many Jews as possible. Later, it will be necessary to hold diplomatic discussions with the British and the Arabs, so that if it is possible to establish a state there, it will arise on a peaceful basis. I have no desire to send 500,000 American troops to keep the peace in Palestine."

The late summer was a tense period for the British government. A British intelligence officer informed Ben-Gurion that the government was about to formulate its Palestine policy and was maintaining total secrecy. August and September were nerve-racking for the Zionist leaders who were in London awaiting the government decisions. On 20 September, Ben-Gurion's bitter forebodings were confirmed. A furious friend of Weizmann's wrote in her diary: "[Chaim and Moshe Sharett] told me this government has gone back on all Labour policy and intends to go on with the White Paper policy, with certain concessions! ... They will not agree to any negotiations on [the] basis of [the] White Paper ..." The following day, the Jewish Agency Executive members in London met for a closed meeting. Ben-Gurion adopted an aggressive stance, calling for the immediate publication of a forceful statement to include the sentence: "The gates of Palestine cannot remain closed and will not remain closed." He also proposed breaking off talks with the government (with the sole exception of a scheduled meeting between Weizmann and Bevin), launching a public campaign in Britain and America, convening the Palestine Jewish assembly, and taking action in Britain and America in support of immigration and defense.

Even though he agreed with most of Ben-Gurion's proposals, Weizmann was doubtful whether such "steps can now be of use". But Ben-Gurion was convinced that the time was ripe for concrete action. On 29 September, he flew to Paris and on 1 October he sent a coded telegram to the head of the Haganah headquarters instructing the Haganah to institute an armed uprising against Britain.

This cable was sent without Weizmann's knowledge. It would not be difficult to imagine how furious Weizmann would have been had he read the secret instructions for "sabotage" and "reprisal" against those killing Jews and for armed immigration. In his operational orders to Moshe Sneh, Ben-Gurion went far beyond anything he had previously outlined to his colleagues in London. He did not delude himself that the armed struggle could drive the British out of Palestine, but he hoped that it would provoke such deep sympathetic response in world public opinion that Britain would be forced to alter its policy. With that end in mind, he told a press conference held in Paris that "the acts of the new British government are a continuation of Hitler's policy of hostility".

As he led his people into an armed struggle, Ben-Gurion became a unique personality, changing identities as easily as others change jackets. In London, he was the chairman of the Jewish Agency Executive, an official personage engaged in regular formal contacts with the British government. In Paris he was the head of the Palestinian insurgency movement, mobilizing personnel, arms, and money and working out stratagems for striking at the same British government whose offices he had visited the day before and whose representatives he would meet again the next day.

On 5 October, while Ben-Gurion was on his way back to London from Paris, Weizmann met with the British foreign secretary, Ernest Bevin. The official topic of their meeting was the issue of immigration certificates. Bevin, short and stocky with a broad face, was a man who radiated force and uncompromising obstinacy. A letter from the Zionist institutions had already notified him that the Jewish Agency refused to receive the meager allocation of certificates stipulated in the White Paper and demanded a quota of 100,000 certificates for the displaced persons in Europe. No sooner did Weizmann enter his office than Bevin flung at him coarsely: "Do you mean that you refuse to accept the certificates? Are you trying to bind me? If it's war you want, we'll meet head on!" When Ben-Gurion heard Weizmann's report, his anger flared up again. At a meeting in the London Zionist offices, he demanded that relations with the British government be broken off, but he faced a united front of Weizmann and his supporters. Nonetheless, it was war Bevin was going to get, whether the Weizmann camp approved or not.

Moshe Sneh, head of the Haganah national headquarters, was already laying the foundations for an alliance with the I.Z.L. and Lehi, which grew into the "Hebrew Resistance Movement". On 9 October, Palmach units raided the Atlith detention camp and liberated 200 of the illegal immigrants being held there. Then, on the night of 1 November, the Hebrew Resistance Movement carried out its first large-scale operation against the British government: units of the Palmach, I.Z.L. and Lehi raided the country's railroads, damaging them at 153 points, and blew up coastguard boats that were used to pursue illegal immigrant ships. It was clear that the underground had carefully avoided bloodshed, and Ben-Gurion sent a letter of congratulations to the Haganah headquarters. But Weizmann's reaction was quite different. He was not content before the Zionist office in London issued a statement condemning the action. Drafting the statement took a long time, and it was not completed "before Chaim threatened to resign unless he added the word 'disgust' in addition to 'condemn'".

Late in the evening on 12 November, Ben-Gurion arrived back in London. Weizmann had in the meantime left for the United States bitter and disappointed in both the Jews and the British. The following day, Ben-Gurion and Moshe Sharett received an urgent summons to the Colonial Office, where the colonial secretary, Hall, presented them with a copy of the statement Bevin would deliver to Parliament a few minutes later. The British government had decided to send a commission of inquiry – to which the Americans would be invited to send representatives – that would determine whether there was room for the displaced Jews of Europe in Palestine or whether they would have to be accommodated elsewhere. Until the committee's findings were published, immigration would continue at the pace previously determined – 1,500 certificates a month.

At a press conference held after making his statement, Bevin spoke crudely. Regarding Zionist plans to build up Palestine's absorptive capacity, he declared that this was "eighty per cent propaganda and twenty per cent reality" and added that he was very anxious "lest the Jews in Europe should over emphasize their racial status . . . if the Jews, who have suffered so much, try to push to the head of the queue, there is a danger of a renewed anti-Semitic reaction throughout Europe".

Bevin's announcement and his accompanying remarks provoked furious reactions. Violent demonstrations broke out in Palestine, and the crowds attempted to set fire to government buildings. Furious at the British, President Truman made it quite plain that he did not intend the Jews to be resettled elsewhere and that he maintained his demand for the transfer of 100,000 Jewish refugees to Palestine. Returning to Palestine at the end of November – a month of violent clashes with the British police that left nine Jewish dead – Ben-Gurion made his response to Bevin before the Elected Assembly of Palestine Jews:

I want to address a few words to Bevin and his colleagues. We, the Jews of the Land of Israel, do not want to be killed. We wish to live. In defiance of the ideology of Hitler and his disciples in various lands, we believe that we Jews, like Englishmen and others, also have the right to live, as individuals and as a people. But we too, like the English, have something that is more precious than life. And I want to tell Bevin and his colleagues that we are prepared to be killed, but not to concede three things: freedom of Jewish immigration; our right to re-build the wilderness of our homeland; the political independence for our people in its homeland.

The situation in Palestine deteriorated to the point where the British government issued severe Emergency Regulations. Curfews, arrests, and searches became a daily occurrence throughout the country. Sentences of death or life imprisonment were imposed on Jews caught in uniform or carrying arms. The British Sixth Airborne Division, which had a heroic record during the Second World War, now became an instrument of anti-Jewish repression. Cynically Ben-Gurion wrote that Palestine would, indeed, become "a national home for the British army in the Middle East".

In anticipation of the arrival of the Anglo-American Commission of Inquiry early in March 1946, however, the Hebrew Resistance Movement ordered a halt to the violence. Weizmann arrived from London and his testimony before the commission was dignified and impressive. Ben-Gurion also delivered a powerful address:

I saw the blitz in London . . . I saw the Englishman whose land and liberty is dearer than his life. Why do you presume that we are not like you? We, too, have things that are more precious to us than our lives. In this country and in other countries, there are hundreds of thousands of Jews who will give their lives – if that is required – for the sake of Zion and for the sake of the Jewish state.

In April the commission left for Lausanne to frame its recommendations. Its report, published on 1 May, rejected the demand for the establishment of a Jewish state and recommended a trusteeship over Palestine (in practice, the extension of the British Mandate); but it also called for the abolition of the Land Regulations and the White Paper, and its principal recommendation was for the immediate issue of 100,000 immigration certificates to Jewish refugees.

Weizmann and his supporters, including several outspoken activists, welcomed the report. Ben-Gurion, on the other hand, did not conceal his disappointment. He regarded the recommendations as "a camouflaged and sophisticated repetition of the White Paper". But almost immediately the entire subject became irrelevant. The recommendations were unanimous, and Bevin had promised the commission members that if their findings were unanimous, he would carry them out. But Bevin and Attlee simply went back on their promise. Attlee contended that carrying out the transfer of refugees would require him to send an additional British division to Palestine and demanded, as a pre-condition, the disbandment of the Jewish underground. Bevin added that the immigration of 100,000 Jews would step up anti-Semitic feelings in the British army and require the outlay of another £200 million. With that they promptly buried the report.

Britain's refusal to fulfill its clearly stated commitment caused deep disappointment within the Zionist movement. From Paris, Ben-Gurion gave instructions for the resumption of the armed struggle. Five days after Bevin's speech, the Resistance Movement carried out one of its most impressive operations: the demolition of fourteen bridges that linked Palestine to the neighboring countries. The British response was to escalate the tension to its peak. On 29 June 1946, the mandatory authorities launched Operation Broadside, which became known among the Jewish population as "Black Saturday". On that day, Palestine was paralyzed by 17,000 British troops, backed by tanks and armored cars. The borders were closed, telephone lines cut, and a general curfew was imposed. Hundreds of Jewish leaders suspected of links with the Haganah were arrested and their homes were searched. The detainees included members of the Jewish Agency Executive. Ben-Gurion was in Paris at the time; Moshe Sneh got a last-minute warning from Haganah intelligence and managed to evade the police; other Haganah leaders also went underground; and Dr Weizmann was not harassed. But kibbutzim all over the country were searched for Palmach members; thousands of people were taken to detention camps where some were beaten and tortured and three were killed. The Haganah leaders who had gone underground managed to meet and decided to respond to the British actions by stepping up their campaign. The meeting approved several operations, including an attack on the King David Hotel in Jerusalem. But with Ben-Gurion out of the country, there was now a factor which had not been taken into account: Dr Chaim Weizmann.

Weizmann was a fierce opponent of violent methods. He sent his aide, Meyer Weisgal, to Moshe Sneh with the demand "that the Haganah cease all armed action of the Resistance Movement until the Jewish Agency Executive, which will meet with as wide a representation as possible, deliberates and decides on future policy". Weizmann contended that "in politics, it was usual for the president to be the supreme commander of the armed forces. I have never used this authority, and it never occurred to me to intervene in your affairs. This time, for the first and only time, I utilize this prerogative and call upon you to halt all operations." This message was not so much a demand as an ultimatum. Weizmann threatened that if Sneh did not resign immediately, he himself would resign and publicize his reasons for doing so. Sneh tendered his resignation, slipped out of the country, and within a few days joined Ben-Gurion in Paris.

"Black Saturday" was more than an offensive operation to break the Resistance Movement. It was part of a carefully planned British campaign to strike hard at the activists and leave them leaderless while encouraging the moderates who supported cooperation with the British. The "Black Saturday" action undoubtedly advanced the first aim; Weizmann's intervention against the Resistance Movement and Sneh's resignation, indicated that the second aim also had a good chance of success. The High Commissioner quickly invited Weizmann for a talk and "hinted at the need for the establishment of a new leadership, even going so far as to mention the names of desirable leaders". Dr Weizmann did reject the High Commissioner's proposal and raised the question of whether to establish a new leadership at a meeting held in Tel Aviv.

Far away, in the Royal Monceau Hotel in Paris, Ben-Gurion fully comprehended the motives of the mandatory government. At a mass rally, he warned: "An attempt has been made to set up a leadership from the 'right wing' of the Jewish community in Palestine. The British government has erred. There will not be a single person, from the right or from the left . . . who will agree to participate in the Jewish Agency as a Quisling or a Petain." During those days, Ben-Gurion received a far-reaching proposal from his neighbor in the hotel, Ho Chi Minh. The two leaders became friends, and Ho readily suggested the establishment of a Jewish government in exile, to take up residence in Indo-China. But matters unfolded otherwise.

Ben-Gurion's isolation in Paris grew during July, after a dramatic event took place in Jerusalem. A unit of the I.Z.L. blew up the southern wing of the King David Hotel, which housed the government offices. In spite of the telephone warnings to evacuate the building, hundreds of people were inside when the bomb went off. The powerful explosion demolished the five storeys of the wing, and some ninety persons died. The calamity shocked the Jewish community deeply. In Paris, Ben-Gurion denounced the I.Z.L. for the operation, but the storm of rage spread rapidly, and spokesmen in both Houses of Parliament specifically denounced Ben-Gurion after the explosion. The moderates in Palestine denounced the activists with unprecedented fury, and the King David explosion served as a catalyst for the establishment of a coalition against militant Zionism.

Ben-Gurion seemed to understand that in the present state of confusion with his policy under severe attack, it would require only a slight tremor to destroy the unity of his camp. Accordingly, he acted with great caution. He did not demand the resumption of the armed struggle, nor did he confront Weizmann and the moderates. On the contrary, he did everything in his power to prevent, for the time being, "upheavals in the movement and a sharpening of internal differences". He devoted his attention to the forthcoming meeting of the Zionist Executive in Paris, where he hoped for a victory, even if he had to pay a heavy price for it.

Ben-Gurion's policy at the meetings of the Executive was complex, evasive, and often in direct contradiction to views he had previously expressed. Even though he was in favor of continuing the armed struggle, he did not object when the majority proposed to freeze operations until the Zionist Congress met. He accepted a far-reaching political compromise when Nahum Goldmann proposed that "the Executive is prepared to discuss the proposal to constitute a viable Jewish state in a sufficient portion of the Land of Israel". This was a revolutionary statement implying partition. For the first time since the adoption of the Biltmore Program, someone dared to propose the partitioning of western Palestine. Ben-Gurion's response was even more astounding. He declared that he accepted the principle of partition, but when the proposal was put to the vote, he abstained. The Executive adopted the principle of partition, while Ben-

Gurion retreated from the Biltmore Program's territorial definition of the Jewish state.

Ben-Gurion would never have capitulated to Goldmann without a fight had he not essentially agreed with him. There is no doubt that Ben-Gurion was ready to accept a partition proposal, but for the record he refrained from voting for it. It should be stressed that both men knew there was a good chance of gaining Truman's support for a partition plan that would result in the establishment of a Jewish state. The Executive adjourned for a few days and Goldmann flew to America to persuade the three-man committee established by Truman to formulate American policy on Palestine to adopt the partition plan. On 9 August, he met with the president's assistant, David Niles, "who informed [him], moved to tears, that the president had accepted the entire plan and had instructed [Dean] Acheson to transmit an appropriate message to the British government". On 13 August Goldmann returned to Paris, and the Executive resumed its meetings. They ended on 23 August by setting the seal on the new Zionist policy of partition.

In the autumn of 1946, Chaim Weizmann was tired and disappointed. The British leaders with whom he held talks were not the same men he had grown to know between the two world wars. They were tougher, fearful of every word the Arabs said, and unfaithful to their promises. Nor were the Jews the same as they had been. Their forceful demands for the immediate creation of a state grated on Weizmann's ears. He would reply, with justice, that he wanted a state no less than they; but he continued to believe in the patient, gradual approach, while they were infected with the messianic virus spread by Ben-Gurion. Weizmann was ailing. He had recently undergone a series of painful eye operations and was almost blind. He was seventy-two years old, and on several occasions in 1946 he had announced that he would not stand for re-election as president of the Zionist Organization at the forthcoming Congress in Basel.

The truth was that Weizmann was determined to remain the head of the Zionist movement, while Ben-Gurion was equally determined to unseat him. In mid-September, Weizmann sent Ben-Gurion a friendly letter, addressing him as "my dear Ben-Gurion" and announcing that he agreed completely with everything decided in Paris. Ben-Gurion's reply was even more friendly and, displaying especial consideration for Weizmann's infirmity, he made the letter easier to read by writing it in large, clear characters. "Very dear Dr Weizmann," he wrote, ". . . Wherever you are, you shall be accompanied by the love and respect of my colleagues and myself." Weizmann replied in a similar vein, but he dropped one hint about his political plans in a seemingly incidental sentence: "I understand it is the intention to settle the question of elections [to the Zionist executive bodies] before the congress begins. That is an excellent idea if it can be carried through. It would save a great deal of trouble and excitement." Ben-Gurion indeed had a plan to prearrange the elections, but not in the manner that Weizmann envisaged. He wrote to Weizmann: "Perhaps I shall soon depart – briefly – for America." "Soon" was not quite accurate; in fact, he took off for the United States a few hours after completing his letter to Weizmann.

Ben-Gurion's purpose was to build an alliance against Weizmann with Abba Hillel Silver, the dynamic and aggressive leader of the American Zionists. Silver's views were maximalist, and his messianic belief in the establishment of a Jewish state was on a par with Ben-Gurion's. He was a strong, domineering man who tolerated no opposition; compromises were beyond him, and he struck at his adversaries without mercy. Two such strong personalities as Ben-Gurion and Silver could not long co-exist without engaging in a struggle for the leadership. But during the war years, the two established a progressively strong alliance in opposition to the conciliatory line followed by Weizman and Dr Stephan Wise. It was Silver who gave the American Zionist movement its aggressive, mass character. Thus when Ben-Gurion set off for the U.S. in semi-secrecy one of his aims was the establishment of the Silver–Ben-Gurion front for the forthcoming Zionist Congress.

The atmosphere in Basel was gloomy as the Congress delegates began to assemble from all over the world. Veteran Zionists sought in vain for familiar faces among the national delegations. There could not have been a more somber expression of the holocaust that had overtaken the Jewish people than the absence of hundreds of Zionist activists last seen at the Geneva Congress a few days before Hitler's columns poured into Poland. While the number of East European delegates had diminished, there was an increase in the delegates from the United States, symbolizing the shift in the focal points of Zionism and the Jewish people.

The debate between Ben-Gurion and Weizmann on Zionist policy began in the Congress plenum. In his opening address, Ben-Gurion announced his readiness to accept the principle of partition. Stressing the Jewish people's right to the whole of Palestine, he nevertheless added that "we are prepared to discuss a compromise arrangement if, in exchange for the reduction in territory, our rights are immediately extended and we are granted national independence". Later in the debate, he praised the slogan of "resistance" – by which he meant armed struggle – but defined its limits and dissociated himself from terrorism. He spoke with great emotion and dignity of the struggle and of illegal immigration.

This [resistance movement] is a new event in the chronicles of Israel. There are Jews in the Diaspora for whom immigration to Palestine is a matter of life and death. For them, the Land of Israel is not Zionism, it is not ideology, it is not a plan, but a vital need, a condition for survival. The fate of those Jews is in the Land of Israel or death. That, too, is power.

Weizmann presented the opposing view in a no less brilliant speech:

I listened to the powerful speech of my friend Ben-Gurion about resistance. He said some would fall, but the others would live. I hope so; but it can take another form. Many more may fall, and then what will happen to the Jewish people, what will happen to Palestine if we upset the basis on which we have built this thing by our efforts and by our blood and toil? . . . Those who attack the government just expect the government to hit back. We complain that they hit harder and we feel it more. What else can we expect? We should have known that before.

In the course of Weizmann's distraught words, an incident broke out. He accused those American Zionists who supported the struggle of remaining content with moral and financial support while sending others to the barricades, whereupon one of the delegates shouted at him: "Demagogue!" Weizmann responded angrily: "Calling me a demagogue. I am one of those who have gone through all the agonies of Zionist work. This man that hurled that epithet at me should know that every farm-house and in every stable in Nahalal and every building down to the tiniest workshop in Tel Aviv or Haifa contains a drop of my life's blood."

The delegates broke into stormy applause and most rose to their feet. Weizmann went on:

I warn you against false taking short-cuts, against following false prophets and will-o'-the-wisp generalizations and against the falsification of historical facts. This is my temperament. I do not believe in violence. I was brought up in a liberal era, which has vanished and is lost forever, and we have emerged into a brutal period. But even though other nations may permit themselves brutal methods, I do not know whether we can . . . "Zion will be redeemed through righteousness" and not by any other means.

It was a brilliant speech, but it did not alter the basic facts: the means proposed by Weizmann were different – indeed, diametrically opposed – to those of Ben-Gurion. Weizmann wanted a confrontation with Ben-Gurion and a clear-cut decision between them.

The struggle around the election of a new Executive and president went on far from the Congress hall. Before the Congress opened, Ben-Gurion summoned several members of Mapai to his room in the Three Kings Hotel and suggested "electing Weizmann honorary president". Most of the

Palestinian Mapai members went along with the idea, but the members of the Diaspora parties connected with Mapai (who constituted a majority in the faction) inclined toward Weizmann. During the Congress, in an atmosphere of heavy tension, the Mapai faction convened again, but Ben-Gurion did not appear. "Suddenly there was a rumor that Ben-Gurion refused to attend," related Shimon Peres, one of the Palestinian delegates.·

Paula came in and said: "Ben-Gurion is leaving!" . . . We went to the Three Kings Hotel . . . knocked on the door, [but] there was no reply. We opened the door and saw Ben-Gurion packing his suitcase . . . He turned to us and said: "Did you come to leave with me, or are you staying?" When we asked him: "Where are you going?" he said: "The Zionist movement has betrayed its tasks. It is not establishing a state. The majority is prepared to make peace with the British. I am in despair. I am going to organize a new Zionist movement." We told him to come with us to the meeting of the Mapai faction. If he got a majority, we would all stay. If [he got only] a minority, we would all get out.

Finally, Ben-Gurion agreed to return to the Congress hall, where the Mapai faction was meeting. The caucus lasted all night, but in the morning Ben-Gurion gained a majority, and Mapai voted in favor of an activist Executive. At the same time, efforts continued to persuade Weizmann to accept the post of honorary president. He refused adamantly. "I have enough honor," he told anyone who approached him on this matter.

In the end, Weizmann's candidacy was not put to the vote at all, for he made it conditional upon the Congress's unambiguous decision in favor of participating in the British government's forthcoming London Conference, and that proposal was defeated. It was a vote of no confidence in Weizmann. He did not even submit his candidacy for president. Ironically, this decisive vote saw the collapse of Ben-Gurion's coalition with Silver. The Mapai world faction decided by a majority vote to support participation in the London Conference. Ben-Gurion and the Palestinian delegates decided to accept the majority's decision and voted in favor of Weizmann's proposal. Thus they actually had no part in his downfall.

Out of respect for Weizmann, the Twenty-Second Congress decided not to elect a president. It chose a Zionist Executive with nineteen members, six of them from the United States. Ben-Gurion was again elected to head the Executive, and was given the defense portfolio. Weizmann returned to London beaten and embittered. It was the end of an epoch. Militant Zionism had come out on top after a decade-long struggle between giants.

Even after his defeat, Weizmann remained a major political figure. For a time he tried to organize a comeback and overthrow Ben-Gurion, but his followers did not respond to his appeal. He was to be much more successful in the diplomatic field, where his personal stature provided him entrance to the White House, and he succeeded in influencing President Truman's attitude toward the creation of the State of Israel. After the state was established, Weizmann was elected its first president. But he complained bitterly about his restricted powers and accused Ben-Gurion of turning him into "the prisoner" of his residence in Rehovot.

It was now in Ernest Bevin that Ben-Gurion found an adversary of his own measure. The foreign secretary was strangely indifferent to the fate of the Jewish people after the terrible holocaust it had endured. During the thirties, he had been pro-Zionist, but now that he discovered the Arab aspect of the problem, he adopted a new policy. He did not comprehend the demand of hundreds of thousands of refugees to go to Palestine because he regarded them as he did other European war victims. He was incapable of grasping that they could not integrate themselves back into Europe and rebuild their lives there. Nonetheless, it was not essential for Bevin to make himself the object of such hatred in Palestine and arouse such protest in world opinion. But he had a number of traits that were clearly to blame for the deterioration of relations between Britain and the Jews of Palestine during the three years after the Second World War.

Like any other strong, obstinate man, once Bevin made a decision, he was not prepared to change his mind. The sharper the attacks on his policy, the harder his heart and the heavier his hand. Faced with illegal immigration and insurrection, he sent in more and more troops, stepping up repression. The protests in Palestine and the United States aroused a latent anti-Semitic complex in him. At a Labour Party conference, he accused the Americans of "trying to help the Jews emigrate to Palestine because they do not want them in New York". This was sufficient provocation for the American press to make unflattering comparisons between him and Adolf Hitler; and while Bevin was in New York for the United Nations Assembly, the police were forced to smuggle him out of a baseball stadium to save him from the fury of the crowd. Bevin converted a stance that may have been inevitable, as far as Britain was concerned, into a policy of hatred and repression. His tough attitude pulled the rug out from under the pro-British members of the Zionist movement and pushed its leaders into ever more militant and extremist positions.

Bevin was the moving spirit behind the Anglo–Arab–Jewish conference, which the British government convened at the end of January 1947. Right from the start the talks were doomed to failure. The Palestinian Arabs were represented by a delegation from The Supreme Arab Committee, and, under the guidance of the mufti, they presented an extremist, uncompromising position, demanding a total ban on Jewish immigration and the immediate establishment of an independent state in Palestine. They also adamantly refused to hold any face-to-face meetings with the Zionists. Bevin ruled the roost, rejecting outright any Jewish demand for partition or abolition of the White Paper. He contended that such moves would be unacceptable to the Arabs. There was no hope of compromise between the two positions.

On 7 February an official envelope containing His Majesty's Government's final offer was delivered to the Zionist office in Great Russell Street. The proposal consisted of a plan to divide Palestine into self-governing cantons, but most of the country would be closed to Jewish immigration or settlement. The British suggested that 96,000 Jews be allowed to immigrate in the course of two years, but subsequent immigration would depend on the decision of the High Commissioner. "This proposal will be rejected vigorously!" shouted Ben-Gurion. "The bait of 4,000 [certificates] a month for two years will not make us change our minds."

Four days later, both the Arab and Jewish delegations rejected Bevin's proposals. In response the foreign secretary announced that "since the proposals put forward by His Majesty's Government have not been accepted as the basis for further negotiations, His Majesty's Government has decided to hand the whole problem to the United Nations". Bevin had conceded defeat. "An episode has come to an end," wrote Ben-Gurion, "perhaps the great episode of the Mandate . . . We are now standing before a great, hard and decisive battle."

This was the end of an epoch in Ben-Gurion's life. The abortive London Conference was the last political struggle into which he flung himself prior to the establishment of the state. Ben-Gurion had a wonderful and unique instinct. At every period of his life, he sensed where the center of gravity lay and hurled himself into that sphere of activity. In December 1946, the state was still remote; in February 1947 it was still out of sight. But Ben-Gurion was convinced that it was an historical necessity; that its birth would provoke the invasion of Arab armies and a bloody confrontation; and that it was vital to prepare for that war. Thus Ben-Gurion left the political arena and devoted himself to studying military problems.

Upon returning to Palestine, Ben-Gurion halted the armed struggle and froze the operations of the Resistance Movement. He had already said that struggle was "only a means for us". Now the most fitting means was non-violent struggle: illegal immigration and settlement. But the dissident organizations again swept the country with a wave of terrorist attacks. Palestine looked like an armed camp, with 100,000 British troops conducting arrests, searches, and even executions. Mandatory-government quarters fenced off behind barbed wire, walls, sand bags, and machine-gun positions, gained the name of "Bevingrad". The I.Z.L. and Lehi stepped up their attacks, mining and demolishing and killing, and the Haganah, in disgust, again undertook counter-action.

On 28 April 1947, the General Assembly of the United Nations assembled in New York to discuss the Palestine question. At the beginning of July, together with a long row of witnesses, Ben-Gurion appeared before the United Nations Special Committee on Palestine (U.N.S.C.O.P.), sent to Palestine to investigate a solution to the problem. "Gentlemen," he addressed the eleven emissaries of the U.N., "I ask you a question. Who is willing and capable of guaranteeing that what happened to us in Europe will not recur? Can the conscience of humanity . . . absolve itself of all responsibility for that Holocaust? There is only one security guarantee: a homeland and a state." He understood that the tragedy of the European DPs was the most convincing argument in favor of the establishment of the state. Consequently, he helped persuade the U.N.S.C.O.P. members to take in the most shocking "testimony" they were to record during their mission – the fate of the immigrants on the ship *Exodus*.

In its better days, the *Exodus* had been an unpretentious river steamer that carried 600 passengers up and down the Mississippi. Now, Haganah emissaries had lined her with wood and steel plates, crammed her with 5,000 Holocaust survivors, and hurled her against the British naval blockade. At sea, the ship hoisted the blue-white flag and adopted the symbolic name of *Exodus Europe 1947*. It was a provocative, demonstrative cruise toward the coast of Palestine, with British planes circling overhead and destroyers lurking on the horizon, while the whole world held its breath to see the outcome of the confrontation. Before it even reached Palestinian territorial waters, the ship was intercepted by British warships. After a battle, which left three dead on board, the *Exodus* was towed into Haifa, where the immigrants were forcibly disembarked and loaded onto three British prison ships, which set sail back to Europe. The death of the three immigrants and the tragedy of the 5,000 refugees were not in vain. The scene at Haifa was witnessed by agitated members of U.N.S.C.O.P. Now Ben-Gurion was certain that the Jewish state was at the threshold.

Several days later, U.N.S.C.O.P. published its findings. The majority report recommended the partition of Palestine into an Arab and a Jewish state with Jerusalem to be placed under international supervision. The debate on the U.N.S.C.O.P. recommendations lasted for months, while the Jewish Agency delegation conducted a nerve-racking campaign to ensure the support necessary for the program to be adopted. On 29 November 1947, the fateful vote was taken at the United Nations Assembly at Lake Success.

That night Ben-Gurion went to sleep early. He was staying at a hotel on the shores of the Dead Sea, and at midnight, someone knocked on his door to awaken him. Outside he saw workers drunk with joy, dancing on the shore. The U.N. General Assembly had voted for partition, and the British Mandate would end on 14 May 1948. "That night, crowds danced in the streets," recalled the Old Man. "I could not dance. I knew that we faced war and that in it we would lose the best of our youth."

Even before there was a state, the war erupted.

9

The War before the War

From the establishment of the Sonnenborn Institute in New York to his request for the defense portfolio of the Jewish Agency Executive, Ben-Gurion had long been forecasting and planning for the war he knew the Arabs of Palestine and the neighboring countries would declare on the nascent Jewish state, when – and if – it came into being. While the Zionist world was preoccupied with the struggle to end the Mandate, Ben-Gurion was one of the very few with the foresight to begin preparing for the post-Mandate crisis. His warning of an imminent war suddenly took on a more realistic coloring after U.N.S.C.O.P. recommended partition; and by the time the U.N. General Assembly voted to partition Palestine into two states, the die was cast.

When Ben-Gurion asked the Jewish Agency Executive to entrust him with the defense portfolio, his ambitious demand provoked some ironic comments. Was it feasible for an elderly political leader, without any military background, to change overnight into a military strategist? Those who doubted the Old Man's capacity for learning the art of war underestimated Ben-Gurion's phenomenal powers of concentration. In the months following the Zionist Congress in Basel, he dedicated himself almost completely to studying military problems. In his study on the second floor of his Tel Aviv home, he started his "seminar". Each morning he opened his journal and began interrogating Haganah commanders. With astounding dilligence he noted down every detail, from the number of men at their disposal to the amount of arms and ammunition concealed in caches. Every so often, he would leave his private headquarters and tour the various Haganah units and their arms. When he was alone, he spent his time reading the works of the great military theorists, military handbooks, and Haganah publications.

The Haganah had acquired the reputation of a huge secret organization – all-powerful and lavishly equipped. As far back as 1943, secret British intelligence memoranda had put the number of Haganah members at between 80,000 and 100,000. It was a long way from these legends to reality. The Haganah units – which included 9,500 teenagers in the Gadna youth corps – numbered 45,337 members at the beginning of May 1947. But even this figure was misleading, since only 2,200 members of the Palmach were fully mobilized. Most of the other Haganah members underwent only occasional training and were totally unprepared for operations of a military nature. Even the Palmach had never conducted maneuvers at a battalion level.

The weapons available were even more disappointing. On 12 April 1947, the Haganah possessed 10,073 rifles of various types; 1,900 sub-machine-guns, mostly of poor quality; 444 light machine-guns; 186 medium-caliber machine-guns; 672 two-inch mortars; 96 three-inch mortars; 93,738 hand-grenades; and 4,896,303 bullets. It did not have any heavy machine-guns, not to mention such heavy arms as tanks, cannon, planes, or warships. Neither its manpower nor its weapons were ready for war with regular armies. Ben-Gurion discovered a further weak point. All operational planning was based upon the assumption that the worst danger facing the Jewish community in Palestine was an uprising of the local Arabs, and it was this threat alone for which the Haganah was prepared. Its commanders did not consider a more serious eventuality: an attack by regular Arab armies.

Such a coordinated attack was Ben-Gurion's basic assumption when he instituted his "seminar" and it led him to the decisive question: was the Haganah capable, of its own accord, of converting itself into a regular army? At the end of the first phase of his "seminar", Ben-Gurion's conclusion was negative. He therefore decided to approach the pool of military men with whom he had not yet consulted: veterans of the British army and the Jewish Brigade. Having failed to find seasoned soldiers in the Haganah, he hoped to find them among the men who had served in a real regular army. As he turned in this direction, however, the Old Man found himself in a hornets' nest.

"In the Haganah," he wrote, "I found two parties: the 'Haganah' party and the 'army' party, with little trust between them." The "army party" was almost absent from the upper ranks of the Haganah command. Many of the Haganah members who had remained in Palestine during the war displayed a cold, even hostile, attitude toward those of their comrades who had enlisted in the British army. Haganah veterans were contemptuous of their military mannerisms as well as their ideas and demands regarding training, structure, and equipment – all of which were appropriate for a regular army but not an underground organization. The army veterans fought back. Having acquired know-how, they tried to apply it; but they were often placed under Haganah commanders whose military training was poorer than their own.

At the end of May 1947, the Haganah command presented its military plans to Ben-Gurion.

Two forces are required: (1) A defense force of 15,000 men as static garrisons, and nine battalions (700 men each) for mobile regional defense; together, 21,300 men. (2) An offensive force consisting of fifteen small brigades of 2,000 men each and a strike force of six battalions with 4,500 men; together, 34,500 men.

Ben-Gurion welcomed the proposal for the establishment of a defense force, an offensive force, and a strike force, but he was critical of other aspects of the plan. Ben-Gurion wrote:

In the absence of heavy armament, at that time, they proposed an increase in light equipment: rifles, sub-machine guns, hand-grenades and machine-guns . . . I considered it urgent to acquire heavy armament: tanks, half-tracks, cannon, and heavy mortars for the land forces; war planes for the establishment of an air force; torpedo boats and other vessels for a navy. I was very surprised to find a lack of understanding on the part of several Haganah chiefs as to the need for heavy armament. . . .

Because of his disappointment in this plan, Ben-Gurion sought proposals from more experienced officers. He approached two former Jewish Brigade officers and asked them to draw up plans for the establishment of an army. "In total secrecy, I was summoned to Ben-Gurion," Chaim Laskov related. "I was asked what needed to be done and in what sequence. I presented a plan . . . We needed twelve large brigades, an air force, armor, artillery, and so many rifles, so many gallons of fuel, and so much ammunition." The discrepancies between the two plans, and Ben-Gurion's growing certainty that army officers alone were capable of preparing the Haganah for its new tasks, led him to place his trust in the Jewish Brigade veterans. But as he was aware of the violent objections such a step would arouse in the Haganah command and in the political power centers, he stopped short of appointing British army veterans to take command of the Haganah.

Instead, Ben-Gurion made a number of fundamental changes in the Haganah command. The head of the national command, Ze'ev Shefer, was forced to resign. Back in December 1946, in the course of the Zionist Congress, Ben-Gurion had summoned Ya'akov Dori and Israel Galili to Basel for a series of conversations. Dori was a veteran of the Jewish Legion and one of the founders of the Haganah. Galili was one of the chief functionaries of Faction B, which had become Ahdut ha-Avodah, and in Ben-Gurion's eyes this was a grave drawback. At the same time, he acknowledged Galili's gifts, which had raised him to the senior officer in the Haganah's national command. Now, in the spring of 1947, he appointed

Galili head of the national command and made Dori commander-in-chief. That summer, he summoned the former chief of operations, Yigael Yadin, a thirty-year-old archeology student, to his headquarters. The tall young man, who was well versed in Haganah affairs, was re-appointed to head the Operations Branch in the national command.

In the course of the summer of 1947, Ben-Gurion had a growing feeling that neither the Zionist movement, the Jewish community in Palestine, nor the Haganah were sufficiently aware of the dreadful dangers in store for them. His sense of foreboding was powerful, but he failed to impress his premonitions on his listeners. Some of his warnings were dismissed as fantasies. Even at a closed session attended by some of the Haganah leaders, the military chiefs spoke only of weapons suitable for platoons or sections; no one mentioned support weapons. Ben-Gurion listened carefully and suddenly asked: "And what about cannon? And airplanes?" For a moment, there was silence in the room. The men looked at one another; several of them had to control themselves to keep from laughing. "He's crazy," someone whispered. "What's he talking about? We're speaking of Stens and rifles, and he dreams of cannon and airplanes." Ben-Gurion went on: "There's going to be a war. The Arab countries will unite and . . . there will be battlefronts. This will no longer be a war of platoons or sections. It is essential to set up a modern army. It is essential to think of the requirement of a modern army."

Indeed, in mid-September, even before the U.N. partition vote, the Arab League's Political Committee decided to commit all the political and military resources at its disposal to preventing the implementation of the U.N.S.C.O.P. recommendations. Arab capitals were deluged with radio broadcasts and newspaper articles carrying statements by political and military leaders that they would shortly go to war against the Jews of Palestine. In this clearly bellicose atmosphere, Ben-Gurion stepped up preparations to attain two objectives: the establishment of a regular army and acquisition of heavy armament. The Haganah command presented a draft budget for training and military equipment, asking for £1 million – or double the previous year's sum. Furious, Ben-Gurion sent the budget proposal back and prepared one of his own that came to over £3 million.

Without wasting a moment, Ben-Gurion also channeled funds to arms purchases. On 30 September, he sent his assistant, Munia Mardor, to Europe to seek out sources of arms supplies. Three days later, Ben-Gurion decided to purchase airplanes and recruit military experts from abroad. On 6 October, he summoned the head of Ta'as, the local arms and munitions works, and told him to order all the raw materials he required immediately. "The money is at [your] disposal."

During these same October days when he was making one important decision after another, Ben-Gurion also adopted the most important strategic decision of the War of Independence: no settlement would be abandoned, even if it were included within the boundaries of the Arab state. The Haganah was thus required to disperse its forces all over the country and maintain access routes to and contact with every settlement. He also indicated that if the partition resolution were not to the liking of the Zionist leadership, the latter would attempt to extend the boundaries of the Jewish state. The phrase "we shall not lay down territorial boundaries" spoke for itself.

On 7 November 1947, the Haganah published its order concerning "the national structure", thereby laying the foundations for the establishment of the Israel Defense Forces.

Three weeks later, the U.N. General Assembly voted for the partition of Palestine and the War of Independence began with irregular warfare.

The fighting did not commence overnight. On hearing of the U.N. vote, the Arab Higher Committee proclaimed a three-day strike. Incidents grew progressively graver, sudden clashes erupted between Jews and Arabs, and small battles were fought using antiquated light arms. But the Arabs were disorganized. A motley mixture of bands operated throughout the country without any coordination and sometimes in open mutual hostility, due to the scheming of Arab rulers. The principal leader of the Palestinian Arabs was the mufti of Jerusalem, who had reappeared in the Middle East after spending the Second World War in Hitler's camp. Haj Amin al-Husseini aspired to establishing an independent Palestinian state; he was not interested in regular Arab forces entering the country for fear that they would deprive him of power after their final victory. Indeed, King Abdullah of Transjordan planned to annex the whole of the area allocated for the Arab state to his own kingdom. He did not want the mufti to emerge victorious and was not inclined to help him. Abdullah even conducted secret negotiations with representatives of the Jewish community. Within Palestine itself, the Arabs were divided between the mufti's supporters and his opponents. The bands that infiltrated across the borders were not free of this internal bickering; and there was open hostility between the mufti and Fawzi Kaukji, who led the Arab Army of Liberation; composed of volunteers from the Arab states. On the other hand, the mufti enjoyed the support of the heads of the Palestinian bands and a battalion of Egyptian Moslem Brotherhood volunteers that reached the Negev.

In many cases the British army, which was still stationed in the country, intervened in Arab–Jewish clashes, adopting a clearly pro-Arab posture. Sometimes, they disarmed Haganah members and handed them over to an

Arab mob, which brutally murdered them; on other occasions they confiscated the meager arms of Jewish convoy escorts, while armed Arabs
moved about and conducted their operations at will. All these acts, together
with the British refusal to place a port at the disposal of the Jews in accordance with the U.N. resolution, left a sense of bitter resentment in the
Jewish community. After thirty years of rule, Britain terminated its
presence in Palestine in an ugly manner, which Winston Churchill denounced as Bevin's "dirty war" against the Jews of Palestine.

In November 1947, after the U.N. resolution, Ben-Gurion summoned
Ehud Avriel to his office. Avriel was thirty, Viennese-born, and a member
of Kibbutz Neot Mordechai. During and after the Second World War, he
stood out as one of the most capable of European emissaries sent by the
Haganah and the illegal immigration underground. When Avriel arrived at
his office, Ben-Gurion looked at him gravely: "We must change our
tactics," he said, explaining that it was no longer sufficient to smuggle arms
into the country haphazardly. From his shirt pocket, Ben-Gurion pulled
out a tiny note that had been folded and refolded. It specified the types and
amounts of arms he wished to acquire immediately: "10,000 rifles, 2·5
million cartridges, 500 sub-machine-guns, 100 machine-guns." Avriel
flew to Geneva and on to Paris. In the French capital he met – fortuitously,
as it appeared – with a contact of the Czech government who invited him to
fly to Prague and buy the arms from government sources there. After
several weeks of negotiations, Avriel signed the first purchase agreement
with Czechoslovakia covering 4,500 rifles, 200 machine-guns, and 5 million
cartridges. Theoretically, the agreement was drawn up between Czechoslovakia and Ethiopia, since Avriel used the official stationery of the Addis
Ababa government, which had served him well on previous missions for the
Haganah and the illegal immigration network. But without any doubt,
Czechoslovakia's consent to sell arms to the Palestine Jewish community
was influenced by Moscow. After the Communist takeover in the February
1948 "Prague coup", the flow of arms to Palestine was stepped up to
include planes and heavy machine-guns. By the end of May 1948, Avriel
was to have bought 24,500 rifles, over 5,000 light machine-guns, 200
medium machine-guns, 54 million cartridges, and 25 German Messerschmitt planes left over from the world war. However, due to the strict
controls imposed by the British authorities, most of these arms did not
reach the country until after the establishment of the state. In the meantime, the Haganah was obliged to operate with the meager arms it possessed.

Ben-Gurion knew no rest in his efforts to acquire every type of arms and
he gave no rest to others. He spurred on the scientists laboring to develop a
flame-thrower; gave orders to find the secret of bulletproof glass; demanded

details on experiments with explosives and secret weapons. He was ambitious, and his demands frequently alarmed his subordinates. He instructed Pinhas Sapir to issue an immediate order for steel to armor-plate vehicles. "Shall I order 200 tons of steel?" asked Sapir. "Order 500 tons!" was the reply. "But the Haganah needs 300 armored cars," said Sapir. "In my view, at least a thousand!" Ben-Gurion retorted.

Yet arms purchases on this scale, the investments in local production, and the financial requirements of the growing army all called for enormous sums – and there was no money. Ben-Gurion decided to fly to the United States to try and raise $25–30 million from the Jewish community there. To his surprise, this proposal encountered vigorous resistance. Golda Meir came forward and offered to undertake the mission: "What you are doing here," she said to Ben-Gurion, "I can't do. But I might be able to do what you want to do in America. I suggest that I go." Ben-Gurion did not want to hear of it. "I need you here," he said. Golda was directing the Jewish Agency's Political Department in Jerusalem in the absence of Moshe Sharett, who was in New York conducting the campaign at the United Nations. "In that case," said Golda, "let's put it to the vote." A vote was taken, and Golda's proposal was approved, and the following day she took off for the United States. She did not even have time to go to Jerusalem to pick up warm clothes, had no luggage, and her wallet contained only $10. A few days after arriving in the United States, Golda appeared at a Jewish meeting in Chicago. She delivered an impromptu address that electrified her listeners. For two months, she traveled all over the United States, raising money for what Ben-Gurion termed "The Iron appeal". On her return, she brought about $50 million, almost twice as much as she had hoped for. Ben-Gurion told her: "One day, when history comes to be written, it shall be said that there was a Jewish woman who found the money which enabled the establishment of the state."

In the course of the winter of 1947–8, a series of military setbacks plagued the Jewish community, and morale was further undermined by the tremendous explosions set off in the courtyard of the Jewish Agency's headquarters – the symbol of Jewish power – and in downtown Jerusalem and Haifa, causing scores of deaths. During that winter the Arabs grasped that their strategy of attacking individual settlements would not work. They raided Jewish suburbs and outlying settlements, inflicting casualties on their inhabitants; but in every case, they were beaten back and forced to flee for their lives. At the same time, however, they discovered the weak point of the Jewish community: communications. In January and February, the Arab bands stepped up their attacks on convoys traveling from the center of the country to Jerusalem, the Negev, and Galilee. In March, the battle for the roads became the decisive trial of strength between the opposing armed forces.

The Jews lacked an effective response to these tactics. At first the convoys were escorted by "armed" guards – usually carrying revolvers or Stens concealed under a girl's clothes in order to evade the strict searches conducted by the British army. But when well-armed Arab bands took up positions along the roads and put up barricades, Stens were of little help. The Haganah tried various ruses: using detours and dirt-tracks, traveling at unexpected hours of the day, armor-plating vehicles, and breaking down barricades with special armored cars. But the Arabs also improved their tactics. They employed electric mines, laid ambushes, took control of large areas along the roadsides, and spread out along the route. In the course of a single week in March 1948 alone, over 100 Jewish combatants were killed in various parts of the country. Most of the supply convoys were ambushed and destroyed, leaving the Negev, Jerusalem the Etzion bloc south of Jerusalem, and part of Galilee cut off.

At the same time, the Jewish community suffered a further blow from an unexpected direction. On 13 February, Moshe Sharett sent Ben-Gurion a report filled with anxiety. "The Americans want to do an about-face" he wrote. In conversation with Jewish leaders, the secretary of state, George Marshall expressed the opinion that partition had been "an error". "Marshall is disappointed in the strength of the Haganah," Sharett continued. "He was sure we would strike at the Arabs and frighten them off." The Arabs' furious refusal to accept partition, the bitter fighting in progress in Palestine, and the United Nations' inability to impose its decisions deepened the wariness of the American policy-makers. There were also pressures – from oil interests, the Pentagon, State Department officials, and powerful British forces – urging the United States to withdraw its support of partition or at least see to it that the Negev was removed from the projected Jewish state.

February witnessed the "Prague coup", as a result of which Czechoslovakia finally joined the Soviet camp. This event jolted the leaders of the United States and increased their fears of Soviet penetration into sensitive areas under Western influence. The panic in American government circles was immediately felt in Washington's Middle East policies: the partition resolution had to be rescinded to prevent the Soviets from entering the region.

On 19 March, Warren Austin, head of the United States delegation to the United Nations, raised an unexpected proposal for the establishment of a "provisional trusteeship" for Palestine under U.N. auspices to keep the peace and give Jews and Arabs an additional opportunity to reach agreement. In effect, this suggestion implied abrogation of the partition resolution. The Jewish state was to die before it even came into being. Ben-Gurion's response was sharp:

The American statement harms the United Nations more than us. . . . [It is] capitulation to the terrorism of Arab bands armed by the British Foreign Office and allowed into the country under its protection. . . . The establishment of the Jewish state was not, in fact, subject to the United Nations' resolution of November 29 – even though that resolution was of great moral and political value – but to our ability here in this country to achieve a decision by force. By means of our own strength, the state shall arise, even now. . . . We will not consent to any trusteeship – neither provisional nor permanent, not even for the briefest period. We will no longer accept the yoke of foreign rule, whatever happens.

As usual, however, Ben-Gurion gave his true answer to America – and to the whole world – in deeds. His first act was political: the establishment of a thirteen-member provisional government known as the People's Administration. This was followed by a military move. It now became vital for the Jews to take the military initiative and put an end to the series of setbacks.

For some time, it seemed as though Ben-Gurion had missed his opportunity. The week following the American statement was the worst of the war. There were signs of disintegration and confusion in various circles of the Jewish community and its leadership. "This is the most terrible day since the fighting began," Ben-Gurion wrote Sharett on 28 March. "The convoy from the Etzion bloc is still floundering in the network of barricades, under savage Arab attack, while the British army, which set out towards it today, continues to play its diabolical game." The following day, a convoy from the coast took a beating at Bab el-Wad, a narrow pass entering the Judean Hills toward Jerusalem, and was forced to turn back. Jerusalem was cut off. Ben-Gurion decided that this was the moment to launch a decisive battle against the Arab bands.

That evening, the heads of the Haganah assembled at Ben-Gurion's home. Suddenly, Ben-Gurion asked: "Well, what about Jerusalem?" Yadin reported that a force of 500 men had been assembled – the largest force ever deployed by the Haganah. But Ben-Gurion did not rest content. "At the moment there is one burning question," he said, "and that is the battle for the road to Jerusalem . . . [yet] the manpower Yigael is preparing is insufficient. Now, that is the decisive battle. The fall of Jewish Jerusalem would be a death-blow to the Jewish community." He began to throw out figures that were truly fantastic: 2,000 men with 2,000 rifles. He imposed his will on his listeners. "This time – for the first time, perhaps – I am taking advantage of my prerogative to issue an order: in two days' time, at dawn, you must concentrate 2,000 combatants at the start-line." At the conclusion of the deliberations, it was decided that 1,500 men would take part in the operation, which was given the code name "Nahshon".

The principal question remained: Who would carry out Operation Nahshon? The high command had no forces available. Most of its combatants and weapons were dispersed all over the country. Ben-Gurion therefore decided that part of the arms and the troops were to be withdrawn from the settlements and the battlefronts and assembled into a strike-force to carry out the operation. It was a daring solution, but also a desperate gamble. Regional and unit commanders were astounded, but they obeyed orders. The units began to mass at a kibbutz in the foothills of Judea at dawn. Every moment, new problems arose. The task-force was the size of a brigade, but no one knew how to deploy a brigade, and it was decided that the units would go into action in battalion formation subject to the commander of the task-force. There were problems of logistics and supplies. Hitherto, Haganah units had operated using settlements as their starting points and as evacuation and supply bases; it was now necessary for the first time to organize an independent supply system. One commander confiscated arms from settlement armories, while trucks coming into Tel Aviv were stopped, requisitioned and loaded with supplies. These trucks were to be the first convoy to break through to Jerusalem.

Something close to a miracle occurred that night. The first plane carrying light arms from Czechoslovakia arrived with 200 rifles and 40 machine-guns, which were issued to the units that same night. A day later, there was another "miracle": the *Nora*, carrying a cargo that included 4,500 rifles, 200 machine-guns, and 5 million cartridges from Czechoslovakia, broke through the British blockade and cast anchor at Tel Aviv port. The precious cargo lay underneath tons of onions, which served as camouflage. Within two days, the ship was unloaded and the arms managed to reach some of the units taking part in Operation Nahshon.

The operation brought salvation to Jerusalem. In a series of actions, the troops took the strong-points overlooking Bab el-Wad, while a Palmach unit captured the Castel hill, which controls the road to Jerusalem. During the night of 5 April, the first convoy broke through to Jerusalem, followed five days later by a second convoy. On 13 April, a convoy of 235 vehicles reached the city. On 20 April, Ben-Gurion also drove up to Jerusalem, accompanied by several other members of the provisional government. From a military viewpoint, the final result of Operation Nahshon was quite limited: the Jerusalem road was only opened for a brief period before being blocked again. But, during the few days that it was open, Jerusalem was supplied with arms, food, and reinforcements, which enabled the city to hold out for an extended period. On other planes, however, the operation's successes were so significant that it has been referred to as "a revolution", "a turning point", and as "the most important operation in the War of Independence". It symbolized and heralded the emergence of new strategies and military patterns in Haganah operations. It was also of far-reaching political importance, since widespread fears that the Jewish powers of resistance were at breaking point were shown up as exaggerated. Operation Nahshon was the military answer of the Jewish community, to the American "trusteeship" proposal.

Operation Nahshon was also of far-reaching importance for Ben-Gurion himself. This was the first strategic decision he had personally undertaken in the course of the fighting. It was a brilliant decision, both militarily and politically. From Operation Nahshon, Ben-Gurion emerged as a true military leader. His gamble signaled the beginning of the second phase of the irregular war (which went on up to the Declaration of Independence), marked by the initiative passing to the Jews. The sporadic successes of various Arab units failed to dispel the atmosphere of collapse and defeat that overtook the Palestinian Arabs. The most prominent example of Arab demoralization was in the flight from Haifa, where the Arabs constituted a majority. Tens of thousands of Arabs fled the city after the Haganah take-over, with only a few thousand remaining. "A horrifying and fantastic sight," Ben-Gurion noted in his journal after touring the abandoned Arab quarters. "A dead city. A corpse city. How could tens of thousands of people leave their city, their homes, and their possessions in such panic with no adequate reason? What brought about this flight? Was it only an order from above? Was it fear?" On the face of it, "an order from above" was the principal reason for their flight. Haifa's Arab population fled by the thousands after the Arab Higher Committee forbade its leaders to sign a capitulation agreement with the Haganah. But there is no doubt that the panic-stricken departure of the Arabs of Haifa, Tiberias, and other areas stemmed from a different reason – Dir Yassin.

Dir Yassin, a small village on the outskirts of Jerusalem, was attacked by troops of the I.Z.L. and Lehi on 9 April, while Operation Nahshon was at its height. A vehicle equipped with a loudspeaker was brought up to broadcast warnings in Arabic and did so until it slid into a ditch. Whether the Arabs heard the warnings or not, they did not flee, and a gun battle broke out with the attacking force. The battle went on for hours, and the Jews did not find it easy to win. In the course of the fighting, but principally at its conclusion, the attackers carried out a ferocious massacre of the villagers who fell into their hands. Most of the inhabitants were killed in or around their homes; a minority – mostly women and girls – were taken by truck to the Old City. By all indications, the I.Z.L. and Lehi did not premeditate a massacre; but the heat of battle, the stubborn resistance they encountered, their anger at the deaths of their comrades-in-arms, and their hatred of the Arabs aroused a wave of mass hysteria whose toll was about 245 dead, including elderly people, women and children.

The news of the killings at Dir Yassin spread like wildfire throughout the country. Descriptions of the atrocity, somewhat spiced by Oriental fantasy, were broadcast by Arab radio stations, printed in newspapers and pamphlets, and passed on by word of mouth, sowing terror among the Arabs. Inhabitants of various Arab villages had begun to flee even before Dir Yassin; now a panic-stricken exodus erupted.

The leadership of the Jewish community was shocked by the events at Dir Yassin. The Haganah spokesman, the Jewish Agency Executive, and even the Chief Rabbinate issued horrified denunciations of the massacre. With Ben-Gurion's approval – some say, on his initiative – the Jewish Agency sent a telegram to King Abdullah expressing its profound shock at the incident. At the time, Abdullah maintained secret contacts with senior representatives of the Jewish community's leadership with the aim of partitioning the country between the sides: Abdullah would annex the territory designated for the Palestine Arab state without objections from the Jews in exchange for his undertaking not to go to war against the Jewish state. Ben-Gurion feared that Dir Yassin would fan the flames in the Arab camp, building up pressure on Abdullah to hurl the redoubtable Arab Legion into the battle. It is doubtful whether the telegram helped to calm matters down. A few days after Dir Yassin, the Arabs took terrible vengeance on the Jews, laying a murderous ambush for the convoy that regularly made its way to the Hadassah Hospital on Mount Scopus. Many of the passengers were burned alive inside the ambulances and other vehicles carrying them. Over seventy Jews, including many well-known doctors, nurses, and university employees were killed in the attack; among them was a young student who was engaged to Renana Ben-Gurion.

As the month of April sped past and the conclusion of the British Mandate approached, Ben-Gurion was confronted with two internal crises that almost sabotaged the long-awaited establishment of the state. The first grew out of a difference of opinion about the structure of the army that eventually developed into what has been dubbed "The Generals' Mutiny". It began with Ben-Gurion's decision to abolish the post of head of the national command, a position wedged in between the General Staff and the defense minister. With the establishment of national formations for the army, Ben-Gurion felt that there was no longer any need for this kind of intermediary. But his decision flared into a serious controversy because the occupant of the post, Israel Galili, was a member of a rival

political party, Mapam, which held the loyalty of many of the Haganah's
top commanders.

Since the outbreak of the world war, Faction B, which broke away from
Mapai and became Ahdut ha-Avodah in 1944, had exercised growing
influence within the Haganah command. In 1948, Ahdut ha-Avodah united
with another left-wing party, Hashomer Hatzair, to create Mapam (the
United Workers' Party), which had strong pro-Soviet leanings and opposed
Mapai on a number of fundamental political issues. The majority of the
Haganah's senior commanders were members of Mapam, so that when
Ben-Gurion decided to abolish Galili's post of head of the national com-
mand, the issue soon turned into a political timebomb.

Israel Galili was then thirty-eight years old and his advance in the
Haganah hierarchy had been swift. Since Ya'akov Dori, recently appointed
commander-in-chief, was a sickly man frequently absent from his post, the
heads of the Haganah had grown accustomed to approaching Galili and
regarded him as an authority on military matters. Galili was renowned for
his wisdom and shrewdness, and he was popular with his subordinates. It
is doubtful whether Ben-Gurion foresaw how violent a political storm his
removal would provoke.

On 26 April 1948, when Ben-Gurion notified Galili of his decision to
abolish the post of head of national command, Galili objected, and the two
men held a number of talks in an attempt to resolve the crisis. The disagreement erupted into a fully fledged crisis on 3 May, when, hoping to put an
end to the controversy at a stroke of the pen, Ben-Gurion sent a curt
official letter to the General Staff: ". . . The post of head of the national
command is hereby abolished, and Israel Galili's appointment to the post is
terminated. The staff of the security forces will henceforth receive its
instructions exclusively from the director of security [Ben-Gurion himself]
or his representative."

Galili was shocked by Ben-Gurion's unexpected step, as was the General
Staff. When the letter was read out at a meeting of the General Staff,
tempers flared up and several "department heads" (as the Haganah leaders
were called) immediately threatened to tender their collective resignations.
Shortly afterward, a delegation of department heads presented itself to
Ben-Gurion and urged him to leave Galili at his post, since he was, in
effect, acting as commander-in-chief. Ben-Gurion asked Yigael Yadin to
act as commander-in-chief until the ailing Dori returned to his post, but
Yadin refused. In the end, after considerable effort, a loose arrangement
was patched up: without consenting to an official appointment, Deputy
commander-in-chief Zvi Ayalon agreed to serve as "an address" for a few
days. But at a meeting of the People's Administration convened that day,

Ben-Gurion was bitterly attacked by the Mapam representatives, and Mapam's official, *Al Hamishmar* predicted that his acts would lead to "a personal dictatorship".

On 5 May, ten days before the Mandate was scheduled to terminate, the mutiny in the General Staff was renewed. Once again, a delegation approached Ben-Gurion and renewed pressure for Galili's reinstatement. Yadin urged that Galili act as commander-in-chief for a week, and Ben-Gurion agreed "on condition that he serves as the acting commander-in-chief, not as head of the national command – not even provisionally". Then Ben-Gurion summoned Galili and asked him to continue at his post until matters were settled. But Galili demanded his reinstatement as head of the national command, and Ben-Gurion refused.

The crisis was at its peak. On 6 May Galili sent a long letter to the members of the Jewish Agency Executive describing his dismissal and the abolition of his post. That same day, at noon, the heads of the Haganah mutinied and presented Ben-Gurion with an ultimatum: "The heads of departments consider it essential to restore [Israel Galili] to his post until final arrangements are made. If this matter is not settled within the next 12 hours, the heads of departments will cease to consider themselves responsible for the conduct of affairs." This was clearly an attempt to subject the civilian authorities to a military *diktat*.

One hour after receiving the letter, Ben-Gurion summoned the five department heads for a talk. He stood firm in the face of the threats of collective resignation and adamantly refused to reinstate Galili as head of the national command. But, intent on appeasing the heads of the General Staff, he undertook a tactical withdrawal, promising that Galili would be restored to the General Staff, without his duties being specified. The department heads returned to their posts, and the next day, Galili agreed to Ben-Gurion's offer. Ben-Gurion capitulated on one matter: he restored Galili to a central position in the Haganah command. But he did not renew the post of head of national command and did not specify Galili's authority. With this, the first phase of the confrontation came to its conclusion.

Ben-Gurion consented to a truce in his struggle against Galili for by then far more fateful questions stood on the agenda: would the Jewish community be able to withstand the Arab armies that were threatening to invade Palestine? Would it be able to withstand American pressure to refrain from proclaiming its independence? Would the state of Israel arise or not?

As the final day of the British Mandate approached, there were increasing doubts among the leaders of the Jewish community about whether to proclaim independence. In Mapai itself, opinions were divided. Most of the rank-and-file members unhesitatingly stood behind Ben-Gurion, who was working for an immediate proclamation of independence. But several of the party's principal leaders hesitated or even opposed that policy. Even Moshe Sharett was undecided. Of the four Mapai representatives in the provisional government, Ben-Gurion was the sole activist.

On 11 May 1948, Mapai's Central Committee convened to deliberate the question. At the first session, Ben-Gurion delivered a fiery address, prophesying "we shall stand every test". After he finished, while other members had taken the floor, Golda Meir entered the hall. Her appearance caused Ben-Gurion considerable excitement, for he knew that she had just returned from a clandestine journey to Amman, where she met King Abdullah in a last-minute attempt to reach a non-aggression pact with him.

This was not Golda's first meeting with the king. In November 1947, she met him secretly; and Abdullah told her that he would not take part in any Arab attack against the Jews and would always remain their friend. In fact, once Mrs Meir signaled the king that the Jews would not interfere with his annexation of territory delineated for the Arab state of Palestine, the talks ended with an informal non-aggression pact. But during the spring of 1948, there were clear signs that Abdullah was changing his policy. The Transjordanian king controled the strongest Arab army in the Middle East – the Arab Legion – and the other Arab states exerted powerful pressure upon him to join the battle. Early in May 1948, Ben-Gurion had come to the conclusion that the Jewish state would be attacked from all sides as soon as it was established. The following days bore out his pessimistic predictions. Early in May, the Egyptian government unexpectedly decided to join in the invasion of Palestine. In Damascus, officers from several Arab armies prepared a coordinated invasion plan. In the meantime a French source reported that "the Anglo-Transjordanian treaty contains a secret article [promising] the crown of Palestine to Abdullah; and that Saudi Arabia, Syria and Egypt have decided: (1) Abdullah was to enter [Palestine] to fight the Jews. (2) They would assassinate him. (3) They would set up a mufti government in Palestine." Against this background, it had been decided that Mrs Meir should again meet Abdullah.

At their meeting Abdullah raised a new proposal to avoid war: Palestine would not be partitioned, and the Jews would gain autonomy in part of the country. Within a year, the country was to be united with Transjordan and there would be a joint parliament in which the Jews had 50 per cent of the members. Golda rejected the proposal outright. "There will be a war," she said, "and we will win. But we can meet again after the war, and after there is a Jewish state." She returned to Tel Aviv while the Mapai Central Committee meeting was in progress and sent a brief note to Ben-Gurion, who had been waiting impatiently for her arrival: "We met in friendship.

He is very concerned, and he looks terrible. He did not deny that we had talked and [reached] an understanding regarding a desirable settlement, namely that he would take the Arab portion, but now he is only one of five." Ben-Gurion immediately left the Central Committee meeting for Haganah headquarters and ordered his commanders to make plans for a battle against an all-out Arab invasion.

Golda's somber tidings were not the only bad news to descend on Ben-Gurion that turbulent day. All afternoon and evening, he awaited the arrival of Moshe Sharett, on his way from Washington after an important talk with the American secretary of state, George Marshall. Partial reports on their conversation did not augur well. Marshall had received Sharett on 8 May 1948, after sharp U.S. warnings to the Jews to postpone the proclamation of their state and to consent to a truce. Sharett told Marshall that there was little chance of the Jewish Agency consenting to a cease-fire, adding that there was considerable probability of "a deal between Abdullah and the Jewish Agency". But there was another, deeper reason for shunning Marshall's suggestion: "We will be held to blame by Jewish history if we consent to any postponement in proclaiming our state without the certainty that the state will indeed be proclaimed after the postponement," Sharett told him. "The United States government voted for us, and we shall never forget it. But we have fought our war alone, without any help. The United States has deprived us of arms, military instruction, and even steel plating to armor plate our civilian buses. Now we are not asking for help. We are asking [you] to refrain from intervening."

Marshall responded with a warning: "It's not up to me to advise you what to do. But as a military man, I want to tell you: don't rely on your military advisers. They're intoxicated with success after their victories. What happens if there is a protracted invasion? Are you considering how that will weaken you? . . . If you turn out to be right, and you proclaim your Jewish state, I shall be happy. But it's a very grave responsibility."

Sharett took his leave of Marshall, saying "We attach great importance to [your] views, and if [you] hear that we have decided otherwise, [you] should know that we have not done so out of disregard for [your] counsel."

Sharett's proud and forceful statements were a cover for a profound inner disquiet and grave uncertainties. David Hacohen, who was waiting for Sharett at a New York airport, later recalled: "He drew me into a telephone booth and said: 'Marshall said that he was talking to me as a general, as a military man. We'll be annihilated!' I'm not saying that Moshe told me we should not proclaim the state. But he was terribly shaken . . ." Then Weizmann contacted Sharett with words of encouragement: "Don't let them discourage you. Either the state is established now or, God forbid, it will never be established!"

Heavy hearted, Sharett flew back home. During his protracted journey, he appears to have formulated his view: he would recommend postponing the proclamation of the state, in accordance with Marshall's proposals. Late on the night of 11 May he arrived at Ben-Gurion's home. Ben-Gurion related:

Moshe came into my room and gave me a detailed report on his talk with Marshall. He told me of his warnings that we would be annihilated and his suggestion that we postpone the proclamation of the state. At the end of our talk, he added four words: "I think he's right." I stood up and locked the door. And then I said to him: "Moshe! I ask you to give a full and precise report of your conversation with Marshall [to the Mapai Central Committee] exactly as you reported to me. But you're not going out of here before you promise me one thing. Those last four words you said ['I think he's right!'], you won't say them at the Central Committee!" Moshe agreed.

That evening, a large crowd congregated at the hall in which the Mapai Central Committee met. The members of Mapai, who respected Sharett's sagacity, waited expectantly to hear his words. They had heard rumors of his doubts in view of the enormous pressures to which he had been subjected in the United States. When Sharett finally appeared, he was welcomed with great excitement. And when he stood up to address the meeting, he kept his promise to Ben-Gurion. "Not only did he keep his promise," said Ben-Gurion, "he delivered an address strongly in favor of the establishment of the state." The fact is that Sharett's address was balanced. First he depicted the very real danger that the United States would not come to the aid of the Jewish state if the Arab invasion did take place. But at a certain point, he did a turnabout, proclaiming, "The risk involved in postponing the proclamation of the state, or of independence, is graver than the risk in taking the step. . . . The future we face is very harsh and grave, but it appears that we have no choice but to march forward."

His words provoked astonishment. The opponents of an immediate proclamation had suddenly been deprived of the banner around which they hoped to rally. The debate on the issue, which went on into the night, was agitated and fierce but there was a clear majority in favor of establishing the state. The meeting ended with the election of a seven-member committee to formulate the Central Committee's views. Five of the committee's members were in favor of an immediate proclamation of the state; two others were outspoken opponents. It was decided to reconvene the Central Committee the following evening.

May 12 was a fateful day. At dawn the Arab Legion launched its attack.

Even though the Mandate had not yet ended and the British army was still in the country, the beleaguered Etzion bloc of settlements was subjected to an onslaught by hundreds of Legionaries with armored support, backed up by thousands of armed villagers. From afar, the leaders of the Jewish community watched helplessly as the handful of Jewish defenders put up their last fight. Ben-Gurion spent most of the day at a meeting of the People's Administration, which sat for eleven hours discussing the fateful decisions that had to be made. That session was the moment of truth for the Jewish community. Here and now, it was necessary to decide on the establishment of the Jewish state.

After Golda Meir reported on her talks with Abdullah, Moshe Sharett described the American proposal regarding a cease-fire. Several of those present were inclined to accept the proposal; consequently, they asked that before a vote was taken, a report be delivered on the military situation. Ben-Gurion summoned Yadin and Galili. Yadin described the military situation in somber colors, speaking of the dangers of invasion and of the changes likely to occur with the entry of foreign forces. "To put it cautiously," he said in closing, "I would say that at this moment our chances are very balanced. To be more frank, I would say that they [the Arabs] have a considerable advantage." Israel Galili also pointed out the enemy's superiority in heavy armaments. "If the confrontation occurs during the coming week, the situation will be very grave." At the same time, he pointed out that the situation was likely to change with the arrival of the arms which had been purchased abroad.

The candid but grave statements of the two military experts had a harsh impact on the meeting. When Ben-Gurion's turn came to address the meeting, he had to make a supreme effort to instill confidence and faith in those members overcome by doubts. Step by step, he led his listeners to the single inevitable conclusion:

... If we are left with no more than the arms we possess now, our situation will be very perilous. But it can be assumed that from this aspect our situation will improve. ... If we manage to bring in [to the country] not even everything we have, but, let us say, 15,000 rifles and a few million cartridges (we have more than that somewhere) and the cannon and the bazookas and the war planes fitted with cannon and machine-guns and bombs (and all that is stored away somewhere) our situation at the beginning of the fighting would be completely different. We would be able to land a powerful blow to the Arabs at the opening of their invasion and undermine their morale.

As night fell, an incessant flow of reports poured in from the battlefronts: clashes on the road to Jerusalem; bitter tidings from the Etzion bloc, negotiations for surrender in Jaffa. The time had come to reach a decision.

The issue put to the vote was whether to accept or reject the United States' proposal for a cease-fire. Consenting to a cease-fire meant postponement of the proclamation of the state. Six members voted against the cease-fire and in favor of proclaiming the state immediately, including Ben-Gurion and Sharett. Four members voted to accept the American proposal and postpone independence, including two leading Mapai members. It was decided that the Jewish state would be established on 14 May.

This decision was followed by another debate on the decisive issue of whether the Proclamation of Independence should specify the boundaries of the state. Ben-Gurion certainly did not want to issue a specific declaration that would curtail his aspirations to extend the boundaries of the state. He proceeded to reveal some of his ideas to his colleagues: "If the U.N. does not come into account in this matter and they [the Arab states] make war against us and we defeat them . . . why should we bind ourselves?" By a single vote, five to four, his view was adopted: the state's boundaries would not be mentioned in the Proclamation of Independence.

That evening, the Mapai Central Committee convened for a third time and approved the text of the proclamation presented by the formulation committee. The largest party within the Jewish community decided to advise the People's Administration "immediately to proclaim the termination of the Mandate and the establishment of the Jewish state and its provisional government". "Under existing circumstances," Yigael Yadin was to comment later, "the decision on the proclamation was solely due to David Ben-Gurion. In its significance and its impact, that decision was comparable to thousands of [military] operations."

On 13 May, the Jewish community was highly excited as rumors spread about the imminent Proclamation of Independence. But the excitement and jubilation were mixed with growing apprehension in view of the reports of the battle at the Etzion bloc, which housed 550 people. At 4.30 p.m. news arrived of the fall of Kfar Etzion. After a brief consultation, Ben-Gurion, Levi Eshkol, and Galili decided to send a telegram to the defenders of the other settlements in the bloc saying that if they were unable to keep on fighting, they should destroy their weapons and hoist the white flag. The decision was painful and depressing. Bad news also came in from the Negev: the Egyptians had attacked Kfar Darom in great force. The atmosphere at the General Staff was gloomy. A last-minute appeal arrived from Abdullah, who repeated his proposals to Golda Meir, but his suggestion was rejected.

That evening, the People's Administration held its final meeting to decide on the text of the Proclamation of Independence. A committee headed by Moshe Sharett presented to the People's Administration a draft proposal on which Sharett himself had done most of the work. The wording of the declaration was borrowed from that of the Mandate; "In as much as . . ." its style was rather legalistic and flowery; and it was very long. It also made mention of the United Nations partition plan. Ben-Gurion objected to various rhetorical expressions and any specific reference to the partition plan. That evening, he sat down in his study and rewrote the declaration. Under his hand, the text took on a completely different character: more vigorous, firm, and bold. He trimmed the text of superficial flourishes, shortened it, and deleted any reference to the partition plan. At two o'clock in the morning, Ben-Gurion's aides brought in a telegram with the news that "hoisting the white flag at Kfar Etzion led to the defenders being massacred by the Arabs".

That night, Ben-Gurion slept about two hours. He rose at seven o'clock, as was his habit, and drank a cup of black coffee while seated at the kitchen table and studying papers and messages. It was his routine way of starting the day. Nothing in his behavior indicated any particular excitement. Ben-Gurion was already at his office when just after eight he heard the drone of a plane in the sky. This was the light plane carrying the British High Commissioner, General Cunningham to Haifa, where he was to board H.M.S. *Euryalus* and wait in coastal waters till the termination of the Mandate. At midnight, on the night of 14–15 May, the British Mandate over Palestine would come to an end. Because of the sanctity of the Sabbath, it was essential to issue the Proclamation of Independence before darkness fell.

Secretaries, stenographers and officials were engaged in frantic preparations for the proclamation. Eminent persons from all sections of the population had been invited to the ceremony, due to be held at four o'clock that afternoon at the Tel Aviv Museum. Flags and furnishings were hurriedly brought to the hall. Ben-Gurion put on a white shirt, a dark suit, and a tie, and at four o'clock his black car halted at the steps leading to the museum entrance. Even though the site of the ceremony had been kept a strict secret, the street was crowded, and there was a throng of journalists and photographers present. In some mysterious fashion, thousands of Tel Aviv citizens had found out where the ceremony was to be held, and they hurried to be present – even if at a distance – at the event that would make them into a free people.

As Ben-Gurion and Paula got out of the car, a policeman posted on the pavement saluted. Momentarily, Ben-Gurion froze, drew himself up stiffly, and returned the salute proudly and vigorously. Then, at a run, he climbed the steps to the museum's main entrance. At precisely four o'clock, he struck the table with his gavel. The audience arose and spontaneously burst into *Hatikva*, the anthem of the Zionist movement. Ben-Gurion picked up two typewritten pages of the text of the Proclamation of Independence and began to read it out.

In clear, powerful words, the text described the exile of the Jewish people, its yearnings to return to its homeland, the emergence of the Zionist movement, the "pioneers, immigrants and defenders" who came to the Land of Israel. The proclamation referred to the Balfour Declaration, depicted the Holocaust and the war which the Jews had waged against the Nazis. It was only as Ben-Gurion read the proclamation that the Jews of the Land of Israel learned the name of their new country: the State of Israel.

When Ben-Gurion ended, the audience rose to its feet and broke into cheers. The excitement spread outside the hall. Ben-Gurion's voice – gruff and familiar – emerged from radio receivers all over the country. An entire people drank his words in thirstily. Thousands of listeners heard the proud sentences and the tidings which bore intoxicating hopes and as horrifying dangers. Not only sentimentalists felt a lump in their throats, and tears in their eyes.

Thirty-seven minutes after his entry, Ben-Gurion struck the table with his gavel. "The State of Israel has arisen!" he called. "This meeting is now closed." In his diary, he jotted: "At four the Proclamation of Independence. Throughout the country, there is profound joy and jubilation, and once again, as on 29 November I feel like the bereaved among the rejoicers."

10

The Fight for Survival

Was Israel a reality? On 14 May the armies of Lebanon, Syria, Iraq, Transjordan, and Egypt poured into Palestine – and the young state had yet to establish a national army. The Arab Legion commanders' operation forecasts predicted that the Jewish state would fall within a few days.

That night, Ben-Gurion was woken twice. At 1 a.m. the head of the Haganah's Communications Department came to inform him that President Truman had decided to extend *de facto* recognition to the State of Israel. (Two days later, the Soviet Union accorded Israel *de jure* recognition.) At 4.30 a.m. he again entered the Old Man's bedroom to report that Israeli representatives in the United States urged Ben-Gurion to address the people of the United States in a direct radio broadcast. Ben-Gurion hurriedly dressed, and as dawn was breaking he was driven to the Haganah radio station. He began to speak as soon as the link-up was made, and suddenly the roar of engines was heard, followed by powerful explosions. At first light, Egyptian planes swooped down on Tel Aviv and dropped their bombs on the nearby Dov Airfield. Speaking like a seasoned radio commentator, Ben-Gurion informed his listeners that at that very moment enemy planes were bombing Tel Aviv. When he finished the broadcast, he returned home unescorted in an open jeep. "From all the houses, people in pajamas and nightgowns were gazing out, but there were no signs of panic. I felt that these people would stand their ground."

The first days of the state's existence were filled with horror. In the north, there were bloody battles against the Syrians and the Lebanese; in Jerusalem, the Arab Legion had reversed earlier Jewish gains and cut the route to Mount Scopus; Egyptian forces captured a strategically located police fortress in the northern Negev. The enemy was in control in the air, and a heavy bombing raid on Tel Aviv's central bus station left forty-two dead. The planes that Ehud Avriel had bought in Czechoslovakia had yet to arrive, and the arms shipments were still in European warehouses or on board ships at sea. Ben-Gurion's immediate aim was therefore to gain time. He knew that each additional day brought further prospects of the long-awaited arms arriving and rejected all appeals to evacuate embattled settlements.

This strategy involved heavy casualties. On 19 May, a day after a heavy Syrian attack was launched, a delegation from the Jordan Valley settlements came to request help from Ben-Gurion. Yosef Baratz, one of Ben-Gurion's old friends, demanded cannon, planes, and reinforcements. "There aren't any," Ben-Gurion replied. "There aren't enough cannon. There aren't enough planes. There is a shortage of people on all fronts. The whole country is a battlefield. We are unable to send reinforcements." On hearing this, one of the men in the delegation burst into tears: "Ben-Gurion, are you saying that we are going to abandon the Jordan Valley?" Years later, Ben-Gurion told a friend: "You cannot imagine what I felt seeing him cry. He stood before me, a sturdy, grown man, sobbing like a child. And there was nothing I could promise."

Concealing his own feelings, Ben-Gurion sent his three friends to Yadin. The chief of operations told Baratz, "We know the situation quite well. There is no solution other than to let the Arabs approach to within twenty or thirty yards of the gateway and then to fight . . . against their armor." Yadin proposed that they attack the tanks with Molotov cocktails. Choking down his tears, Baratz replied: "Yigael, is it feasible to take such risks and to allow them to reach the gateway of [Kibbutz] Degania?"

"Yes," said Yadin. "There's no alternative. Admittedly, it's a very risky method, but it's the only way."

But Yadin nonetheless went to see Ben-Gurion. Four 65-millimeter mountain cannon, without sights, had just arrived in the country. By virtue of their antiquity, they were referred to as "Napoleonchiks". Yadin urged Ben-Gurion to send them to the Jordan Valley settlements. Ben-Gurion refused, since he wanted them for the battle to open up the Jerusalem road. The two men quarrelled fiercely; in the end, they compromised. Ben-Gurion consented to send the cannon to the Jordan Valley for twenty-four hours; after that, they were to be transferred to the central front. In a heroic battle at the gateway to Kibbutz Degania, the defenders halted the enemy armor and repulsed the attack. The cannon also went into action, and the panic-stricken Syrians hastily withdrew. With some satisfaction, Ben-Gurion noted in his diary: "The four guns sent to the Jordan Valley have improved morale in our settlements." But the objective situation was as grim as before.

The worst day of all was 22 May. From the south, an Egyptian armored column lunged towards Tel Aviv. The Egyptians also entered Beersheba and attacked a number of settlements to the north. One after another, the Arab Legion captured the Jewish quarters at the edge of Jerusalem and was now threatening the entire Jewish section, bombarding it incessantly. Legion units also held the Latrun police fortress, which controlled the road to Jerusalem. In the center of the country, there was concern that the Iraqi expeditionary force, together with the Legion, would break through the Jewish defense lines and reach the sea, thereby cutting the state in two.

Ben-Gurion spent that entire night in feverish consultations with members of the General Staff. "There was nothing left to fight with," a Mapai leader later related. "That Saturday night was the most critical moment . . . Ben-Gurion stalked about like a wounded lion. All the craftsmen were mobilized into battalions to defend Tel Aviv. That evening, one of the heads of the staff said to me: 'Another seventy-two hours and it will all be over!'" But after that sleepless night, matters improved slightly. In Jerusalem, the Legion's attack was halted; the Egyptians failed to advance any further, despite the heavy pressure they were exerting.

Another day had passed, and despite the bitter tidings from the battle-fronts, Ben-Gurion could see a spark of hope. The first German-made Messerschmitts arrived from Czechoslovakia, and under a cloak of complete secrecy five Czech technicians arrived and began to assemble the planes. Jewish planes finally launched their first bombing sorties in the south, on the Jerusalem front, and in other sectors. In addition, a ship was approaching with 5,000 rifles and 45 cannon aboard. "That will be the beginning of the turning point!" Ben-Gurion wrote jubilantly.

By 24 May, Ben-Gurion felt sufficiently confident to present his strategic aims to the General Staff:

> I proposed that, as soon as we received the equipment on the ship, we should prepare to go over to the offensive with the aim of smashing Lebanon, Trans-jordan and Syria. We have to hold on in the Negev. The plan for this week: the liberation of Jerusalem and its environs. The battle for Jerusalem is the most important, both morally and politically – and, to a large extent, militarily too. . . . The weak point in the Arab coalition is Lebanon [for] the Moslem regime is artificial and easy to undermine. A Christian state should be established, with its southern border on the Litani River. We will make an alliance with it. When we smash the [Arab] Legion's strength and bomb Amman, we will eliminate Transjordan, too, and then Syria will fall. If Egypt still dares to fight on, we shall bomb Port Said, Alexandria, and Cairo.

These astonishing statements disclosed Ben-Gurion's private train of thought. Perhaps his last sentence was the most revealing: "And in this fashion, we will end the war and settle our forefathers' accounts with Egypt, Assyria, and Aram." Ben-Gurion regarded history as a living entity; to him, nations were collective entities that acted, thought, and remembered in terms of hundreds and thousands of years. The kingdom of Israel had been cut short long ago. Now that it had risen again, it found itself facing the same enemies. Their states bore different names and their peoples had changed beyond recognition; but in the final analysis, they were the same empires with which "our forefathers" had accounts, and now was the time to settle them.

In strategic terms, Ben-Gurion believed the most dangerous enemy was the Arab Legion and that an Israeli victory was possible only if the Legion were eliminated. After Abdullah's army was overcome, the other enemy forces would collapse. He had a further reason for directing the main thrust at the Legion, and that was Jerusalem. After the onslaught by the Arab armies, Ben-Gurion told a Cabinet meeting that "the 29 November resolution has died". If the partition boundaries were dead and the internationalization of Jerusalem had become a fading dream, Jerusalem had to become part of the Jewish state. But that would only be possible if the Arab Legion was defeated, since King Abdullah likewise regarded Jerusalem as his principal objective. Ben-Gurion regarded Jerusalem as the symbol of Jewish sovereignty and eternity. He even believed that if the city fell, the whole state might go under.

For the most part, the General Staff did not share his views. "Ben Gurion did not know Jerusalem's powers of resistance," contended Yadin, who was the Old Man's principal opponent. "He exaggerated in his fear that the city would fall within two or three days. I thought that the Egyptians were the most dangerous enemy, and I gave priority to the south."

On 22 May, the situation in Jerusalem deteriorated dramatically. A telegram notified Ben-Gurion that the Legion was capturing village after village in the vicinity. Ben-Gurion was horrified. "I demanded that, without delay, a military column be sent to Jerusalem, with all the units that are trained and armed . . . The units are to receive all the weapons available. The armored cars are to be transferred immediately. They are to take . . . all the surrounding villages and break through to Jerusalem."

A stormy argument broke out between Ben-Gurion and Yadin. An immediate attack on the Jerusalem road required a frontal assault on the Latrun police fortress, which controlled the route. The Legion had occupied this fortress with strong and well-trained forces, backed by armor and artillery. The Haganah, on the other hand, had no forces available. The only force not in action at that moment was the newly formed 7th Brigade. At the last moment, Ben-Gurion personally reinforced the brigade with hundreds of untrained recruits, immigrants just off the ships. They had never held a rifle in their lives; they spoke a motley of languages and did not understand Hebrew. Frantically, their officers tried to give them basic weapon training, and the recruits parroted a number of basic Hebrew commands. In Yadin's view, the 7th Brigade had yet to become a combat unit, but Ben-Gurion did not take his objections into account. On the evening of 22 May, he called an urgent staff meeting. When he found out that the 7th Brigade's 3,000 men had been confined to their camp for three days, Ben-Gurion erupted in anger: "Three thousand soldiers are idle in their camps; nine thousand 'soldier days' have already been wasted at a time when Jerusalem can fall at any moment!"

Ben-Gurion proposed that the operation to open the road to Jerusalem be undertaken by the 7th Brigade, reinforced by a battalion from the Alexandroni Brigade. The commander of Alexandroni expressed his fear that this would weaken his forces, which faced the Iraqi army; the Iraqis might break through and cut the link between Tel Aviv and Haifa. But Ben-Gurion was not deterred: "I'm prepared to take responsibility for the risk," he said.

The attack was scheduled for the night of 23 May. However, in the course of the day, it transpired that the brigade was not yet prepared, and it was impossible to attack that night. With great effort, Yadin managed to persuade Ben-Gurion to postpone the operation by twenty-four hours. Ben-Gurion was experiencing growing tension. Talks had already commenced about a truce, and if fighting were halted while the Jerusalem road was in the Legion's hands, the city would remain cut off and its population's morale could break. From Jerusalem itself, the news was grave. The Legion's shells were landing everywhere, and food and water were being rationed out in tiny amounts. The Jewish Quarter of the Old City, which had been cut off from the rest of the Jewish neighborhoods, was sending out desperate appeals for help. All kinds of defeatists were beginning to talk of "compromise", of "saving human life", and various other terms that signified one thing: capitulation.

On the eve of the operation, Yadin flew to the Kibbutz where the assault forces were massing. His impression was that the brigade was in a state of chaos. Together with its officers, he came to the conclusion that it was essential to postpone the attack for a few days. He returned to Tel Aviv and tried to convince Ben-Gurion that the operation had to be put off. Ben-Gurion's response was laconic: "Attack, whatever the cost."

The Jerusalem road winds through a broad valley at the foot of the Latrun heights, which are dominated by the police fortress. Nearby is the picturesque Trappist monastery surrounded by vineyards. The view from the heights was of an open field covered with ripening corn; and it was from there that the Arab Legion observed the assault column ponderously making its way toward its objective as dawn broke on 25 May. The Legion's artillery and machine-guns poured a murderous barrage at the attackers, who suffered heavy losses. Many of the untrained men lost their heads, withdrew and began to flee. The day began with a burning easterly wind, and as the fleeing soldiers stumbled through the wheat field, they were harassed by thirst and swarms of tiny flies. From the hillsides came crowds of Arab villagers armed with rifles and daggers, eager to kill the wounded soldiers. With great difficulty, some of the officers managed to get themselves organized enough to cover the retreat of their troops. The assault ended in disaster, and the casualties numbered nearly 200. The 7th Brigade was badly mauled in its baptism of fire, and the long convoy of trucks standing by to carry provisions to Jerusalem remained where it was.

That night, Ben-Gurion was eager to find out when it would be possible to mount another attack on Latrun. Like a bulldog, he stuck to his resolve to attack Latrun as many times as necessary until the road to Jerusalem could be opened. He even sent the newly assembled Messerschmitts to bomb Latrun and the neighboring Arab village of Emaus. Shocking news arrived from Jerusalem: the Old City's Jewish Quarter had fallen to the Legion and its defenders had been taken captive. In the meantime, the U.N. was pressing for a truce. On 30 May, Ben-Gurion again hurled his army against Latrun – and again, he failed.

After the battle, Mickey Marcus, the veteran American colonel who had just assumed command of the Jerusalem front, sent a telegram to Yadin: "I was there and I saw the battle. The plan was good. The artillery was good. The armor was excellent. The infantry was disgraceful."

But Ben-Gurion did not give up. On 9 June, he hurled in two additional brigades, with Yigal Allon commanding the operation. At operation headquarters was Yitzhak Rabin, the commander of one of the reinforcement brigades. It was a last attempt to capture Latrun before the month-long truce went into effect. But this attack also ran aground. The Latrun fortress remains intact, as a reminder of the army's most painful setback in the War of Independence.

Nevertheless, Jerusalem was saved. Three members of the Palmach had discovered a hill route that by-passed Latrun, running exclusively through Israeli-controlled territory. When Ben-Gurion learned of this on 2 June, he immediately gave orders to pave a road for food convoys to Jerusalem. Feverish work commenced, and part of the route was made fit for vehicles; but one section, where there was a 375-foot climb up the sharp slopes of a rocky hillside, could not be paved. Hundreds of Tel Aviv civilians were mobilized and put to work every night, carrying vital equipment and supplies along the new route. Convoys of mules and jeeps were also organized. Finally, work began on paving a road. By the time the truce was declared, Jerusalem was no longer cut off.

On 11 June 1948, the Jews and Arabs laid down their arms for four weeks, and the "peace emissary" appointed by the Security Council, the Swedish Count Folke Bernadotte, reached the country and immediately began to work for a prolonged truce between the warring sides. The commander of the northern front described the onset of the truce as "manna from heaven". The existence of Israel was no longer in danger. But just as the tortuous tension lifted for a while, the state faced its gravest test – not in war against the Arabs, but in a sudden outbreak of fighting among the Jews.

"Altalena", the literary pseudonym of Vladimir Jabotinsky, was the name given to an old U.S. Navy landing vessel purchased by the National Liberation Committee (the I.Z.L.'s supporters in the United States). The day after the proclamation of the state, the I.Z.L.'s commander-in-chief, Menahem Begin, approached Ben-Gurion's aides and offered to sell the vessel to the government and use the proceeds to buy arms. But the men in charge of weapons purchases rejected the proposal. So the I.Z.L. command decided to fill the ship with about 1,000 immigrants and a large amount of arms and sail it to the Israeli coast. According to I.Z.L. sources, the arms loaded on the ship in southern France included 5,000 rifles, 3,000 bombs, 3 million cartridges, hundreds of tons of explosives, 250 machine-guns, mortars, bazookas, and other light arms. About 850 immigrants also embarked on the ship, which set sail on 11 June.

The operation was in open defiance of the laws of the land and a flagrant violation of I.Z.L. undertakings, for on 1 June, Begin had signed an agreement with the provisional government, requiring I.Z.L. members to join the Israel Defense Forces in battalion formations and take an oath of loyalty. Their arms and other military equipment were to be handed over to the army high command, and the I.Z.L. and its separate command were to terminate their activities in the State of Israel and in the areas of jurisdiction of the Israeli government (a provisional I.Z.L. command – to operate for one month at most – would supervise the battalions' enlistment in the army). The I.Z.L. also undertook to cease its arms-purchasing activities abroad.

In the meantime, the first truce had been proclaimed, and on the night of 15–16 June, Menahem Begin met with representatives of the Defense Ministry. The following morning, Levi Eshkol and Israel Galili reported to Ben-Gurion on the ship, which was due to arrive in a day or two. To Ben-Gurion, it was self-evident that the arms on the *Altalena* would immediately be delivered to the army, and he turned his attention to finding a way for the ship to be unloaded without arousing the suspicions of the U.N. observers. That same day, however, Begin asked that 20 per cent of the arms be set aside for I.Z.L. forces in Jerusalem. The city had yet to be included in the Jewish state and held the status of a *corpus separatum*, which was to come under international rule. Since Israeli sovereignty did not extend to Jerusalem, the I.Z.L. and Lehi continued to operate there independently. In view of this legal situation, the 1 June agreement did not apply to Jerusalem, and Galili informed Begin that he accepted the proposal.

Then, however, Begin came up with a new proposal: the remaining 80 per cent of the weapons should be used, first of all, to arm the I.Z.L. units that had joined the Israel Defense Forces; only what remained would then be handed over to the army. Galili adamantly rejected this idea, but he realized that the I.Z.L. people "are now inclined to independent action". That same night, Galili again contacted Begin, who informed him that the I.Z.L. intended to store the arms in its own armories. The arms would be issued to the I.Z.L. units in the army at a special ceremony to be attended by a member of the I.Z.L. provisional command. This conversation marked the breakdown of the agreement between the I.Z.L. and the Defense Ministry.

On Saturday, 19 June Galili reported on the latest talk with Begin. He contended that "a new and dangerous situation has arisen: a demand for a kind of private army, with private weapons, for certain units in the army". Ben-Gurion decided to bring the matter before the Cabinet, which met on 20 June in an atmosphere of suspicion and anxiety. Alarming information was pouring in: the *Altalena* was rapidly approaching the Israeli coast, while hundreds of soldiers – members of the I.Z.L. – had deserted their units and were heading for the coast to help unload the ship. The crowd waiting on the shore near the settlement of Kfar Vitkin was headed by Menahem Begin and his colleagues from the I.Z.L. command. Political leaders, heads of the labor parties, and the army high command all reverted to their age-old fear that the "dissidents" would stage an armed revolt to seize power or establish a separate Jewish state in Jerusalem and Judea. "There are not going to be two states," Ben-Gurion declared at the Cabinet meeting, "and there are not going to be two armies. And Mister Begin will not do whatever he feels like. We must decide whether to hand over power to Begin or to tell him to cease his separatist activities. If he does not give in, we shall open fire!"

Israel Galili and Yigael Yadin were summoned to the Cabinet meeting, and Galili reported that the ship was due to arrive at nine o'clock that evening. Yadin announced that 600 men were in the area and a further two battalions could be brought up. At this point, one of the ministers advanced a proposal consisting of a single sentence: "The government charges the defense minister with taking action in accordance with the laws of the land."

"Taking action means shooting," declared Ben-Gurion.

Yet the proposal was adopted unanimously. The Cabinet ordered the General Staff to assemble a force to take counter-action. "The officer in charge should endeavor to avoid the use of force, but if his orders are not obeyed, force will be employed." Ben-Gurion and his aides immediately drove to the General Staff headquarters to work out the details of the operation. Ben-Gurion was "very excited". He said to Yadin: "If these people [the members of the Cabinet] have decided on it, we must act quickly." Ben-Gurion himself was obviously surprised by the Cabinet decision. By this time, the *Altalena* had cast anchor off Kfar Vitkin. Hundreds of people waiting on the beach welcomed her with great enthusiasm. Using improvised means, they began to unload the arms and ammunition.

That night, Galili and Yadin reached the headquarters of the Alexandroni Brigade, not far from Kfar Vitkin. The brigade commander immediately ordered some of his units to surround the area where the *Altalena* lay at anchor. Pinhas Vazeh, who accompanied Yadin and Galili, set off for the beach to talk to Begin. I.Z.L. men placed him in a jeep and drove him to the beach. On arrival, he told the I.Z.L. leaders he had come to invite Begin to meet Israel Galili. But Begin said he was not prepared to go to Galili. "If Galili really wishes to meet Begin, let him come here. Begin is prepared to meet him here on the beach." Vazeh returned to report to his superiors. Since the I.Z.L. leaders refused to meet the government representatives, it was decided to send an ultimatum. At 1.15 a.m. on 21 June, the commander of the Alexandroni Brigade sent the following message to Menahem Begin:

... I have been ordered to confiscate the arms and war material that have reached the coast of the State of Israel ... on behalf of the government of Israel. You are requested to fulfill this order immediately. If you do not consent ... I shall immediately employ all the means at my disposal to implement this order ... I must inform you that the whole area is surrounded by fully armed military units and armor, and the ways are blocked. ... You are hereby given a ten-minute delay for your reply.

Begin rejected the ultimatum, demanding that the brigade commander come to him under a white flag. The commander refused. Israel Galili, who was in no haste to carry out the ultimatum's threat, reported to Ben-Gurion. The prime minister replied with a most forceful message: "This time, it's impossible to compromise. Either they accept *orders* and carry them out, or [we] shoot. I am opposed to any negotiations with them and to any *agreement*. The time for agreements has passed . . . If force is available, force must be employed without hesitation." In his own handwriting, Ben-Gurion added: "*Immediately!*"

The situation was turning into a crisis at Kfar Vitkin and on a country-wide scale. Officers and men with I.Z.L. affiliations deserted the Alexandroni Brigade in an attempt to join their encircled comrades on the beach. From the sea, two ships of the Israeli navy and several motorboats closed in on the *Altalena*. In the course of the morning, the ship was discovered by U.N. observers, but I.Z.L. soldiers prevented them from approaching the beach and continued unloading the vessel. The same morning, the provisional government issued a statement stressing the firm resolve of the government and the army command "to stifle this dastardly attempt" to defy the authority of the state and to provoke "a disgraceful *attentat* from within".

At evening, a gun battle broke out between the I.Z.L. units and the army. As darkness fell, the *Altalena* quickly steamed out to sea, with Menahem Begin and a group of his followers on board. The naval vessels pursued her as she sailed south toward Tel Aviv. The fighting on Kfar Vitkin's beach went on, and only the next morning did the 300 I.Z.L. soldiers there surrender to the regular forces. But the most tragic phase of the confrontation broke out when the *Altalena* reached the coast off Tel Aviv.

The *Altalena* reached Tel Aviv after a bizarre all-night pursuit, during which it exchanged fire with pursuing Israeli naval vessels. The High Command ordered the commander of the flotilla to prevent the ship from reaching Tel Aviv at all costs, but it was already too late. At dawn, when its black silhouette became visible off Tel Aviv, reports of the *Altalena*'s arrival spread like wildfire, and hundreds of I.Z.L. sympathizers began to stream to the beach, joined by I.Z.L. soldiers who had deserted their units. There were almost no army units loyal to the government in the city. Many I.Z.L. supporters jumped into the sea, trying to swim to the ship or to reach her in light boats. The confrontation had now reached its crucial point. Would the state remain silent in the face of this defiance? Would these fiery passions spark off a civil war?

At dawn, Shmuel Yanai, the Navy's chief of operations, was ordered to rush to General Command headquarters. Upon entering the hall there, he encountered a strange sight. All the army's senior commanders sat silently on chairs along the walls. In the center, Ben-Gurion was striding about "like a lion in a cage". His expression was furious as he marched back and forth from wall to wall, his hands clutched behind his back, muttering to himself.

Yanai was brought before him, and Ben-Gurion asked him, "as a naval expert", what to do about the ship.

I put forward all kinds of ideas: lobbing smoke bombs to force her to pull out, seizing the ship from boats, unloading its cargo ... Ben Gurion dismissed all my proposals with a wave of the hand. I was off target. Only later on did I understand what he wanted to hear from me – what his true aim was: he wanted to destroy the ship. The vessel ... had become the pretext for fraternal strife. He wanted to destroy it to remove the issue over which people were prepared to fight. Later on, there would be arguments, mutual recriminations – but there would no longer be a pretext for fighting.

That morning, Ben-Gurion issued written instructions to Yadin: "You are to take all [necessary] steps: concentrating army [units], fire-power, flame-throwers, and all the other means we possess in order to bring about the ship's unconditional surrender. All these forces *will be employed* if instructions are issued by the government."

The Cabinet was convened for an emergency session. Some of the ministers displayed uncertainty, anxiety, and even fear. A number were inclined to negotiate with the I.Z.L., and give in here and there so as to avoid fraternal strife. But Ben-Gurion spoke with considerable heat: "What has happened ... endangers the state ... This is an attempt to destroy the army, and this is an attempt to murder the state. On these two points there cannot, in my opinion, be any compromise. And if, to our great misfortune, it becomes necessary to fight over this, we have to fight." When the Cabinet put the issues to the vote, it decided to demand that the I.Z.L. hand over the ship to the government, with force to be employed if necessary. Ben-Gurion immediately ordered Yadin to take action in accordance with the Cabinet decision.

The *Altalena* lay at anchor off the Tel Aviv coast, and the few army units present attempted to prevent the I.Z.L. sympathizers, who included armed soldiers, from approaching the beach. But the crowd exerted growing pressure, and the ship also lowered a boat with armed men. In the end, shooting broke out. It was a horrifying sight. A gun battle was in progress in the heart of Tel Aviv under the very eyes of dazed citizens, foreign observers and journalists, and U.N. personnel. Yigal Allon, commander of the Palmach, was placed in command of the operation. "Ben-Gurion called me in for a personal talk," Allon related. "Addressing me in a dramatic tone, he said, gritting his teeth: 'Catch Begin! Catch Begin!'"

Allon now asked for a cannon "to threaten to sink the ship". As the *Altalena* was loaded with explosives and lay less than 350 feet from the beach, the inhabitants of the streets near the sea were evacuated. At four in the afternoon, Ben-Gurion ordered Yadin to shell the ship. The first shell missed its target, but the second one struck the ship's hold, and fire broke out. As a thick cloud of smoke mounted, the ship was rapidly evacuated. A few moments later, there was a tremendous explosion. Afterward the fighting on the shore died down. Fourteen I.Z.L. men and one Palmach soldier were dead and dozens were wounded.

That night, the entire nation listened tensely to a two-hour address by Menahem Begin transmitted by the I.Z.L.'s underground radio. In the course of his broadcast, Begin lost control of himself, breaking into bitter tears and cursing Ben-Gurion as "that fool, that idiot" who had "plotted" to murder him. He claimed that the *Altalena* had been shelled with the intention of killing him personally and boasted that "a wave of his finger" would have sufficed to eliminate Ben-Gurion, had he so wished. He warned Ben-Gurion and his followers that "if they raise their hands against anyone of us, they are doomed. Those who do not instantly release our officers and soldiers, they are doomed." At the same time, he warned his own men: "We will not open fire. There will be no fraternal strife while the foe is at the gateway." That same turbulent night, the I.Z.L. published a statement, filled with hatred and incitement. It called Ben-Gurion a "crazy dictator", his Cabinet "a government of criminal tyrants", "traitors", and "fratricides". The statement withdrew the previous order to I.Z.L. troops to join the army and take the oath of loyalty to the government. "The I.Z.L.'s officers and men will prefer to go to the concentration camps that the crazy dictator is certain to establish."

At a meeting of the People's Council convened that evening, Ben-Gurion made his reply: "With one rifle, one can kill several persons; with 5,000 rifles [the number on the *Altalena*] one can kill an entire community!" His conclusion was incisive: since the arms were not destined for the army, their destruction was fortunate. He concluded with a sentence that made him eternally detested by the I.Z.L.: "Blessed be the cannon that shelled that ship!" Those words becoming the rallying cry in the furious campaign that I.Z.L. supporters conducted against Ben-Gurion for a generation. To them, the *Altalena* and its cargo of arms were sacred; to him, the cannon that destroyed it was sacred – and they would never forgive him for it.

The dramatic incident of the *Altalena* was over, and Ben-Gurion had quelled a mutiny on the right. But he was still not in firm control of the armed forces, and not long after the sinking of the *Altalena* he was confronted by a renewed flare-up of the Generals' Mutiny. There was growing resentment in the General Staff over Ben-Gurion's intervention in every matter: operations, appointments, deployment of forces, arms, allocations, right down to the most minute details. Many of the senior officers could not come to terms with this state of affairs, and there were frequent disagreements between the Old Man and Yadin and other commanders.

In the course of the fighting, Ben-Gurion became increasingly conscious of the urgent need to carry out a far-reaching reorganization of the army's structure. Aside from the purely military purpose of this move, he wanted to diminish Mapam's influence by removing from senior positions several Mapam officers who had failed to prove themselves in battle. In addition, the upper echelons of the army were still largely filled by veterans of the Haganah and the Palmach, and now Ben-Gurion was resolved to fill some of the top posts – department heads and front commands – with professional non-party officers who were veterans of the British army.

On 24 June, Yigael Yadin presented Ben-Gurion with his plan for reorganizing the army and appended a list of officers whom he proposed to appoint to command brigades and fronts. The overwhelming majority were Palmach men and members of Mapam. Yadin's draft appointments had been approved by Israel Galili. But Ben-Gurion did not approve of most of the suggestions and immediately prepared an appointments list of his own. He proposed that three British army veterans be made department heads in the General Staff and a fourth, Mordechai Makleff, be given command of the crucial central front.

Instantly, the storm clouds gathered. "This morning, when I notified Yigael . . . of my conclusions," Ben-Gurion noted, "[he] threatened me with upheaval and destruction in the old manner." The confrontation focused on Mordechai Makleff's appointment as front commander. Makleff possessed all the qualities Ben-Gurion was looking for: he was young, he had been an officer in the British army, and he was not a member of any party. Yadin valued the young officer, but did not consider him sufficiently gifted or skilled to take command of a front. He was also aware that the three front commanders he had proposed were members of Mapam, but he regarded them as the army's most experienced officers. At the general command, the disagreements grew sharper, and Ben-Gurion again summoned Yadin back to his office. "I explained that now, after the establishment of the army, the composition of the staff is strange . . . There isn't a single soldier there. It is vital to change that . . ." Disregarding Yadin's objections, Ben-Gurion drew up the list of appointments and signed it.

The following day, a storm broke at the General Staff. Yadin and the Mapam members all submitted letters of resignation and asked to have them forwarded to the Cabinet. Ben-Gurion immediately summoned

Yadin and characterized the letters of resignations as "a political mutiny in the army" and as "a matter of unparalleled gravity". He warned that such a mutiny was "liable to endanger the battle, which is a fight for life or death". If he insisted on resigning as chief of operations, Ben-Gurion said he would accept his resignation. "But it is my duty," he added, "to inform him that I regard it as grave sabotage ..." Yadin replied: "As chief of operations, I shall not take responsibility for a decision of this kind. If you insist, I shall resign. You can send me as a soldier, but you can't force me to take responsibility."

At the subsequent Cabinet meeting, Ben-Gurion spoke with considerable severity. He criticized the Palmach for its insubordination, flung out angry accusations about political meddling in the army, and offered his resignation if his plan were not adopted. Ben-Gurion demanded the formation of a ministerial committee to study the affair and present its recommendations. He also defined the price of the mutiny: Israel Galili's dismissal.

The Cabinet decided to set up a five-man ministerial committee to examine the state of affairs in the high command. Its deliberations were conducted in a dramatic atmosphere. Within eight days, the truce was scheduled to end on all fronts. The heads of the departments in the General Staff remained defiant. Mapam conducted a bitter propaganda campaign against Ben-Gurion in the media, accusing him of hatred for the Palmach, of attempting to starve it by depriving its units of essential supplies, and of hatred for the Mapam kibbutzim.

In the course of a few days, the committee heard highly secret testimonies on the crisis in the army. Galili criticized Ben-Gurion severely for his sins of omission. Yadin testified about Ben-Gurion's incessant intervention in operational decisions and severely criticized his policy in the battle for Jerusalem.

The inquiry demonstrated the severe lack of trust characterizing Ben-Gurion's relations with some of his senior officers, and there was a growing feeling that his reorganization proposals should not be implemented and that the existing situation should be frozen. On 6 July the committee drew up its findings, and they were a slap in the face for David Ben-Gurion. The report revived the post of head of national command. The director-general for military affairs – Israel Galili – would be placed between the defense minister and the chief of staff, precisely as he had demanded. The report boxed Ben-Gurion in on both sides: *vis-à-vis* the army, by means of directors-general; toward the government by means of the war cabinet. Ben-Gurion read the report through, got up, and went home. That evening, he notified the Cabinet that he was resigning from his posts as prime minister and minister of defense. In his letter of resignation, he added: "In order to save the government's valuable time, I beg you to shelve the proposals for the organization of the Defense Ministry – if the intention is a Defense Ministry which I head."

The members of the committee were dazed by the Old Man's ultimatum. The chairman, Gruenbaum, began to retreat, considering "a complete withdrawal" from the whole inquiry; other ministers tried to persuade Moshe Sharett to take over the premiership, but he refused. When Gruenbaum met with members of the General Staff and informed them of the gravity of the situation, they also beat a retreat, announcing that they would obey every order coming from the government and would not resign, even if the order were not to their liking. Gruenbaum warned Galili that "he would, apparently, be the victim" if Ben-Gurion returned. Galili announced that he was prepared to step down from his post if necessary.

In the meantime, the situation was bizarre. The premier and defense minister, having resigned, remained at home and no longer dealt with current business. Some of the General Staff officers, headed by Yadin and Galili, were in a similar position of having tendered their resignations. Yigael Yadin felt "terrible" and set off for Ben-Gurion's home, resolved to "break the ice", Paula barred his way, intent on preventing him from going up to Ben-Gurion's room. "It's no good," she told him angrily, "he won't see you." But he went up anyway.

Ben-Gurion was lying in bed, on his side, facing me. As soon as he saw me, he turned to the wall, with his back to me. He was sulking. He did not speak. I said: "Listen, Ben-Gurion. I – who am I? You're in charge. You won't be forgiven for this state of affairs. If we can't talk – throw me out! Dismiss me! But the truce is ending. How can you carry the responsibility? I propose a compromise: for the time being, we won't appoint front commanders . . . The principal problem is Jerusalem . . . I propose that we appoint Yigal Allon to command Operation Larlar [aimed at occupying towns, on the way to Jerusalem]. After that we'll see."

He turned over toward me, slowly, and said: "I agree, I agree." With that, the matter ended.

The final scene in the crisis took place at the Cabinet meeting on 7 July, Ben-Gurion did not attend the meeting, which was presided over by Sharett. For many hours, the Cabinet squirmed and wriggled, while its members protested at being coerced, presented with an ultimatum, a "*diktat*". They criticized Ben-Gurion's character, his disobedience towards collective decisions; they denounced him for his inability to work with others, for not getting on with the General Staff, for his responsibility for the Latrun debacle, for his outrageous appointments. And then, with something like a secret sigh of relief, disguised by their desire to capitulate with honor, they asked Ben-Gurion to come back, flinging the recommendations of the five-man committee into the wastepaper basket.

Ben-Gurion's victory was the end of the "mutinies" in the army. From this point onward, he was to receive a free hand in running defense matters. He was generous enough to permit a ministerial committee to assist him; but he remained the supreme commander and conducted the War of Independence right up to the end, as he had hoped. The man who paid for the confrontation was Israel Galili. Formally, he was not dismissed, and he continued to work in the Defense Ministry. But his post was an empty one, and his position was gradually undermined. In September, he finally left the Defense Ministry and returned home to his kibbutz.

In the course of the four-week truce, Israel's army had undergone a complete revolution. Large quantities of arms were brought into the country and additional forces were recruited. "At the termination of the first truce," Yigael Yadin related, "we took the initiative into our own hands; and after that, we never allowed it to return to the Arab forces." On 8 July, twenty-eight hours before the end of the truce, the Egyptians launched a surprise attack in the south, and fighting flared up again. It soon became evident that the war had taken on an entirely new character.

The fighting lasted only ten days, but it brought Israel some significant gains. Large areas were occupied in Galilee and the Jerusalem area, and the Jerusalem corridor was broadened. B-17 (Flying Fortress) bombers purchased abroad bombed Cairo and Raffiah on their way to Israel. The following day, they bombed the El Arish airfield, while a Dakota dropped its bombs on Damascus. When the second truce came into effect, a completely new situation had come into being. The Israeli victories during these ten days of fighting astounded the Arabs and the outside world, and the new truce was proclaimed for an unlimited period of time.

As Ben-Gurion saw matters at this time, any attempt to achieve peace would require Israel to pay a high price in territorial terms. The pressures exerted by the U.N. and the Western Powers were liable to bring about a political setback, in spite of Israel's military victory. His forebodings were borne out when the "peace envoy", Count Bernadotte, presented his plan on 16 September. Israel was highly suspicious of the tall, bony Swedish count for Bernadotte was decisively under British influence and right from the start he based his efforts on changing the U.N. partition map to Israel's detriment. His initial peace plan wiped the Palestinian Arab state off the map and proposed an economic, military, and political alliance between the Jewish state and Abdullah's kingdom. Bernadotte demanded that the refugees be permitted to return and he proposed that the Negev be severed from the Jewish state and ceded to the Arabs, in return for which the Jews would receive western Galilee. He also proposed that Jerusalem be granted to the Arabs, with the city's Jewish population being given municipal autonomy. The Israeli government rejected Bernadotte's proposals, and the Arab states did likewise.

On 16 September, Bernadotte advanced a new set of proposals, some of which were a repetition of his former plan. Withdrawing his previous idea of granting Jerusalem to the Arabs, he returned to the internationalization plan under U.N. supervision. This proposal was also rejected by both sides. But a tragic event, which occurred one day after he presented his plan, suddenly lent it great moral force. On the afternoon of 17 September, a convoy carrying Count Bernadotte and the heads of his staff set out through the streets of Jewish Jerusalem for a meeting with the Israeli governor of the city. As they passed through an outlying neighbourhood, the street was suddenly blocked by a jeep. A group of armed masked men appeared and opened fire on the convoy. One of them poked a sub-machine-gun through the window of Bernadotte's car. After killing a French officer, the assailant inflicted fatal wounds on Bernadotte. The killers then jumped into their cars and fled.

Ben-Gurion learned of the astounding murder at six that evening, when he received telegrams from Jerusalem. Sealed envelopes dropped outside the foreign consulates in the city contained letters from an organization calling itself The Fatherland Front, which proclaimed that its members had carried out the assassination. A quick investigation discovered that The Fatherland Front was a cover for a group of Lehi extremists who had been issuing threats on Bernadotte's life because of the far-reaching Israeli concessions demanded by his peace plans.

Within a few hours, news of Bernadotte's death had spread throughout the whole world, provoking expressions of anger and disgust. The Israeli leadership was also in an uproar. Ben-Gurion's proposal was adopted there and then: the dissident organizations in Jerusalem must be dissolved and their remnants in the rest of the country smashed. As soon as he received the first telegram, Ben-Gurion summoned the head of the Internal Security Services and the commander of the Military Police and ordered them to arrest all members of Lehi throughout the country. He also decided to undertake vigorous measures against the I.Z.L., even though he knew they were not involved in the assassination. Three days after the assassination, the underground organizations had been completely disbanded throughout Israel.

The Bernadotte assassination had a bizarre sequel. Seventeen years later, the present author found the names of the three Lehi members suspected of the murder on a page in Ben-Gurion's journal dated 19 September 1948.

One was a man with whom Ben-Gurion had grown friendly in later years. When the author approached Ben-Gurion with the passage and asked, "Did you know this?" the Old Man was surprised and said, "No. Let's ask him." The friend was called in for a confidential talk, and when he left Ben-Gurion told the author, "He confessed." The Old Man never revealed the secret to anyone else, and over the years he grew even closer to the confessed assassin. The former premier and the former terrorist were to spend many more quiet hours together, united by their affection and by the terrible secret that once threatened the very foundations of the newborn state.

Tempers ran high after Bernadotte's assassination. Within a few days, the U.N. General Assembly would renew its deliberations concerning Jerusalem and the Negev. The Bernadotte plan constituted a severe menace to Israeli interests on both points, and it seemed likely that the United Nations would try to impose painful concessions on Israel. Ben-Gurion knew that the only way to prevent such a development was to take immediate military action which would establish *faits accomplis*. He found a pretext in the enemy's violations of the truce.

Naturally, Ben-Gurion's prime objective was Jerusalem. On 26 September, the premier presented a plan for a daring military operation. He proposed to attack the Arab Legion and take the entire southern portion of the West Bank (Judea) from Jerusalem to the partition line in the northern Negev. He came to the Cabinet meeting convinced that the operation would be approved. The pretext for it would be the Legion's demolition of the Latrun pumping station, which deprived Jerusalem of its water. Ben-Gurion had already given orders to the army to prepare for the attack. His plan was imaginative, but most of the ministers opposed it on political grounds, and when it came to the vote, he found himself in the minority. He left the Cabinet meeting in a sombre mood, and ordered Yigael Yadin to call back the forces prepared for the operation. Later, he was to term the Cabinet's decision a matter for "wailing for generations", "because, in the existing situation, Jordan is in control of the hills of Judea, and all the roads to Jerusalem, as well as the Old City itself". Below the Cabinet decision, he wrote, "The proposal to renew the battle for the city is not yet for publication, because I do not want to shame those members of the provisional government who were opposed to it."

Despite the Cabinet's rejection of his proposal, Ben-Gurion drew up a plan for a new offensive: to launch an attack in force against the Egyptians and liberate the Negev. The Negev was cut off, and only an improvised air-lift employing crude desert air-strips brought in supplies, ammunition, and reinforcements. Ben-Gurion decided to place the operation under the command of Yigal Allon and already had a plan prepared. A supply convoy would set out for the Negev and the Egyptians would undoubtedly stop it, thereby infringing the truce; whereupon Israel would respond with a general offensive along the whole southern front.

Although Yigael Yadin was heartily in favor of the Negev operation, Ben-Gurion knew he was in for another sharp confrontation in the Cabinet. Having learned from his earlier setback, he now assured himself of the support of his own party's ministers before presenting the plan to the government. Thus when he entered the Cabinet meeting, he could presume that he had a good chance of gaining a majority for his proposal this time.

Outlining the plan, he expressed his belief that it would be feasible to destroy the Egyptian forces in seven days fighting. "If the battle is limited to the south," he said, "we shall seize the breadth of the Negev as far as the Dead Sea and the Red Sea, and we might be able to enter Hebron and Bethlehem, too, if [enemy] forces do not come from the north." In the discussion, most of the ministers expressed their support for the operation, and it was scheduled to begin on 14 October, under the name Operation Ten Plagues. But just as during the first truce, there was a fierce internal confrontation right before the attack was launched – the trial of strength with the Palmach.

Originally the crack shock troops of the underground Haganah, the Palmach, was an anomaly in the Israel Defense Forces. The other "private armies" – the I.Z.L. and the Lehi – had been fully integrated into the army, and the Haganah itself had, of course, become the basis of the broad-based national armed forces. Yet the Palmach's independent command continued to exist. Now Ben-Gurion decided to take his final step and dissolve it. The Palmach had been of great assistance to him in his conflict with the "dissidents" – during the first truce, when he grappled with the I.Z.L. and during the second one, when he broke up the underground organizations following Bernadotte's assassination. But once these internal matters were under control, Ben-Gurion progressively reduced the authority of the Palmach command and even detached some of its units. Now he was to take the final step.

On 29 September, Ben-Gurion informed the General Staff of his decision to dismantle the Palmach command and issued the necessary instructions to the chief of staff. At the same time, he waited for an appropriate moment to put the order into effect. That opportunity arose as soon as the Cabinet approved the offensive against the Egyptians. On the eve of the renewal of hostilities, the chief of staff sent a dispatch to Palmach headquarters, worded in accordance with Ben-Gurion's instructions explaining why there was no further need for a separate Palmach command

and making it clear that Palmach units would henceforth be directly under the command of the General Staff.

At this point, Mapam, the self-same party which had hitherto denied any special ties to the Palmach, took vigorous action. It's leaders decided to appeal against the ruling. Yet they did not do so before any state forum, such as the Cabinet or the State Council, but approached the Executive Council of the Histadrut Labor Federation. In doing so, they reduced a political decision of the civil administration into a party squabble within the broader labor movement."

Thus at the very time that forces in the south were deploying for a surprise attack on the Egyptian lines, the leaders of the labor parties met to argue about the fate of the Palmach. The debate was attended by the chief of staff, the commander of the Palmach, and even by Yigal Allon, who was supposed to be in command of the operation in the Negev. The exchanges were bitter and turbulent. Ben-Gurion characterized Mapam's actions as "a danger to the integrity of the state, the greatest danger that has arisen since the establishment of the state". One Mapam leader painted an apocalyptic picture.

The right wing has no inhibitions. The moment it can seize power, it will do so. The moment the Palmach is eliminated, there will be a left-wing clandestine [movement] in the army. There will [also) be a Fascist underground ... By eliminating the Palmach, the labor movement in the Land of Israel is, with its own hands, sawing away one of the strongest branches that guarantee our safety ...

With one exception, however, all the members of Mapai rallied around Ben-Gurion and hit back fiercely at Mapam. The debate raged on for two whole days. At its conclusion, a majority of sixteen to eight supported Ben-Gurion's step.

The Palmach command carried out the order and dispersed; and neither the Palmach nor Mapam undertook any step against the government's authority. But the Mapam leaders and the commanders of the Palmach remained resentful. They regarded Ben-Gurion as a destructive foe who had smashed one of the most splendid creations of the country's pioneering youth. Just as I.Z.L. members never forgave Ben-Gurion for the *Altalena* episode, the Palmach's veterans did not forgive him for dissolving their command. But that was not the end of the affair. Ben-Gurion's final aim was to dissolve the Palmach as a whole, not its command. At war's end, the Palmach brigades were also disbanded, in spite of the Old Man's previous promises to the contrary. The final dissolution of the Palmach infuriated its commanders. After the war, most of its officers and others who had not actually served in the Palmach but were Mapam sympathizers left the army. Their departure was a severe blow to the quality of the army and its operational effectiveness during the period following the War of Independence.

On 15 October the supply column that initiated Operation Ten Plagues set out for the Negev, and the Egyptians obligingly played the role cast for them by attacking the convoy in full view of the U.N. observers. The army immediately went into action in the first Israeli operation bearing all the hallmarks of a full military offensive. The force employed was of division size, and the attack commenced with an air strike at the El Arish airfield. Operation Ten Plagues included the bitterest and fiercest battles of the War of Independence, marked by hand-to-hand combat with firearms, knives, fists, and teeth.

On 19 October, while the fighting was raging at full force, the Security Council convened and called for an immediate cease-fire. Ben-Gurion delayed the Israeli reply, so as to gain another day or two to complete the operation. Meanwhile, in a nightmarish step-by-step battle, Israeli forces succeeded in opening up the road to the Negev, which had been cut off for eight months. In a surprise attack launched during the night and going on into the early morning, they also wrested Beersheba out of Egyptian hands. This success had a great impact, in Israel and abroad and further demoralized the Egyptian army. In the afternoon, fighting ceased.

With operations in the south at a successful conclusion, Ben-Gurion turned his attention to the north. The head of Northern Command was given permission to go into action. Here, too, the pretext for the attack was found in truce violations on the part of Kaukji's Army of Liberation. In a brilliant lightning operation, Northern Command's forces took sixty hours to liberate the whole of central Galilee and invade Lebanon, capturing fourteen Lebanese villages before halting at the Litani River.

The good news from Galilee fortified Ben-Gurion's self-confidence and goaded the ambition he had been cultivating in recent months: to take the West Bank and thus have the whole of the historic Land of Israel under Israeli rule. But the news from the U.N. meeting in Paris was worrying. The British and Chinese representatives in the Security Council had tabled a vigorous resolution demanding an Israeli withdrawal to the lines it occupied prior to 14 October. That alone deterred Ben-Gurion. In the meantime, Ralph Bunche demanded that Israel evacuate its positions in the Negev, and withdraw from Beersheba, where an Egyptian governor was to be appointed. Britain demanded that the Negev be ceded to Transjordan; the Soviet Union supported a return to the 29 November boundaries; and the United States was in favor of negotiations between Israel and the

Arabs for a territorial compromise. Ben-Gurion was prudent in his dealings with the U.N., but he refused to give up a single inch of the territory occupied in the Negev.

On 16 November, the Security Council called on Israel and her Arab opponents to initiate talks for an armistice agreement. Egypt announced her refusal to negotiate with Israel, and at the end of December, Ben-Gurion gave orders for the final operation in the south: Operation Horev. In the first phase, the plan called for driving the Egyptians completely out of the Negev; the second phase called for encircling the Gaza Strip and annihilating the Egyptian forces there. Five brigades were massed for the operation under the command of Yigal Allon.

In the course of Operation Horev, Israeli forces penetrated the Sinai peninsula and were a stone's throw from El Arish on the Mediterranean coast. Its occupation would have completed the encirclement of the Gaza Strip. The fighting precipitated an internal crisis within Egypt, and it seemed as though nothing could save the country from a complete military and political collapse. But on 31 December, there was a dramatic turnabout. American Ambassador James MacDonald delivered an urgent message to the Israeli government warning that Britain would take armed action against Israel, by virtue of the Anglo-Egyptian Defense Treaty, if Israeli forces remained on Egyptian soil. Ben-Gurion, who was then in Tiberias, immediately issued orders for the withdrawal of the Israeli forces from Sinai. Later the same evening, MacDonald himself arrived in Tiberias bringing Ben-Gurian a note from President Truman threatening "a reconsideration of the Israeli government's application for admittance to the United Nations and . . . of the relations between the United States and Israel . . . to prevent extension of the conflict". Ben-Gurion was angered by the harsh tone of the note: "Is it necessary for a mighty power to use such a tone in addressing a small and weak state?" he asked. Unofficially MacDonald admitted that he was surprised by the wording of the note and remarked that it seemed that the president was under considerable pressure. As for the demand itself, the prime minister said that "following the liberation of the Negev, our army crossed the border for the purpose of maneuvers, but it has already received instructions to return".

Although the crisis was actually over, Britain nonetheless took the opportunity of making her presence felt by appearing on the battlefield during the final hours of the fighting. In the afternoon, Spitfires carrying British markings appeared over the Israeli formations, apparently to make sure that they were indeed pulling out of Sinai. Ground fire was opened up on them, and Israeli fighters scrambled to intercept them. Three Spitfires were shot down. A few hours later, British planes again appeared over the

Israeli positions. Once again, the Israeli planes set out to meet them, this time downing another two planes. Reports of the air actions caused Ben-Gurion great concern at the prospect of a clash with Britain. Nothing happened, however. On the contrary, President Truman severely condemned Britain for sending planes to the combat area. There was no confrontation with Britain.

On 13 January, armistice talks were inaugurated with Egypt at the Roses Hotel in Rhodes. When Egypt abandoned the battlefield, the Old Man turned his glance back to the east. He was still inclined to believe that it would be necessary to wage a further battle for the entire city of Jerusalem and the northern West Bank (Samaria). Yet Ben-Gurion was drawn in two conflicting directions. On the one hand, there was the need for peace. On the other, he sensed that without war he would not remove the Iraqi army from its present lines near the sea, where it constituted a menace to Israel; nor would he succeed in liberating the routes to Jerusalem. He decided to relinquish the military option on one condition only: if he could achieve a real peace with Transjordan. In the course of January, Moshe Dayan and Eliyahu Sasson held secret meetings with King Abdullah at his palace, and the king expressed his readiness to reach a peace settlement with Israel. One of the subjects discussed was a Transjordanian outlet to the sea by way of Gaza, but Abdullah was vigorously opposed to Israeli control of the Um Rashrash (Eilat) area on the Red Sea shore.

When the Armistice Agreement was signed with Egypt at the end of February, Ben-Gurion felt that it was time to establish further *faits accomplis* to the east. He gave orders for a military operation to occupy Eilat. Two brigades set out secretly, following different routes, toward the Red Sea. On 10 March, both reached Eilat without encountering any resistance. Near two wretched hovels standing on the shores of the picturesque Gulf of Aqaba, the soldiers hoisted an improvised Israeli flag, its colors daubed on in ink. Thus, by use of his army, Ben-Gurion gained what Abdullah had refused to grant him.

Finally, Ben-Gurion relinquished his intention of occupying the northern West Bank in view of a diplomatic success: the Iraqi army decided to hand over its positions to the Arab Legion and return home. Dayan informed King Abdullah that Israel would consent to this change only on condition that the borderline be changed to Israel's advantage. The Jordanians consented, also agreeing that the whole railway line to Jerusalem be included in Israeli territory. On 3 April, an Armistice Agreement was signed with Transjordan. Ten days before, an armistice had also been agreed upon with Lebanon, and the agreement with Syria was signed on 20 July. The War of Independence was at an end.

Soon after, Ben-Gurion was asked by a young writer: "Why didn't you liberate the whole country?" The Old Man replied: "There was a danger of getting saddled with a hostile Arab majority ... of entanglements with the United Nations and the Powers, and of the State Treasury collapsing. Even so, we liberated a very large area, much more than we thought. Now, we have work for two or three generations. As for the rest – we'll see later ..." The realist in him had triumphed over the visionary and the statesman had gained the upper hand over the conqueror. But he had not fully relinquished the dream.

A few months later, the Old Man set out on his "great trek to Eilat", accompanied by officers of the General Staff. As they passed through the Jordan Rift Valley, Ben-Gurion stood gazing at the Mountains of Edom beyond the Jordanian border. Near by stood a young general whom Ben Gurion admired.

"How would you take those hills?" Ben-Gurion asked.

The general began to analyze the problem, explaining the route he would take and the forces he would use. Suddenly, he stopped and asked in astonishment: "Why do you ask? Do you want to conquer those hills?"

Offhandedly, the Old Man muttered: "I? No. But *you* will conquer them."

The Heroic Years

Before the War of Independence had come to an end, Ben-Gurion had already begun to direct his overflowing energies to the next objective. He underwent an abrupt metamorphosis and began to dedicate himself to the purpose for which all his previous deeds had laid the groundwork: the Gathering in of the Exiles.

There were prominent members of Mapai, and of the Cabinet, who feared that unrestricted immigration would lead to the collapse of the state. Logically, they were right. How could a state with 700,000 inhabitants absorb hundreds of thousands of immigrants every year? Ben-Gurion, however, paid no heed to his colleagues' counsel. Almost single-handed, he coerced Mapai, the Cabinet, and the Jewish Agency into adopting their most important decision since the establishment of the state: to open the gates to mass immigration. "If such immigration was to succeed," he later wrote, "it would not be to my credit. Immigration was borne along by the historical forces of distress and pressure and hope, and thousands of people were engaged in organizing and fostering it. But if it should fail, and undermine the state – as many people predicted, not without reason – only I would be to blame."

The target set by Ben-Gurion was to double the population of the state within four years, and this mass immigration unfolded as a splendid, exciting epic. The flow of immigrants began while the War of Independence was at its height. Over 100,000 Jews arrived between 14 May and 31 December 1948. While fighting for its very life, the state found the inner resources to care for them, house them, and provide them with a livelihood. In 1949, the flow turned into a flood: 239,576 immigrants reached the country that year; in 1950, 170,249; in 1951, 175,095. Within four years, 686,748 immigrants entered the country, and, together with natural increase, they helped to boost the population by 120 per cent. Ben-Gurion's objective had been achieved in full.

At first, the immigrants were housed in abandoned British army camps, wooden huts, or deserted Arab villages. These were followed by tattered tents, canvas structures, tin shacks, and transit camps that sprouted up throughout the country. In winter, the heavy rains and cold spells brought floods and epidemics; in summer, the sun beat down mercilessly on the camp dwellers. At one stage, about 200,000 people were living in tents, and sometimes two families shared a single tent. The whole country was covered with transit camps, crowded housing estates, and hastily erected, ugly little towns. And the State Treasury was empty.

The Israeli government made desperate efforts to obtain loans, credits, grants from foreign governments, and donations from Diaspora Jews. Time and again, the money ran out and the government's warehouses were left bare of basic foodstuffs. On several occasions, the country's population was dependent upon a ship bringing a cargo of wheat or flour; had it been delayed, the outcome would have been hunger. Heavy taxes were imposed on the population and severe austerity and rationing were employed to cut down on private consumption and reduce the state's expenditure in foreign currency. Rationing of vital commodities naturally gave rise to a flourishing black market, but Ben-Gurion recruited the services of the police, the Internal Security Service, and public and state bodies to put down its activities and personally headed the body established to fight it. Later, he was to contend that the first four years of the state's existence were "the greatest years in our history since the [Maccabean] victory over the Greeks, 2,113 years before the rebirth of the state in our times".

Nevertheless, these "great years" also brought him some bitter disappointments. In the elections held on 25 January 1949, Mapai gained 46 of the 120 Knesset seats. Mapam, which had challenged Mapai's hegemony, won only 19 seats, while the Religious Front got 16 and Herut (the Revisionists' party) received 14. Ben-Gurion's dream of building a broad coalition was soon dashed. The most painful refusal came from Mapam, stemming principally from its tough, blindly pro-Soviet line and its harsh criticism of Mapai's policies. As a result, Ben-Gurion was obliged to rule by means of a narrow coalition consisting of Mapai, the Religious Front, and the Progressive Party. It was a loose partnership that fell apart repeatedly, making it necessary to disperse the Knesset within two years of its constitution. The Second Knesset – elected in 1951 – also witnessed repeated Cabinet crises.

Despite the backdrop of an unstable parliamentary situation, the prime minister had not only to deal with a highly unusual domestic program but begin to establish a clear-cut foreign policy. The first challenge from the international community came late in 1949, when the United Nations General Assembly decided to discuss the question of internationalizing Jerusalem. The notion had been a stipulation of the original November

1947 partition resolution, but in the meantime the war had established
certain facts on the ground, and Jerusalem was divided between Israel and
Abdullah's Kingdom of Transjordan. Suddenly the Jerusalem question was
raised again, and on 5 December, Foreign Minister Moshe Sharett phoned
from New York to inform Ben-Gurion that the internationalization proposal was likely to gain a majority. Israel advanced a counter-proposal
whereby the city would remain sovereign territory of the two states that
occupied it but the Holy Places would be subject to international supervision. The Israeli delegation cabled Ben-Gurion to inform him that "our
proposal . . . has prospects of receiving only one vote – that of the Israeli
delegation". Ben-Gurion was sitting in his study reading the Bible when
the cable arrived. When his secretary informed him that only Israel's vote
was guaranteed for the proposal, he glanced at the open Bible and said,
"Yes, but that is the vote that counts!"

That statement was an indication of his intentions. On 9 December,
when the General Assembly put the matter to the vote, the internationalization proposal was adopted. The resolution placed Israel in a difficult
situation: failure to react, would imply acceptance of the U.N. decision.
Once again, Ben-Gurion acted in characteristic fashion: he established
faits accomplis.

On 10 December Ben-Gurion proposed to the Cabinet that the capital be
transferred to Jerusalem without delay. The Cabinet's deliberations were
stormy. Most of the ministers supported Ben-Gurion's view, but several
hesitated. In a cable from New York, Moshe Sharett tendered his resignation as foreign minister. Without informing his Cabinet colleagues of
Sharett's resignation, Ben-Gurion cabled back to say that he refused to
accept it. Three days later he told the Knesset in the course of the War of
Independence, when Jerusalem was under siege, the government had been
obliged to take up its temporary seat in Tel Aviv.

But the state of Israel has, and will have, only one capital – Jerusalem the
eternal . . . Since fighting ended, we have continued the transfer of the government to Jerusalem . . . There is no longer any obstacle [to prevent] the Knesset's
return to Jerusalem, and we propose that you decide accordingly.

World reaction to the Israeli decision was furious. France hastened to
submit a resolution condemning Israel; the Vatican was up in arms; and
the Catholic states issued sharp protests. But after the shouting died down,
no one made a move to prevent the implementation of the Knesset resolution. A few days later, trucks loaded with furniture, papers, and office
equipment, began to transfer various ministries to the capital. Only two
ministries remained in Tel Aviv: the Defense Ministry, to keep it far from

the border; and the Foreign Ministry, because of Sharett's fears that diplomats would refuse to come to Jerusalem. Sharett kept the Foreign Ministry in Tel Aviv for a long time, and it was only under Ben-Gurion's angry pressure that he transferred it to Jerusalem in 1953.

"Why did I think we could do it?" Ben-Gurion said years later. "First of all, I knew we had an ally – Transjordan. If *they* were permitted to hold on to Jerusalem, why weren't *we*? Transjordan would permit no one to get them out of Jerusalem; consequently, no one would dare to remove us. I also knew that we would come to no harm. I was convinced that [the U.N. warnings] were no more than talk . . ."

It may have been their joint opposition to the internationalization proposals that brought Jordan and Israel so close together. In fact, on the very day the Knesset decided to transfer the capital to Jerusalem, a secret meeting in Amman produced a Jordanian–Israeli document that was the closest thing to a draft peace treaty Israel ever achieved. But, the agreement did not remain in force for very long. While he was initialing it, Abdullah warned his guests that "he is not completely master of his own home, and he has to receive the approval of the British representative in Jordan". Indeed, when the British raised objections, the king told the Israelis that the agreement should be regarded as void. In October 1950, however, there were renewed contacts regarding a peace treaty and the talks went on until early in 1951. There were many difficulties over minor problems arising from the Armistice Agreement with Jordan, and Ben-Gurion began to entertain doubts about the prospects for a peace settlement. He came to the conclusion that Jordan would not make peace with Israel as long as Britain withheld its support for such a move. "In effect," he said to his aides, "the Legion is a British army, and Abdullah is on Britain's payroll." Then, unexpectedly, on 20 July 1951, Abdullah was assassinated at the gateway to the Al-Aksa mosque; the killer was a fanatical follower of the mufti of Jerusalem.

Abdullah's assassination was symptomatic of the upheavals then sweeping the Arab world, partly stemming from the Palestine problem. A few days before, the Lebanese stateman Riad Sulh was also assassinated in Amman (he, too was in favor of a settlement with Israel). Syria plunged into a prolonged period of instability, and in Egypt there was growing unrest, which would lead to the military coup a year later. All attempts to make peace between Israel and the Arab states ended in failure. The endeavors of the U.N. Conciliation Commission came to a sad end. The conference that convened in Lausanne in 1949 dispersed without having achieved any results, due to the inflexible attitude of the Arab representatives. Talks held in Paris also broke down. The U.N. efforts having failed, the Western Powers decided on a step to stabilize the situation in the Middle East. On 25 May 1950, the United States, France, and Britain issued a joint declaration offering guarantees for the *status quo* in the Middle East. They proclaimed that they would preserve an arms balance between Israel and her neighbors and oppose any use of force in the region.

The Tripartite Declaration did not dispel Israeli fears. Ben-Gurion grew progressively more concerned about Israel's survival, and the breakdown of the peace talks with the Arabs created a situation analagous to that in effect during the British Mandate: being in a minority *vis-à-vis* the Arabs, the Jews needed the support of a foreign power. Ben-Gurion did not believe that Israel would be able to hold out alone forever and searched about for other means of guaranteeing his country's security. Once again he grasped the necessity of an alliance with a foreign power to ensure that the Arabs would not be able to destroy Israel. But which Power would ally itself with Israel?

Because of its long association with the Middle East – and Palestine in particular – Great Britain seemed to be the most likely candidate to Ben-Gurion. With the Korean War at its height and tension rising between the two world blocs, there were widespread fears that a third world war was about to break out. Key strategic regions suddenly took on redoubled importance in the eyes of Western military leaders, and one of these areas was the Middle East.

On 17 February 1951, Sir Brian Robertson, commander of the British forces in the Middle East, arrived in Israel on a tour. In the course of talks with him, Ben-Gurion asked: "What are your plans in the event of a war with the Soviet Union?"

"Russia will probably thrust southward toward Iraq," Robertson replied. "We shall advance northward from our bases in Egypt by way of Israel, Jordan, and Iraq."

Ben-Gurion was indignant. "How can you talk that way? Is Israel in your pocket? Do you think we're a British colony? Or a state under your control, like Jordan? Israel is small, but it is independent. Before deciding to turn it into a 'transit route' for your armies, you must come to an agreement with us."

There was considerable tension in the room, and Sharett flung worried glances at Ben-Gurion. Finally, the British general said: "I'm sorry. I'm a soldier. That is a political question."

Unexpectedly, Ben-Gurion said: "It is possible to establish a different relationship between Israel and Britain. Why shouldn't we join the British Commonwealth? You have more in common with us than with Ceylon.

We could establish an interrelationship like the one you have with New Zealand."

The other participants were astounded. Never, in any forum, had Ben-Gurion hinted that he was interested in joining the British Commonwealth. Robertson was both surprised and embarrassed by the proposal. However, on military matters his views were clearer: he wanted to reach an agreement with Israel on the establishment of British air and naval bases in the country, as well as military repair and maintenance workshops, industries, and supply dumps. The idea was to the liking of some of the army commanders. "Our isolation was burdensome," said Chief of Staff Mordechai Makleff. "There was a suggestion making the rounds that we would give the Negev to the British for a military base [to] protect the Suez Canal, because it was clear that the British would evacuate Egypt. In the same fashion, we also wanted to reach an agreement with N.A.T.O."

Robertson returned to London and reported on his talks with Ben-Gurion. In the meantime, a far-reaching change had occurred in Britain: on 9 March 1951, Ben-Gurion's "greatest enemy", Ernest Bevin, resigned his post as foreign secretary (he died five weeks later). His successor, Herbert Morrison, sent a highly significant message to Ben-Gurion:

... We understand from General Robertson's report that ... U.K.–Israel relations should be established on such a basis that Israel would in an emergency act, and be treated by the U.K., as if she was a member of the Commonwealth ... We believe that it is possible to establish a relationship between our two people which ... shall constitute a bond between us and which shall be capable of progressive development. In our view, this must be a gradual process and one which comes about naturally as a result of continual contact with exchanges of views and individual acts of cooperation in the military field ...

Ben-Gurion received this message at the end of April, but he did not reply. Disappointed at the evasive wording of several passages, he came to the conclusion that "Morrison is a fox, and should not be trusted". At the end of October, however, when the Conservatives won the general election and Winston Churchill returned to power, Ben-Gurion felt able to reply to Morrison's message. At the end of November, he signed a letter addressed to Sir Anthony Eden, the foreign secretary in Churchill's new Cabinet:

He wrote We are willing to do our share in safeguarding the interests of our two countries and to promoting the aims of the free world in the Middle East. ... To enable us to play our role effectively, it will be necessary to strengthen our industrial potential, to develop means of transport and communication ... to improve the training and equipment of our armed forces ... and to provide stocks of food and fuel. In our view direct conversations on concrete plans might well be initiated between our governments.

Ben-Gurion made no further mention of joining the British Commonwealth and referred only to military cooperation, along the lines of Morrison's proposal.

Eden's reply arrived only at the end of January 1952: "His Majesty's
Government agree to your suggestion that direct conversations on specific
matters should now be initiated . . . [and] accordingly suggests that a small
British mission should visit Israel for the purpose of exploratory discussions
of the type mentioned in your message . . ." The British delegation arrived
only in October, and Mordechai Makleff was charged with conducting the
talks, which dealt with the subjects Ben-Gurion had listed in his letter.
When the talks ended, it was decided to hold a further meeting in Britain.
But this second meeting was never held, and gradually the matter faded
away. "The British Foreign Office was against the idea right from the start,"
said one of Ben-Gurion's aides, "and it never had a chance."

With his hopes of an alliance with Britain frustrated, Ben-Gurion now
turned his sights on the United States, where he had received an enthusiastic welcome during a tour in May 1951. But in November 1952,
Eisenhower was elected president, and with the onset of a Republican
administration, there were heavy forebodings in Israel. Many people were
convinced that the Americans would adopt a policy of appeasing the Arabs
and would be prepared to supply them with arms to guarantee a rapprochement. The first test of United States' intentions was timed for the spring,
when the new secretary of state, John Foster Dulles, toured the Middle
East.

In preparation for the visit, Ben-Gurion presented his foreign policy
views to Mapai's Political Committee, which heard him expound a
vigorously pro-American line. He stated that if global conflict broke out,
Israel would not be able to remain neutral, both because the various sides
would not show any consideration for her neutrality and because Soviet
occupation, even temporary, would mark "the end of the state and of
Zionism". Ben-Gurion stressed Israel's great value to the West in the
event of war, because of the state's military strength, whereas in peacetime,
the Arabs' power was greater, because of their political strength. He
therefore wanted to place the principal stress on convincing the United
States to make Israel into "the base, the workshop, and the granary" of the
Middle East. "Granting bases to friends and allies does not harm our
sovereignty," he said. ". . . We have to explain [to the Americans] that the
whole of Israel – strengthened, in military and industrial terms – is a base
. . . available to the free world on a day of need." Ben-Gurion was now
prepared to go further than ever before in identifying Israel with the West,
so as to make America into the prop he sought. His statement featured a

contention that was to become the cornerstone of his future policies: Israel is the bastion of the West in the Middle East.

The prime minister did his best to expound this thesis to John Foster Dulles, when the latter reached Israel on 13 May; but his efforts were in vain. Shortly after returning to the United States, Dulles told a Senate committee: "Our basic political problem . . . is to improve the Moslem states' attitudes toward the Western democracies, because our prestige in that area has been in constant decline ever since the war."

Thus the United States also turned its back on Israel. The small state remained without protectors or allies. It also remained in alarming financial straits, and it was clear that the country could not continue to maintain a hand-to-mouth existence indefinitely.

In September 1950, Ben-Gurion had summoned the heads of American Jewry to Jerusalem and proposed that they raise a $1 billion loan from the Jews of the United States and other Western countries. In May 1951, he flew to the United States to inaugurate the Israel Bonds campaign at a mass rally in New York's Madison Square Garden. The campaign enjoyed enormous success, but the money it brought in was not enough for a long-term stabilization of the state's feeble economy. Israel needed prolonged and massive financial help. At this critical point, the first faint prospects of reparations from Germany appeared on the horizon.

On 12 March 1951, Israel submitted a claim for $1·5 billion for the Jewish property pillaged by the Nazis. The claim was submitted to the Four Powers occupying Germany, but the Big Four refused to deal with it. The only chance of receiving reparations was by conducting direct negotiations with the German authorities. Chancellor Konrad Adenauer, the leader of the newly constituted German Federal Republic, expressed his readiness to pay reparations to the State of Israel, which represented the heirs of the Nazis' victims. But the issue provoked unprecedented protests and demonstrations of horror from all sections of the Israeli public. In view of the enormous sensitivity of the matter, Ben-Gurion had to fling the full weight of his personal authority into the scales. He did so willingly. Many of his colleagues, including leaders of his own party, suffered deep spiritual agony. They were torn between the need to build up the state and their reluctance to take "unholy" money from the murderers of six million Jews. But not Ben-Gurion. "In a single sentence, the reason lay in the final injunction of the inarticulate six millions, the victims of Nazism, whose very murder was a ringing cry for Israel to rise, to be strong and prosperous, to safeguard her peace and security, and so prevent such a disaster from ever again overwhelming the Jewish people."

Early in December, Ben-Gurion held a talk with Dr Nahum Goldmann, chairman of the Jewish Agency, who was about to set off for a secret meeting with Adenauer. The two men decided that they would agree to a sum of $1 billion as a starting point for negotiations. "Only if there were such a declaration of intent would Ben-Gurion regard it as a basis for asking the Knesset's approval for talks between the State of Israel and Western Germany." Goldmann left Israel on 4 December, and two days later he met with Adenauer in London. There and then, Adenauer signed a letter in which he agreed to accept the Israeli claim of $1 billion as the basis for negotiations. On 10 December, Goldmann returned to Israel and delivered the letter to Ben-Gurion. On the strength of the document, the prime minister decided to raise the matter before the Cabinet and the Knesset.

The whole country was in uproar as the date of the Knesset vote approached, Mapam and Herut organized protest rallies, and various reports indicated that the right wing intended to perpetrate terrorist acts. The Cabinet faced broad opposition in the Knesset backed by the sense of pain and humiliation experienced by hundreds of thousands of Israelis. On 7 January, these feelings erupted in full force. Knesset members arriving for the fateful vote had to make their way through police barriers and barbed wire fences. As evening fell, Ben-Gurion arose to make his address in an atmosphere of unprecedented tension. His statement was largely factual. Without employing rhetorical flourishes, he described the government's efforts to gain reparation payments from Germany by means of the Occupying Powers and the Israeli view presented in its note to the Four Powers.

Over six million Jews were put to death by torture, starvation, massacre, and mass suffocation. . . . Before, during, and after this systematic mass murder, came the pillage – this too, on an unprecedented scale . . . A crime of such enormous proportions can have no material compensation. Any compensation, of whatever size, is no restitution for the loss of human life or expiation for the sufferings and agonies of men and women, children, old people and infants. However, even after the defeat of the Hitler regime, the German people . . . continues to enjoy the fruits of that massacre and pillage, of the plunder and robbery of the Jews who were murdered. The government of Israel considers itself bound to demand of the German people restitution for this stolen Jewish property. Let not the murderers of our people also be the beneficiaries of its property!

As Ben-Gurion was delivering his address, a few hundred yards from the Knesset, Begin spoke before a mass rally. In an emotion-packed speech, in sharp contrast with Ben-Gurion's address, Begin whipped up the emotions of his listeners.

When you fired at us with a cannon, I gave an order: No! Today, I shall give the order yes! This will be a battle of life and death ... Today, the Jewish premier is about to announce that he will go to Germany to receive money; that he will sell the honor of the Jewish people for monetary gain, casting eternal shame upon it ... There is not one German who did not murder our parents. Every German is a Nazi. Every German is a murderer. Adenauer is a murderer. All his aides are murderers. But *their* reckoning is money, money, money. This abomination will be perpetrated for a few million dollars....

The crowd's spontaneous eruption of emotions was heightened further by Begin's demagogy: "According to reports we have just received, Mister Ben-Gurion has stationed policemen armed with grenades and tear-gas made in Germany – the same gas that suffocated our parents." He threatened to launch a campaign of violent resistance, declaring that he and his colleagues were prepared to go to "concentration camps, torture chambers". "Freedom or death!" he cried. "There is no way back!"

From the rally, Begin went to the Knesset to make his speech. An impassioned crowd marched in his wake, crushing through the police barricades and pelting the Knesset, with stones. Ninety-two policemen and thirty-six civilians were injured. The shouts of the mob, the sounds of the clashes, and the wail of ambulance sirens added a further dramatic dimension to the debate going on within the building. While Mapam leader Ya'akov Hazan was making his speech bitterly denouncing the government, a Herut Knesset member rushed into the chamber shouting: "They're using gas! Gas against Jews!" Two communist members shouted: "Blood is being shed outside! It's impossible to continue the session!" A woman member fainted. Shouts, threats, and curses filled the chamber, together with whiffs of tear gas. The floor was littered with stones and shattered glass. The right- and left-wing extremists seemed set on disrupting the Knesset session. At 7 p.m. Ben-Gurion called in the army to restore order. He managed to keep his temper till Begin arose to make his speech – whereupon the two men began a furious exchange. When the speaker of the Knesset tried to silence Begin, the latter replied: "If I don't speak, no one shall speak!"

At this moment of storm and confusion, Ben-Gurion felt that it was vital to speak clearly to his people, and provide it with vigorous leadership. On 8 January, he broadcast a short radio address.

Yesterday a dastardly hand was raised against the sovereignty of the Knesset – the beginning of an attempt to destroy democracy in Israel ... The leader and organizer of this "revolt", Mr Menahem Begin, stood in Jerusalem's Zion Square yesterday, inciting the crowds ... I do not dismiss Mr Menahem Begin's proclamation that he is preparing for a battle of life or death. As premier and defense minister, I feel duty-bound to say to the people [have] no fear! The state possesses sufficient forces and means to protect Israel's sovereignty and freedom and to prevent thugs and political assassins from taking control and [foil] pro-longed acts of terror within the state ... The state of Israel will not be turned into Spain or Syria.

The Knesset debate raged on for two days longer, but passions gradually cooled. On 9 January, a roll-call vote was taken. Both camps mobilized all their forces: a Mapai member who was abroad at the time was summoned to fly home; a Herut member suffering from the after effects of a heart attack was brought in on a stretcher. By a vote of 61 to 50, the government's proposal was adopted, and a month later, the reparations agreement was signed, with the West German government undertaking to provide Israel with $715 million worth of goods and services over a twelve-year period. The German government committed itself to pay a further $107 million to a committee representing world Jewish organizations. The reparation payments would thus reach a total of $822 million.

It was not by chance that 1953 was the year when Ben-Gurion collapsed under the burden of accumulated weariness. Five years after the establish-ment of the state, all the great challenges had been faced and decisions had been reached on all the fateful matters that would determine the character of the state and shape its future. The prime objective – mass immigration and doubling the population within four years – had been attained in full. At the end of 1952, the flow of immigrants diminished, and the absorption of immigration became a matter of routine. The bitter confrontation over the reparations agreement was a matter of the past. The army had been unified by legislation and creation of permanent structures. Israel's political path had been clearly defined since she had abandoned her policy of "non-alignment" and adopted a pro-Western posture. Peace negotia-tions with the Arabs had failed, and Israel had come to terms with the fact that she would have to depend upon her military prowess for a long time to come. By and large, the heroic period of Israel's rebirth may be considered to have come to an end.

Ben-Gurion had played a decisive role in all these developments. The frequent Cabinet crises; the bitter disagreements within his own party; the daily needs, which required him – with all his penchant for clear-cut decisions – to seek compromises and half-way arrangements all caused him profound frustration and sapped his strength. When the Cabinet secretary, Ze'ev Sharef, was asked late in 1953 why Ben-Gurion had decided to resign, he replied: "The Messiah arrived, he gathered in Israel's exiles, he triumphed over all the peoples around, he conquered the Land of Israel ... and then he had to take his seat in a coalition ..."

During this period, Ben-Gurion took a number of leaves of absence, in Israel and abroad, during which he tried to withdraw completely from his customary hypercharged routine. Late in November 1950, he went on a three-week vacation to Greece, England, and France, accompanied by Elkana Gali and Ehud Avriel. While in England, he "vanished" from the journalists, immediately giving rise to rumors that he was conducting secret contacts with British and other statesmen. In fact, he had slipped away to visit the bookshops in Oxford and Cambridge.

The tour ended with a few days' rest on the French Riviera, and Ben-Gurion even permitted himself to indulge in a little "mischief". One day, he and his companions drove towards Monaco on the twisting, dangerous road running along the cliffs. Suddenly, he decided that the time had come for him to learn to drive. He regarded driving as one of the hallmarks of modern man and did not conceal his envy of his aides, who possessed this skill. He stated that, he wished then and there, to learn to drive, and nothing the two men could say would change his mind. The Old Man clutched the steering wheel and the luxurious vehicle lurched forward. At the last moment, his aides managed to send their escort car ahead to clear the way, while Elkana Gali and Ehud Avriel leaped onto the narrow running boards holding on to the door with one hand and desperately waving to approaching cars to halt or pull over with the other. In Ben-Gurion's grasp, the car wobbled drunkenly all over the road. After a short drive, the Old Man gave up, but it was a long time before Avriel and Gali recovered from the most dangerous ride they had ever experienced.

That evening, the two men decided to compensate themselves by relaxing at the Monte Carlo casino. In a brief consultation, they decided to wait until Ben-Gurion went up to his room to sleep. But Ben-Gurion did not display the slightest intention of going to his room. Innocently, he watched them exchange nervous glances. Suddenly, his eyes gleamed mischievously, and he said: "You want to go to gamble at the casino, right? And you want to win, too? Come, let me teach you how." Sitting down beside them, he picked up a pen and a sheet of paper and explained his "secret system" for winning at roulette. The two men gazed at him in utter astonishment. Had he learned this system during a private vacation on the Riviera a few years before? Or at some other place during the course of his travels? The Old Man would not disclose his secret, but the two men were even more astonished to reach the casino's roulette tables and discover that his system worked!

Neither trips abroad nor occasional days of rest in the country could overcome Ben-Gurion's weariness. Consequently, Ben-Gurion arrived at the conclusion that he had "to leave this work for a year or two, or longer".

Yet it is questionable whether fatigue was the only reason for Ben-Gurion's resignation. Together with the feeling that he needed a vacation from his work in the Cabinet, Ben-Gurion appears to have come to the conclusion that he was personally obliged to apply himself to some pioneering undertaking. In order to face up to the challenges of the times, the state was in need of a large-scale volunteer movement to undertake ventures that were beyond ·the capacity of governmental agencies: settling desert areas, immigrant absorption, closing social gaps. Ben-Gurion understood that for all his official authority, he could not send people to such tasks from the Prime Minister's Office. He had to step forward and lead them personally.

This idea gradually took root in Ben-Gurion's mind. Without being conscious of it, he began to hunt about for a new target through which he himself could fulfill what he demanded of others. He found that target in the spring of 1953, while driving back from Eilat. In the heart of the Negev, he saw a number of huts and a group of young people working nearby. He approached and asked them what they were doing there. They told him that they had served in this area during the War of Independence and had decided to set up a new kibbutz – Sdeh Boker. This was the challenge. To found a new kibbutz in the heart of the Negev, to begin from the very beginning!

Progressively, his resolve hardened: he would leave the government and join Sdeh Boker. But, prior to his resignation, he wished to make certain that he was leaving the state well organized and not facing any danger. He thought that he could withdraw for two years, having come to the conclusion that the Arabs would not launch the second round of their war against Israel before 1956. He decided to prepare a detailed defence plan for the period of his absence. On 19 July 1953, he departed for a three-month vacation and spent most of his leave touring army units all over the country. He planned a reshuffle of the senior command and worked out a program for improving security and strengthening the armed forces. On 18 October 1953, his eighteen-point program was complete.

Satisfied, the Old Man now addressed himself to more practical matters. In the presence of his secretary, Yitzhak Navon, he stood up and measured the dimensions of his study. On a sheet of paper, he sketched a rectangle, carefully noting the length and breadth. Then he gave the sheet to Navon and said: "These are the measurements. Tell them to build the hut accordingly."

"What hut?" Navon asked, bewildered.

"In Sdeh Boker," said Ben-Gurion. "I am going to settle down there."

Spreading like wild-fire, the rumor aroused consternation. The Old Man's foes mocked the report; his supporters and admirers sensed anxiety and fear. What would they do without him? Who could imagine the State of Israel without Ben-Gurion? But he paid no need to the appeals of his colleagues, delegations, or newspaper editorials. On 2 November, he tendered his written resignation to the president and went on to take his leave of the army, of his party, and of the Cabinet. On 7 November, he gave up the post of premier and broadcast an impassioned farewell, quoting from the Book of Psalms (131: 1): "Lord, my heart is not haughty, nor mine eyes lofty; neither do I exercise myself in great matters, or in things too high for me."

12

Sdeh Boker

Upon his departure from the government, Ben-Gurion handed over the premiership to the successor his party had chosen: Moshe Sharett. The relationship between the two men went back to the beginning of the century, and Sharett for many years held Ben-Gurion in total awe. "Your esteem for me is my moral backbone," he wrote to Ben-Gurion in 1937.

For me you are not just a senior colleague in my work, not just the leader of the movement which is my life's home. For me, you are a man whose personal moral authority I accepted when I was yet on the threshold of my youth ... I shudder to think what would have happened to me if you had not been at my side and before me ... I want you to know what you are for me, and what I wish you to be till the end of our paths.

From the very first, however, Sharett's feelings were not requited: Ben-Gurion wrote to Paula of Sharett:

He is not a man of vision ... At times he fails to find his way in complex matters ... he is incapable of deciding on matters demanding great intellectual and moral courage. But he knows his job, he is gifted with many talents ... and I believe that he knows himself to be in need of guidance.

Sharett was not carved from the same kind of tough material that molded Ben-Gurion's powerful, decisive personality. His political views were more moderate, and he was also more skeptical than Ben-Gurion, avoiding oversimplification of issues. He attached great value to the written and spoken word, and was congenial in manner, not harsh or extreme like Ben-Gurion. Pioneering endeavors and the eagerness to establish *faits accomplis* – the very kernel of Ben Gurion's Zionist philosophy – were important to him, but he did not approach them with the same uncompromising zeal. The differences in the two men's opinions found their expression in one of Ben-Gurion's best-known sayings and in Sharett's comment on it. In 1955, Ben Gurion declared: "Our future depends, not on what the *goyim* [nations of the world] say, but on what the Jews do!" Sharett's subsequent comment was: "Correct. But it is also important what the *goyim* do!"

Arguments about "What will the *goyim* say?" were the key to many of the disagreements which progressively poisoned the relationship between Ben-Gurion and Sharett in the course of the fifties. Sharett was worried about U.N. resolutions of condemnation and stuck obstinately to the view that "without the U.N. resolution, the state would not have come into being". Ben-Gurion held that "the State of Israel exists solely due to the people of Israel, and primarily, due to the army".

The growing rift between the two men was no trifling matter. On the one hand, there stood a charismatic leader, a man of enormous power, a magnetic, overwhelming character. The man who confronted him was far weaker, and lacked those powers of leadership, that dimension of greatness and vision which had brought Ben-Gurion to the top. In their arguments and confrontations, Sharett was burdened by a painful sense of inferiority and anger with regard to his older colleague. As for Ben-Gurion, when he decided to resign as premier in 1953, a heavy burden of bitterness overlaid his relationship with Moshe Sharett – the successor he did not want.

During the leave of absence Ben-Gurion took before his resignation, Moshe Sharett acted as premier and Pinhas Lavon as defense minister. It was only on 5 October that Ben-Gurion notified the Mapai ministers he was resigning "for two years". Sharett joined with his colleagues in trying to persuade Ben-Gurion to retract his decision, but he did not really attach much hope to these efforts. Yet he did not foresee that the succession to Ben-Gurion held agonizing frustrations in store for him. First of all, he was disenchanted with the new defense minister whom Ben-Gurion had brought forward. He was similarly dissatisfied with the character of the new chief of staff, Moshe Dayan. In fact, Sharett's problems began while he was still acting premier.

On 12 October 1953 infiltrators from Jordan slipped into an Israeli village and flung a hand-grenade into one of its houses, killing a woman and two of her children. The incident provoked great anger in Israel, and leading circles entertained a growing conviction that it was essential to strike a hard blow at the Jordanians. That day, Ben-Gurion was touring in the north, where a large-scale military exercise was in progress, accompanied by his deputy, Pinhas Lavon, Chief of Staff Mordechai Makleff, and Chief of Operations Moshe Dayan. On receiving the news of the raid, the four men held an impromptu consultation at the side of their jeep. Ben-Gurion listened, but he did not contribute to the discussion. Formally, he was on leave of absence and Lavon was the acting defense minister, so Ben-Gurion decided to remain silent.

It was decided to mount a reprisal action – the largest ever undertaken by the army. The target selected was the village of Kibiya, which served as a base and haven for infiltrators. The plan was to send a unit into the village to blow up several dozen houses. As the reprisal was intended to be painful, it was decided to inflict a relatively large number of casualties on the Jordanians – ten to twelve.

Moshe Dayan set off immediately for General Staff headquarters to draw up the operational order. Right from the start, the operation was intended as vengeance for the dead woman and her children, and as a warning to the Jordanians that Israel would no longer sit by idly.

From the General Staff the order was forwarded to Central Command which decided that a company of paratroopers was to undertake the operation. The company was placed under the command of a young major by the name of Arik Sharon.

No one consulted Moshe Sharett, the acting premier. Lavon only notified him casually of the projected operation. Sharett did not object to this bizarre procedure, but the following morning, he was beset by grave doubts. He called Lavon in for a talk, and when he objected to the proposed operation, Lavon countered "B-G. does not agree with you". At the end of the meeting, Sharett wrote to Ben-Gurion asking him to return to head the Cabinet, "because I will not preside over its meeting next Sunday".

While Sharett was writing his letter, the paratroopers and soldiers from "Unit 101" were already forming up. Zero hour was set for 9.30 that evening. About one hundred soldiers converged on Kibiya in small detachments loaded down with some 1200 pounds of explosives. The Jordanian soldiers began to flee in panic. When the order was given, the paratroopers stormed the village and about twelve Jordanians, most of them soldiers, were killed. The villagers began a panic-stricken flight, taking their women and children to the neighboring towns. No one stood in their way. The departure of its inhabitants left the village in darkness and silence, broken only by a monotonous Oriental melody undulating from the café's ancient radio, which its owners had not troubled to turn off before fleeing. This now provided the background music for a series of explosions. The paratroopers did not search the houses marked out for demolition. They broke in, laid the charges, and withdrew. In one case only did the demolition officer hear the sound of crying from within a house after he had already lit the fuse of his charge. Running inside, he found a little girl hiding in a corner and managed to get her out and to send her off toward a nearby village.

As they destroyed house after house, it never even entered the para- troopers' minds that they were unwillingly perpetrating a massacre. Dozens of women, children, and old people were crouched in cellars, on upper stories, and under beds. They made no sound, and no one noticed their presence. The explosions went on for three hours; after demolishing about forty-five houses, the unit withdrew to Israeli territory. On his return, Arik Sharon reported that the enemy had suffered ten to twelve fatal casualties. Dayan sent him a note in his own handwriting: "There's none like you!"

The following day, when the Jordanians returned to the village, the horrifying truth came out. Seventy corpses were found in the rubble, including dozens of women and children. The atrocity aroused world-wide abhorrence. There was considerable confusion in the army too. No one had foreseen that the action would lead to an outcome of this kind. Moshe Sharett was aghast. In its embarrassment, the General Staff decided that the army spokesman would not issue any statement on the operation. The Cabinet and the Knesset were shaken by the tumult in world public opinion and by the disgust the action had aroused among Israelis and their leaders. Winston Churchill sent a personal message to Ben-Gurion, deploring the operation. For several days, the Cabinet remained undecided on how to deal with the crisis.

On 18 October, Ben-Gurion returned from his leave of absence, and presided over the Cabinet meeting. On being asked whether he knew of the Kibiya raid, he answered innocently: "I was on leave, and no one has to ask me whether or not to undertake a reprisal raid. If I had been asked, I would have said: 'Do it!' " Referring to this reply, Mordechai Makleff commented: "Strictly speaking, Ben-Gurion was right." Indeed, Ben-Gurion had been on leave, and was not consulted. But he knew about the operation.

Ben-Gurion added: "What I knew about this operation was what I heard from the acting minister of defense, [namely] that the operation had been carried out by inhabitants of the border settlements." On his initiative, a statement to this effect was issued in Israel and distributed abroad. The raid had been carried out not by the army, but by border settlers acting on their own initiative. Despite Sharett's objections, Ben-Gurion insisted vigorously that the army must not admit its responsibility for the operation.

Later, he was to confess to one of his confidants that he had lied, but he explained his motives for doing so. "Have you read Victor Hugo's *Les Misérables*?" he asked.

There's a description in the book of the wanted prisoner's flight from the officer pursuing him. He hides in a room where a nun is seated. The police officer enters the room and asks the nun: "Have you seen the prisoner?" and she answers: "No." Never doubting her word, he leaves the room without conducting a search. As for the nun, she committed no sin in lying, because her lie was designed to save human life. A lie like that is measured by a different yardstick.

Ben-Gurion believed that under certain circumstances, it was permissible to lie for the good of the state. But Moshe Sharett was astounded by his behaviour. "I told Zipporah [his wife] that I would have resigned if it had fallen to me to step before a microphone and broadcast a fictitious account of what happened to the people of Israel and to the whole world."

The Kibiya operation had far-reaching military consequences, and the army came to the conclusion that future reprisal raids should be directed against military, not civilian, targets. However, the principal lesson from the episode stemmed from the discovery of startling deficiencies in communications between the country's leaders and in their ministerial responsibility. Sharett, who was officiating as acting premier at the time of the action, failed to get Defense Minister Lavon to consult him or report to him.

Perhaps Ben-Gurion – who implicitly backed Lavon – saw this incident as a taste of things to come and perceived the dangers in Sharett's weakness. At any rate, when the Mapai Political Committee convened on 2 November, Ben-Gurion proposed that Levi Eshkol replace him as premier and that Pinhas Lavon take over as defense minister. The moment Ben-Gurion announced his proposals, it became clear to all that he did not have a sufficiently high opinion of Sharett to entrust him with the premiership. Within hours, the story became public, and the whole country knew that Ben-Gurion did not want Sharett to be his successor. Eshkol, however, refused to undertake the premiership. There was growing pressure from Sharett's friends, and Mapai found itself in grave confusion. In mid-November, a three-man committee began sifting candidates for the post of premier. Its members met with Ben-Gurion and convinced him to back Sharett's candidacy. Other opponents of Sharett also withdrew their objections. The only person who opposed Sharett vigorously and systematically all the way was Pinhas Lavon.

On 14 December 1953, Paula and David Ben-Gurion set off for Sdeh Boker. Secretaries, military policemen, and security guards helped to load several trucks with furniture, suitcases, household utensils, bundles, and, above all, many hundreds of books. A whole entourage of journalists and friends accompanied the Ben-Gurions to Sdeh Boker. After taking his leave of his escort, the Old Man stripped off his dark suit and tie and put on a thick, coarse winter uniform. This change of clothes was symbolical of the change in his life-style. The newly arrived kibbutz member set off for his first day's work, which consisted, of all things, of hauling manure – precisely what he had done on his first day in Petah Tikva, forty-seven years earlier.

At Sdeh Boker, Ben-Gurion received dozens of letters daily from all over the world. With characteristic diligence, he did not leave a single letter unanswered. He also received many visitors every day – invited and uninvited; there were delegations, prominent personalities, statesmen, journalists, and youth groups. They swallowed up the precious time he had set aside for reading, writing and work. It is amazing that he still found time and strength to engage in agricultural work.

He was very earnest in his attitude to kibbutz life and to his status as a rank-and-file member. He asked the members of the kibbutz to call him "David", and not "Ben-Gurion".

He derived great satisfaction from his work. Every evening he went to the notice board in the dining room to find where he had been posted in the work roster. At first he engaged in spreading manure and plowing, but realizing that this would soon sap his strength; the kibbutz entrusted him with caring for the small meteorological station. Most of the time, he was put to work with the sheep.

He felt well, and his health improved somewhat. His face and hands were tanned, and he was full of energy and vitality. He also slept better.

Many citizens wrote, pleading with him to return to the national leadership. Over and over again, his replies set out his pioneering motives. He wrote a Tel Aviv resident:

I am happy and content, that I am still capable of working in the Negev Desert, and helping a group of wonderful young people who have undertaken a great and arduous task: to turn the desert into (the Garden of) Eden. I consider it a great privilege to take part in this bold venture ... It is possible [for me] to help in building up the country not only by standing at the head of the government.

Yet he could not fully divorce himself from that position. A stream of high-ranking visitors constantly came down to Sdeh Boker – ministers, army officers, senior officials, and party leaders – all of whom sought Ben-Gurion's counsel on internal and foreign policy. One of the reasons for this – probably the most important – was Moshe Sharett's lack of authority and leadership. Ben-Gurion's absence was keenly felt, particularly as the situation along Israel's borders deteriorated. Murderous infiltration raids from Jordanian territory multiplied, reaching a horrifying peak with the murder of eleven passengers on a bus ambushed by an Arab gang in the Negev. In early autumn, the situation on the Egyptian border also worsened, and there were a number of violent clashes there.

To aggravate the situation, there were fundamental disagreements between Prime Minister Sharett, who favored a moderate policy, and Defense Minister Lavon, who headed the activist camp. In addition to this clash on principles, there was also a bitter personal confrontation between the two men, and soon their relationship became intolerable. At the same time, there were grave misunderstandings between Lavon and the chief of staff, Moshe Dayan, as well as with the Defense Ministry's director-general, Shimon Peres. Both of these men – Ben-Gurion's disciples and outspoken activists – backed Lavon against Sharett on political and military issues; but there was nevertheless a sharp crisis in relations between each of them and Lavon. Before long, a hair-raising epidemic of clashes and accusations overtook the nation's leaders. It was not only Ben-Gurion's absence that caused this uproar. Clearly, the atmosphere at the top was being poisoned by the character of Pinhas Lavon.

Ben-Gurion may have been satisfied with his appointee as defense minister, but his colleagues were aware of several traits that had escaped the Old Man. The forty-nine-year-old Lavon was excessively sarcastic, and his barbs were painful. He was arrogant, egotistical, and openly disdainful of others. While he was still only acting defense minister, Lavon made Sharett's life a misery, treating him with open contempt, and not bothering to consult him or report to him. He did not even trouble himself to notify Sharett of a reprisal raid ahead of time. Zvi Maimon, who acted as the Cabinet's stenographer, told one of Ben-Gurion's aides:

It is hard to see [Sharett] unable to control his Cabinet colleagues, but it's even harder to see [Lavon] making his life a misery. The presence of [coalition] ministers does not hinder this "devil" in his diabolical verbal tricks . . . there is no justification for the venomous verbal freedom he permits himself to display toward the premier.

In addition to Mapai leaders, the outgoing chief of staff, had warned Ben-Gurion against Lavon. Ben-Gurion asked him candidly, "Why don't you want Lavon?" Makleff replied that Lavon "did not know how to treat soldiers", adding that he was "a dangerous man. . . . On one occasion, Lavon told me that it was necessary to stir up trouble between the Americans and the Jordanians by sabotage operations in Amman." Later, Makleff recalled his words as a kind of prelude to the Lavon Affair.

Lavon appeared to have undermined his position himself. His unconcealed cynicism and haughtiness deterred even his own friends, and at the end of July 1954 matters again reached a head. Several Mapai leaders – including Eshkol, Golda Meir, and Zalman Aranne – came to see Ben-Gurion, complaining bitterly of the relationships between Sharett and Lavon. Ben-Gurion jotted a laconic note in his journal: "I advised Eshkol to have an open talk with Pinhas. Eshkol promised." What Ben-Gurion did not record in his diary was the message Eshkol was to pass on to Lavon. But Nehemia Argov, Ben-Gurion's closest aide noted in his diary: "Eshkol told P.L. that B.-G. said he would not be premier, and B.-G. said he did not stand behind him . . ."

In effect, Ben-Gurion had now withdrawn his backing for Lavon. He had given up hope of Sharett right from the start; now he was disappointed in his own appointee. The two men were to remain on good terms. But in the summer of 1954, Ben-Gurion appears to have concluded that the leaders who had replaced him were a complete failure and his choice of Lavon had been a mistake.

Two principal groups now began a campaign to restore Ben-Gurion to power, each one motivated by its own interests. One group consisted of "the young men": several of Ben-Gurion's aides (Nehemia Argov, and Yitzhak Navon); several of the senior officials who had worked under him (Shimon Peres, Teddy Kollek, and Ehud Avriel); and Moshe Dayan. Singly and together, this group repeatedly launched its forays into Sdeh Boker in the hope of convincing Ben-Gurion to return. Ben-Gurion was more profoundly impressed by the growing pressure of his old Mapai colleagues. The first delegation turned up in July 1954. "They came to demand my return," Ben-Gurion summarized their conversation. But in his characteristically fiery manner, he declared: "I shall not return . . . I have returned to Sdeh Boker, and here I will stay." He gave a similar reply to Zalman Aranne and Golda Meir when they came to him with the same request.

Such was the atmosphere as 1954 drew to a close: powerful external pressures; border tensions and gropings for a new political direction; loss of public confidence in the nation's leadership; and political and military leaders locked in bitter feuding in an atmosphere of suspicion and slander. Worse still, elections were in the offing, and there was a widespread search for a strong, credible leadership that would display inspiration and initiative. And then, like a *deus ex machina*, act one of the Lavon Affair erupted.

In the spring of 1954, Gamal Abdel Nasser assumed full powei in Egypt, after a bittter behind-the-scenes struggle. To keep Egypt in the pro-Western camp, the United States exerted pressure on Britain to withdraw from the country. The matter appears to have been settled during Prime Minister Winston Churchill's talks with President Eisenhower in Washington on 25–9 June 1954. (The Anglo–Egyptian agreement was ultimately signed at the end of July.) While these negotiations were in progress, there was great concern in Israel over the forthcoming British evacuation of the Canal Zone. The accepted view in Israel was that the presence of British forces in the Canal Zone was a damper on possible adventurous tendencies in the Egyptian regime. The British withdrawal would also give an immediate boost to Egypt's military potential, through the acquisition of airfields, military installations, and arms dumps along the canal.

Certain circles in Israel decided that it was vital to make every possible effort to dissuade Britain from evacuating the Canal Zone. At the last moment, Defense Minister Pinhas Lavon and the chief of military intelligence, Benyamin Gibly, who were on close personal terms, seem to have decided to take unconventional action to foil the evacuation or, at the very least, delay it.

The groundwork appears to have been laid years earlier. Back in 1951, an Israeli intelligence officer named Avraham Dar slipped into Egypt bearing a British passport with his alias, John Darling. Posing as a businessman, he succeeded in recruiting a group of young Jews – members of Zionist youth movements – and forming them into a clandestine network of two cells: one in Cairo, the other in Alexandria. The cell commanders were issued with transmitters to keep contact with Israel.

During the first part of 1954, a new commander was appointed to replace Avraham Dar. The members of the network knew him as "Robert". He arrived with a German passport made in the name of Paul Frank and masqueraded as a businessman. His real name was Avry Elad; Viennese-born, he had served in the Palmach, reaching the rank of major (though he was demoted to the rank of private for stealing a refrigerator). In 1953, he was recruited for work in military intelligence, and his former rank was restored to him. Elad was sent first to Germany to build up a false identity. Then he set off for Egypt. Another Israeli officer remotely linked with the network, came to Egypt on a German passport made out in the name of Max Bennet and posed as an artificial-limbs expert.

With the British evacuation of the Suez Canal imminent, Israeli intelligence circles came up with an idea to prevent or delay the withdrawal. They proposed a series of sabotage acts directed primarily against Western embassies and other institutions, such as libraries, cultural centres and consulates. These acts would be interpreted by the British government as being perpetrated either by the Egyptian government itself or by the fanatically nationalist Moslem Brotherhood. In either case, the attacks would demonstrate that the regime was weak, incapable of maintaining order, and not to be relied upon to keep agreements it signed. The British government would be obliged to reconsider the evacuation plan or even cancel it.

In retrospect the plan appears astonishingly naïve and dangerous. Those who thought it up appear to have lacked any political understanding. Even when it was raised, there were objections from the small circle who knew of it. But the head of military intelligence, who supported the idea, submitted it to the defense minister, who took a liking to it. (Lavon himself had once come up with a similar idea for operations in Amman to sow discord between Jordan and the United States.) During the spring of 1954, Lavon and Gibly discussed the plan in a favorable light. The defense minister gave it his full backing, but he was not requested – possibly, because of his support was known – to give verbal or written instructions for its implementation. This unanimity was to be of great significance at a later stage.

On 26 May 1954, the deputy chief of military intelligence set off for Europe to meet Avry Elad in Paris. Speaking on Gibly's behalf he ordered Elad to return to Egypt and have the cells attack Egyptian, British, and American targets in Cairo and Alexandria. Further instructions would be sent, in code, in a cooking recipe broadcast on the Voice of Israel's program for housewives.

Elad returned to Egypt on 25 June and within a short time his people went into action. On 2 July, three young men from the Alexandria cell dropped medium-sized parcels containing incendiary bombs into mail boxes in a Cairo post office. On 14 July, members of the cells in Cairo and Alexandria deposited improvised incendiary bombs in the American libraries in each city; in both cases, small fires broke out but were quickly extinguished. On 23 July, Elad ordered his subordinates to attack five objectives simultaneously: two movie theaters in Cairo, two in Alexandria, and the luggage depository in Cairo's railway station. The bombs were packed in spectacle cases, and that evening there was a fateful mishap. One of the incendiary devices went off prematurely in the pocket of Philip Nathanson, a member of the Alexandria cell, just as he was about to enter the Rio Cinema. An Egyptian officer saw the young man writhing with pain, as smoke poured out of his pocket. Assisted by several policemen, the officer seized him and, after extinguishing the blaze, placed him under arrest. That same night, several members of the cell were arrested. In the next few days, the whole network was captured, Max Bennet among them. Avry Elad was not touched, even though he was the commander of the group and all the threads led to him. Unhurriedly he wound up his affairs, sold his car, and set out for Europe two whole weeks after the commencement of the arrests.

The first reports on the arrests reached the head of military intelligence that same evening, and the news placed him in a quandary. Had the operations been successful, he would have gained considerable standing with the defense minister, who had backed him all along. But now that they had misfired, the blame rested entirely with him. The defense minister had, admittedly, encouraged him and supported the idea; but he had not given specific instructions to execute the plan. Without informing the defense minister that the operations in Egypt had been already carried out and their perpetrators caught, Gibly approached Lavon with the proposal that the plan be executed. The defense minister approved the proposal, without realizing that his order was retroactive.

On 25 July, the Arab communications media announced the capture of a Zionist network that had tried to set fire to movie theaters, and may have been responsible for the fires in the American libraries. Gibly sent a note to Lavon notifying him that "our people" were among those arrested in Alexandria. The defense minister read the note and signed it. The report confirmed that the operation had failed, but that, after all, was the risk involved in clandestine actions. Two weeks later, on 8 August, Gibly presented a detailed written report on the capture of the network. As far as Lavon was concerned, that was the end of the affair.

On 24 August, Moshe Dayan came to visit Ben-Gurion, shortly after returning from abroad. After their meeting, Ben-Gurion wrote in his journal: "He told me about a strange order by P.L. – during his [Dayan's] absence – for an operation in Egypt which failed (they should have known that it would fail) – criminal irresponsibility!" This was Ben-Gurion's first knowledge of the mishap in Egypt, and this was his verdict on Lavon's actions. Until mid-October, Ben-Gurion does not appear to have talked to anyone about the affair. But on his 68th birthday, he confided in Nehemia Argov. "For the first time, I talked with the Old Man on the horrifying subject named Lavon," Argov wrote in his diary. "The Old Man analyzed the Egyptian matter: 'It was not the defense minister's business to decide on this [operation]. By what right did he take it upon himself to decide and act independently in an out-and-out political sphere?'

Clearly, as early as October, Ben-Gurion regarded Lavon as being to blame for the debacle in Egypt.

On 11 December 1954, the second act of the tragedy began with the opening of the trial of "the Zionist agents" in Cairo. The trial set off a storm in Israel, and the papers were filled with reports from Egypt. On reading them, the defense minister was surprised to learn that the sabotage attacks had been launched prior to his approval. He called in the chief of military intelligence, who asserted vehemently that Lavon had approved the operations at a meeting held on 16 July. This was clearly a lie, since Lavon's order was given on 23 July; but to protect himself, Gibly now claimed to have received the order a week earlier. The defense minister looked in his diary and discovered that they could not have discussed the matter on that day because he did not see Gibly then. However, Lavon was no wide-eyed *ingenu*. Seeing that Gibly was trying to pass the blame onto him, he decided to hit back in the same fashion. He claimed that he only met the head of military intelligence on 31 July – in other words, a week after the network's capture – and it was then that Gibly got the order out of him.

This second lie also failed to stand up. The hand-written memorandum dated 26 July in which Gibly notified the defense minister that "our people" had been arrested in Alexandria – turned up in a file in the minister's office. From then on, Lavon adopted new tactics: he totally denied issuing the order and denied that he had at any time approved execution of the operation. He approached Moshe Sharett and asked him to set up a commission of inquiry to examine the matter. Sharett agreed.

The commission was composed of former Chief of Staff Ya'akov Dori and Supreme Court Justice Yitzhak Olshan. One of the witnesses summoned to appear before them was Avry Elad, who was then in Europe. His testimony constituted a threat to the chief of military intelligence. If Elad told the truth, he would reveal that he had received instructions to undertake sabotage operations while he was still in Europe in May and June – long before Gibly's talk with Lavon. The intelligence chief's loyal assistant, Mordechai Ben-Tzur, therefore sent Elad a sealed envelope containing a letter from Gibly and himself. Notifying Elad that he would soon be summoned to Israel to give testimony on the debacle in Egypt he ordered him to deny carrying out the attacks on the Alexandria post office and the American libraries on 2 and 14 July. In addition, he told him to amend his diary and reports accordingly. The purpose of the letter was to induce Elad to testify that the operations began after 16 July – the day when Gibly had talked with Lavon and received permission to undertake the attacks. When Elad returned to Israel, he was met at the airport by Gibly's subordinates, who briefed him on how to testify before the Olshan–Dori Commission and prepared him for his meeting with Moshe Dayan and Pinhas Lavon. Elad delivered his false testimony just as Ben-Tzur had instructed him in his secret letter.

That testimony was of decisive importance for a further reason. While operations in Egypt were in progress, Gibly wrote to Chief of Staff Dayan, who was touring the United States, and informed him of the attacks. The letter was dated 19 July 1954. Dayan read the letter and destroyed it. Later, those investigating the episode claimed that the copy of the letter in military intelligence files had been forged on orders from Gibly. The secretary retyped the letter and in the section describing the operations in Egypt, she added the words: "on Lavon's orders" – backing up Gibly's contention that he had received the order on 16 July and supporting Elad's false testimony before the Olshan–Dori Commission.

In the meantime, the Cairo trial had evoked considerable upset in Israel.

On the eve of the trial, an Egyptian Jew by the name of Karmonah committed suicide. (Another version is that he was beaten to death by the Egyptian police.) On 21 December, Max Bennet committed suicide in prison. A young woman among the accused made two suicide attempts. The months of December 1954 and January 1955 were a bitter nightmare for the country's leaders and for the few others in on the secret. On the one hand, they launched a desperate campaign in the world's capitals to try and save the defendants in Cairo. On the other hand, the Olshan–Dori Commission uncovered a horrifying web of lies, intrigues, and poisoned relationships at the top of the defense establishment.

On 27 January 1955, the Cairo military tribunal issued its verdict: two of the accused were acquitted for lack of evidence; six were sentenced to long periods of imprisonment (from seven years to life); and two others, Shmuel Azar and Dr Moshe Marzouk, were sentenced to death. The urgent pleas of heads of state, clergymen, and intellectuals from all over the world were of no avail. On 31 January the two men were hanged in the courtyard of Cairo prison.

Lavon had placed great hopes on the Olshan–Dori Commission, but its inquiry back-fired on him. He soon discovered that all the witnesses – with one exception – were against him. He was also aware that the chiefs of military intelligence were falsifying evidence against him. As his tension increased, Lavon was pushed to extremes. He confided in a faithful friend that Dayan and Peres "had conspired to bring about his elimination from public life", adding that "unless he succeeded in proving his innocence in the Cairo affair, he would commit suicide". Lavon was to repeat his suicide threat several times during the next few days, and his impassioned words had a profound impact on his colleagues in the Mapai leadership. When the investigation ended there can be no doubt that the Mapai ministers' inability to decide what to do about Lavon stemmed from their awful fear that he would kill himself.

The Olshan–Dori Commission functioned for ten days, in total secrecy. Interim reports convinced Sharett that the commission would find Lavon to blame. But on 13 January, when the commission submitted its findings to Sharett, its conclusions were indecisive. "We find it impossible to say more than that we were not convinced beyond all reasonable doubt that [the chief of military intelligence] did not receive orders from the defense minister. At the same time, we are not sure that the defense minister did give the orders attributed to him."

Anxiously, Sharett awaited Lavon's response to the commission's findings. His forebodings came true. On 18 January, Lavon marched into his room and gave vent to his terrible anger. "I witnessed an outburst of blind fury," Sharett wrote. Lavon launched a wild attack on the commission's findings, referring to them as "a mendacious document" and as "a crying injustice". He delivered personal attacks on the commission's members and finally announced that he would demand a parliamentary inquiry. Astounded, Sharett tried to refute his charges, reminding him how pleased he had been with the commission's members and warning him that a parliamentary inquiry implied publication of the whole matter. For his part, Lavon stated that "there are situations in which a man stops considering the world's reactions".

In a state of great upset, Sharett summoned his close friends in Mapai. Most of them condemned Lavon; only Eshkol opposed his dismissal, urging Sharett "to bear the situation, and do everything possible to reduce the damage". They concluded their discussion with the decision to consult Ben-Gurion. These decisions of the Mapai leadership were adopted in a veritably clandestine manner. At the time, the Lavon Affair and its ramifications were the most closely-guarded secret in Israel. Not even Cabinet ministers and Knesset members knew what was happening at the top.

On 1 February, a "high-level" delegation set off for Sdeh Boker to consult Ben-Gurion. His opinion was: "He [Lavon] must go!" Lavon learned of their visit that same evening. The next day, a newspaper printed a report on the consultations held at Sdeh Boker concerning "internal changes among Mapai Cabinet ministers". It was a heavy blow to Lavon. The following day, he submitted a letter of resignation to Sharett. This would appear to have ended the internal crisis. But there was a catch in Lavon's letter: "I reserve [the right] to bring the reasons for my resignation to the knowledge of the party and the Knesset Foreign Affairs and Defense Committee. I am not prepared to take public blame for the Egyptian affair and no party discipline will oblige me to . . ."

Determined to prevent publication of the whole matter, the Mapai leaders reconsidered their intention of dismissing Lavon, and asked him to remain. This was what Lavon had been waiting for. He now revealed a plan he had presented to Sharett while the investigation was still in progress: the dismissal of Shimon Peres and Benyamin Gibly and sweeping changes in the Defense Ministry.

Sharett was prepared for far-reaching concessions to appease Lavon. On 11 February, without notifying the chief of staff, he summoned Gibly. According to Nehemia Argov:

The premier told him it was clear that he, Benyamin [Gibly] had not committed the actions [in Egypt] without an order, but he ought to have decided to prevent the action even if he received such an order from the defense minister. Consequently, he was bound to resign as chief of the [Intelligence] Department.

Benyamin was astounded. He answered something or other, saying that this was an injustice. If he were dismissed, he would make the reasons for his dismissal known; he would not resign of his own accord.

The premier called in the chief of staff [Dayan] . . . and told [him] that Lavon had made a condition for remaining [at his post] namely the dismissal of Benyamin and Shimon [Peres]. Accordingly, [Gibly] would have to go. The chief of staff said to Sharett: "Five Jews have concluded that Lavon has to go: Sharett, Dori, Olshan, Sha'ul [Avigur] and Ben-Gurion. They have recognized the disaster going under the name of Lavon. And after that instead of being given the push, he demands innocent victims. What justification is there to explain such a deed? If there is no other way, and it's decided that Lavon has to remain, that's possible, on one condition: *status quo* all the way. No concessions to Lavon. If he doesn't want [that], let him go. There is no room for any concessions whatsoever. I will not be ordered to dismiss Benyamin [Gibly] of my own free will.

Sharett retreated. He had already summoned Peres to a meeting, which he now called off. Instead he opted to freeze the situation. No one would go; no one would resign. Lavon now had his back to the wall. On 17 February, he submitted a final letter of resignation. That day, Ben-Gurion wrote in his black notebook:

It was a "wakeful" day, if that adjective can be applied to a day. At eight in the morning, Nehemia [Argov] arrived. Moshe [Sharett] asked him to come to me as soon as possible and inform me that P.L. insists on [tendering his] resignation and presenting his allegations to the Cabinet and the Foreign Affairs [and Defense] Committee. Sha'ul [Avigur] refuses to accept [the post] (there is no other candidate).

Argov was followed by a influx of delegations. In his diary, Ben-Gurion recorded: "Lavon is definitely going, and there is no one [to replace him]. They propose that I return. I was overcome. I decided that I must accept the demand and return to the Defense Ministry. Defense and the army precede everything."

The news was met with an enthusiastic welcome. That same night, the final news broadcast reported that Ben-Gurion was returning to the government as defense minister. Moshe Sharett worded an enthusiastic telegram to Sdeh Boker:

Admire your step as a model of noble citizenship and testimony to profound comradeship among us. I know what you sacrifice. Let the enthusiasm of the nation and the army be your consolation. I will come to you on Sunday after the Cabinet meeting. Be strong! Moshe.

Ben-Gurion was back.

13

The Winds of War

Enthusiastic crowds cheered Ben-Gurion when the newly reappointed defense minister appeared outside the Knesset on 21 February 1955, and strode inside, accompanied by Paula. He looked tanned and healthy, wearing khaki clothes under a short winter coat with a flannel collar. His restoration as defense minister sparked a victory procession, and a great wave of popular admiration was directed at him. Ben-Gurion himself, however, was less enthusiastic about his return to the Cabinet. "If I were not concerned over the military situation," he wrote, "one hundred bull-dozers could not have gotten me out of Sdeh Boker."

The day before the Old Man came to Jerusalem, Sharett had gone to see him at Sdeh Boker. The Ben-Gurions, in working clothes, and Sharett, wearing a dark official suit and a tie, exchanged smiles before the press cameras. The outward impression was one of complete harmony, but the true state of affairs was quite different. During that meeting the premier and his defense minister withdrew for some tough talking on the relation-ships between their respective ministries. The following day, Ben-Gurion sent Sharett a formal, harshly worded letter demanding that a distinction be made between Sharett's status as prime minister and his additional post of foreign minister. "Since the two posts are now merged," he wrote, "a consultation with the prime minister is also a consultation with the foreign minister. But consultation with the foreign minister is one thing, and con-stant intervention by the foreign minister and his subordinates in defense matters is quite different. I shall not consent to such a thing." Ben-Gurion stated that if he were to learn in the near future "that the Foreign Ministry intervenes in defense matters . . . and the premier supports the inter-vention . . . as premier, you will have to take over the defense portfolio from me or appoint someone else in my place".

The letter caused Sharett "regret and disappointment" and he wrote back to Ben-Gurion: "Is there indeed such little hope of reaching an un-derstanding and arriving at an agreed conclusion?" On his return, Ben-Gurion told the Cabinet secretary: "Sharett is cultivating a generation of

cowards. I won't let him. Infiltrators are on the prowl, and we are hiding
behind fences again. I won't let him. This will be a fighting generation."

During the night of 23 February, a group of infiltrators on a mission for
Egyptian intelligence made its way over the border from the Gaza Strip,
broke into the guardroom of a governmental scientific institute and stole all
the documents stored there. Later they ambushed a Jewish cyclist on the
road and murdered him. Another group of infiltrators ran into an Israeli
patrol, and one was killed. A search through his clothes turned up a report
on traffic on the highways of southern Israel. Four days later, Ben-Gurion
and Dayan came to the prime minister's office in Jerusalem and proposed a
reprisal action against Egypt. They suggested attacking an Egyptian army
base near Gaza, and Dayan estimated enemy losses at ten. Sharett gave his
permission for the operation, which was subsequently code named "Black
Arrow". It was carried out by 149 paratroopers under the command of
Arik Sharon.

The dimensions of the operation mushroomed unexpectedly, as a result
of Egyptian reinforcements approaching the camp, and eight paratroopers
were killed in the clash. But their victory was complete, and the Egyptian
army suffered a crushing setback. The following day, the Egyptian radio
reported thirty-eight dead and over thirty wounded. Sharett was "horrified"
and characterized the report of the battle as "stunning". He sent off a
worried note to Ben-Gurion, giving vent to his fears of what lay in store for
Israel as a result and warning of the reactions of the U.N. and the United
States. Ben-Gurion sent back a brusque reply. "Our isolation is not a
result of [the operation]; it came [about] earlier, when we were as pure as
doves."

Overnight, the Gaza raid set off a sharp escalation of military tension
between Israel and Egypt. The Egyptian leaders feared that Israel planned
to launch a full-scale war against them. Nasser later stated that "the nightmarish night" of the Gaza operation led him to adopt two far-reaching
decisions: to set up suicide units (*fedayeen*) for the purpose of launching
raids from Gaza into Israel; and to furnish his army with ample amounts of
modern arms. He described the Gaza raid as the "turning point" in
Israeli–Egyptian relations, putting paid to any prospects of peace. But a
cautious analysis of the military and political circumstances of that period
casts grave doubt on the accuracy of this oversimplified claim. The decisive
event that induced Nasser to seek arms and political backing from the Iron
Curtain countries took place in Baghdad on 24 February, four days before
the Gaza raid: the establishment of the Iraqi–Turkish alliance. This
alliance was the kernel of the famous Baghdad Pact, which – with British
participation and the blessing of the United States – constituted "the

northern tier" against the Soviet Union. Nasser was fiercely opposed to the treaty, and its conclusion late in February was in fact the "turning point" that induced him to seek out friends and arms elsewhere. The Gaza raid only gave added urgency to Nasser's search for new allies and arms suppliers.

Upon returning to the Defense Ministry in 1955, Ben-Gurion took action to intensify military tension – not with the aim of provoking an overall confrontation, but, on the contrary, in the hope of forestalling it. He believed that if Israel were to strike back hard against Egyptian provocations, Egypt would be frightened off and curb its behavior. Yet the Egyptian response to the Gaza raid was to aggravate the situation along the Gaza Strip. On the night of 24 March, a group of infiltrators slipped across the border and made its way between the immigrant settlements scattered all over the northern Negev. Ten miles from the border, the infiltrators saw festive lights and heard the sounds of song and laughter: the Kurdish immigrants living in Moshav Patish were celebrating a wedding. Silently, the infiltrators approached the open space where the wedding was being performed and suddenly stormed forward, firing their sub-machine-guns and lobbing hand-grenades. Within seconds, the celebration turned into a scene of horror. Wounded villagers writhed in pools of blood. The laughter and singing were replaced by cries of pain. People were fleeing in all directions. One of the village guards attacked the raiders and drove them off. When the shooting died down, the toll was one dead and twenty-two wounded.

After the Patish raid, a prominent journalist asked Ben-Gurion why he followed a policy of reprisals. The Old Man replied that one of the reasons was to deter the enemy. "But there's a further reason," he added "an educational and moral reason."

Look at these Jews. They came from Iraq, from Kurdistan, from North Africa. They come from countries where their blood was unavenged, where it was permissible to mistreat them, torture them, beat them . . . They have grown used to being . . . helpless victims . . . Here we have to show them that . . . the Jewish people has a state and an army that will no longer permit them to be abused . . . We must straighten their backs . . . and demonstrate that those who attack them will not get away unpunished; that they are the citizens of a sovereign state which is responsible for their lives and their safety.

The Patish action shocked Ben-Gurion. On 25 March, he submitted a far-reaching proposal to Moshe Sharett: immediate military action "to drive the Egyptians out of the Gaza Strip". Sharett was vigorously opposed to the idea, but Ben-Gurion did not give up. At the next Cabinet meeting, he formally tabled the proposal. Some of his opponents brought up political and military contentions; others were deterred by the thought of incorporating such a large Arab minority into Israel's population. When the vote was taken at a further meeting, on 3 April, the proposal was defeated.

Ben-Gurion suddenly found himself in a minority in the Cabinet. For many months, he would be obliged to display the utmost restraint and bow to the wishes of the moderate coalition headed by Sharett.

The rejection of the proposal nipped Ben-Gurion's warlike impetus in the bud. It also cut short his tenuous truce with Moshe Sharett, and the relationship between the two men now deteriorated dramatically. Their disagreements became widely known as a result of an aggressive speech Ben-Gurion delivered in public containing statements opposed to Sharett's views. An irritated Sharett reminded Ben-Gurion that he had advised him to speak differently. Ben-Gurion replied: "I did not say what you advised me to say, because your words were not to my liking." The prime minister's frustration grew particularly sharp because Ben-Gurion made no secret of his intentions. In a further letter he proclaimed, with painful candor:

After further consideration of the matter, I have decided from time to time to give *public* expression to my views on the main issues of foreign policy (without attacking the position adopted by the government, and without disagreeing with your public[ly expressed] opinions) for we are facing elections; under certain circumstances, I may be charged with forming the government, and I shall do so; I am bound to inform the people of the basic guidelines of the foreign policy I shall pursue.

The results of the Knesset elections held at the end of July displayed a clearly activist trend and were interpreted as an expression of disappointment in the Sharett government's lukewarm policies.

On 12 August, Ben-Gurion officially consented to undertake the formation of a government. While Mapai was overjoyed by his decision, Sharett seethed with anger. He had come to the conclusion that Ben-Gurion wanted a different foreign minister,

...obedient and submissive, a hired professional whose function it is to word, to explain, and to justify the policy of his tyrannical master. ... Should I accept this humiliating verdict? Should I permit my dignity to be trampled ... violate my conscience? ... For the first time, I realized that I had no place in Ben-Gurion's Cabinet.

However, declarations were one thing and deeds another, for when Ben-Gurion approached him, Sharett's resistance was short-lived. Ben-Gurion presented an ultimatum: he would not take on the post of prime minister unless Sharett agreed to be his foreign minister. Sharett consented.

Even before Ben-Gurion could resume his premiership, however, there was a fateful incident on the Egyptian border. An Egyptian strong-point opened fire on an army patrol on the border road, and the patrol stormed the strong-point, killing three Egyptian soldiers. The Egyptians hit back by sending *fedayeen* as far as twenty-five miles into Israeli territory, where they murdered six civilians, attacked military vehicles, and tried to demolish the broadcasting installations. In the eyes of Ben-Gurion and Dayan, Israel could no longer maintain restraint. However, in view of Sharett's objections to reprisal raids, Dayan presented the Cabinet with a plan for an action on a limited scale: demolition of the bridges on a main road inside the Gaza Strip. The operation was approved, and the assault force set off. But late that night, Sharett gave orders for the operation to be called off and for the assault force to be recalled.

Dayan submitted his written resignation to Ben-Gurion who was still serving in his capacity as defense minister, and in hearty agreement, Ben-Gurion brought Dayan's letter to the Cabinet. "Either the Sharett line, or the Ben-Gurion line," he told his fellow ministers, "because following them both alternately causes nothing but damage." He stalked out of the Cabinet meeting, left his office, and went home. Sharett capitulated, and that same day, he reconvened the Cabinet, which now approved a large-scale reprisal operation proposed by Dayan. After a prolonged period of restraint, the army was charged with launching the largest action since the raid on Gaza.

That night, Israeli paratroopers blew up the headquarters of the Palestinian Brigade in the Gaza Strip, killing thirty-seven Egyptian soldiers. The Egyptian reaction was furious. The following day, reinforcements were rushed to the Gaza Strip, and there were extended exchanges of fire along the border. Egyptian airplanes penetrated Israeli air-space, and in a brief dogfight Israeli planes downed two Egyptian Vampires. Then, on 12 September, Nasser unexpectedly issued new regulations tightening the blockade of the Tiran Straits and extending it to the air-space above the straits. With tension at its height, astounding news came out of Cairo: the Czechoslovak–Egyptian arms deal.

Negotiations over the arms' deal had been going on for months. In April 1955, Nasser approached Chinese premier Chu En Lai at the Bandung Conference and asked for his aid acquiring arms from the Soviet Union. Chu complied with the request and a few weeks later notified Nasser that the Soviets approved of the idea. Beginning on 21 May, Nasser entered into negotiations with the Soviet ambassador to Cairo. Wary about penetrating an area hitherto considered a Western preserve, the Soviets wanted the deal arranged through Czechoslovakia. Thus the negotiation were transferred to Prague in August 1955, and a month later the deal was finally signed.

Publication of the Czech arms deal sent shock waves running throughout the West. In contrast, a wave of "joy bordering on ecstasy" overtook the Arab world. Nasser appeared as the champion of the Arab world, the idol of millions, the man who would avenge their honor after years of humiliation by the imperialist powers. He also inspired millions of Arabs with the hope that Israel's destruction was imminent. Indeed, the quantities of weapons promised to Egypt totally demolished the tenuous arms balance in the region. At the time, the amounts appeared positively legendary: about 200 jet fighters and bombers (Mig-15 and Ilyushin-28); 230 tanks, 230 armored troop carriers, 100 self-propelled guns, and 500 other cannon of various types, as well as torpedo boats, destroyers, and six submarines.

There was profound anxiety in Israel when details of the deal became known. Suddenly, the danger of Israel's destruction by the Arab states had become very real. In a spontaneous display of voluntary sacrifice, tens of thousands of citizens contributed money, jewelry, and various valuables to the Defense Fund for the purchase of arms. Messages and emissaries were sent off to the capitals of the Western world in quest of arms to restore the previous balance between Israel and Egypt.

Outgoing prime minister Sharett set off for Europe on a last-minute mission to meet the foreign ministers of the four Great Powers (who were conferring in Paris and Geneva) and ask them for arms or for action to foil the Czech deal. His hopes were dashed. With the exception of French Premier Faure's promise to deliver Mystere 4 fighter planes (whose implementation was delayed, not unintentionally), Sharett brought nothing back on his return to Israel.

The prime minister designate did not expect Sharett's trip to produce any results and he did not wait for his return before sending an urgent summons to the chief of staff, Moshe Dayan, who was vacationing in Paris. On Dayan's arrival, Ben-Gurion instructed him immediately to prepare an operational plan for three contingencies: occupation of the Gaza Strip; an offensive into northern Sinai; and the capture of the Tiran Straits to break the Egyptian blockade and ensure freedom of navigation in the Red Sea. The stress was on the third of these operations.

Ben-Gurion was in a warlike mood. When he mounted the Knesset rostrum on 2 November 1955, to present his new Cabinet, his tough speech – and the military action against Egyptian strong-points on the Negev border that followed it – marked the beginnings of a change in the government's political and military policies. Following the Czech–Egyptian arms deal, the growing menace from the south, and the blockade of the

Tiran Straits, Israel took a path that was to lead to a pre-emptive war. Ben-Gurion did not confess as much, but his acts in the coming year were to pave the way for the unavoidable confrontation with Egypt.

From October to December 1955 Ben-Gurion was in a difficult quandary. He was torn between adopting the military solution proposed by the army and launching a political campaign to acquire arms, by virtue of which he hoped to avoid the necessity of a pre-emptive war. In a statement issued on 9 November, President Eisenhower announced that the United States was prepared to consider requests for arms needed "for defensive purposes". Ben-Gurion began to entertain hopes – however faint – of acquiring American weaponry. Consequently, when Dayan flew to Sdeh Boker on 13 November to discuss the operation for seizing the Straits of Tiran, he found Ben-Gurion reserved. The first date set for the operation was the end of December. However, Ben-Gurion asked Dayan to postpone it to the end of January. "We may get American arms," he said.

Dayan did not let up, and early in December there were further discussions about the Tiran operation. In the end, Ben-Gurion presented Dayan's plan to the Cabinet on 5 December. The proposal was defeated for the Cabinet decided that the moment was not opportune and that "Israel will take action at the place and time she finds fit." For the time being, at least, the military options were off. Once again, Ben-Gurion's hopes depended on arms from and alliances with the West.

The idea of an American "guarantee" had become one of the main objectives of Israeli foreign policy many months before the Czech–Egyptian arms deal. On his return to the Cabinet in February 1955, Ben-Gurion supported the establishment of a defense pact with the United States. Abba Eban sponsored the idea and conducted months of negotiations in Washington. The proposal he crystallized was that Israel would undertake not to employ force to change her boundaries and the United States would commit herself to come to Israel's aid "insofar as the president's constitutional powers permit". While the Americans did not treat this as a practical proposition, they used the idea as an inducement – at times, as a threat – to get Israel to behave in a manner which suited their purposes.

In April, Sharett approached Secretary of State Dulles with the proposal that the United States guarantee Israel's territorial integrity and arm her to keep pace with the supply of weapons reaching the Arab states. But the Americans made consideration of the issue subject to conditions which could be considered restrictions on Israeli sovereignty. Negotiations to overcome these obstacles went on throughout the summer of 1955, since Ben-Gurion fully supported the idea of a pact and was even prepared to offer the Americans military bases in Israel. However, the talks faltered in mid-autumn, and the idea was finally dropped.

The failure of the defense pact to materialize was only one of a series of disappointments the United States inflicted on Israel. Even when the Czech–Egyptian arms deal was made public, the United States refused to supply Israel with arms. In effect, the United States was determined to reach an overall settlement in order to defuse the situation in the Middle East – even at Israel's expense. In an address to the American Foreign Policy Association Dulles revealed a plan for an international loan to enable Israel to pay compensation to the refugees; American financing for water and irrigation projects to rehabilitate the refugees; American guarantees for treaties to prevent the use of force to change Israel's borders with her neighbors and United States assistance in solving the problem of those borders "as the existing lines . . . were not intended to be permanent boundaries". A few weeks later, in a speech to the Knesset, Moshe Sharett proclaimed: "No unilateral cession of territory can be considered." But this did not prevent British Prime Minister Eden, in his famous Guildhall speech, from proposing extensive Israeli concessions as part of a compromise between the 1947 partition plan and the 1949 armistice lines.

Above all, however, it was the menace inherent in Soviet penetration of the Middle East that concerned the United States most. The American policy-makers believed that Soviet plans could be foiled by an agreement between Israel and Egypt, which would void the Czech–Egyptian arms deal and bring Egypt back into the Western fold. Thus in January 1956, under conditions of total secrecy, the American government sent a high-ranking emissary to the Middle East to try and pave the way for such an agreement.

The envoy, Robert Anderson, was a personal friend of the president and had served as secretary of the navy and secretary of defense in Eisenhower's Cabinet. Bearing letters of recommendation from the president to Nasser and Ben-Gurion, Anderson first flew to Cairo, where he held a top-secret meeting with Nasser. Then he flew to Israel by private plane via Athens, and arrived in the country under a heavy veil of secrecy. Not even the Cabinet knew of his presence or his talks with the prime minister.

First, Anderson reported on his meeting with Nasser, who had assured him of his desire for peace but had stipulated as a pre-condition the solution of two problems: refugees and territory. He insisted that the refugees be granted "a free choice" between compensation and repatriation to Israeli territory and that territorial continuity between Egypt and Jordan be assured by severing a portion of the Negev from Israel and handing it over to the Arabs. Ben-Gurion was skeptical about the sincerity of Nasser's desire for peace and totally rejected proposals for territorial concessions. As for the refugees, he stated that giving them a "free choice" implied "the influx of a Fifth Column, which would destroy the Jewish state from within". At the same time, he urged Anderson to organize a secret meeting between Nasser and himself or Sharett. "If Nasser takes part in person and the whole extent of the problem is examined, it is possible for peace to be achieved within ten days," he said and recommended that such a meeting be held in Cairo, where total secrecy could be maintained. The American envoy was somewhat skeptical of the suggestion. "You people move much faster here," he told the Israelis cautiously, "and you have clearer ideas of what is feasible."

Anderson was right. On 25 January, when he flew to Cairo to report to Nasser on his talks with the Israeli leaders, the Egyptian president became evasive. He expressed his fears of a face-to-face meeting, because "he does not want what happened to [King] Abdullah, to happen to him". On substantive issues, Nasser's views remained unchanged.

Once again Anderson flew to Israel by way of Athens, and on 31 January he reported to Ben-Gurion and Sharett on Nasser's response. Overcoming his disappointment, Ben-Gurion adopted a conciliatory tone. He proposed a cease-fire agreement in the Gaza Strip to be backed up by establishing direct contact between local commanders. Once again he, however, pressed for a direct top-level meeting, promising that if he met Nasser, he would propose "things that Nasser doesn't even think of. Most important things." For his part, Sharett expressed his willingness to come to an arrangement with Jordan over dividing sovereignty in Jerusalem.

Anderson headed back to Washington to report to the president. With him, Ben-Gurion sent a note expressing his disappointment at Nasser's refusal to conduct direct negotiations and, referring to the Czech arms deal, again asking for defensive weapons. In his reply, Eisenhower conceded that "the talks of my emissary to the Near East did not make progress toward settling the problems facing us, as you had hoped". Yet his answer to the request for arms was evasive.

When Anderson returned to the Middle East to renew his talks in Cairo, there was a disappointment in store for him. Nasser adamantly opposed any direct contact with Israelis. His position had hardened on other issues as well. Once again, he insisted on solving two principal issues: "free choice" for the refugees and Israeli territorial concessions. Anderson flew to Jerusalem and effectively conceded that his mission had failed. "Mister Prime Minister," he said to Ben-Gurion, "I have done what I could . . . I have never seen him so emphatic as on this question of personal meetings. I cannot give you any assurance concerning a direct meeting at any foreseeable time." The only proposal Anderson could put forward was that he continue to mediate between the two governments.

Sharett and Ben-Gurion were bitterly disappointed, and their frustration was heightened by another setback: just two days before Anderson's arrival, President Eisenhower had rejected the Israeli request for arms. Once again, through Anderson, Ben-Gurion asked the Americans for arms, but this time his words contained an implied threat. "Let us assume that, after you present your report, we receive a negative answer, or no answer at all [to our request for weapons]. Then we shall have one single duty: to safeguard our security. Nothing else will engage our attention." His words were a preliminary warning of the pre-emptive war soon to be launched against Egypt.

By its short-sightedness, the United States actually pushed Israel into the pre-emptive war that Ben-Gurion was trying to avoid. Clearly, the United States was principally to blame for the menacing situation that arose in the Middle East in the spring of 1956 and paved the way for the Sinai Campaign.

With the onset of spring, war clouds again gathered over the Middle East. All three of Israel's borders were now ablaze. In the north, the Syrians shelled Israeli fishing and police boats on the Sea of Galilee. On the eastern border, tension rose as a result of internal upheavals in Jordan, where pro-Nasser elements were gaining strength. The Egyptian forces in the Gaza Strip fired incessantly, and early in March large Egyptian forces massed in northern Sinai and instigated border incidents. At one point an artillery battle, started by the Egyptians, was fought across the Gaza Strip border. In response to their heavy casualties, the Egyptians again sent *fedayeen* to sow death and destruction inside Israel. War with Egypt seemed likely to break out at any moment, and U.N. Secretary-General Dag Hammarskjold met with Ben-Gurion and Nasser in a desperate effort to halt the hostilities.

This was one of the most difficult periods in Ben-Gurion's career. On the one hand, he had to contend with a dithering Cabinet, most of whose members followed the foreign minister in opposing vigorous action. On the other, he had to restrain the pressing demands of Chief of Staff Dayan for a pre-emptive war against Egypt before it was too late. Through the gathering clouds of war, there was a single ray of light for Israel. While the clashes on the Egyptian border were at their height, a dozen Mystere 4 fighter planes landed at an Israeli military airfield. A new source of arms, supplies had been opened up for Israel – France.

The background to the establishment of France as Israel's principal supplier of arms began shortly after Ben-Gurion's return to the Defense

Ministry early in 1955. From then until 1 April 1956, when the first French planes landed in Israel, Shimon Peres, director-general of the Defense Ministry, conducted a thorough campaign in French government circles and laid the groundwork for what grew into a flourishing relationship between the two countries. Twice the government of premier Edgar Faure promised everything from light tanks and cannon to jet fighters, and twice delivery was frustrated. At the end of November 1955, however, Faure's Cabinet fell, and following the French elections in January 1956, Guy Mollet was summoned to form a new Cabinet. It was Mollet's rise to power that marked the decisive turning point in Franco–Israeli relations.

Both of the principal partners in Guy Mollet's coalition supported Israel – each for its own reasons. The socialist ministers, headed by Mollet and Foreign Minister Christian Pineau, entertained considerable sympathy for Israel and for their sister-party, Mapai. The socialists' principal coalition partner was the Radical Party, headed by Bourges-Maunoury which was principally concerned with the Algerian problem. Most of its political moves were dictated by hatred for Nasser, who was the main supplier and supporter of the Algerian F.L.N. rebels. Thus, Israel faced a new French government prepared to do far more for her than any of its predecessors. The first indication was the Mystere sale.

Contacts between the two countries' defense ministries grew in February and March, so that by the time Shimon Peres arrived in Paris for extended talks with Defense Minister Bourges-Maunoury, there was growing inclination on both sides to establish direct links between the two defense ministries and armies, by-passing the respective foreign ministries altogether. On 23 April, Peres and Bourges-Maunoury signed an agreement for the delivery of an additional twelve Mystere 4 planes. However, the decisive step toward the establishment of the French–Israeli partnership was taken a month later. At the end of May 1956, Peres submitted an ambitious proposal to Ben-Gurion: the conclusion of an unwritten pact with France against Nasser. When Ben-Gurion expressed his support for the idea, Peres flew to Paris and met with Bourges-Maunoury. This time, he proposed a massive delivery of arms to Israel and preparations for joint action against Egypt. Bourges's response was favorable, and they decided to hold further secret talks in France within a few days.

It was inevitable that the initiatives of the Defense Ministry in dealing with a foreign government would aggravate the tension between Ben-Gurion and his foreign minister. Because the extent of Peres's contacts with Bourges-Maunoury and their agreement to by-pass their respective foreign ministries were unknown to Sharett, he viewed Israel's increasingly stringent responses to Egyptian provocation as detrimental to French support. On the face of things, he appeared to be right; and when the French foreign minister cancelled a trip to Israel as a result of the bloody clashes on the Gaza border early in April 1956, Sharett was at the peak of his exasperation with the prime minister. But Ben-Gurion knew that Israeli–French collaboration was conditional upon Israel's readiness to go to war against Egypt. It was clear to him that eventually the Cabinet would be forced to choose between Sharett's policy and his own. But, for all his prestige, and with all his harsh decisiveness, not even Ben-Gurion could just stand up and demand Sharett's resignation. Consequently, he seized on a chance pretext: the need "to revive the party".

In May 1956, a meeting was held at Ben-Gurion's Jerusalem home concerning the appointment of a new Mapai secretary-general and the necessity that a party leader of the first rank take the post. As various names were brought forward in the course of the discussion, Sharett said, "jokingly": "Well, perhaps *I* should become the secretary of the party."

"Everyone laughed," wrote Golda Meir, "except Ben-Gurion, who jumped at Sharett's little joke."

"Marvellous!" he said at once. "A wonderful idea! It will save Mapai." His colleagues were taken aback, but gradually they came round to thinking that this was, indeed, a good idea. A day or two later, Ben-Gurion asked Golda: "Don't you think it's a good idea for Moshe to become secretary of the party?"

"But who will be foreign minister?" she asked.

"You," he said calmly.

Golda could not believe it. She tried to argue with him, explaining why it was impossible, but the Old Man did not budge. "That's it," he said.

On the afternoon of 2 June, two Mapai leaders, Pinhas Sapir and Zalman Aranne went to see Sharett. On seeing them, Sharett "erupted". According to Sapir, "he knew that this was the end" and shouted: "I know why you've come: to slaughter me! I agree." A short time later, the news was brought to Ben-Gurion.

Sharett's resignation opened up the way for one of the most highly secret – and fateful – steps in the chronicles of the State of Israel: the unwritten pact with France. Sharett resigned on 19 June 1956. Just three days later, on the night of 22 June, a French Nord aircraft took off from an airfield north of Tel Aviv carrying Moshe Dayan, Shimon Peres and Chief of Intelligence Yehoshafat Harkavi. They were welcomed in Paris by representatives of the French army and by Colonel Louis Mangin, head of the French defense minister's bureau. Together, they set out for an ancient château where the secret Israeli–French conference was to be held, and were joined by several generals from the French high command, including Generals Challe and Lavaud, as well as a representative of the French intelligence agency, the S.D.E.C.E. The two delegations discussed ways of containing Nasser and perhaps even causing his downfall. They decided to recommend immediate massive French arms deliveries to Israel; exchange of intelligence information and close cooperation in intelligence; and planning practical operations up to, and including, war.

After overall agreement had been reached on guidelines, the Israeli demands were presented: 200 AMX tanks, 72 Mystère 4 planes, 40,000 75-millimeter shells, 10,000 SS-10 anti-tank missiles. To the Israelis, these were astronomical figures, but the French representatives did not bat an eye. It was agreed that the arm s should be delivered in total secrecy, and the French representatives promised to do their utmost to ensure that the deliveries were made within the coming months, even if they had to be withdrawn from French army units. The price settled on was $80 million.

On 25 June, the Israeli delegation returned home feeling satisfied with itself. In response to their report, Ben-Gurion mused, "This is a somewhat perilous adventure, but what can we do? Our whole existence is like that." He did not reveal the matter to the Cabinet, confiding solely in Foreign Minister Golda Meir and in Finance Minister Levi Eshkol, who had to raise the money to pay for the arms.

Ben-Gurion spent July in tense expectation and preparations for the new arms. During the night of 24 July, the first shipload reached Israel and was unloaded under a heavy mantle of secrecy. To the handful of men in on the secret, that was an unforgettable night. But the rest of the world remembers that week for a different event: On 26 July, two days after the first shipload of arms reached Israel, Nasser proclaimed the nationalization of the Suez Canal. It seemed that this time he had gone too far. News of the nationalization sparked off a wave of anger in Western capitals. Political and military consultations were quickly launched between France and Britain; military and naval forces were placed on alert; in the British army's Operations Room in London, French and British staff officers planned a joint invasion to take place in September. The objectives were Alexandria and Cairo.

Within a few days, however, the plans for an immediate invasion of Egypt were shelved because the United States was emphatically opposed to the use of force in the Middle East, and Dulles exercised his powers of moderation on Paris and London. On his recommendation, an international conference was convened in London on 16 August to discuss the future of the Suez Canal. The meeting terminated after adopting Dulles's plan for the establishment of an international body to manage the canal.

Australian Premier Robert Menzies flew to Cairo to inform Nasser of the conference's decisions, but on 9 September, Nasser rejected them. Undeterred, John Foster Dulles called a second conference in London on 19 September, which founded the Canal Users' Association, a group of maritime nations that would supervise the management of the canal and collect transit dues. But the association was likewise stillborn. Dulles's declaration that it was not the U.S.'s intention to take ships through the canal by force reassured Nasser and dissolved his fears of a foreign military invasion. In despair, France and Britain appealed to the United Nations Security Council.

Dulles may have believed that he had achieved his principal aim: preventing the immediate outbreak of war and gaining time for tempers to cool and for the British to lose their warlike determination. As far as the British are concerned, he seems to have been right. But the French were determined not to lose this unique opportunity to topple Nasser. They gave up hope on the Americans and sensed that the British were retreating from their previous militant stance. Left with only a single way of guaranteeing the success of their operation, the French turned to Israel.

Ben-Gurion's first reaction to the idea of military action together with the Western Powers was very prudent. On 2 August, when Dayan told him that "the French are asking for details on our ports and airfields", he replied that "if the French want such information, we must provide it willingly; altogether we must treat them as brothers all along the line". At the same time, however, he tried to cool Dayan's excitement, warning him that Eden would not take action against Egypt without United States assistance, and "there is no hope of that scoundrel Dulles supporting any daring action against the Arabs and the Russians".

Early in September, the French began to give serious consideration to the idea of Israel joining a military venture about a week after the attack was launched. The head of the Defense Ministry's purchasing mission in Paris sent a cable to this effect after a conversation with Abel Thomas and Louis Mangin, and Ben-Gurion gave orders for an immediate reply stating that, Israel was prepared to cooperate. On 18 September, Shimon Peres set off for Paris, ostensibly to deal with arms purchases. In effect, he intended to take advantage of his visit to interest the French leaders in a joint policy vis-à-vis Egypt. In Paris, he met with Bourges-Maunoury, who confided his doubts about British readiness to undertake military action against Egypt and hinted at a joint French–Israeli action. When Peres cabled a report of his conversation to Ben-Gurion, the Old Man's reply diplomatically encouraged pursuance of the suggestion. Peres lost no time in transmitting this reply to Bourges-Maunoury. The following day,

22 September, the French defense minister consulted the principal members of his Cabinet, who approved steps for joint action with Israel against Nasser.

When Peres returned to Israel, Ben-Gurion noted the main points of his report in his diary, including the French desire to have "a delegation of three – including at least one minister – to come on Saturday to hold discussions with Guy Mollet, Pineau and Bourges-Maunoury for cooperation on a basis of parity".

At the termination of the next Cabinet meeting, Ben-Gurion invited a few of the ministers to his office and told them of the French proposal. Several expressed their fear that all the Arab countries would join in the fighting and "volunteers" might be dispatched from the Communist countries. "My view," wrote Ben-Gurion, "was that this was our first opportunity to find an ally . . ."

All the fears exist, but they will also exist when we stand alone and Nasser tries to annihilate us. Yet we will undertake this partnership only on a number of conditions: (1) That France has advance knowledge of our limitations in the air and in armor; (2) that Britain does, indeed, stand behind France, and the [operation] is carried out with the knowledge of the United States; (3) that we receive the coast of the Tiran Straits . . . Here is born the first earnest alliance between us and a Western power, and under no circumstances must we decline it.

A few days later, a high-level Israeli delegation, including Cabinet ministers Golda Meir and Moshe Carmel and Moshe Dayan and Shimon Peres, set off for negotiations with the French leaders. They were awaited by Foreign Minister Christian Pineau and Defense Minister Bourges-Maunoury, as well as political and military aides, and at a later stage the talks were also attended by Commander-in-Chief Ely and a number of French officers. Pineau inaugurated the first session with a political survey and expressed the French view that the operation should be launched in mid-October, before the American presidential elections, explaining that electoral considerations would prevent Eisenhower from opposing the operation. But he revealed his apprehensions that the British would abandon their decision to take part in the operation. Pineau wished to know whether Israel would be prepared to undertake the operation with France alone, in the event of Britain withdrawing its agreement. Such an operation, he said, could be carried out in one of two ways: either Israel fought alone, with France extending military assistance; or Israel and France launched a coordinated attack.

Golda Meir who replied on behalf of Israel, stressed Israel's desire to act jointly with France. At the same time, she requested guarantees that

Britain would not take action against Israel (under the terms of the Anglo–Jordanian Defence Pact) if fighting flared up on the Jordanian border. She also asked about the attitudes of the Soviet Union and the United States. Pineau replied that France did not believe the Soviet Union would intervene; the United States would adopt a passive role, "and the French do not recommend that either France or Israel approach [the Americans] on this matter".

Pineau's statement marked the first shadowy emergence of the idea of "the Israeli pretext" – that is, an Israeli attack on Egypt would serve as an excuse for France and England, or for France alone, to intervene, to protect the canal, so to speak, from the warring sides. In the course of the coming weeks, this idea was to become the backbone of the joint plan. Pineau stated that if the British grasped that Israel was prepared to act alone during the first phase of the operation, "this will improve the chances of a favorable decision by the British Cabinet . . ."

Following instructions, the Israelis replied that they were in favor exclusively of a coordinated operation launched simultaneously. Dayan received the impression that, in the final account, the French would not act without the British. "We sensed that Ben-Gurion was right in saying that if Britain withdrew, France would follow in her footsteps."

The afternoon's talks were devoted to the military aspects of the operation and the question of whether Israel could replace Britain as France's ally. It was decided to hold a further meeting with the French commander-in-chief to discuss operational questions and that when the Israelis returned home, they would be accompanied by a number of French officers who would inspect the army and examine the quality of the Israeli bases. The following day in a meeting with French Commander-in-Chief Ely, Dayan advanced a suggestion for dividing up the combat sectors: Israel would operate in Sinai to the east of the Suez Canal, and France in the Canal Zone.

When the conference came to an end, Golda Meir held a personal meeting with Guy Mollet at the premier's office, stressing that the Israeli Cabinet had yet to decide on any action. At the same time, Moshe Dayan and the French commander-in-chief agreed that 20 October was a feasible date for launching the attack, on the assumption that with the Security Council debate ending on 12 October and a resolution being adopted by 15 October, the Israeli army would complete the mobilization of its reservists by 20 October. On the night of 1 October, the Israelis returned home accompanied by a French survey mission. Immediately after his return, Dayan called together the General Staff to forewarn them of a possible operation against Nasser. The projected date: 20 October 1956.

As soon as they landed, the delegation presented its report to Ben-Gurion, but his reaction was not enthusiastic. The following day, he formulated his views on a French–Israeli operation. "My conclusions are unfavorable . . . stemming from the assumption that the English will not take part and will not permit the French to operate from Cyprus." He intended to express these views to General Challe, one of the leaders of the French Survey mission and also planned to write to Guy Mollet and present his misgivings about the proposal. But before doing so, he expounded them to Golda Meir and Moshe Dayan. The chief of staff disagreed with Ben-Gurion and asked him not to reveal his objections to the French. "It would be easy now to extinguish this tiny flame of [French] readiness to go to war against Nasser," said Dayan, "but it will be impossible to rekindle [it]." Dayan thought that Ben-Gurion's fears of Egyptian bombing raids on Israeli towns were exaggerated. Employing "a sharp tone", he asked the Old Man to display restraint in his projected talk with Challe. "Three months ago, we would have regarded a situation in which France was prepared to join us in taking military action against Egypt as a dream; and now, when this is happening in reality, we are liable to draw back." Far more confident of Israel's military strength than Ben-Gurion, Dayan was genuinely afraid that the prime minister's apprehensions could foil the operation.

Shortly afterward, Ben-Gurion received Colonel Mangin and General Challe, but he followed Dayan's counsel and did not express his objections to the French–Israeli plan. At the same time, he put his visitors through a characteristically thorough interrogation regarding their plan. He wanted to know what French forces would be employed, from which bases they would start out, whether the navy would take part, where the paratroopers would set out from, etc. Although Ben-Gurion took his leave of his visitors by expressing "the thanks of the whole Jewish people" for their help, his misgivings remained. Their conversation had shown him that the French did not have a well-thought-out plan to carry the war to its conclusion and that they were not certain of British intentions. Since he entertained the well-founded fear that France would not act without Britain, his opposition to the plan grew stronger. All the same, the following day he was in a calm mood and agreed with Dayan that joint operational planning with the French was to be continued, though "the plan was not to be implemented without Britain's approval".

The Suez crisis was entering its conclusive stage. As foreseen, the U.N. Security Council debate ended with a Soviet veto on the Anglo–French proposal for internationalization of the canal. The following day, 14 October, General Challe and Labour Minister Albert Gazier (acting in place of Pineau) flew off for an urgent meeting with Prime Minister

Anthony Eden at Chequers. The main topic of the talks was General Challe's presentation of the "Israeli pretext", whereby Israel would launch a war against Egypt, giving Britain and France an excuse to intervene. According to his plan, Israel would occupy most of the Sinai peninsula and France and Britain would take position along the Suez Canal under the pretense of protecting it against the belligerents. The idea caught Eden's imagination. He decided to fly to Paris, accompanied by Foreign Secretary Selwyn Lloyd, and on 16 October the prime ministers and foreign ministers of the two countries sat down for their decisive meeting.

After five hours of talks, the two states agreed to adopt the idea of "the Israeli pretext". The British were prepared to assure Israel that they would not come to Nasser's assistance if war broke out between Egypt and Israel, and even handed the French a written declaration to that effect to pass on to Jerusalem. But if war broke out on Israel's eastern border, they would not refrain from coming to the aid of Jordan, with which England had a valid defense treaty. Finally, the British did not object to talks being held between France and Israel during the next few days, and after some misgivings, they consented to send a representative to high-level talks between France and Israel in Paris.

The first cable describing the contents of the Anglo–French talks reached Ben-Gurion on 17 October, and he was totally opposed to the proposal. "I answered that the British proposal cannot be taken into consideration, and if Mollet, knowing this, still thinks it worthwhile that I come, I shall be prepared to go after Sunday." The next day, when Mollet replied that the French were still in favor of a meeting, Ben-Gurion decided to go to France. But he still clearly intended to reject what was now being referred to as "the British proposal" (namely the notion of an "Israeli pretext", which was actually a French idea). He had been insistent on quashing the notion the day before; but Moshe Dayan made a sober analysis of the situation and told the prime minister: "England and France do not need us for the military battle . . . The only [useful] trait we possess in this matter – the only one which England and France lack – is our ability to provide them with the pretext they need to go to war. This is the only thing that can serve us as an entry ticket into the Suez battle."

On Sunday 21 October, General de Gaulle's private plane landed in Israel, carrying Generals Challe and Mangin. Clearly, the two men had been sent to soften up Ben-Gurion for his meeting with Guy Mollet and prepare him to accept the "British" plan. In an aura of complete secrecy, Ben-Gurion entered his car and set off for the airport. Yet his patience ran out when Dayan and Peres told him of their conversations with Challe and Mangin and reported that the Anglo–French position was unchanged.

Ben-Gurion's temper flared up. He wanted to stop the car and return to Tel Aviv. "In that case, what is the trip for?" he growled. "I am afraid that it can only spoil our relations with France." Ben-Gurion met the two French envoys at the steps to the plane. Fighting down his anger, he told them: "If you intend to present the British proposal to us, the only benefit of my journey to France [will be] that I will make the acquaintance of your premier."

14

The Sinai Campaign

After a flight lasting seventeen hours, the DC-4 landed on the rainswept runway of the Villacoublay airfield, and the visitors were received under conditions of complete secrecy. Cars were waiting to carry them to a beautiful villa in Sèvres where the conference was to be held.

On their arrival Ben-Gurion and his companions were invited to lunch. Guy Mollet, Christian Pineau, and Bourges-Maunoury arrived while the meal was in progress. After making one another's acquaintance, the Israelis and their French hosts sat down at a round table and the Sèvres Conference opened. Ben-Gurion spoke first, expressing his vigorous opposition to the British plan. "Instead, I proposed a plan for settling all the issues in the Middle East – not immediately, but after extensive discussions with the United States and England. I called the plan 'fantastic' but feasible, as long as the English display goodwill and good faith – which I doubt."

Ben-Gurion spelled out the details of his plan. "Before all else, naturally, the elimination of Nasser." After that, the partition of Jordan, with the West Bank going to Israel and the East Bank to Iraq. Lebanon's boundaries would also be moved, with part going to Syria, and another part, up to the Litani River, to Israel; the remaining territory would become a Christian state. In newly expanded Syria, the regime would be stabilized by being placed under a pro-Western ruler. Finally, the Suez Canal would enjoy international status, and the Straits of Tiran would be under Israeli control. Ben-Gurion stressed that his plan would "satisfy the needs of England, France and Israel – as well of Iraq and Lebanon".

In spite of its practical elements, the plan did not evoke any interest from Ben-Gurion's French colleagues. Politely, Guy Mollet commented that "the plan is not fantastic, and he was prepared to accept it". But he immediately turned back to the subject at hand, stressing that "time is pressing with regard to Nasser and the Canal". Christian Pineau commented that Ben-Gurion's notion was "over-ambitious", and likewise he stressed the advantages of immediate action. The United States was currently involved in the presidential elections; the Soviets were embroiled in Poland and Hungary. Even the weather demanded a swift decision: at the end of October, the autumn storms would sweep the Mediterranean, impeding large-scale operations.

Focusing on the heart of the matter, Pineau explained that Britain would not be able to take action without a pretext; it was therefore vital for Israel to launch the attack. Obviously, Israel was undecided because of security considerations. But France was prepared to give Israel guarantees, and that was why Ben-Gurion had been invited to Paris.

Still, Ben-Gurion did not retreat. He stressed the danger of Soviet volunteers coming to the Middle East and noted that Eisenhower, whose election campaign was being conducted under the slogan of "peace at any price", would feel freer after the elections. Once again he expressed his fear that if Israel launched the attack, the world would denounce her as the aggressor and he depicted the horrors of Israel's cities being attacked by Egypt's Soviet-built bombers. Then he reverted to his original proposal: the operation should be launched at a later date, after American neutrality was assured and after Britain had been convinced to adopt the overall plan.

The two sides were deadlocked, and the Israelis and French alike were disappointed. Bourges-Maunoury joined in by stating categorically that if the operation were not launched within a few days, "France would have to withdraw from it." He explained that France would not be able to keep dozens of ships, and its reservists, on standby. "In three months' time, the military and political situation may be easier, but France will then stand aside. We are unable to wait any longer. The beginning of November is the final date." At the same time, he offered French planes and ships to protect Israel's skies and shores.

For the first time, Ben-Gurion retreated from his opposition to immediate action, agreeing to launch the operation in the near future "if, after we begin in the early morning of D-Day, following presentation of an ultimatum to Egypt, [the French] bomb the Egyptian airfields". He appealed to the French to work out a three-sided plan, persuade the British to take up "full partnership", and carry out the operation in the forthcoming week. The French noted that such a move would require changes in the original plan and stressed that it would be very difficult to convince the British.

Thus the first session of the conference closed without any results. Yet the participants did not disperse, for a "senior representative" of the British government was due to arrive at any moment, and it seemed clear that his reactions and views would settle the fate of the joint operation. "There were guesses whether it would be Salisbury, Butler, or Lloyd," wrote Ben-Gurion. "It turned out to be Lloyd."

No one was pleased by the arrival of the British Foreign Secretary. When Lloyd entered, accompanied by his private secretary, Logan, both men looked embarrassed and sullen. It was as though a chilly breeze accompanied them into the villa. The congenial atmosphere generated by the French and the Israelis suddenly became stiff and formal. The encounter between Ben-Gurion and Lloyd at this tripartite "collusion" conference was etched into the memories of its participants The two men exchanged a cool, official handshake. Everyone observed their mutual suspicions, which neither man bothered to conceal. Ben-Gurion felt as though Lloyd "tried to treat him as a subordinate". "Britain's foreign secretary may well have been a friendly man, pleasant, charming, amiable. If so, he showed near-genius in concealing these virtues," Dayan wrote of the meeting. "His whole demeanor expressed distaste – for the place, the company, and the topic."

Lloyd first closeted himself with his French colleagues for a report on the Israeli position. His response was unfavorable. The Israelis and French alike sensed that the matter was hopeless. "Ben-Gurion said he was not prepared to accept the British proposals and he had better leave for Israel in the morning," wrote Dayan. "Bourges-Maunoury for his part, announced that he would have to consider disbanding his Suez units by the end of the week unless a positive decision were taken quickly."

But the champions of the operation had not given up. "To my astonishment," wrote Ben-Gurion, "I was invited to a three-sided conversation in another room." The Old Man was accompanied by Dayan. Lloyd spoke first, presenting the British position. After proving conclusively that the Suez problem had, in effect, been solved in his talks with Egyptian Foreign Minister Fawzi – hinting thereby that England had no interest in military action, certainly not with the assistance of Israel – he pointed out that the one aim justifying such action would be the overthrow of Nasser. This should be accomplished in the manner advanced by the British and French: an Israeli invasion of Sinai, reaching the Suez Canal within two days, whereupon an Anglo–French ultimatum would be presented to both sides to pull back from the canal. If the Egyptians refused, France and Britain would invade, occupying the Canal Zone and overthrowing Nasser.

Ben-Gurion's reply was "firm and brief". He totally rejected Lloyd's proposal, and, again stressing the danger of Egyptian bombing raids on Israel's cities, demanded that the British and French begin their attacks on Egyptian airfields the day after the Israeli attack. Yet Ben-Gurion had now taken another step back from his original position by agreeing that Israel would be the first to launch the attack. All he wanted to gain now was a shortening of the time lapse between the Israeli attack and the beginning of the Franco–British operation and assurances that the Egyptian airfields

The Old Man and his diary

Ben-Gurion and Paula with two lambs and two young kibbutz members at
Sdeh Boker

Golda Meir and Pinhas Lavon

Prime Minister Moshe Sharett invites Ben-Gurion to join his Cabinet as Defense Minister after the dismissal of Pinhas Lavon

Ben-Gurion, accompanied by Paula, returns to the Defense Ministry

Ben-Gurion, in army uniform, visits Moshav Patish after the murderous
Fedayeen raid

Ben-Gurion on the day he received an honorary doctorate from Brandeis
University

ABOVE LEFT Miss Doris May

ABOVE RIGHT The two "Old Men": Ben-Gurion and Charles de Gaulle

BELOW Ben-Gurion and Konrad Adenauer during their meeting in New York

Chief of Staff Moshe Dayan with Shimon Peres (left, then director-general of the Defense Ministry) and Teddy Kollek (then director-general of the Prime Minister's Office). All three were to follow Ben-Gurion out of Mapai and join Rafi

Ben-Gurion lunching with his old rival Menachem Begin after the Six Day War. General Ezer Weizman is seated between them

The Founding Father in his old age

In his study at Sdeh Boker

The Old Man and the wilderness of Zin

The army says farewell to its founder

would be bombed. He was also concerned over the eventuality of full-scale fighting going on for two days, in which case Israel would be condemned and might run the risk of confrontation with volunteers from the Soviet bloc.

At this point, Dayan raised a proposal aimed at bridging the gap between the two sides. He suggested a limited Israeli operation in the vicinity of the canal – a paratroop drop, for example. Israel would announce the action, whereupon the British and French governments would immediately call upon Israel and Egypt to pull their forces back from the Canal Zone in order to safeguard the functioning of the waterway. The Egyptians would undoubtedly reject this demand, and at dawn Britain and France would immediately begin attacking Egyptian airfields. Lloyd did not reject Dayan's proposal outright, but he demanded that instead of a small-scale action, there be "a real act of war". Otherwise Britain would be condemned for her intervention. "I asked: Why should [we] take upon ourselves an operation for which we shall be condemned?" Ben-Gurion recorded. "[Lloyd] said that Nasser was our foe, and denied our rights. I said: He has done that for years, and no one protested. Lloyd conceded the justice of my concern over the bombing of Tel Aviv and Haifa and [our] airfields, but remained opposed to the operation."

At dinner as well, Selwyn Lloyd did not curb the hostility that had marked his behavior. One of the participants said: "He was angered and embittered at the fact that he, the foreign secretary of Great Britain, was obliged to sit face-to-face with Ben-Gurion, the premier of Israel, on an equal footing. . . . He seemed humiliated at having to meet in secret with the Israelis, and, on top of that, joining them in preparing an attack on the Arabs, his country's friends." Even when Ben-Gurion asked him good-humoredly as to when British history began, Lloyd referred him to his secretary, Logan. "That's what I need him for," he said sourly.

After dinner, the conference resumed, and at midnight Lloyd took off for London to present the new proposals to the British Cabinet. After seeing him off, Pineau told Ben-Gurion that "he does not trust Lloyd, and he will fly to London tomorrow evening", to talk with Lloyd (and Eden) about the plan. Ben-Gurion was more pessimistic than the others. "I am afraid that Pineau's journey will be in vain, after Lloyd gets a [British Cabinet] decision to his liking, contrary to the French view and to our view."

Ben-Gurion was quite right with regard to Lloyd. The British foreign secretary returned from Paris with the impression that the operation would be called off and was pleased at the prospect. But his joy was premature. Anthony Eden was in a belligerent mood and decided to make another attempt to reach an understanding with Israel.

International developments strengthened Eden's resolve. The Jordanian elections resulted in a decisive victory for the pro-Nasser elements and the new premier announced his intention of abrogating the Anglo–Jordanian defense treaty and of bringing Jordan into the Egyptian–Syrian joint command. These events confirmed Eden's contentions that Nasser was forcing England out of the Middle East and that, consequently, it was essential to depose him.

At midday on 23 October, the Franco–Israeli talks were resumed and instantly plunged into a severe crisis. General Challe proposed a Machiavellian scheme to permit the French and British air forces to intervene on Israel's side as soon as fighting began: the Israeli air force would stage a bombing attack on Beersheba that night and the Egyptians would naturally be held to blame. Thereafter, the French and British air forces would immediately go into action. Furiously, Ben-Gurion stood up, his face flushed with passion. He asked for his words to be translated literally. "On my own behalf, I announced, as a Jew, that I was not prepared to assist in [an act of] deceit toward the world. . . . We believed in the justice of [our cause]. And when we fight, we will fight [on the basis of] this belief. But I do not see how we can deceive the world and stage such a thing." He shouted angrily: "To lie to the whole world to make the matter easier and more convenient for Britain? That, no! Never!"

In somber mood, the Israeli delegation met for consultations in order to summarize its final views to Pineau before his departure for London. This meeting was the most decisive of the Sèvres Conference, Peres suggesting sending a ship through the Suez Canal. The Egyptians would obviously stop it, providing the pretext for Israeli military intervention, followed by Franco–British intervention. Dayan reiterated his original proposal: to drop a paratroop battalion, under cover of darkness, about thirty miles from the Suez Canal. That night, an armored column would break through to southern Sinai and link up with the paratroopers. Thirty-six hours later, the French and British would intervene, whereupon the whole of the Israeli army would go into action. Dayan held that the paratroop battalion's descent into Sinai and the attack on border strong-points by an armored brigade would give the Egyptians the impression that this was a large-scale raid, not all-out war. The danger of being drawn into extensive fighting, and above all the danger of Egyptian bombing raids on Israeli civilian centres, would be minimal. At the same time, such an operation should satisfy the British demand for a "pretext".

Ben-Gurion made no comment on Dayan's proposal, but gave him permission to present it to Pineau, who carefully noted down the main points and promised to convey them to the British. Dayan also laid down the price for Israel's participation: England and France were to recognize Israel's right to hold on to certain sections of Sinai after the fighting in order to ensure freedom of navigation to Eilat.

That same evening, Pineau took off for London, where he closeted himself with Eden for a long talk and presented the "Dayan plan". Eden accepted it. "I think I can get it passed," he told Pineau. Meanwhile, in Paris, while Peres, Dayan, and their aides went off to relieve the tensions of the past two days in a cabaret Ben-Gurion remained in Sèvres on his own. For him, this was the decisive night. "Somewhere, someone would have to make the decision," Peres wrote. "He had to make a clear-cut decision that contained the menace of annihilation. None of us envied him the long evening that lay before him."

The following morning, Peres and Dayan were told to report to Ben-Gurion immediately. They reached the villa in Sèvres anxious to hear what he had to say. Had he decided in favor of war, or not? Ben-Gurion was sitting calmly in the villa's beautiful garden holding a list of questions. "As he read them to us," wrote Dayan, "my mind grew steadily easier . . . It was evident that he had reached a positive decision on our joining the operation."

Ben-Gurion had, indeed, decided in the affirmative. That morning he wrote in his diary:

I have weighed up the situation and if effective air measures are taken to protect us during the first day or two until the French and British bomb the Egyptian airfields, I think the operation essential. This is a unique opportunity [in that] two powers . . . will try to eliminate Nasser and we will not face him alone as he grows stronger and conquers all the Arab countries. The operation required of us is on the order of a "raid" – though with larger forces this time – and if it succeeds, we will obtain freedom of navigation in the [Tiran] Straits, for we shall seize Sharm el-Sheikh and the island of Tiran . . . and the situation in the Middle East may change in accordance with my plan.

Ben-Gurion flung a series of questions at his aides and finally asked Dayan to sketch out the operational plan. As there was no paper in the garden, Peres "sacrificed" his packet of cigarettes to the Sinai operation. Emptying out its contents, he carefully ripped the pack and opened up the cardboard rectangle, on which Dayan sketched a rapid outline of the Sinai Peninsula. He drew a dotted line through the centre of the peninsula to indicate the route to be followed by the planes that would drop the paratroopers over the Mitla Pass. In the north, he drew a second line, parallel with the Mediterranean coastline, to show the route of the armor that would break through toward the canal. A third line ran along the coast of the Gulf of Akaba ending in an arrow pointing at Sharm el-Sheikh.

Jokingly, Ben-Gurion, Moshe Dayan, and Shimon Peres appended their signatures to "the first map of the Sinai operation".

Ben-Gurion's territorial ambitions were not limited to Sharm el-Sheikh and the island of Tiran, though he preferred not to reveal them to his aides. In effect, he wished to detach the Sinai peninsula from Egypt and annex it to Israel. Guy Mollet heard of this idea in a private conversation he held with Ben-Gurion during the early afternoon. Ben-Gurion said that large quantities of oil had been discovered in western Sinai "and it is worthwhile detaching the peninsula from Egypt, to which it never belonged – the English filched it from the Turks when they thought they had Egypt in their pockets". Ben-Gurion tried to gain Mollet's support for the idea by suggesting joint exploitation of the oil. According to Ben-Gurion, Mollet displayed "interest" in the proposal.

After a late lunch, Pineau arrived back from London, where he had succeeded in gaining Eden's support for the plan. At a meeting of the inner Cabinet held that morning in London, the three senior ministers had joined Eden in approving the plan, contrary to the views of Lloyd. Two men had come back from London, with Pineau: Logan (Lloyd's secretary) and Patrick Dean (the British assistant foreign secretary) since it was decided that Lloyd would not represent England in the final stages of the tri-partite negotiations in Paris. The three delegations convened at the round table in the dining room for their conclusive meeting.

In the course of the discussion, Ben-Gurion demanded French and British recognition of Israel's right to occupy the island of Tiran per-manently. "For us," he said, "[the] Suez [Canal] is not so important. Our Suez is the Tiran Straits, and we want to occupy the Eilat coast as far as the isles in the south, the isles included." At the end of the discussion, Ben-Gurion proposed drawing up a protocol of joint program, "that the three sides will sign and that will be approved by the three governments".

The document was drawn up within two hours. It stated that the army would launch its operations during the afternoon of 29 October, in the vicinity of the canal. The following day, the governments of France and Britain would send "appeals" to the governments of Egypt and Israel. Egypt would be urged to cease-fire immediately, withdraw its army to a distance of ten miles to the west of the canal, and consent to a temporary occupation of key points along the canal by France and Britain in order to ensure freedom of navigation in the waterway. The appeal to Israel would also include a demand for a complete cease-fire and the "withdrawal" of its forces to a distance of ten miles to the east of the canal. The two govern-ments would demand compliance with their appeals within twelve hours; if one of the belligerents should refuse, the French and British would take the necessary measures "for their demands to be accepted". At the same time, it was specified that the Israeli government would not be required to fulfill the terms of the appeal addressed to it should Egypt refuse to do the same. If Egypt did not observe the terms of the appeal, French and British forces would attack during the morning of 31 October 1956.

Israel would take the Tiran Straits and the islands of Tiran and Snapir, in order to ensure free navigation in the straits. She would not attack Jordan in the course of the operation; but if Jordan should attack Israel, the British government would not come to the Jordanians' aid.

These were the main points of the tripartite agreement. Separately, France promised to send Israel a squadron of Mysteres, and a squadron of Sabre F-86 fighter bombers. In addition, "volunteer" crews would be sent to man the Israeli Mystere planes for which the Israeli air force lacked crews, and French warships equipped with anti-aircraft guns would be sent to Israel and stationed near Haifa and Jaffa.

The agreements were signed at seven o'clock that evening, at an impromptu ceremony. Christian Pineau signed on behalf of France; Patrick Dean for England; and Ben-Gurion for Israel. The Sèvres Conference was at an end. Just before midnight, the DC-4 took off from the Villacoublay airfield. Once again, Ben-Gurion was alone with his thoughts. As dawn was breaking, he wrote: "Yesterday was, perhaps, a great day . . . If, on arriving home, we find the ratification of the British government, we will face great days in our history. But I am highly doubtful whether London's approval will be forthcoming."

At midday, when the French plane landed at an Israeli air force base, Dayan immediately rushed off to the General Staff to supervise planning and mobilization by citing the danger of a clash with Jordan, in view of the imminent entry of an Iraqi division into Jordan and Jordan's adherence to the Syrian–Egyptian joint command. Late the next evening, Ben-Gurion received official confirmation of the Sèvres protocol. In spite of the tripartite conferences at Sèvres, Anthony Eden had decided to ignore Israel entirely and write a non-commital letter to Guy Mollet alone. But Mollet was unwilling to go along with such hypocrisy and had Eden's letter photostated and sent on to Ben-Gurion. Eden's letter stated:

Her Majesty's Government have been informed of the course of the conversations held at Sèvres on 22–4 October. They confirm that in the situation therein envisaged, they will take the action decided. This is accordance with the declaration enclosed with my communication of 21 October. [Eden was referring to his first communication to Pineau, in which he had detailed the points of agreement regarding joint action with France and Israel.]

"A typically ambiguous British Foreign Office letter," Ben-Gurion fumed and worded his reply to Mollet: "If the conclusions have been ratified by the two governments, they are ratified by the Israeli government as well."

Ben-Gurion was determined to keep his ministers ignorant of the details of the agreement with France and Britain, and particularly about his journey to France and the signing of the Sèvres protocols. He preferred to tell those ministers who were not yet in on the secret that on Sunday he would propose military action against Egypt to be launched on the following day; and according to a prior understanding, France and Britain would address appeals to both sides on Monday and go into action against Egypt on Wednesday morning. The only ministers in whom Ben-Gurion did not confide in advance were those of Mapam, for fear that someone might leak the secret to the staff of the Russian embassy. Only on 28 October, just before the decisive Cabinet meeting, did the prime minister invite the Mapam representatives and unfold the plan. They asked for time for consultations, and upon returning they announced that they were opposed to the operation and would vote against it but would "bear responsibility" as members of the Cabinet. When the time came to vote on the proposal, the Mapam ministers were alone in their opposition.

Nothing could now halt the thrust of history. Ninety thousand reservists had been mobilized, French combat squadrons landed on Israeli airfields, and three French warships approached the Israeli coast. Heavy Nord-Atlas transport planes set off from bases in North Africa and landed in Israel after a stopover in Cyprus, where they took on equipment and technicians. Total secrecy was preserved right up to the very last moment.

Ben-Gurion looked calm and confident, but the terrible tension he was under found a unique outlet: his temperature shot up. Immediately after returning home from the Cabinet meeting, he collapsed into bed. While he lay there, leaders of the opposition parties – with the exception of the Communists – came to see him in succession. He informed them all of the projected operation in the hope of gaining wide parliamentary support for the secret Cabinet resolution. The opposition leaders received his announcement "willingly and gave their full approval". There was an element of drama in Ben-Gurion's meeting with his bitter rival, Menahem Begin, who now sat at his bedside congratulating him warmly on his decision.

At the last moment, however, Ben-Gurion's plans encountered a single vigorous opponent: the president of the United States. At eight o'clock on Sunday evening, 28 October, the American ambassador arrived at Ben-Gurion's Tel Aviv home with a brief message from President Eisenhower classified as "secret". Referring to previous communications between the two leaders, in which Ben-Gurion had expressed his concern at the Iraqi army's possible entry into Jordan, Eisenhower countered:

So far as I am informed, there has been no entry of Iraqi troops into Jordan . . . I must frankly express my concern at reports of heavy mobilization on your side, a move which I fear will only increase the tension which you indicate you would like to see reduced. . . . I remain confident that only a peaceful and moderate approach will genuinely improve the situation and I renew the plea which was communicated to you through Secretary Dulles that there be no forcible initiative on the part of your government which would endanger the peace and the growing friendship between our two countries.

Ben-Gurion read the message and promised to send an early reply. The American ambassador tried to gauge his intentions by means of a trick question: should American nationals in Israel be evacuated? The Old Man replied that he could express no opinion on the matter. The Americans still didn't suspect that Israel intended to take action in the south. They were keeping their eyes on the eastern border. That same day, Abba Eban was summoned to the State Department, and on the wall of Dulles's office, he found an enormous map of Israel and Jordan. The Americans were convinced that Israel intended to take action against Hussein.

Before Ben-Gurion had time to reply to Eisenhower's note, a second secret message from the American president was delivered to him.

This morning I have received additional reports which indicate that the mobilization of Israel's armed forces is continuing and has become almost complete . . . I have given instructions that this situation be discussed with the United Kingdom and France, which are parties to the [1950 Tripartite] Declaration, requesting them to exert all possible efforts to ameliorate the situation.

The note concluded with a further appeal to the Israeli government "to do nothing that would endanger the peace". The sentence mentioning Eisenhower's approach to France and England proved how mistaken the United States president was in his assessment of the situation.

Just before midday on 29 October, Ya'akov Herzog, Ben-Gurion's newly appointed political adviser, brought the prime minister the reply he had drafted. It depicted the "expansionary policies" followed by Colonel Nasser, which had provoked "unprecedented tension in the area"; Egypt's re-armament with massive amounts of Soviet arms; her threats to annihilate Israel; the *fedayeen* forays; and the blockade of the Suez Canal and the Tiran Straits. The establishment of the Egyptian–Syrian–Jordanian joint military command was described by the note as "creating a ring of steel around Israel's borders". The most important section of the message was its conclusion:

... with Iraqi troops poised in great numbers on the Iraq–Jordan frontier, with the creation of the joint command of Egypt, Syria and Jordan, and with the renewal of the incursions into Israel by Egyptian gangs, my government will be failing in its essential duty if it were not to take all necessary measures to assure that the declared Arab aim of eliminating Israel, by force, should not come out.

The note contained no undertaking to refrain from going to war. Furthermore, any experienced political observer would have immediately grasped that it heralded an imminent attack.

Indeed, at 4.59 p.m. 395 Israeli paratroopers jumped out of the transport planes that had flown so low to evade Egyptian radar that they almost scraped the tops of the Sinai ridges. News agencies flashed the sensational report all over the world: Israel had gone to war. In Washington, in the midst of a conversation in which Abba Eban was expounding Israel's peaceful intentions, Under Secretary of State Rountree received a slip of paper just ripped from the teleprinter. After glancing at the note for a moment, he told Eban drily: "I think our conversation has become somewhat academic." In New Delhi, on his way to talks with Nehru, Moshe Sharett bought a paper whose headlines heralded the news. In world capitals Israeli ambassadors were brought in on the great secret. The Sinai Campaign had begun.

30 October was the day Ben Gurion feared most, for the operational plan required Israel to bear the whole burden of the fighting on her own and in danger of Egyptian bombing raids. But the Egyptian air force proved itself to be a "paper tiger". With the exception of one sole Ilyushin bomber that slipped into Israeli air-space by night, Nasser's pilots were too wary to approach Israel's borders. Nonetheless, in his Tel Aviv home Ben-Gurion waited impatiently for the Franco–British ultimatum, which was delayed by a few hours. The Old Man was filled with anxiety! "I was not sure that Eden would keep his part of the arrangement," he wrote. Finally, however, late that evening, Ya'akov Herzog arrived bearing the ultimatum and a draft reply. By late that night, the Israeli and Egyptian replies reached the French and the British. Israel accepted the appeal; Egypt rejected it; and France and Britain announced that they intended to take action during the coming hours.

31 October passed in tense expectancy as Israel waited for the British and French to go into action. During the evening, Ben-Gurion's irritation grew as it became clear that his allies' bombing attacks had yet to commence. The drama was heightened by an urgent phone call from air force commander Dan Tolkowsky, who had received reports from a reliable source that the Egyptians were planning to bomb Tel Aviv. He asked for permission for an immediate raid on the Cairo-West airfield. Ben

Gurion's reply was a vigorous negative: "As long as the Egyptians do not bomb our population centers, or our rear airfields, we will not do so either." He preferred to wait for the British and French bombing raids. At long last, after a nerve-racking wait, the report arrived: the French and British had commenced their bombing attacks. Ben-Gurion heaved a sigh of relief. "Even though [Eden] was twelve hours behind time," he wrote "and I was filled with anxiety that Tel Aviv or our airfields would be bombed, [our] partners kept their principal engagements." Now the most difficult battle would begin, not on the battlefields of Sinai but in the political arena. As an urgent meeting of the U.N. Security Council was convened, President Eisenhower again exerted pressure on Israel. His assistant, Sherman Adams, called Rabbi Abba Hillel Silver and asked him to contact Ben-Gurion immediately and tell him:

... the president proposes that Israel immediately offer to return to the border, since it has completed its task, namely elimination of the *fedayeen* bases. If Israel does so, the president will immediately issue a declaration of profound admiration and firm friendship toward her.

Eban immediately cabled the message to Ben-Gurion. But Ben-Gurion did not halt the army. At the Security Council, France and Britain vetoed the draft proposals submitted by the United States and the Soviet Union for an immediate cease-fire and for Israeli forces to withdraw to the border. President Eisenhower kept up his pressure. This time he personally called Abba Hillel Silver, reiterating his proposal to "issue a most friendly declaration in a broadcast scheduled for that evening".

Meanwhile, at 5 p.m. on 31 October, the British air force began bombing Egyptian airfields. It was a *de luxe* onslaught, however. The British were careful to broadcast prior warnings from Cyprus radio, giving the ground crews time to take cover in shelters and pilots time to fly their planes to the safety of airfields in the south or in other Arab countries. Egyptian armored forces moved into the cities, taking up positions at street corners or in parks. The bombing attacks therefore produced ludicrous results. But Israel's purpose was achieved. From that moment onward, pressure on Israel decreased considerably as the spotlights of world public opinion were focused on France and Britain. Eisenhower stopped harassing the Zionist leaders; the French and the British – above all, Anthony Eden – now became the prime targets for his anger.

After the Security Council's failure to impose a cease-fire, Yugoslavia sponsored an emergency session of the General Assembly. Within twenty-four hours, the Assembly adopted a resolution calling for a cease-fire and a Israeli withdrawal. Only five states voted against it: England, France,

Israel, Australia, and New Zealand. The resolution inspired Israel's leaders with a sense of urgency. They estimated that Israel had forty-eight hours to bargain with the United Nations. It was therefore essential to complete the occupation of Sinai – above all, of Sharm el-Sheikh at the Straits of Tiran – within the next two days. Indeed by 3 November, the greater part of the Sinai Peninsula was in Israeli hands, and on 5 November, the army took Sharm el-Sheikh and the islands of Tiran and Snapir. It was also the day when the British and French at long last commenced their landing in Egypt. Yet 5 November also marked the most alarming development in the war: the Soviet Union intervened in the crisis.

On the previous day, Soviet forces finally succeeded in crushing the Hungarian revolt, so that the U.S.S.R. was now free to tackle the Middle East. On 5 November, Soviet Premier Marshal Bulganin despatched sharply worded notes to France, England, and Israel. The notes to England and France defined the Anglo–French operation as aggression and contained implied threats of employing Soviet nuclear missiles against the two countries. At the United Nations, news of the imminent outbreak of a world war spread like wildfire. Pressure on France and Britain for an immediate cessation of operations grew considerably. The presidential elections were to be held the following day, and Eisenhower phoned Eden incessantly, urging him to halt the fighting. Sick, nervous, and depressed, Eden was increasingly unable to withstand this growing pressure. The United States also exerted heavy financial pressure on England by manipulating the currency markets and placing sterling in danger of collapse.

Bulganin's message to Israel was brutal in tone:

The government of Israel is criminally and irresponsibly playing with the fate of the world and with the fate of its own people. It is sowing hatred of the State of Israel among the Eastern peoples, such as cannot but leave its mark on the future of Israel and places in question the very existence of Israel as a state . . . Being vitally interested in keeping the peace, and ensuring peace in the Middle East, the Soviet government is at this moment taking steps to put an end to the war and to restrain the aggressors.

Ben-Gurion's first reaction to the threats contained in the Soviet note was a display of cool restraint. However his concern was far deeper than he allowed to show. "If [Bulganin's] name were not appended [to the note], I could think it had been written by Hitler, and there is no great difference between those hangmen," he wrote. "[What] worries me [is the fact] that Soviet arms are pouring into Syria, and it may be thought that the arms are accompanied by 'volunteers'."

Unaware of the Soviet threats, Israel rejoiced. The Sinai Campaign had ended in a crushing victory. The Sharm el-Sheikh blockade had been broken, and the Egyptians' heavy cannon, which controlled the straits approaches, had been blown up. Some 6,000 Egyptian prisoners were crowded into cages and detention camps, as against only four Israelis taken prisoner by the Egyptians. Israel's losses were relatively light – 172 dead. The Egyptians had lost between 1,000 and 3,000 dead. Ben-Gurion shared in the general jubilation. "At first," he wrote, "the matter looked like a daydream; then like a legend; finally, like a series of miracles."

That same day, Britain and France capitulated in face of growing international pressure. During the afternoon, Eden phoned Mollet and notified him of his intention of proclaiming a cease-fire. The French Cabinet also decided to halt operations. Fighting stopped at midnight. The canal had not been taken, and the Franco–British operation had ended in humiliating failure.

7 November was Ben-Gurion's great day. For the moment, the sober, restrained statesman had vanished, and he did not heed the counsel of his aides. At 11 o'clock that morning, a triumphant Ben-Gurion stepped up to the Knesset rostrum. He had yet to recover from the illness that kept him to his bed throughout the fighting. But a man like Ben-Gurion would never forego a victorious address to Israel's Knesset, whose hall was packed to overflowing.

"The revelation of Sinai has been renewed in our time by our army's thrust of heroism," he said at the beginning of his address. "This was the greatest and most splendid military operation in the chronicles of our people, and one of the greatest in the history of the nations." He made an oblique reference to his dream of annexing the Sinai Peninsula, saying: "Our army did not infringe on Egyptian territory . . . Our operations were restricted to the Sinai Peninsula alone."

On top of its passionate nature and its fiery biblical analogies, Ben-Gurion's address focused on a number of prinicpal points:

(1) The Armistice Agreement with Egypt is dead and buried, and will not be revived . . . (2) Together with the agreement, the armistice lines between us and Egypt have also given up the ghost. . . . (3) We do not want a perpetuation of the anarchy [characterizing] our relations with Egypt, and we are prepared for negotiations for a firm peace . . . (4) We are prepared for similar negotiations with each of the other Arab states . . . (5) Israel is not prepared, under any conditions, that any foreign force, whatever its name, be stationed within her boundaries or in any of the territories occupied by her. (6) Israel will not fight against any Arab state, or Egypt, if she is not attacked by them.

Ben-Gurion's words displayed clear intentions of annexing Sinai and the islands in the Gulf of Akaba. But, even more than Ben-Gurion's address to

the Knesset, what remained in everyone's memory was a single phrase from
his message to the victory parade held at Sharm el-Sheikh: "Yotvat [the
island of Tiran]," he proclaimed passionately, "will once more become a
part of the Third Kingdom of Israel!" If only for a single day, the Third
Kingdom of Israel had arisen.

The following day, the term vanished. It did not make its appearance in
Ben-Gurion's writings, nor was it mentioned in his memoirs. Israel awoke
to gloomy, fearful realities that made the previous day's triumphant
jubilation sound as though it came from a different world. This bitter
awakening began with the first foreign reactions – all unfavorable and
angry – to Ben Gurion's Knesset speech. By ninety-five votes, with
Israel alone voting against, the United Nations General Assembly decided
that Israel had to withdraw from Sinai unconditionally. Ben-Gurion
learned of the resolution on the morning of 8 November, but he did not
seem particularly concerned. Then two decisive events led him to renewed
reflection – the vigorous intervention of the United States and of the
Soviet Union.

First, he received an urgent message from President Eisenhower who
was overwhelmingly just reelected for a second term of office and was free
to adopt harsh measures. It was the most sharply-worded American
message ever sent to Israel:

Any decision on the part of the Israeli government [not to withdraw from
Egyptian territory] is likely to undermine the urgent efforts being made by the
United Nations to restore peace in the Middle East, and it could not but bring
about the condemnation of Israel for infringing U.N. principles and instructions . . . It would be a matter of greatest regret to all my countrymen, if Israeli
policy on a matter of such grave concern to the world *should* in any way impair
the friendly collaboration between our two countries.

The president put on a show of force to back up his words. The Israeli
minister in Washington was warned by the State Department that Israel
was endangering world peace.

This is the gravest situation the free world has ever been in, not only with
regard to the future of the Middle East, but of the whole world. It is obvious
to us that the Soviets are taking advantage of this situation for disastrous purposes. If that should happen Israel would be the first to be swallowed up.

Under Secretary of State Hoover reeled off American threats against
Israel should she refuse to withdraw: cessation of all governmental and
private aid from the United States to Israel (U.J.A. income included);
United Nations sanctions; the chance that Israel might be expelled from
the United Nations. In addition, the Americans made it quite clear that

they would not intervene on Israel's behalf in the event of an attack by Soviet "volunteers".

Ambassador Abba Eban hastened to phone Ya'akov Herzog and notify him of the American threats. In his diary, Ben-Gurion wrote:

> Eban phoned me, filled with fear. His cables also sow fear and terror. Hoover has warned [Minister Reuven] Shiloah that they will sever all links with us, cut off all aid, and perhaps even expel us from the U.N. They seem to be in terror of Russia. According to reports, large amounts of arms, and volunteers, are pouring into Syria.

Indeed fear of Soviet intervention overtook the whole world. The panic was heightened by a series of reports of a Soviet military presence in Syria and Egypt. The greatest concern, however, was aroused by reports leaked from C.I.A. sources in Paris; the Soviet Union intended to annihilate Israel completely in a massive air strike to be launched within twenty-four hours.

Ben-Gurion was affected by the general panic, though he tried not to show it. He wrote in his diary:

> It was a nightmarish day. From Rome, Paris, and Washington there is a succession of reports on a stream of Soviet planes and "volunteers" to Syria, on a promise to bomb Israel – airfields, cities and so on – if the Syrians and Jordanians go to war against us . . . There may be a great deal of exaggeration in these reports, but Bulganin's note to me . . . and the Soviet tanks' rampage in Hungary testify what these Communist Nazis are capable of doing.

It appeared as if Israel were suddenly on the brink of annihilation. But the Soviet threat on 6 and 7 November was no more than a scare tactic, a brilliant exercise in psychological warfare. The reports of a Soviet military presence in the Middle East were all false. In his memoirs, Khrushchev boasted of having disseminated false reports of Soviet "volunteers" heading for the Middle East. But no one knew that on that "nightmarish" 8 November. Israel's leaders foresaw catastrophe overtaking their country, while the world faced the danger of nuclear war. France, Britain, and Israel had gone to war on the tacit assumption that the United States would afford them protection from any Soviet attempts to intervene. Matters turned out to be otherwise. An enraged Eisenhower withdrew American guarantees, and Israel was left isolated and vulnerable. On entering Ben-Gurion's office, Dayan found him "very pale, and as angry as a wounded lion".

"The wounded lion" did his best to conceal his fears of a Russian onslaught, but some of his aides and Cabinet colleagues could not restrain themselves. His office was filled with frantic advisers and officials conducting hasty consultations amidst an atmosphere of tension and despair; the telephones never stopped ringing, while cables from all corners of the world brought a stream of ominous tidings. Several ministers were loud in their demands for an immediate withdrawal. The pressure from all sides, particularly the Soviet threats and the threat of a world war, undermined Ben-Gurion's decisiveness. "He courageously bowed his head to realities," Herzog related, "and consented to withdraw – without a peace treaty."

He had been frightened by the Russian threats, but it was to the Americans that he resolved to capitulate. That day, Ben-Gurion worded two letters in reply to the notes from the American and Soviet leaders. His communication to Bulganin was cold and proud, and contained no undertaking to withdraw. It was to Eisenhower that he disclosed his intention to withdraw. Even here, however, he did so in conjunction with a desperate last-minute effort to ensure some gains for Israel. Ben-Gurion had not yet given up his ambition of annexing the straits, and perhaps the Gaza Strip as well. He also hoped to extract a commitment from the U.N. that in pulling back, the Israeli army would be replaced by an international force, not by Egyptian troops. Finally, he hoped for an undertaking that the United States would work for a final peace settlement in the Middle East.

At nine o'clock in the evening, Ya'akov Herzog phoned Eban in Washington and asked whether it would be possible to get American consent to Israel's withdrawal being made conditional on the entry of an international force (rather than the immediate unconditional withdrawal demanded by the United Nations). Eban called back a little more than two hours later to report that Dulles had agreed to such a formula. It was then that Ben-Gurion and Herzog worded the key sentence in the letter to President Eisenhower: "We shall readily withdraw our troops as soon as a satisfactory arrangement has been reached with the United Nations regarding the entry of an international force into the Suez Canal Zone." Ben-Gurion further stated: "Neither I, nor any other authorized spokesman of the Israeli government has ever said that we intend to annex the Sinai Peninsula."

In the meanwhile, an entire people sat with its ears glued to the radio. Since early evening, the citizens of Israel had been informed that Ben-Gurion was about to broadcast an address to the nation. Finally, Ben-Gurion went on the air after midnight. He spoke in a weary, restrained tone, and many sensed undertones of disappointment and pain. He read out the letters from Bulganin and Eisenhower and his replies. From his note to Eisenhower, his listeners grasped the decision: the army was going to withdraw from Sinai. At the conclusion of his statement, Ben-Gurion addressed the soldiers: "There is no power in the world that can reverse your great victory . . . Israel after the Sinai Campaign will never again be the Israel [that existed] prior to this mighty operation."

The following day, Ben-Gurion received a cable of appreciation from Eisenhower congratulating him on his decision to withdraw. Bitterly, Ben-Gurion wrote: "Can I send him a cable of appreciation for his behavior during this crisis?"

What of his dream of "the Third Kingdom of Israel"? Ten years later, in a moment of candor, Ben-Gurion confessed his error in making that speech. "I made a few mistakes in that speech, saying that the Armistice Agreement was dead and buried, that Egypt would not be allowed to return to Sinai. I went too far . . ." He fell silent for a moment, reflecting, and then added: "But you see . . . the victory was too quick. I was too drunk with victory."

With the terrible tension broken, the whole world waited expectantly for Israel to fulfill her undertaking to withdraw from the territories she had occupied. But Ben-Gurion adopted a different tactic. He hoped that, when freed of the nightmare of Soviet threats, the United Nations would adopt a more balanced attitude toward Israel. Delay would also give Israel a chance of explaining her views in the United States and of gaining the sympathy of American public opinion. The second aim of his procrastination was to make withdrawal into a bargaining card, permitting Israel to make certain concrete gains in exchange for the territory she held. There was a third purpose, which he kept secret, revealing it only to his confidants. In conversation with Dayan, Ben-Gurion said: "There's no way of knowing, but I think we may not have to withdraw from the Tiran Straits and Gaza."

On 15 November, Israel announced that withdrawal had commenced; but it was 3 December before her forces had pulled back to thirty miles from the canal. At first, Ben-Gurion hoped that this initial withdrawal would suffice for an indeterminate period of time. But a week later, France and Britain notified the United Nations that they would evacuate all their forces from the Canal Zone by 18 December. Pressure on Israel increased, and Ben-Gurion undertook to withdraw fifteen miles per week. At the same time, the army did everything to delay the advance of the U.N. forces and the entry of the Egyptian army. Israeli units plowed up the Sinai highways, pulled down telegraph poles and dismantled the railway tracks. Amidst bitter disagreements with Secretary-General Hammarskjold and with the United States, Israel withdrew as far as El Arish. By mid-January under growing external pressure, she pulled back to her last line, and the army deployed along the Palestine mandatory borders (which included the Gaza Strip) and at Sharm el-Sheikh.

In a cable to Eban, Ben-Gurion wrote: "I shall suggest to the Cabinet [that we] consent to any arrangement in Sinai if we are forced to, but under no circumstances to give in over the Tiran Straits and the islands (which, incidentally, do not belong to Egypt) and the [Gaza] Strip . . . [They] are vital [to us] and we will accept death rather than surrender." Ben-Gurion had resolved to fight to the end. He told his confidants that he would not withdraw from Gaza and the straits, even if America "blew up" and imposed an economic and financial embargo.

Eisenhower's position hardened in the course of January, and in early February he personally intervened in the crisis by sending Ben-Gurion a sharply worded note:

It is my earnest hope that this withdrawal will be completed without further delay. Such continued ignoring of the judgement of the nations, as expressed in U.N. resolutions, would almost surely lead to the invoking of further U.N. procedures that would seriously disturb the relations between Israel and other member nations, including the United States.

This was a clear threat that sanctions would be imposed. Ben-Gurion, who had been unwell for weeks, erupted into anger. "Ya'akov," he called to Herzog, "write and tell him to bomb us with guided missiles! He has atomic missiles; why shouldn't he fire them at us? Let them carry out their sanctions!"

Somewhat less excited, but no less angry, he worded his reply to Eisenhower:

In your letter you referred to the possibility of U.N. "procedure" being invoked against Israel for not having carried out in full General Assembly resolutions. No such "procedures" have ever been invoked against Egypt, which for years has violated Security Council resolutions and the U.N. Charter and continues to do so . . . Is it conceivable that the United States, the land of freedom, equality and human rights, should support such discrimination and U.N. "procedures" be invoked to force us back into a position that would again expose us to murder and blockade? . . . Our people will never accept this, no matter what sacrifice it may entail.

In mid-February the conflict between Eisenhower and Ben-Gurion sharpened. Eisenhower decided to appeal directly to the American people in a radio and T.V. broadcast:

If we consent that an armed attack can gain the attacker's objectives, that will mean we have turned back the clock of international order . . . I believe that, for the sake of peace, the United Nations has no choice but to exercise pressure upon Israel to obey the resolutions about withdrawal . . . Should a nation which attacks and occupies foreign territory in the face of U.N. disapproval be allowed to impose conditions on its own withdrawal ?

Both Israel and the United States were now deployed for the final trial of strength between them: the General Assembly meeting on 26 February. At the last moment, however, there was yet another unexpected development. On the morning of 27 February, Ben-Gurion wrote in his journal: "There is a report from New York of some unexpected proposal by Pineau, but we have not received its contents." That evening, Eban cabled the substance of the proposal submitted by Pineau, who was in Washington together with Guy Mollet: Israel would proclaim full withdrawal from Gaza on the strength of the "assumption" that U.N. forces would take over full powers of military and civilian administration in the Strip and would remain there until a peace settlement was concluded. If Egypt caused any violations of this arrangement, Israel would retain the right of self-defense. The United States and other countries would inform the Assembly that they confirm the Israeli "assumption", thereby giving international backing to the Israeli position. As for the right of self-defense, Israel would be entitled to exercise it if the Egyptian army returned to the Strip or if freedom of navigation were impeded. Pineau and Mollet had submitted this proposal to the United States government, which approved it.

Ben-Gurion summoned an urgent Cabinet meeting for that same evening, and the French proposal was adopted. That night, Ben-Gurion cabled detailed instructions to Eban, and the following day an Israeli delegation headed by Eban worded a joint document with a group of American experts headed by Dulles. They also worked out the scenario for the conclusion of the General Assembly debate. The Israeli foreign minister would submit a declaration, whose main points were worked out at this joint meeting; she would be followed by the United States' representative, announcing his country's favorable view of the "assumptions" included in the Israeli declaration. After that, the maritime states would declare their support for freedom of navigation in the straits. This scenario would remove the crisis from the sphere of the General Assembly, and thereby avoid a vote in the body where the Soviet bloc and the Afro–Asian countries together comprised a majority and were liable to foil the proposed agreement.

1 March was the decisive day, and Ben-Gurion was again confined to his bed. That evening, shortly before Golda Meir was scheduled to make her address to the Assembly, he invited a number of generals to his home. He sensed a moral and national obligation to try and convince the men who, in his eyes, represented the victors of the Sinai Campaign. Without any embellishments, he described the risks that Israel was taking upon herself

in consenting to withdraw. "I told [the Cabinet] that this is a gamble, but it's a known risk; we may have to fight again . . . [and] when we have to fight again, the whole of the United Nations will not back us. But [we will have the backing of] enough states sufficient to enable us to do so with greater peace of mind." Ben-Gurion stressed that he had been prepared to face sanctions. But if Israel rejected Pineau's proposal, she would run the risk of cutting off the flow of French arms, and there would not be a single state in the world to supply Israel with weapons. "Tomorrow," he concluded, "there won't be dancing in the streets. I can imagine that in the army itself . . . there will be great sorrow. But I am sure that in six months' time . . . ships will come, tankers . . . [work] will begin on constructing a railway, American, French, English, Italian and Ethiopian ships will come – [and] there will be rejoicing . . ."

No less than he attempted to convince his officers, Ben-Gurion appeared to be trying to convince himself that this was the only road open to him. In describing the forthcoming political moves at the General Assembly, he enumerated the setbacks in store for Israel's enemies, Nasser above all. "Nasser may not long survive what is going to happen at the United Nations in an hour's time," he said. "Today, his destiny has turned. He will not fall at eleven o'clock tonight, it doesn't go that fast, but I think his fate is going to be settled today. This act [at the United Nations] signifies the elimination of Nasser, but that is not accomplished in a single hour."

Ben-Gurion erred. Nasser was not about to fall. On the contrary, he knew of the "plot" that was brewing. Neither Hammarskjold nor Dulles was prepared, at any time, to agree with the Israeli "assumption" that Egypt would not return to the Gaza Strip, and Dulles's promises to Israel were nothing more than a smokescreen. All this was to become clear to Israel that same evening in an unexpected and painful manner.

At the appointed hour, Golda Meir mounted the speaker's rostrum at the General Assembly and announced the evacuation of Gaza and of the Tiran Straits, in accordance with the Assembly's decision concerning the stationing of U.N. troops. Having completed her address, she returned to her seat, and U.S. Ambassador Henry Cabot Lodge rose to declare the United States' agreement with the Israeli "assumptions", in accordance with the pre-arranged scenario. But his words were not in accordance with the text agreed upon. "To my astonishment," wrote Golda Meir,

I heard him reassure the United Nations that . . . the future of the Gaza Strip would have to be worked out within the context of the armistice agreements. Perhaps not everyone at the United Nations that day understood what Cabot Lodge was saying, but *we* understood all too well. The U.S. State Department had won its battle against us, and the Egyptian military government, with its garrison, was going to return to Gaza. There was nothing I could do or say. I just sat there, biting my lip, not even able to look at the handsome Mr Cabot Lodge while he pacified all those who had been so worried lest we refuse to withdraw unconditionally.

The United States' representative was followed by the delegates of several other countries, who expressed their agreement with Israel's "assumptions" about freedom of navigation in the straits, in accordance with the original scenario; but as far as the Gaza Strip was concerned, Israel had clearly been tricked.

When Ben-Gurion learned of this development, he erupted into rage, and at first, he wanted to call off the withdrawal. He immediately summoned the Cabinet for a special meeting, the first to be held on the Sabbath since the establishment of the state. The Cabinet instructed Eban to present an immediate demand to Dulles for a clear declaration that the Egyptians would not return to Gaza. But the United States evaded making such a statement, and Ben-Gurion had to make do with the letter Eisenhower sent him that evening: "I believe . . . that Israel will have no cause to regret acting in accordance with the vigorous feelings of the whole international community," wrote Eisenhower. Referring to "the hopes and expectations" which found their expression in the words of Israel's foreign minister "and others" he stated: "I believe it is reasonable to entertain such hopes and expectations . . . and I want you to know that the United States . . . will seek that such hopes prove not to be in vain."

Ben-Gurion attempted to seize on these words, and in his reply to Eisenhower, he again urged that the Egyptians should not return to Gaza. But it was too late. In keeping with her undertaking, Israel withdrew from the straits and the Gaza Strip. Within a few days, Egyptian military government was restored to Gaza. Ben-Gurion ranted and raved, but he did not respond with a military strike. "I do not have the heart for an operation in Gaza," he told the chief of staff. Ben-Gurion bowed his head to the *fait accompli*. At the conclusion of the political battle, the Cabinet, the army, and the whole of Israel were left with the bitter taste of a political setback.

In the short run, the prime minister appeared to have lost the diplomatic battle, and a splendid military victory had been turned into a political defeat. Israel's territorial aims had not been attained; Nasser had not been overthrown; Israel had been identified with the imperialist states; her relations with the United States had gone through a severe crisis; and her relations with the United Nations and its secretary-general were in a state of open tension and mistrust. The Egyptian army returned to Gaza, and the southern settlements again faced the same dangers as before.

So it appeared in the short view. But as time went by, the Sinai Campaign brought Israel rich dividends, first and foremost ten years of peace. One after another, her borders fell silent. The *fedayeen* did not return to Gaza, and the other borders enjoyed a kind of *de facto* peace. The sense of insecurity, and the menace to the very existence of their state, were wiped from the minds of the Israelis. Ben-Gurion's vision of the future of Eilat was also largely realized. Its port became the southern gateway to Israel, freedom of navigation was guaranteed, an oil pipeline was laid from Eilat to the Mediterranean coast, and a significant boost was given to the development of the Negev.

The Sinai operation also brought about an unprecedented upsurge in Israel's foreign relations. Contrary to the predictions of all the experts, who foresaw that Israel would be isolated and shunned by the African and Asian states, precisely the opposite occurred. Those same young African and Asian nations which had condemned Israel in the United Nations, or those which achieved their independence at that time, regarded her as a symbol and a model. From every corner of the world, African, Asian, and South American delegations came to Israel to request technical, agricultural, and military assistance. The Sinai Campaign inaugurated a new epoch in Israel's foreign relations, and links with Third World countries reached their high point during the years 1957–67.

Israel's relations with the Western Powers also prospered. The Sinai Campaign made the American leaders aware of the dangers of Soviet penetration of the Middle East. During the next few years, Egypt, Syria and Iraq identified with the pro-Soviet camp, while Israel's growth as a stable Western democracy and an obstacle to Soviet influence fortified American–Israeli relations. The alliance struck between France and Israel on the eve of the Sinai Campaign was extended and strengthened. For the next ten years, Israel had no difficulty in buying arms from France. The French also helped Israel construct the large atomic reactor at Dimona and served as a loyal political backer for many years.

Internally, the Sinai Campaign boosted the power of Mapai, and strengthened Ben-Gurion's position. It was an "elixir of youth", which restored Ben-Gurion's strength and fortified his status as leader. The Sinai Campaign inaugurated the Golden Age in the chronicles of the State of Israel. It was also to be Ben-Gurion's Golden Age as a national and political leader.

15

The Golden Age

On Thursday, 28 August 1958, Ben-Gurion, as usual, attended the weekly meeting of the General Staff. That evening several of his close aides came to his home; and following their instructions, he put on khaki uniform, as he always did when setting off to observe army maneuvers. Behind-the-scenes rumors made the rounds that day that Ben-Gurion was going down to the Negev to witness secret trials of new military equipment. At nine o'clock that evening, a Defense Ministry aide came to Ben-Gurion's home and escorted the Old Man to his car but it did not set off toward the Negev. Following a circuitous route, it drove to Lod airport, entering by a side entrance. On the darkened runway were a number of figures, including Foreign Minister Golda Meir and Yitzhak Navon. The whole retinue clambered into a large military aircraft that was warming up its engines at the edge of the runway. At quarter to ten, the plane took off, flew out to sea, and then turned north. As he had done two years before, Ben-Gurion was setting out on a journey whose details were a closely guarded secret and would remain so for many years. In the course of his trip, Ben-Gurion was to meet the leaders of another state and conclude a treaty of friendship and cooperation.

Ben-Gurion's flight was preceded by a chain of tempestuous events. In August 1957, Syria became the target of massive Soviet penetration. Large amounts of Soviet arms were unloaded at the port of Latakia, and military experts flowed in from the Soviet Union. It seemed only a matter of time before Syria was drawn into the Soviet camp. At the same time, there was growing tension along Syria's border with Israel. A series of incidents instigated by the Syrians left dead and wounded on the Israeli side, but Ben-Gurion decided to exercise restraint. He had no intention of attacking Syria but hoped that the Powers – particularly the United States – would cause the overthrow of its pro-Soviet regime. He wrote to Secretary of State Dulles.

The establishment of Syria as a base for international Communism is one of the most dangerous events that has befallen the free world in our time ... I believe that the free world should not and need not acquiesce in this situation.

But everything depends upon a firm and purposeful position taken by the United States as the leading power among the free nations. If you adopt this line, Syria's neighbours other than Israel, together with rebellious elements in Syria, would certainly take measures to root out the danger . . . I feel bound to recommend such a course with the greatest solemnity and conviction. You may be assured that Israel would do nothing to embarrass the progress of such an action.

His hopes were not groundless. He knew that America was planning a coup in Syria, by means of Turkey, Iraq, and Jordan. But the plot failed. The United States made vain efforts to exert pressure upon Syria by dispatching the Sixth Fleet to the area and concentrating Turkish, Iraqi, and Jordanian army units on Syria's borders. Israel took no part in these American moves, but early in the autumn of 1957 Ben-Gurion made renewed efforts to break down American reservations. He sensed that this was an opportune moment. The Soviet Union had launched its satellite, Sputnik, arousing great concern in the West; and the governments of Syria and the Soviet Union had issued threats against Turkey, to which the United States granted public guarantees. Israel was disturbed to note that, even with the growing Soviet danger, she was not among those states whose existence the United States was prepared to guarantee. Ben-Gurion instructed Golda Meir to meet with Dulles and discuss an American warning to the Soviet Union regarding the existence of Israel. He also renewed the Israeli request for American arms, as well as assistance in extending the country's ports and airfields "so that we can play a role in emergencies". He was staking a great deal on the anti-Soviet motives guiding United States policy in the Middle East. But Golda Meir's conversation with Dulles did not yield hoped-for results.

While Israel endured endless frustration at the hands of the United States, however, Ben-Gurion secretly established a clandestine alliance in the Middle East. In the most profound secrecy, a specter-like organization was born, and extended until it formed a ring around the Arab Middle East. The terms "clandestine" and "specter" are no exaggeration. In the course of several years, Israel conducted intensive activity throughout the Middle East under a mantle of almost total secrecy. Using different disguises, traveling under false names, by indirect routes, Ben-Gurion's emissaries repeatedly flew off into the night for the capitals of Israel's new allies. This clandestine endeavor covered various spheres, most of which are classified to this day. The full operation became known under the name of "the periphery alliance".

The story began before the Sinai Campaign, when Israel secretly built up a special relationship with two Middle Eastern states: Iran in the north and Ethiopia in the south. Nasser's subversive activities and his expansionist ambitions aroused growing concern in both countries – and not in them alone. A number of additional states, including Sudan, were anxious over Egypt's appetite for power. Then came the Sinai Campaign, and the set-back Israel inflicted on Nasser produced unexpected reverberations throughout the Middle East and its surrounding countries. States that had cowered in fear of Nasser's ambitions suddenly discovered that there was a country capable of defeating him. Leaders worried about Communist penetration under Nasser's sponsorship learned that there was a state with the ability to check the Soviets. Concern was particularly acute in Ethiopia, an isolated Christian country in Africa that experienced rising anxiety in the face of Nasser's Pan-Islamic and Pan-African expansionism. Shortly after the Sinai Campaign, a high-ranking Israeli emissary arrived in Ethiopia and met with Emperor Haile Selassie to discuss joint political action against Nasser's subversion, as well as cooperation in economic development. The plan they adopted called for sending Israeli experts to Ethiopia and Ethiopian students to Israel and the establishment of joint projects and courses.

At the same time, Israel was turning its gaze to the east, and extensive activity was initiated in Iran, which was likewise interested in blocking Nasserist and Communist influence in the Middle East. The country faced severe problems in the fields of agriculture and scientific development, and Israel was prepared to offer assistance. After a number of Israeli emissaries were sent to Iran, relations grew steadily closer. In January 1958, Ben-Gurion wrote to the shah and made reference to the benevolent policy of the ancient Persian king Cyrus toward the Jews. In his reply, the shah stressed that "he cherished the memory of Cyrus' policy and intended to continue this ancient tradition".

The unwritten alliance with Iran became the cornerstone for the establishment of a triangle. In April 1958, veteran Israeli diplomat Eliyahu Sasson held a meeting with the Turkish foreign minister, who expressed his government's considerable disquiet over developments in Syria. In the course of 1957, the Turks sensed a clear threat against their country's security when an alliance was established between their northern neighbor, the Soviet Union, and their southern neighbor, Syria. The Turkish and Israeli representatives agreed on a timetable and agenda for further high-level meetings.

In light of these promising links with states to the north and south, Israel came up with the overall plan for a "periphery pact": the establishment of a bloc of states around the edge of the Middle East – Turkey and Iran to the north and Ethiopia to the south – linked to Israel. This unofficial alliance was of obvious significance to the West. Now, for the first

time, Israel sensed that she had something to offer the Americans. She was
no longer a small, isolated country, but the leader and connecting link of a
group of states (one of which belonged to N.A.T.O. and two others of
which were members of the Baghdad Pact) whose population exceeded
that of all the Arab states together. They were also prepared to go a long
way in collaborating with the Americans against Soviet designs in the
region. Ben-Gurion grasped the great importance of gaining American
political and financial backing for the secret association. He wrote to Abba
Eban, Israeli ambassador to the United States: "If America adopts this
plan – a link between Iran, Turkey, Israel – and, one should add, Ethiopia –
something important may grow out of it." Eban expressed certain misgivings about the alliance's chances of success. But Ben-Gurion was
enthusiastic and, as usual, he galloped ahead. In order to ascertain whether
it was feasible to establish the alliance, he wanted to hold high-level
discussions with the Turkish government.

It is doubtful whether this meeting would have taken place were it not
for the upheaval that struck the Middle East during the summer of 1958,
dragging several states into a powerful maelstrom. In May, civil war broke
out in Lebanon between Christian circles and the Moslems who were
working for Lebanon's integration in a Nasserist Arab bloc. The armed
uprising, which began as an internal conflict, was fanned by the propaganda
of Nasser's agents and nourished by Egyptian and Syrian aid in money,
arms, and combatants. In July, the crisis struck Iraq and Jordan. As the
situation in Jordan deteriorated, with the Hashemite throne endangered by
pro-Nasserist subversion, the Iraqi government sent aid in the form of a
motorized brigade under the command of General Kassem. Halfway along
the route, however, Kassem ordered his soldiers to turn around and storm
Baghdad. Together with his colleagues of the Free Officers group, he
carried out a rapid military coup and seized power.

With the collapse of Iraq, it looked as though all the Western strongholds
in the Middle East were tumbling down in succession. Formerly, the heart
of the Baghdad Pact, Iraq now appeared to be turning into a Soviet satellite.
Her neighbors, Iran and Turkey, were panicstricken upon realizing that
the Soviet ring was tightening about them.

The fall of Iraq almost led to the overthrow of Jordan's King Hussein.
With the collapse of the Hashemite king's Iraqi backers, all the pro-Nasser
elements in Jordan reared their heads. Hussein remained a prisoner in his
palace, protected by a few battalions of British soldiers that England had
hurriedly flown to Amman from bases in Cyprus.

During the first days after the bloody revolution in Iraq, it looked as
though the United States would strike back in force. The following day, the

U.S. announced that, in response to a request by the president of Lebanon, it was landing American troops on the Beirut coast. At the same time, it placed the strategic air command and the air force carriers on emergency alert. Marine units from the Gulf of Okinawa were rushed to the Persian Gulf, and another task force was dispatched to a base in Turkey. The United States hoped that some surviving Iraqi leader would ask for American intervention to save the regime there, but no such request arrived.

The coup in Iraq persuaded the Turkish leaders to overcome their remaining misgivings about strengthening their ties with Israel. "Our emissary was summoned to [the Turkish foreign minister] . . ." Ben-Gurion wrote excitedly in his diary five days after the Iraqi coup,

and [was] told . . . that they are taking action parallel to ours and he will be pleased to see full coordination of our political actions with theirs. We have entered historic times, and the opportunity for such action will not return . . . He also informed me of agreement in principle to hold a meeting of the two premiers . . .

The following day, Ben-Gurion presided over consultations at the home of Golda Meir concerning "tightening links with Iran, Turkey, and Ethiopia with the aid of America, in other words, by pressure upon America and United States pressure and assistance in these countries". Ben-Gurion immediately worded an urgent memorandum to President Eisenhower in which, for the first time, he presented the peripheral pact:

Our object is the creation of a group of countries, not necessarily a formal and public alliance, that will be able to stand up steadfastly against Soviet expansion through Nasser and might even be able to save the freedom of Lebanon and, perhaps, in the course of time, of Syria too. . . . We can carry out the mission . . . since . . . it is a vital necessity for us, as well as a source of perceptible strength to the West in this part of the world.

Enumerating the forms of aid that Israel was capable of offering, he asked the president for American cooperation! "Two things are necessary: U.S. support – political, financial, and moral, and the inculcation of a feeling in Iran, Turkey and Ethiopia that our efforts in this direction enjoy the support of the U.S."

Late in the evening of 24 July, Eban met with Dulles and delivered Ben-Gurion's memorandum. The following day, Ben-Gurion received Eisenhower's initial response: "I am deeply impressed by the breadth of your insight into the grave problems which the free world faces in the Middle

East and elsewhere . . . Since the Middle East comprehends Israel, you can be confident of the United States interest in the integrity and independence of Israel. I have discussed your letter with the secretary of state, who will be writing to you in more detail."

This response came as a disappointment to Ben-Gurion. He had hoped for an invitation to Washington to hold official talks. Dulles and Eisenhower were still cautious. But when Dulles finally did reply to Ben-Gurion, he expressed a favorable opinion and encouraged the prime minister to establish the peripheral pact. Ben-Gurion gave the green light for the operation to be stepped up. On 28 August he took off on his nocturnal flight. Just after midnight his plane landed at a military airfield near Ankara.

Ben-Gurion and his aides were driven to a sumptuous official guest house near the Turkish capital. The following morning, the Turkish premier arrived, accompanied by his foreign minister and a carefully selected retinue of senior advisers. The meeting began with Ben-Gurion presenting a political survey. The topics discussed were cooperation in Western capitals in explaining the dangers of Nasser's expansionist politics; consultations on assistance to Ethiopia and Iran against Nasserist and Communist subversion; Israeli assistance to Turkey in industrialization; joint scientific research; and the extension of trade between the two countries. At midnight Ben-Gurion's plane took off again. "At half past two in the morning, we landed at the military airfield," Ben-Gurion wrote in his diary, "and there, to my surprise Ezer (Weizman) was waiting; he drove me to the Sharon Hotel." None of the hotel's guests or staff who chanced to see the prime minister so late at night was surprised to see him dressed in khaki, coming "directly from maneuvers in the south". In fact, Ben-Gurion was already toying with the idea of paying a similar clandestine visit to Ethiopia.

The secret pact concluded in 1958 with Turkey, Iran, and Ethiopia was long lasting. It was not fortuitous that the shah told a French journalist in 1960: "Of the two candidates in the United States presidential elections, Nixon and Kennedy, I prefer Kennedy – not so much because of his personality as because of his party. In the Democratic Party, the Jews possess considerable influence, and Iran is interested in the consolidation of this influence because of her close ties with Israel." Nor was it by chance that on 14 December 1960, when there was an attempted coup against the Ethiopian emperor, amateur radio operators all over the world picked up the signals sent out by the supporters of the Lion of Judah: "A coup is threatening the throne. Alert the Israelis!"

The Israelis did, indeed, help the emperor retain his throne. In fact the periphery pact held up in spite of the coups that occurred in the region. Links with Turkey did not weaken when the Menderes government was overthrown by a military coup or even when the former premier and foreign minister were hanged by the new regime (though the northern pact lost some of its vitality during the 1960s, when there was an improvement in relations between the Soviet Union and Iran and Turkey).

Despite the encouraging influence of the periphery pact, early in 1960 Ben-Gurion decided that, in view of the generally alarming situation in the Middle East, it was necessary to meet with the leaders of the Western states and request arms. In theory, he had no cause for anxiety. France continued to supply arms to Israel; Germany's links with Israel were growing stronger; and Britain had abandoned her previous hostility. There was also a marked improvement in the American posture following the events of 1958; the U.S. even provided Israel with 1,000 recoilless guns – admittedly "light" arms, but the first actual weapons the United States had ever supplied. The American administration also consented to provide secret financing for Israel's purchase of tanks from England and took a very favorable view of Israeli activities in Asia and Africa.

Yet Ben-Gurion's publicly expressed optimism was only a cover for his growing concern. In November 1959, the Old Man was apprehensive of an imminent Egyptian attack; in December, there was grave tension on the Syrian border and two ships carrying cargo destined for Israel were stopped in the Suez Canal. The arms race in progress in the Middle East made him fear that Soviet aid would enable the Arabs to convert their quantities into a new quality.

Since the president of the United States did not see fit to invite him to Washington for an official visit, Ben-Gurion preferred to find some pretext for a trip to America and take advantage of the opportunity to ask for a meeting with Eisenhower. The pretext soon arose when he was granted an honorary degree by Brandeis University. The Israeli embassy in Washington notified the State Department of Ben-Gurion's forthcoming visit, and the president consented to meet him in March.

Ben-Gurion spent eight days in the United States, and his timetable was crowded. He met Jewish leaders in New York and Boston, dined with Dag Hammarskjold, held conversations with Eleanor Roosevelt and Nelson Rockefeller, appeared at receptions and press conferences, met several Senate leaders, and was received at the home of Vice-President Nixon.

Naturally enough, the highlight of his visit was his meeting with President Eisenhower. Their conversation did not produce any encouraging results. Their talk, lasting an hour and a half, was in effect a monologue. Ben-Gurion spoke almost incessantly, with Eisenhower getting in no more than an occasional comment. The prime minister aired his views on various topics, from the situation in the Middle East to relations between the two world blocs. Eisenhower listened respectfully, but when Ben-Gurion touched on the subject of arms, the president told him that the United States would not be "the chief supplier" of weapons to the Middle East, preferring that the European states undertake this task. The United States, said Eisenhower, preferred to act as "arbitrator". At the same time, Eisenhower promised his guest that the United States would protect Israel's existence.

Ben-Gurion was sorely disappointed by the meeting, but another encounter became the principal event of his tour. It was the New York meeting of the two Old Men: Ben-Gurion and Adenauer. Their conversation has rightfully been described as "historic", for it marked the formal reconciliation of the Jewish people, as embodied in the State of Israel, and Adenauer's "new Germany".

Secret plans for a meeting between Ben-Gurion and Adenauer had long been in preparation. On learning that Ben-Gurion did not wish to come to Germany, Adenauer proposed other meeting places – Rhodes, Athens, or Teheran. Finally, on hearing of Ben-Gurion's forthcoming trip to the United States in March, the chancellor proposed that they meet in New York, where he planned a visit at the same time.

Arms and finance were the two principal topics Ben-Gurion discussed with Adenauer in New York. Shimon Peres had notified Ben-Gurion of a secret agreement worked out with the German defense minister whereby Germany would "lend" Israel various types of weapons, or even deliver them free of charge; the weapons included combat and transport planes, helicopters, submarines, air-to-air missiles, and other items of sophisticated equipment. However, this extraordinary undertaking required the approval of the chancellor. The second subject was economic help.

At nine o'clock in the morning of 14 March 1960, Ben-Gurion descended from his suite in New York's Waldorf Astoria Hotel and headed for another suite a few stories below, where he was welcomed by Konrad Adenauer. Some observers described Ben-Gurion's handshake as a gesture of forgiveness, to free Germany of her guilt for her crimes against the Jewish people. This was not how Ben-Gurion saw it. He made a distinction between the crimes of Nazi Germany and the efforts of Adenauer's Germany to atone for them. The two men agreed that the time was not yet ripe for the establishment of normal diplomatic relations between Germany and Israel. Neither public opinion, nor the spirit prevailing in the legislatures of Bonn and Jerusalem were ready for such a step. At the same time, they talked at length about arms supplies and economic assistance. Ben-

Gurion had long resolved to approach Adenauer with a request for a $250 million loan, now that reparations payments were nearing completion. At the last moment, however, pressure from his secretary, Yitzhak Navon, induced him to ask Adenauer for a loan of half a billion dollars, to be made available to Israel over a ten-year period, for industrial and agricultural development, primarily in the Negev. Adenauer consented immediately. "We will help," he said.

Ben-Gurion now went on to military matters. He asked Adenauer for weapons to be supplied to Israel along the lines of Peres's understanding with Defense Minister Strauss. Adenauer knew of these talks and readily gave his approval for sizable amounts of military equipment to be supplied to Israel free of charge. Ben-Gurion left the meeting with a feeling of great satisfaction. He told the journalists waiting outside: "Last summer, I told the Knesset that Germany today is not the Germany of yesterday. After my encounter with Adenauer, I am certain that my judgment was correct."

His judgment was also correct in the need for Israel to find a source of arms other than France, a problem that had long concerned the prime minister. Indeed, two months after Ben-Gurion's meeting with Adenauer, a severe crisis erupted in Franco–Israeli relations when French Foreign Minister Couve de Murville summoned the Israeli ambassador and informed him that the French government had decided not to supply uranium for the nuclear reactor Israel was constructing in the Negev. Furthermore, he demanded that the fact of the reactor's construction be made public and that it be placed under foreign – perhaps international – supervision. Later, de Gaulle was to write in his memoirs: "[We] stopped the assistance . . . for . . . construction . . . of an installation for converting uranium into plutonium from which, one bright day, atomic bombs could emerge."

The news evoked deep concern in Israel, for it not only heralded the effective failure of the plan to establish the reactor, but indicated a fundamental change in the attitude of France, which had up till then assisted Israel in her nuclear-research project. Israel's request for a meeting between Ben-Gurion and de Gaulle was met by a sympathetic response. A week before the meeting, Ben-Gurion sent Shimon Peres to Paris to prepare the ground and map out the topics for discussion with the heads of the French administration.

At four o'clock on the afternoon of 13 June, Ben-Gurion and his aides arrived in Paris and were housed at the Bristol Hotel, a few hundred yards from the Elysée Palace. The prime minister was highly anxious as indicated by his punctilious preparations for the meeting with de Gaulle. He sat up until late at night, filling his note pad with details and figures. The following morning his advisers found him in the same state as they had left him the night before: tense, worried, and surrounded by his notes.

At midday Ben-Gurion's entourage headed for the Elysée Palace. His aides were overcome by the magnificent reception. They mounted the stairway between two rows of Republican Guards in their resplendent uniforms with drawn swords. Before sitting down to lunch, Ben-Gurion and de Gaulle withdrew briefly. This was their first fleeting contact in advance of the meeting they would hold after lunch.

Ben-Gurion, who had been very tense in anticipation of the meeting, was in for a pleasant surprise. "I had a strange image of de Gaulle," he admitted later. "I heard that he is a cold, hard, closed man, and I found a lively, humane man with a sense of humor, very alert, and much kindness. He speaks ironically at times, but it is a friendly irony." De Gaulle wrote: "From the very first moment, I sensed sympathetic admiration for this courageous combatant and champion. His personality symbolizes Israel, which he has ruled since the day he presided over her establishment and struggle."

After lunch, the two men again left their aides and withdrew to the French president's office for their political discussions. Ben-Gurion was well aware of the danger Israel would face if France withdrew from Algeria and did his best to prevent such a withdrawal, but he failed. When he presented his Algerian plan to de Gaulle, the French president replied: "My God, you are trying to establish a new Israel in Africa!"

"Yes!" replied Ben-Gurion, "but there is one difference: that 'new Israel' will be backed by France, with her forty-five million inhabitants and her alliances with the Western countries." Ben-Gurion then told de Gaulle of Nasserist subversion and enumerated Israel's links with the peripheral pact states. De Gaulle displayed particular interest in Israeli fears of an Arab onslaught. "Do you really fear that an Arab coalition might endanger you?" he asked the Old Man.

"There is no need for a coalition," replied Ben-Gurion. "Under certain circumstances, Egypt alone can attack us. I said so to Eisenhower, who made a formal declaration that the United States would not permit Israel to be annihilated."

"Neither will France!" said de Gaulle emphatically.

"I regard your assurance as genuine, as I did Eisenhower's," said Ben-Gurion. "But that does not provide us with any security. The moment Egypt has better planes than we do, we will be in great danger."

"You believe that you are in danger unless you are on terms of parity in armaments?" asked de Gaulle.

"Not so much in quantity as in the quality of arms," Ben-Gurion replied.

"I do not presume that they can overcome you," said de Gaulle.

It was precisely this statement that worried Ben-Gurion. Wherever he visited, he was horrified to hear the legend of "Israel the invincible". Once again, he went to the trouble of explaining Israel's defense problems to de Gaulle. "If [the Arabs] bomb Tel Aviv, we will not be able to mobilize our reservists," he said.

"Did you say all this to Eisenhower?" de Gaulle asked.

"Yes," said Ben-Gurion. "Eisenhower said they cannot be the chief supplier [of arms]."

"Why?" de Gaulle asked.

"Because of international considerations and the international situation," Ben-Gurion replied, telling the French president of Israel's requests to the United States for surface-to-air missiles.

Their talk went on longer than expected. It was about four o'clock, and Ben-Gurion was scheduled to lay a wreath on the tomb of the Unknown Soldier within a few minutes. The principal topics – arms supplies and atomic energy – had yet to be touched upon. De Gaulle himself noted that fact. "How long are you staying in France?" he asked. On learning that Ben-Gurion would remain in Paris a few days longer, he invited him for a further meeting. The two men took leave of one another in great friendliness.

On 17 June, his last day in Paris, Ben-Gurion held his second meeting with de Gaulle. Their talk began with the question of the nuclear reactor. Ben-Gurion understood de Gaulle's reservations about continued participation in the construction of the reactor. He assured the French president that it was not Israel's intention to manufacture nuclear arms, and the two men agreed that Shimon Peres would come to Paris for talks with French ministers in the hope of solving the crisis. In contrast with his reservations on the reactor, however, de Gaulle confirmed continued cooperation in various military spheres. "I think you exaggerate with regard to the danger facing you," he said. "Under no circumstances will we sanction your annihilation. At present, we do not possess great power, but it is growing, and we shall protect you."

Ben-Gurion contended that such help would inevitably come too late. He depicted Nasser's eagerness to annihilate Israel and predicted that if he did manage to acquire modern planes, like the Mig-19, his officers would push him into war.

"You need weapons against Migs?" asked de Gaulle. "For Migs, you need missiles, and we do not possess any." He promised to raise the matter with Macmillan and Eisenhower. As for other arms, "you will receive England's finest Centurions and the best planes we possess".

The two men rose to take their farewells. De Gaulle accompanied Ben-Gurion to his car and during a last handshake, said: "I think our talks were very important and useful. I am glad you came, and that I managed to meet you. And now that we know one another, whenever you have anything [to discuss], you can address me. Write to me personally." De Gaulle told his son-in-law: "Ben-Gurion and Adenauer are the two greatest leaders in the West." Some time later, he characterized Ben-Gurion's personality as "noble", adding that he was "one of the greatest statesmen of our time".

Ben-Gurion left Paris with a profound sense of satisfaction. Admittedly, the nuclear-reactor crisis had not been solved, but de Gaulle had given specific promises with regard to military supplies and assistance. Even more important, the marks of friendship that de Gaulle had showered upon him were like holy gospel in the France of 1960, and extensive assistance to Israel became one of the foundations of the Fifth Republic's policy.

The new atmosphere characterizing Franco–Israeli relations after Ben-Gurion's meeting with de Gaulle undoubtedly helped in resolving disagreements on the nuclear issue. A few months later, Shimon Peres went to Paris for meetings with Couve de Murville, Guillaumat and several of their aides. They concluded an agreement whereby Israel would continue construction of the reactor unaided, while France would not repeat her demands for international control. The French companies linked with construction of the reactor would continue to supply the equipment that had already been ordered. It was also agreed that Ben-Gurion would soon make a public statement about the construction of the reactor and enumerate the research projects to be conducted there. However, before Israel had time to complete her part of the deal, the nuclear reactor set off a grave crisis that reverberated throughout the world.

On 9 December 1960 U.N. Secretary of State Christian Herter sent an urgent summons to the Israeli ambassador to Washington. The Americans had learned that Israel was constructing a nuclear reactor, and the report had evoked great concern in the administration. Moreover, the administration had taken the initiative in convening the Joint Congressional Committee on Atomic Energy to discuss the question. The following day, the *New York Times* carried a fairly vague report on the meeting of the Congressional Atomic Energy Committee. Three days later a short report published in *Time Magazine* disclosed that the meeting had discussed a state that was constructing a nuclear reactor. *Time* added that this state did not belong to N.A.T.O. or to the Eastern bloc. On 16 December, the London *Daily Express* carried a sensational report that Israel was manufacturing a nuclear bomb. Citing British and American Intelligence sources, the report mentioned that there was considerable concern in the West. On 18 December, the *Washington Post* bore the headline: "U.S. officials state nuclear reactor developed secretly by Israel." According to the report official circles in Washington estimated that this reactor would enable Israel to manufacture an atom bomb within five years.

In this fashion, the "Israeli atom bomb" set off a worldwide explosion. Within a short time, further sensational details were made known. Following C.I.A. reports, a U-2 spy plane was sent on a mission over Israel, where it took photographs of a strange group of structures in the Negev. When asked about the purpose of these structures, the Israelis contended that they were a "textile works". However, aerial photographs proved beyond doubt that the structure was a nuclear-research reactor, which the Americans considered perfectly capable of manufacturing nuclear weapons.

Now that the truth was out, Israel no longer denied that she was constructing a nuclear reactor but stressed that it would engage solely in peaceful research. The United States treated these explanations with great suspicion, particularly as all the construction work had been carried out in secret. British and American newspapers posed grave questions as to the character of a nuclear installation secretly constructed in the heart of the desert, camouflaged as a textile works, and protected by soldiers, police roadblocks, barbed-wire fences, and signs forbidding photographs. American concern reached its peak on 19 December, when President Eisenhower called in his close advisers for urgent consultations at the White House.

As sensational headlines piled up in rapid succession, journalists turned their attention to the nature of French aid to Israel. Some newspapers contended that the reactor being built with French help was identical to the one that had served to manufacture the French atomic bomb. The uproar did not subside when the French Foreign Ministry and Atomic Energy Authority published a joint statement confirming that France was assisting Israel with her nuclear program but stressing that this assistance was of a specifically scientific nature and was designed exclusively for peaceful purposes. In Cairo, Nasser declared dramatically that he would mobilize four million soldiers to attack Israel and demolish her nuclear installations.

Ben-Gurion was forced to make some response. On 21 December, he told the Knesset that a research reactor was under construction in the Negev but added that reports of the manufacture of an Israeli atomic bomb were false. His statement, worded in accordance with the agreement between Peres and Couve de Murville, did not calm the storm. The United States now approached Israel employing the sharpest terms. On

3 January 1961, the youthful American ambassador, Ogden Reid, met with Israel's foreign minister and presented five questions on behalf of the State Department, requesting answers to be delivered to him before midnight:

(1) What was Israel planning to do with the plutonium generated by the reactor? (2) Would Israel consent to inspection of the plutonium produced in the reactor? (3) Would Israel permit authorized scientists from the International Atomic Energy Commission, or some other friendly body, to visit the reactor? (4) Was Israel building or planning an additional reactor? (5) Could Israel declare unreservedly that she had no plans to manufacture atomic weapons?

That day, Ben-Gurion and Golda Meir decided not to reply to the American questions by the stipulated hour. The Old Man was infuriated by this disrespectful demand, verging on the crudest form of pressure. After the deadline had passed, he summoned the American ambassador to Sdeh Boker, and spoke to him with great forcefulness. As to the first question, he replied: "As far as we know, those who sell uranium do so on condition that the plutonium reverts to them." In reply to the second question, concerning "guarantees", the Old Man replied: "International guarantees – no. We don't want hostile states meddling in our business." At the same time, he expressed complete willingness to permit visits by scientists from a friendly state, or from an international organization, but not immediately. "There is anger in Israel over the American action in leaking this matter," he said and expressed his view that the visit would be conducted in the course of the year. He answered in the negative about the construction of an additional reactor and concluded by declaring yet again that Israel did not intend to manufacture nuclear weapons.

Then Ben-Gurion added a comment of his own. "On only two occasions in my life have I displayed a sense of self-importance in addressing representatives of foreign countries," he said. "I have spoken in this manner only once before, [saying] that we are only prepared to talk as equals, even though we are a tiny state . . . you must talk to us as equals, or not talk to us at all."

The United States submitted Israel to prolonged pressure to sanction an immediate inspection of the reactor by American scientists. For her part, Israel was not willing to consent immediately for reasons of prestige, and there was a sharp confrontation between the Israeli government and the American administration. In the meantime, John Kennedy had been elected to the presidency, and during his term of office the pressures increased. Finally, in March 1961, Ben-Gurion came to the conclusion that he must go to the United States and meet with the new president.

At the end of May, Ben-Gurion paid a state visit to Canada and then flew to New York. He was very tense in anticipation of his meeting with Kennedy, fearing that the inflexible position adopted by the United States over the nuclear reactor would harm relations with Israel. Before his departure, Ben-Gurion informed de Gaulle, of the explanations he intended to submit to Kennedy, and de Gaulle agreed. Prior to Ben-Gurion's meeting with Kennedy, Israel had permitted two American scientists to inspect the reactor. At the same time, Israeli Cabinet opponents of the reactor's construction stepped up their activities so that if serious differences also emerged during Ben-Gurion's meeting with Kennedy, there would be no doubt that Israel's nuclear program would have to be scrapped. American suspicions grew when it was learned that Israel was displaying an interest in long-range Mirage 4 bombers. To the United States, this looked like an Israeli attempt to acquire delivery systems for nuclear weapons. Various prominent personalities heard Kennedy express his misgivings about Israel's actions. However, when the two leaders met in New York, Kennedy told Ben-Gurion that, after visiting the reactor, his experts were convinced of the accuracy of Israel's explanations: they found that the reactor was designed for peaceful purposes, and did not serve any military needs whatsoever. Ben-Gurion felt a sense of relief. For the time being, at least, the reactor had been saved.

The two leaders' talks were business-like and congenial. Ben-Gurion recalled his first impressions of Kennedy, whom he had met a year previously. "He looked to me like a twenty-five-year-old boy," he said. "I asked myself: how can a man so young be elected president? At first, I did not take him seriously." After discussing the reactor, they went on to the situation in the Middle East. At that time, there was a renewed rapprochement between the United States and Egypt, and Kennedy was eager to propose solutions to defuse the situation in the Middle East. Ben-Gurion raised a proposal whereby the Powers, including the Soviet Union, would issue a joint declaration against the use of force to change the *status quo* in the Middle East, but Kennedy expressed doubts as to whether Khrushchev would go along with such a step. Then Ben-Gurion raised Israel's request for surface-to-air missiles, but he received a negative answer.

Ben-Gurion's companions were impressed by the conversation, and by the personality of the dynamic young president. But the prime minister thought otherwise, since the conclusion of their talks had left a bitter taste in his mouth. He had taken his leave of Kennedy and was turning to go when the president suddenly turned back, laying his arm on Ben-Gurion's shoulder in a gesture of friendship, and asked him to come back into the room for a moment so that he could tell him "something important". When the door closed and the two men remained alone, Kennedy addressed the

Old Man with unexpected candor: "I know that I was elected by the votes of American Jews. I owe them my victory. Tell me, is there something I ought to do?" Ben-Gurion was put off by the question. He had not come to the United States to haggle over Jewish votes, and this kind of political wheeler-dealing was not to his liking. Thus he contented himself with a brief sentence: "You must do whatever is good for the free world." After the conversation, Ben-Gurion told his aides: "To me, he looks like a politician."

That appraisal, and Ben-Gurion's ability to make it from his own unique position, were not lost on his aides, for Ben-Gurion was a true statesman. The Old Man's loyal secretary, Yitzhak Navon, once said, "If you were to ask me what idea underlay all of Ben-Gurion's actions, in a single sentence: The survival of the people of Israel." On what did that survival depend? Ben-Gurion himself gave the answer: "The fate of Israel depends on two things: on her strength and on her righteousness." These were the two imperatives toward which he constantly worked. As a statesman, he spent his whole life fighting for Israel's security, which meant strength in every sense. But he also wished to endow his small nation with dimensions of vision, of a universal message that would make it into a "chosen people" and a "light unto the nations".

If he is to be judged by his achievements, Ben-Gurion enjoyed greater success in the sphere of power than in the world of the spirit. He was a man of extremes, passionate in his feelings, fierce in his feuds, harsh in his battles. "I am a quarrelsome, obstreperous man," he often said. But to the same extent, he was capable of love, admiration, and veneration. He had great respect for Nehru and was deferent to philosophers even when he disagreed strongly with their political views. His comments on Professor Einstein and correspondence with Dr Schweitzer and Bertrand Russell, his dialogues with Israeli philosophers, writers, and scholars all display a profound respect for their personalities and spheres of study. But he kept his most fundamental, spontaneous admiration for an entirely different type of person – the modest and anonymous pioneers and settlers who made the desert bloom.

Ben-Gurion admired courage in all its forms, and was particularly taken by physical bravery. When a rash of "parachute fever" overtook the army the sixty-eight-year-old defense minister even decided to undertake a paratroop course, until Dayan finally talked him out of it, but his own courage found expression in his vision. The objectives he marked out for his people were the products of a venturesome mind that rebelled against convention and smashed existing concepts and limitations. A man lacking his daring would not have been able to lead his people through challenges like the establishment of the state, the formation of an army, settling the Negev, constructing the nuclear reactor, building up an advanced aircraft industry. Each and every one of these steps was taken against the advice of experts of all kinds. Yet his fiery vision did not lead him to build castles in the air. His head was indeed up in the clouds, but his feet were planted firmly on the ground. Ben-Gurion was a dreamer, but his dreams were constructed upon the careful compilation and analysis of the tiniest details and the basic facts that constituted reality. Some regarded him as a contemporary prophet; but this prophet held a slide-rule.

Ben-Gurion kept many of his political objectives so secret that he did not reveal them to even his closest aides. Early in 1957, after the Sinai Campaign, Menahem Begin came to Ben-Gurion's Tel Aviv home. Begin told the Old Man that he had been invited to the United States for a lecture tour, but American Jewish circles were against the tour, claiming that Begin's views on Israel's "historical boundaries" were liable to be harmful. On hearing this, Ben-Gurion made a comment that hinted at his own territorial dreams: "There are things which should be thought about but never spoken about." Later, however, Ben-Gurion came to terms with the *status quo* on Israel's eastern border. Long before the Six Day War, he abandoned his secret plans for further conquests that would lead to the annexation of populated areas to Israel.

Considering his unchallenged position as a national leader and international figure, Ben-Gurion's most unexpected trait was his boyish naïvety. He often displayed the freshness and amazement of a young man. He admired magicians and people who could make rapid mathematical calculations. In the middle of 1959, he even began seeing a clairvoyant, though it is highly doubtful whether he believed in her prophecies. On one occasion, Ben-Gurion cut his hair very short, pulled a beret down over his ears, and began to ask his office staff whether they recognized him, because he wanted to go out into the streets incognito and see "how the Jews live", like the Sultan Haroun al-Rashid in the markets of Baghdad.

At the same time, there were some signs that Ben-Gurion had mellowed with age. During the year they spent in Sdeh Boker, there was a renewal of his intimacy with Paula. When he decided to live in the kibbutz, he told his wife: "You are not obliged to come with me. I am going to the desert, which is a harsh place to live in. Stay in Tel Aviv, if you wish. I will come to see you every two weeks, and you will come to visit me every two weeks." But Paula rejected the idea, and accompanied him to the desert. He was very touched and dedicated one of his later books to her with the inscription: "To Paula, with love. 'I remember thee the kindness of thy youth, the love of thine espousals, when thou wentest after me in the wilderness, in a

land that was not sown' " (Jeremiah 2, 2). During that year, he often sought
her company, and when she went to Tel Aviv for a few days, he felt forlorn.
"The hut has become empty and harsh without you . . . When will you
come back?" In fact, she suffered considerably from kibbutz life. She had
followed her husband to the Negev because she loved him and knew that
her place was beside him; but she missed city life and was often "miserable". Ben-Gurion was not aware of her feelings. Immersed in his own
world – his writing and his books – he could not comprehend the feelings of
those about him.

He devoted little attention to Paula or to his family. He rarely met his
sisters or his brother Michael, who owned a light-refreshments stall in
north Tel Aviv. His own children were married and parents by then, and
Ben-Gurion tried to be a good grandfather, noting his grandchildren's
birthdays in his pocket diary to send them presents and good wishes. His
son, Amos, had married a young English nurse named Mary who had cared
for him during his service in the British army. Paula objected to Amos's
marriage to a Gentile and asked Ben-Gurion to exercise his influence upon
him. But Ben-Gurion did nothing of the sort. While writing to Paula that
he was making efforts "to get him out of the entanglement he has got into"
he gave Amos and Mary his heartfelt blessing. He may have been influenced
by the fact that during that very same period, towards the end of the war,
he himself began a long involvement with a non-Jewish woman: Miss
Doris May.

It is remarkable that Ben-Gurion's deepest and most prolonged extra-
marital relationship was with a woman so distant and different from himself: an Anglo-Catholic who lived in Lancing, a small town on the English
Channel. Though she was linked to the Zionist movement – toward which
she displayed a loyal identification – she was British through and through.
As she herself put it, she was even "in a sense, an 'imperialist' ". His
clandestine relationship with Miss May seems to have given Ben-Gurion
an opportunity to sever his links with his surroundings and drift away to
another world that he shared with no one but her.

Ben-Gurion met Doris May in the 1930s, when she served as Chaim
Weizmann's secretary in the London Zionist Office. Her acquaintances
from that period recall her as a slim, attractive Englishwoman, with a fair
complexion, fair hair, and blue eyes. Her broad face was not beautiful, but
her expression was pleasant. Then, as later in life, she was "imposing" and
"aristocratic" possessing a strong character, considerable intelligence, and
a sharp tongue. At the same time Doris May was well educated, eloquent in
speech and writing, with a natural wit and a charming style. She had
studied ancient and modern languages and English literature at Oxford, but

disregarding her superior education and intellect, she consented to work in Weizmann's office as an ordinary secretary. She had sought after a challenge in life, an ideal to strive for, and had found it in Zionism. Visitors to Weizmann's office would see her making shorthand notes as he dictated, and then typing them up; but on entering into conversation with her, they would unexpectedly discover a wise and refined woman.

In 1940 and 1941, Ben-Gurion spent prolonged periods of time in London, and during the blitz, he would spend his evenings at the Zionist offices, where Doris May taught him Greek. The two also spent many evenings together in the British Museum shelter. He was fifty-three; she was forty-one and a charming woman, towards whom it was difficult to remain indifferent. The pair became intimate. From then on, they kept up close contacts, primarily by means of discreetly forwarded letters and by short meetings – sometimes at intervals of years. The letters they exchanged were restrained in tone, but their personal feelings found expression in the way they addressed one another. Ben-Gurion was in the habit of addressing her as "dearest" or "darling", signing off with "Yours David". She, too, called him "dearest" or "dearest David", and at the end of her letters would add a few warm words like "with much love, as ever" or "yours, as ever". Occasionally, primarily, at the beginning of their relationship, Ben-Gurion's letters contained some muted expression of his feelings for her. He wrote to her in February 1942, three months after leaving her:

I remember the last evening before I left [London] . . . I remember how you felt. This is the way I feel all the time here and perhaps worse. After all, you felt that only in regard to Number 77 [Russell Street] – but you were in England, in your England, in that proud brave and lovely country of yours. I feel here as lonesome as one can feel. I am altogether alone – among so many people – and a desert! [At the end of his letter he referred again to the subject that had brought them together.] In lonely and sleepless nights, I am still with my Plato. I have just finished reading the whole *Politaea*. What a wonderful – and in numerous places modern – book.

Their intimacy was expressed in matters unrelated to their personal relationship. Candidly and at length, he told her of his problems and his uncertainties and described his preoccupations. She would confront him brashly when she disagreed with the political line he had adopted, which she described as

. . . a . . . policy of murder in Palestine [his struggle against the British since 1939] . . . I am afraid you cannot escape responsibility for any of this my dear, and I confess I do not envy you your conscience when you lie awake at night . . . None of this, you may say, is any of my business. But if you employ "goyim", it is only sense to use them and pay some attention to what they tell you . . .

Yet Doris May also shared with "dearest David" the latest about her life at her country home at Lancing.

The garden is untidy, but very very green; and Nicholas (my weekend cat) is blacker and fluffier and handsomer than ever in his new winter coat, which he is growing a month early this year. He's the most charming company imaginable: affectionate, completely independent and highly intelligent about his own affairs. But I expect you still don't like cats – a pity! You don't know what you're missing.

They continued to meet after the war; he met her in London, and, on at least two occasions, he came to see her in Lancing. After "Black Saturday" in 1946, Ben-Gurion was staying at the Royal Monceau Hotel in Paris; he was unable to come to London, and he could only contact Doris May by phone. "It's just silly for you and me to sit on either sides of this narrow ditch of ours," she wrote sadly, "and hold no more communication than if we were respectively exploring the north and south poles . . ." She informed him that ever since the war, she had been planning to visit friends in France. "I had hoped to do it while your 'conference' [of the Jewish Agency Executive, in August 1946] was on in Paris, and to stop over for a night on the way and see you." However, this plan did not work out, due to the pressure of work and "there was never a chance of getting a clear week for gallivanting". She hoped to see him at the Congress in Basel. "That's the only chance I can see of seeing you in the measurably near future."

Her tone changed again the moment she returned to her other role – that of his tutor and mentor in Western culture.

I was interested to hear that you are making Augustine's acquaintance. . . . He's interesting mainly for the influence he had on the thought of the Middle Ages – if you care for that odd, chaotic chunk of history. Myself I think that if you really want a "spiritual home" in history, the period to choose (after the early Greeks) is the Renaissance – French and Italian for preference. The world that began with Rabelais and ended (perhaps) with Shakespeare. A time in the morning of the world, when men's mind reached out to unimaginable horizons, as their bodies went roaming the oceans in absurd cockleshells in search of Eldorado. Not perhaps much fun for your "proletariat" – but what a life could be, and was, lived by the intelligent and adventurous elite! . . . Do you know Villon's "Balade des Pendus"? He was the first – and the fore-runner really – of the French Renaissance poets, and those particular verses of his were, I think, the first verses that ever literally kept me awake at night – when I was about twelve!

Miss May worked in the Jewish Agency's London office up to the establishment of the state. Then she joined the Israeli embassy as a local employee and was appointed secretary to the ambassador. "She was the *grande dame* of the embassy," said one of the diplomats who served there. The embassy heads consulted her on a variety of matters, and she was a kind of institution in her own right. Former heads of the Jewish Agency – now leaders of the state – showered her with warmth and affection on their visits to London, and she was popular with everyone. There were occasional rumors and hints concerning her relationship with Ben-Gurion, but she preserved total discretion and refrained from taking advantage of her unique links with the prime minister. She visited Israel in 1951, and they saw each other again when he came to London. She was very eager to visit Israel again, but she did not ask for his assistance. Instead, she saved up her own salary, and in the summer of 1954, when he was living at Sdeh Boker, she came on another visit. Later, in 1955, when the Old Man returned to his post as defense minister, he was to invite her to come to Israel as his guest for the Independence Day celebrations. She replied that this was really wonderful on his part, but "anyway it would have to be on the defense budget, I suppose, and just think how much more useful an extra . . . gun or two would be!"

During the mid-1950s, Doris May aged and her hearing deteriorated considerably; but her appearance remained imposing, her body was youthful and her voice clear. Ben-Gurion remained close to her, and her advice was of great importance to him, although he did not always follow it. In February 1955, when Ben-Gurion returned to his post as defense minister, Doris May sent him a telegram of congratulations, followed by a short letter:

I waited to wire till I heard you were in fact installed at the Defence Ministry – and confess that I now heave a sigh of heartfelt relief, coupled with a rueful sympathy for you. Still you must know by now that it is your fate to be a galley slave, and that for you there can be no escape . . . Never mind darling, you know you in fact enjoy it, anyhow at times!

Be as kind as you can to Moshe (Sharett) won't you? He does admire you so much – and is so very scared of you! And don't you let our marvellous Army get *too* much above itself. Nobody wants ! I mean, I *hope* nobody wants a military junta sitting in Jerusalem, now or ever.

Bless you, my dear. Be well.

As ever, yours, Doris.

Ben-Gurion responded with a startling offer that indicates how greatly he desired her company:

I don't know what is going to happen after the end of July – after the elections to the Third Knesset . . . If I will have to come back for good, I will insist on your coming to work with me. It is not only your English I will need, but your "feel", although I will not always (or never) accept your advice. But your helpful guidance would certainly be useful. Would you come?

She replied promptly. "Your letter has caused me some heart-searching. But I feel sure you know without being told, that I am, as always, 'yours to command' and I am deeply moved and honoured by your confidence." At the same time, she pointed out that there were reasons making it unadvisable for her to come:

Foreigners on a P.M.'s doorstep are seldom "well-seen". The last thing I would wish would be to give your opponents any excuse for accusing you of being too much tied to the British coat-tail. . . . Finally, do you really *want* "a critic on the hearth"? *Advocata Diaboli*? Even if I 'speak only when spoken to', a constant cold douche of silent criticism? . . .

Well, darling, I've been "thinking aloud" for your benefit. The practical implication seems to be that we should regard the idea of my coming to sit on your doorstep after the elections as a kind of secret hope between us.

Ben-Gurion paid no heed to her warnings. "If I have to come back – you must come and work with me. Don't talk nonsense about 'foreigners' . . . You, a foreigner? You know well that I trust nobody more than I trust you . . . For the time being it is only a dream, but dreams may come true."

The dream did come true, though somewhat belatedly. Ben-Gurion returned to power in November 1955, and a few months later Doris May was pensioned off. In August 1956, she came to Israel to work alongside him. But the hopes she attached to her stay in Israel appear to have been destroyed. After the feverish days of the Sinai Campaign, she was left with little to do. She found no place for herself, nor did she enjoy much attention from Ben-Gurion himself. Her dreams of finding "a niche" to fill were dashed, as were those of rejoining "that inner circle which I once took so much for granted". Disappointed, she returned to England after a few months. Was there also a cooling-off in her relationship with Ben-Gurion? The answer to that question is not clear, but a study of his archives reveals that their correspondence ceased after her return home. They met again in 1966, when she came to Israel to help in editing Weizmann's letters. But this meeting apparently did not lead to a renewal of their former intimacy.

Doris May spent her final years at her little house in Lancing in the company of her books and her cats. At the end of 1968, she suddenly contracted cancer. Within two weeks, her illness overcame her. She died at the age of sixty-nine, far from Ben-Gurion, and took her secret with her to the grave.

Ben-Gurion was also beginning to experience the ravages of age. Ever since an illness in 1955, when he sensed that his physical strength would not last indefinitely, he had begun to worry about his health and to take an interest in questions of life and death. He was careful to have himself examined by specialists whenever he felt unwell and became a model pupil of Dr Feldenkreis, who taught him to exercise and take the daily hike that became part of the Old Man's image. His awareness of his age and the state of his health heightened his interest in biology, and he was particularly preoccupied with the human brain, a subject which caused him some concern. Ben-Gurion had always taken pride in his phenomenal memory, and when he began to forget names or details he grew deeply worried. He called these signs of forgetfulness "age's cry of alarm to the mind".

For thirty years, from his "conquest of the Zionist movement" in 1933 until his resignation in 1963, Ben-Gurion was the leader of the Palestinian Jewish community and the State of Israel. The high point of his leadership, the Ben-Gurion epoch, spans the period between the adoption of the Biltmore Program in 1942 and his first withdrawal to Sdeh Boker in 1953. During this period, he adopted his great historical decisions. His return in 1955 as the leader who presided over the Sinai Campaign and its triumphs gave Ben-Gurion an additional four years of glory, which coincided with Israel's Golden Age in the late 1950s. Nineteen sixty marks the beginning of Ben-Gurion's decline, a prolonged process characterized by sharp ups and downs.

Nonetheless, Ben-Gurion had not lost his incredible will to fight for his beliefs. On his way back after the American visit, he told Mendes France at a stopover in the French capital, "I am returning to the elections [now and] I hope we get 51 per cent of the vote!" The seventy-five-year-old prime minister was determined to stand for another term. The Frenchman shook his head doubtfully. "I don't believe you will succeed," he said quietly. Mendes France proved to be right. Ben-Gurion was returning to face the elections sparked off by a great turmoil in the country. His successes could not conceal the fact that his standing in Israel had been gravely undermined. He, too, was being swept away by the stormy waves of the Lavon Affair.

16

The Hurricane

On 29 October 1957, in the midst of a Knesset debate, a short, swarthy young man leaned out of the Visitors' Gallery and flung a small object onto the Cabinet table in the center of the chamber. Immediately, a powerful explosion rocked the walls of Israel's parliament. The object was a hand-grenade, which exploded near the chair of Religious Affairs Minister Moshe Shapira, wounding him severely. Lighter injuries were inflicted on Golda Meir, and David Ben-Gurion, who was hit by splinters in his arm and leg. The casualties were immediately evacuated to Hadassah Hospital, and the assailant was caught. He was a mentally deranged young man by the name of Moshe Du'ek who perpetrated the attack in revenge for his alleged mistreatment by the Jewish Agency.

The assassination attempt shocked the Israeli public. Horrified, Ben-Gurion's secretary, Nehemia Argov, arrived from Tel Aviv and for several days he scarcely budged from the prime minister's bedside. On Saturday 2 November, after a brief visit to Tel Aviv, Argov was on his way back to Jerusalem when he momentarily lost control of his car and ran into a cyclist. The doctors doubted whether they could save the man, who was married and the father of four. Argov returned to Tel Aviv, locked himself in his room, and shot himself through the head. On his desk, he left two letters: one for his friends; the other, in a sealed envelope, for Ben-Gurion. To his friends, he wrote: "I fear that [the cyclist] will not live . . . Unfortunately I cannot go on living in this situation." But there were many who contended that Argov was equally shaken by the assassination attempt against Ben-Gurion. "He thought that he would reach the high point of his mission in life if someone tried to assassinate Ben-Gurion and he, Nehemia, would protect the Old Man with his body, stopping the bullet meant for him."

Nehemia Argov loved Ben-Gurion with unmatched devotion, and the prime minister trusted him completely. It is doubtful whether anyone on Ben-Gurion's staff was closer to him. The Old Man even obeyed his "orders" – to put on a jacket, rest, or leave some matter alone. Ben-Gurion relied on him to regulate his visitors, sift through his letters, and control his daily timetable. When he was away from his office, he would even ask Argov to forge his signature and sign official documents for him. Most of all, he responded to Argov's love with a deep affection.

No one knew how to tell the Old Man of Argov's tragic death. His aides decided to put off the news for a few days, since Ben-Gurion was still recovering from his shock and injuries, and the bond of silence was shared by the country's newspaper editors: for the first time in the history of the Israeli press, several newspapers printed a special edition consisting of a single copy without reference to Argov's death. It was this copy that was brought to the prime minister. Finally, on 5 November, Shimon Peres, Teddy Kollek, and Moshe Dayan entered Ben-Gurion's hospital room to face the inevitable task: it was Dayan who broke the news.* Ben-Gurion was horrified. Without saying a word, he turned his head to the wall and then slowly shifted around and turned his back on his visitors. No one spoke, and in the heavy silence the sound of a choked sob burst from the Old Man's chest.

Perhaps it was the two tragedies, coming so close together, that left Ben-Gurion with intimations of mortality; or perhaps the time had naturally come for the prime minister to prepare his legacy for his party and his country by assuring the entry of young leadership into their top echelons. At any rate, that same day in his hospital room, Ben-Gurion begged Dayan to remain at his post as chief of staff for an extended tour. But Dayan refused and chose to take up a political career, thereby providing the younger generation of Mapai with the leadership it had been lacking. Three weeks after Dayan's resignation from the army became effective in March 1958, the Old Man summoned the leaders of Mapai's "youngsters" "to clarify [their] mission in the state".

At the [forthcoming Mapai] conference, I intend to speak about the need to bring a new generation into the leadership . . . There is a generation that was born here before the state, and there is already a young generation that was brought up in the period of statehood – all those who were ten years old when the state was founded. These are the people of the future. They have done great things; they fought in the War of Independence and the Sinai Campaign and displayed their abilities. They must be charged with the leadership of the state and the movement – jointly with the veterans, for the time being, but they will not survive long. This change will meet with objections within the party, but they must be resisted.

* Yigael Yadin contends that he was the one who brought Ben-Gurion the bitter tidings.

His closing words were more of an understatement than Ben-Gurion would have dreamed. This meeting with the "youngsters" was the first shot of the bitter war of succession that would rage in Mapai for years to come and serve as the background to the Lavon Affair. His statement shows that Ben-Gurion not only supported the younger generation's assault on the leadership, he actually instigated it. And it proves that the suspicions of the veteran Mapai leaders were quite justified; he had decided gradually to replace them with young blood.

By early November 1959, Ben-Gurion had completed his plans for bringing younger men into the national leadership. The Cabinet he would form after the elections would include three young men: Abba Eban, Moshe Dayan, and Yigael Yadin (Peres being marked for deputy minister of defense). He spoke with Dayan about his plans for the future, but the ex-army chief remained evasive, contending that he did not wish to be elected to the Knesset. All the same, Ben-Gurion decided that Dayan would serve in the next Cabinet as minister of agriculture. Eban was to return to Israel in mid-1959 after an extended tour as ambassador to the United States, but he had already been appointed president of the Weizmann Institute of Science. The Old Man came nonetheless to an agreement with him whereby he would be elected to the Knesset and serve in the next Cabinet as minister without portfolio. Yadin, however, expressed profound misgivings. First, he said, he wished to consolidate his scientific standing; secondly, he would find it hard to accept the party yoke. The Old Man did not give up, and when Yadin asked what post he would be offered, Ben-Gurion replied that "he was being called into the government not as an expert, but as a statesman; consequently, it was not important which ministry would be entrusted to him, but rather his activity in the government as a whole". To get Yadin to join the Cabinet, Ben-Gurion was prepared to go so far as to accept Yadin's refusal to join the party. But, Yadin's decision to refuse the offer was irreversible. His answer caused Ben-Gurion considerable sorrow. In 1964, he wrote to Yadin: ". . . It was my opinion (and it is my opinion now also) that the man worthy of being premier is Yigael Yadin . . . "

Even before Yadin had rejected Ben-Gurion's offer, however, the party rebelled. When Ben-Gurion told her of his talks with the three young men, Golda Meir immediately notified him (not for the first time) that she would not remain in the Cabinet after the elections. Histadrut secretary Pinhas Lavon also challenged the young leaders, and the Mapai Party apparatus, known as the "Bloc", was up in arms. Ben-Gurion failed in several of his attempts to achieve a reconciliation between the older and younger leaders. On the surface, the party retained its inner harmony, but the confrontation actually grew sharper, with the Mapai veterans (headed by Golda Meir, Zalman Aranne, Pinhas Lavon, and Pinhas Sapir) waging a constant battle against their younger colleagues.

With the onset of the 1959 election campaign, Ben-Gurion resolved to win over the country's younger generation of voters with the assistance of the young leadership he had promoted and fostered. Not content with having his young men placed on Mapai's Knesset slate, he took care to stress that they enjoyed his personal backing. It is doubtful whether such displays of support were to the liking of the party veterans. At the same time, they preferred to bury the hatchet until after the elections, giving vent to their indignation only at closed meetings. Ben-Gurion also held a long talk with Golda Meir in an attempt to conciliate her. But all the promises and reconciliations were regarded as worthless by the Mapai veterans in view of the Old Man's declared sympathies for his "young protégés".

The Knesset elections were held on 3 November, and the results showed that Mapai had gained the greatest triumph in its history. Winning seven additional seats, it now had forty-seven Knesset members and reached the pinnacle of its power. Many commentators attributed the stunning victory to the young candidates featured in Mapai's slate. But if anyone thought that the election victory would put an end to the contest between the generations within the party, he was deluding himself. On the contrary, once the elections consolidated the power and standing of the younger leaders, the veterans deployed to protect their positions.

Golda Meir and Zalman Aranhe hoisted the standard of revolt, adamantly refusing to join the new Cabinet. Ben-Gurion devoted his principal efforts to courting them back and to appeasing Pinhas Lavon. It was late November before Golda consented to return to the Foreign Ministry. (The same day, Zalman Aranne also agreed to resume his former post.) But Golda's consent had a price. Ben-Gurion had marked Abba Eban to act as a kind of information minister whose task would be to represent Israeli views abroad. Golda objected violently, even refusing to permit Eban's office to be located in the Foreign Ministry building. Ben-Gurion capitulated. He also found a tenuous *modus vivendi* with Lavon.

Still, internal harmony had not truly been restored, for clashes between veterans and the young leaders went on almost incessantly. Again, Ben-Gurion rose to protect the younger leaders. They held on to his coattails, while he blazed the trail for them. The clashes aggravated the sense of alienation dividing Ben-Gurion from his veteran colleagues, while bitterness and anger gradually replaced the trust and admiration they had showered on him for so long. The battle of the generations within

Mapai is also the principal key to the political events of 1960–5, which have been chronicled in the history of the State of Israel as the Lavon Affair.

One after another, Ben-Gurion's oldest friends and colleagues broke their links with him. The first to stand up as a self-proclaimed foe was Moshe Sharett. Ever since his removal from the Foreign Ministry, Sharett had been a bitter man who felt that he had been dealt with unjustly. In the course of time, his pain turned into a deep grudge against Ben-Gurion. Now that Mapai's leaders were locked in conflict, it was clear that Sharett would not lift a finger to help the Old Man.

Sharett's successor, Golda Meir, also drew away from the Old Man and slipped progressively into the anti-Ben-Gurion camp. In the past, she had been boundlessly devoted to him, and in her political views, she was "more of a 'Ben-Gurionist' than Ben-Gurion himself". But in recent years she had found herself in a nagging dilemma. She continued to admire the Old Man, but the bad blood between the Foreign Ministry and the Defense Ministry and her personal disagreements with Shimon Peres placed her in violent conflict with the younger leaders. Her devotion to the party and her personal loyalty to the men she had worked with for over a generation heightened her dislike for the "youngsters", whom she regarded as cynically ambitious. This led to disruptions in her relationships with Ben-Gurion.

In a heart-to-heart talk two weeks after the elections, Golda poured out her anger to Ben-Gurion. She had not wanted the Foreign Ministry in the first place, she told him, but she had been summoned and loyally answered the call. Yet she soon had the feeling that Ben-Gurion had no faith in her authority. Golda's grievances were well founded. She was foreign minister more for show than in substance. France had been removed from her jurisdiction; she played no part in relations with Germany; she played no more than a marginal role in the establishment of the peripheral pact; and in her work with England and Italy, she was in constant collision with Defense Ministry emissaries (who also maintained direct relations with Burma and other Asian countries and sold arms to South American and African countries). Ben-Gurion personally initiated and conducted all important contacts with the United States, and she did no more than follow his instructions. Later, when Ben-Gurion set off on his tours of Europe and the United States, Golda only accompanied him to one solitary lunch at the Elysée Palace. She seems to have been given a free hand only in developing relations with Africa – and even there only with countries that did not belong to the peripheral pact and did not have training or arms-purchasing links with the Defense Ministry. There is no escaping the conclusion that foreign policy was conducted by Ben-Gurion – at times by means of Golda's ministry, at others by means of the Defense Ministry and its director-general or through clandestine channels.

Other senior party leaders had their own burden of resentments. Like Golda, Aranne, Sapir, and others also regarded Ben-Gurion's efforts to foster younger leaders as a menace to their own posts and standing. He assured them repeatedly that he did not intend to remove them, but they simply did not believe him. The same threat also hovered over Mapai's "Bloc". In the view of the rank-and-file leaders, with their devotion to conventional procedures, the onslaught of the younger generation was a danger to the party's integrity. They deplored Ben-Gurion's support of the young men who had been "parachuted" into the party, regarding it as unwitting aid to the destruction of Mapai.

Thus a broadly based and powerful coalition crystallized in opposition to Ben-Gurion's young protégés and, inevitably, to Ben-Gurion himself. This coalition was joined by a man who had previously provoked the general opposition of the party's leadership: Pinhas Lavon. Six years earlier, Golda, Zalman Aranne, Eshkol, and the party establishment had all objected to Lavon's nomination as defense minister, regarding him as "a catastrophe". They were also the people who ultimately caused his dismissal. But Ben-Gurion had rehabilitated Lavon, entrusting him with the Histadrut and restoring him to Mapai's top leadership. Lavon did not forget how his colleagues had behaved toward him (even in 1960, many of them kept up their criticism of him. But in the confrontation between the veterans and the young leaders, he was one of the establishment's pillars of strength and perhaps its most outspoken representative. There can be no doubt that he was acting under powerful emotional impulses stemming from his hatred for Dayan and Peres, whom he regarded as bearing the principal blame for his personal misfortune in 1955.

This was the situation inside Mapai in the wake of the party's greatest triumph and at a time when Ben-Gurion's prestige was at its peak. Mapai was like a keg of gunpowder. No more than a single spark was needed to set off a tremendous blast that would devastate everything around it. The spark was provided by the Lavon Affair.

Late in 1957, Israeli intelligence agents contacted a German citizen known to be involved in espionage and asked him to carry out missions for them in Egypt. The German declined their offer but said there was someone else who could do the job: a man who had become friendly with a senior Egyptian intelligence officer in 1954. His name was Paul Frank. This "referral" horrified the Israeli agents. "Paul Frank" was the alias of Avry Elad, the Israeli intelligence officer who had headed the ill-fated underground network in Egypt and the only one to escape from Egypt after the 1954 debacle. Elad was indeed in Germany at the time, where he continued to use the cover and the alias he had adopted on leaving for Egypt.

Israeli agents immediately began to scrutinize Elad's actions, and they soon came up with an appalling discovery: he was on close terms with the Egyptian military attaché in Bonn, Admiral Suleiman, and in 1954 this same Suleiman had been one of the chief interrogators of the Israeli network in Egypt. Heads of the Security Services began to entertain frightful suspicions: was Avry Elad a double agent working for the Egyptians? Had he been recruited by Egyptian intelligence as far back as 1954? Had he betrayed his country and denounced the network? Or had he been detained together with the other members of the network and bought his freedom by making a deal with Egyptian intelligence?

These questions suddenly cast new light on a number of riddles that had not been solved in 1954: how could it be that all the operations of the network in Egypt had misfired completely? How did the Egyptians succeed in uncovering the whole network in the course of a few days? How was it that while everything was collapsing around him, Avry Elad could calmly wind up his affairs, sell his car, and leave Egypt unruffled with his secret transmitter in his luggage? The heads of the Security Services decided to bring Elad back to Israel for questioning. He was summoned home on a false pretext and shortly after his return, he was arrested.

A vigorous investigation failed to establish that Elad was, indeed, a double agent. At the same time, it uncovered other crimes Elad had committed against the security of the state. He was put on trial in 1959, accused of "possession of secret documents", and was found guilty. His trial ended in August 1960 with the imposition of a ten-year prison sentence. In the course of the trial, however, Elad revealed that an emissary had been sent to him in Europe with orders for him to commit perjury before the Olshan–Dori Commission and falsify his journal. Elad's revelations led to a clear conclusion: after the capture of the network in Egypt, the heads of military intelligence had instigated forgery and perjury in order to "plant" evidence that it was Defense Minister Lavon who had ordered intelligence chief Benyamin Gibly to carry out the abortive operations in Egypt.

In retrospect, it is clear that proof of these crimes did not in itself clear Pinhas Lavon of his share of the blame or of his own false testimony before the Olshan–Dori Commission. However, at the time, Elad's revelations seemed sufficient reason to clear him completely. The moment it became clear that one of the sides had committed forgery and perjury, it seemed logical to contend that the other side was in the right. In Lavon's view, the evidence was ample grounds to demand that he be cleared.

On Ben-Gurion's orders, a military board of inquiry was set up on 12 September and was instructed to investigate the allegations that documents had been forged and perjured testimony had been submitted to the Olshan–Dori Commission on the orders of Benyamin Gibly or other officers. At the time, Lavon was on holiday in Geneva.

But when he returned to Israel on 21 September, he warned that he would soon issue a number of statements, "some of them pleasant, others perhaps not so pleasant". Lavon clearly did not want any further investigation. He simply wanted his name to be cleared forthwith – and that would be that. Later, his supporters were to claim that he wanted the matter closed because he believed that he had already been subjected to enough misery. But his opponents believed that he was afraid a thorough investigation would show that the intelligence chief's crimes did not in fact clear him of responsibility for the operations in Egypt.

When Ben-Gurion and Lavon met on 26 September, there was a latent tension underlying their friendly gestures toward one another. Ben-Gurion later wrote: "Lavon said to me: 'Call off the [committee of] inquiry and declare that I am innocent and all the blame falls upon [Gibly].' " Ben-Gurion "almost did not believe his ears". He replied: "I did not condemn you [then] and I do not condemn you now. But I am not authorized or empowered to clear you because I am neither judge nor investigator; nor am I entitled to cast the guilt on someone else as long as a trial has not proved his guilt. I did not investigate the Egyptian affair, I simply regarded it as my duty to investigate the falsification of the date on the military intelligence document." Lavon replied that he intended to approach the Knesset Foreign Affairs and Defense Committee. "I did not advise him to do so," Ben-Gurion remarked, "but that is his private affair. I merely told him that I would report the findings of the commission of inquiry to the Cabinet, when they were submitted."

This conversation was the key to the entire 1960 "affair". In the course of their talk, the two men had clashed on principles, as well as on a personal plane. Ben-Gurion, with his profound belief in clear principles of justice and equity, was astounded when Lavon asked to be cleared and thereby close the whole episode. Lavon may have felt so self-confident after the disclosure of the forgeries that he never anticipated his request would be rejected. But a man of Ben-Gurion's moral fiber and natural honesty could not have "cleared" Lavon even if he had wanted to. From the viewpoint of moral principles, Ben-Gurion was perfectly justified. But not from a humane viewpoint. Before him stood a broken man who had borne a sense of bitter pain and searing injustice for five years. Ben-Gurion did not know whether or not Lavon had given that unfortunate order. Was it not his duty as a comrade to give Lavon his full assistance in clearing himself?

Lavon left Ben-Gurion with the feeling that his salvation would not come from the Old Man. Even if his demand were unjust, his premonition was accurate.. Yet Ben-Gurion's behavior displayed another aspect of decisive importance that could be characterized as feebleness, or passivity. He should have foreseen that Lavon's approach to the Knesset's Foreign Affairs and Defense Committee was liable to entail a public scandal. Why did he do nothing to forestall it? Displaying a bizarre apathy, he went on with his business: that evening, he headed for Sdeh Boker to write his customary article for the government annual during the course of the High Holidays recess. That conversation with Lavon may have been symptomatic of Ben-Gurion's advancing age and the weariness he had accumulated during his years of office. Over the past year, his diary had shown signs of confusion and forgetfulness; his imposingly clear memory overlooked events and details of considerable importance. His battle inside the party on behalf of the young leaders and the exhausting 1959 election campaign had sapped his strength, and he was no longer the man he had once been. In contrast, Lavon was aggressive and determined. Spurred on equally by his frustrations and his hopes, he flung himself into the fray to get himself cleared quickly and decisively. Lavon took the initiative, and it was he who dictated the next move.

The following day, the snowball was launched, and it gathered speed and mass at a dizzy rate. One after another, the newspapers joined in the campaign which had no precedent in Israel. A partial and one-sided version of Lavon's talk with Ben-Gurion appeared in the morning papers. Day by day, as revelations multiplied, the headlines grew bigger and the editorials fiercer. Almost all the articles backed Lavon in his demand for "swift justice". There was growing criticism of Ben-Gurion and members of the defense establishment. Lavon dropped broad hints about "Ben-Gurion's young men" – above all, Peres, and, to a lesser extent, Dayan – being his principal opponents. Faced by this tidal wave of attacks and revelations, Ben-Gurion was somewhat at a loss as to how he should respond. He was at Sdeh Boker, and the papers reached him after a delay of hours or sometimes an entire day. His close aides were not at his side: Shimon Peres was in France, immersed in delicate negotiations concerning the Dimona reactor; Yitzhak Navon had taken off for a visit to Persia; Moshe Dayan was in Africa. In almost total isolation, Ben-Gurion tried in vain to halt the rising flood.

He sent three successive letters to Moshe Sharett, asking for information on the mishap in Egypt and the reasons for Lavon's resignation. Sharett hastened to provide the necessary information, and Ben-Gurion slowly began to get to the roots of the affair. But during the crucial days when the storm broke, he stood helpless in the face of the press campaign, incapable of providing the government and his party with the vigorous leadership it required. It was 2 October before he managed to jerk himself awake. He paid a brief visit to Jerusalem, raised "the affair" before the Cabinet, appeared before the Foreign Affairs and Defense Committee, and issued a detailed announcement to the press. But even though the whole country was in uproar, Ben-Gurion still remained calm and he saw no need to launch a counterattack or adopt any new initiative.

At first, Ben-Gurion's relations with Lavon remained correct; but barbed comments gradually multiplied, as did implied insults and indirect accusations. The two men exchanged tensely worded letters, but the real confrontation was sparked off when Lavon appeared in person before the Foreign Affairs and Defense Committee. In the course of three weeks, he appeared before the committee four times, and his testimony caused a sensation that soon set the whole country in uproar. After their first encounter with Lavon, the members of the committee were "upset, agitated, and even shocked". The central topic of his testimony was his version of the "mishap".

Lavon flung grave accusations at the men who had headed the defense establishment at that time, above all Peres and Dayan. He did not accuse them of involvement in the forgeries, but hinted that they took advantage of the plot to settle their accounts with him. Lavon extended his attack on the Defense Ministry, mentioning various matters, connected or unconnected to the "mishap".

A large proportion of Lavon's accusations were false, and many of the details he submitted were distorted or incorrect. Moshe Sharett's testimony on the circumstances of Lavon's resignation refuted many of his charges. After returning from France on 7 November and consulting with Ben-Gurion, Shimon Peres himself appeared before the Foreign Affairs and Defense Committee. Armed with documents and other proof, he disproved each of Lavon's accusations. In growing fury, Ben-Gurion himself sent the committee a number of sharply worded question to present to Lavon. But the counter-testimony was scarcely considered by the committee members, who were dazed by the flow of revelations, by Lavon's furious attacks, and, above all, by the shocking fact that forgery and perjury had been committed by high-ranking officers in the army, the pride of the nation.

Lavon's testimony set off a political earthquake. The opposition parties immediately seized on it to attack Mapai, perhaps even hoping to bring about the government's fall. Unlike the past, when the deliberations of the Foreign Affairs and Defense Committee were top-secret, some unknown hand provided the newspapers with detailed accounts of Lavon's testimony.

Up until then, military censorship had prevented specific details of "mishap" from reaching the public, which did not know what it was all about. Now people floundered helplessly in an attempt to unravel the bizarre terminology used by the censor to label events and protagonists: "the mishap" (the debacle in Egypt), "the senior officer" (Benyamin Gibly), "the senior officer's superior" (Moshe Dayan, who was chief of staff at the time), "the reserve officer" (Colonel Mordechai Ben-Tzur), "the third man" (Avry Elad). Details of the affair remained classified until 1972; prior to that time, the citizens of Israel were unable to decipher the terms, code names, and signals that the opposing camps flung at one another in the press. But the public did understand that there was a terrible crisis in progress at the top levels of the administration and the ruling party. Lavon had suddenly torn up the rules followed by the government, the Knesset, and Mapai.

Lavon's testimony had two immediate results: Mapai's leadership, scandalized by the "factory of horrors" in the committee and in the press, decided to do everything possible to remove the matter from the committee's jurisdiction either by transferring it to the Cabinet or by making immediate concessions to Lavon. At the same time, Ben-Gurion, who was by now furious at Lavon, abandoned his neutral stance and launched an open attack against him.

On 5 October, Ben-Gurion was astounded to read in one of the afternoon dailies entire passages from a letter he had sent Lavon, and he lost his temper. "I do not believe that there is a Holy Ghost at [the newspaper] or that its editorial board contains some prophet who knows hidden matters," he wrote to Lavon. "It is clear to me, without any shadow of doubt, that [the letter] was transmitted to the paper. By whom?"

Thus a sharp confrontation arose between Ben-Gurion and Lavon over an apparently marginal matter. Lavon evaded answering the Old Man's direct question, and Ben-Gurion regarded this as proof that Lavon was lying. A brief letter severed their relations: "Your reply does not in any way answer the question I asked you," Ben-Gurion wrote. "I will not ask again."

The statement was an open declaration of war. Up until this point, Ben-Gurion had contended that he was "outside the quarrel" and wished Lavon success in his efforts. But, when the incident of the letter showed him that Lavon lied and leaked information to the press, he joined Lavon's enemies.

Whether he intended it or not, Ben-Gurion was now a party to "the affair". The moment he openly took sides against Lavon, he weakened the moral impact of his demand for a judicial inquiry. In the public at large, the press, and Mapai itself, there were many who considered Ben-Gurion's demand "an evasion", as Lavon had termed it. The true significance of Ben-Gurion's position did not get through to the public. The picture they saw was of Lavon demanding justice and accusing army officers and the heads of the Defense Ministry of having framed him, while Ben-Gurion obstructed his efforts to clear his name. The Old Man's battle of principle boomeranged because of his hesitation, the inadequate way he presented his position, and, it must be added, because of his hostility toward Lavon.

It is clear why Ben-Gurion so passionately wanted to set up a judicial inquiry in to the entire affair. One can only wonder at the clumsiness of his actions. While proposing to the justice minister that a judicial inquiry be initiated, he told the many people who approached him on the matter that "he would not intervene" in the affair. But at the Cabinet meeting held on 30 October, Justice Minister Rosen submitted a proposal that in no way met Ben-Gurion's demand: he requested that a ministerial committee examine all the material relating to the affair "and decide on a tentative procedure". Ben-Gurion listened to Rosen's proposal and put it to the vote. He did not approve of the idea, but he advanced no objections. In fact he took no part either in the discusion or in the vote. "I will only conduct the Cabinet meeting," he said.

The ministers had worked with Ben-Gurion long enough to know that whenever he opposed a particular resolution, he expressed his opinion clearly and attacked it vigorously. Yet now he sat in silence. He seemed to be trying to cut himself off from the resolution; but his behavior appeared to signal his tacit approval for the establishment of the ministerial committee. At the end of the discussion, a vote was taken. With twelve votes in favor and two abstaining, it was decided to set up a seven-member ministerial committee. Ben-Gurion had not made the slightest move to prevent its establishment. Mapai could breathe freely. The terrifying "affair" had been removed from the Foreign Affairs and Defense Committee and placed in "reliable hands".

The "Committee of Seven", as it was popularly known, held intensive deliberations on the Lavon Affair from 3 November to 20 December 1960. It had been empowered to present no more than procedural findings, that is, the committee was to advise the Cabinet on ways to deal with "the affair". However, Levi Eshkol, thought otherwise. From the first moment, the finance minister opposed any judicial inquiry and was determined to bring the whole matter to a close within the ministerial committee. He loyally fulfilled the mission with which he had been charged by Mapai's establishment – the party apparatus and the veteran leadership: to restore domestic peace within Mapai, to prevent any split or schism, "to guide the ship to a safe harbor". In other words – to put an end to "the affair" even at the price of appeasing Lavon and granting his demands.

With this aim in mind, Eshkol held that the Committee of Seven should reach final conclusions regarding Lavon. This meant that the committee would become a kind of unofficial commission of inquiry, and that is precisely what came about. From its earliest meetings, the committee began to read material and discuss questions of fact related to "the mishap". It overstepped its powers to an excessive degree and began to seek the answer to a question beyond its jurisdiction: "Who gave the order?" As it was not a committee of jurists, but a political forum, it did not follow legal procedures. Furthermore, it diverged from elementary investigatory procedures: its members studied only a part of the documents relating to "the affair"; they held interminable arguments about whether or not the committee was authorized to summon witnesses and ultimately summoned no one (not even people who specifically requested to appear before it). At the same time, Justice Minister Rosen decided to send the attorney-general to Paris to take testimony from Gibly's successor Yehoshafat Harkavi, and from the secretary who had typed the forged copy of "the letter". Exceeding its powers, relying on partial information, failing to hear evidence, under overt pressures to present its findings, and working by haphazard procedures, the committee finally reached its conclusions. What the committee submitted to the Cabinet on 20 December were not procedural proposals for dealing with the affair but a clear-cut verdict: "We find that Lavon did not give the order cited by 'the senior officer' and that 'the mishap' was carried out without his knowledge. . . . Investigation of 'the affair' should be regarded as concluded and completed."

Ben-Gurion read the report in disbelief. "I was particularly amazed," he wrote, "to see the signature of Justice Minister Pinhas Rosen on this document." The infuriated prime minister regarded the procedure followed by the committee as "partiality and half-truths, and the findings lack veracity and justice". He did not take part in the Cabinet vote on the committee's report. Eight ministers voted in favor; four others – including Abba Eban and Moshe Dayan – abstained. Then Ben-Gurion addressed the meeting: "I am addressing the justice minister . . . There is a certain procedure by exclusive means of which the truth can be revealed. Witnesses are cross-examined and confronted with one another, both sides have lawyers, the lawyers examine matters carefully. What is this fear of yours of a judicial commission of inquiry?" His final words produced consternation. "You have made your decisions. There are findings. There is a Cabinet decision approving these findings. The Cabinet has a law of collective responsibility. I am no partner to this responsibility – neither for appointing the committee, nor for its findings, nor for the Cabinet decision – and I will not be responsible for it. For your information: I am no partner of yours. I am not a member of the Cabinet." On 31 January, the Old Man submitted his resignation to the president.

The findings of the Committee of Seven and Ben-Gurion's consequent resignation indicate "a breakdown in communications". Ben-Gurion erred in failing to make it clear to his colleagues, from the outset, that he would not, under any circumstances, accept decisions of the ministerial committee that precluded a judicial inquiry. Admittedly, he had written to Eshkol that "he would draw his conclusions" if no judicial commission of inquiry were established, but Eshkol and the others were convinced that he would come to terms.

Then Ben-Gurion compounded this failure with a grave and fateful error. He combined two struggles, one of which swept away the moral foundations of the other. Each of the causes he fought for was justified unto itself; striving for both simultaneously led to tragedy. While Ben-Gurion continued to campaign for a judicial inquiry into "the affair", he simultaneously embarked on a furious struggle against Lavon, sparked off first and foremost by Lavon's bitter attacks on the defense establishment and the army. Ben-Gurion felt that it was vital to cast out the man who had dared to denigrate the army and the men responsible for Israel's security. But when he flung himself into the fray, the Old Man overlooked his customary distinction between the principal issue and marginal matters and failed to decide whether to concentrate on his battle for justice or on his conflict with Lavon.

He waged both campaigns impulsively, without distinguishing between them. In one and the same letter, or speech, or article, he would call for a fair judicial inquiry that would give both sides an equal chance and launch a furious barrage against Lavon, accusing him of lies, of issuing irresponsible orders, or of indulging in wild slander. To the general public, the two issues sounded like one. Ben-Gurion was demanding a fair trial, but he had already reached his own verdict. One can hardly blame the public for seeing Ben-Gurion as a party to the dispute and his hostility toward Lavon as a cover for "the senior officer". Disdain and mockery of Ben-Gurion were widespread. The public regarded his resignation from office as a response to Lavon's acquittal. His fight against Lavon was regarded as a vendetta.

After the Committee of Seven's findings were submitted to the Cabinet, Ben-Gurion began to hint that Lavon should be removed from his post as secretary-general of the Histadrut. The press interpreted his statement, "I will not sit with Lavon," as a demand that Mapai choose between Lavon and himself. Several of his supporters told journalists that Ben-Gurion would not withdraw his resignation unless the party rallied behind him and dismissed Lavon. In the course of January, some Mapai leaders still hoped to achieve an honorable conclusion to the confrontation between Lavon and Ben-Gurion. Some proposed a "party court" to judge Lavon for his statements, but the proposal was dropped. Another idea raised in Mapai's secretariat, with Ben-Gurion's support, was the establishment of a "test committee" to consider Lavon's statements and issue its verdict; but this idea soon perished. Now that both proposals had fallen, there seemed to be only one way left – harsh, brutal and ugly: Lavon's dismissal without discussion, without trial, without the smallest measure of comradely justice. Mapai members were, for the most part, prepared to adopt this solution in order to appease Ben-Gurion, and Levi Eshkol took it upon himself to procure Lavon's dismissal.

On 31 January 1961, Ben-Gurion submitted his resignation to the president. Two days later, Mapai's secretariat adopted Eshkol's proposal that Lavon be dismissed. On Saturday, 4 February, the party's Central Committee convened and decided to dismiss Lavon. The resolution was adopted over Moshe Sharett's fierce objections. In a secret vote, 159 members were in favor of Lavon's dismissal, 96 were against, and 5 abstained.

This was the end of Lavon. But Ben-Gurion's young disciples, who toiled with great enthusiasm to canvass votes against Lavon, did not comprehend that it was also the end of the Old Man. Lavon's dismissal led to an open schism between Ben-Gurion's camp and the veteran leadership. Furthermore, it undermined the moral foundations of Ben-Gurion's image, destroyed his credibility, and presented him as a vindictive dictator imposing his will on one and all. Ben-Gurion never regained his previous standing in the eyes of his party or his people. Lavon's dismissal marked the beginning of the end of his rule.

A few days after Lavon was dismissed, Ben-Gurion agreed to form a new Cabinet, but he immediately ran into great difficulties. The two other labor parties (Mapam and Ahdut ha-Avodah, which had broken with Mapam and reconstituted itself as an independent party) refused to join the Cabinet under his leadership. There was no choice but to disperse the

Knesset and go to the polls. Less than two years after Mapai's greatest victory, the party – stricken and in disarray – faced new elections.

In elections held on 15 August 1961, Mapai lost five of its Knesset seats. "From the party's point of view," Ben-Gurion wrote, "this is a tremendous victory, after ten months of ruthless slanders ... But from a political viewpoint, these results are a catastrophe."

17

The Parting of the Ways

On 2 November 1961, Ben-Gurion presented his new Cabinet to the Knesset. He would head the Israeli government for another twenty months, a bizarre period that witnessed the progressive decline of his rule. All the trends set into motion by the Lavon Affair would continue and grow sharper, until the prime minister believed that he had lost the backing of his party altogether. The issues during this round were not personal – but they were no less emotional. Ben-Gurion went down to his defeat because of his policy of trust for what he termed "another Germany". Yet like so many issues in Israeli politics, the question of the Israeli government's posture toward Germany was not clear-cut. In fact, the real issue was almost drowned in the hysterical uproar that began with the discovery of a project to manufacture missiles in Egypt.

On 21 July 1962, there was deep consternation in Israel when Egypt launched two types of surface-to-surface missiles, one with a range of 175 miles, the other with a range of 350 miles. A jubilant Nasser told a Cairo crowd that his missiles could hit any target "south of Beirut". What was not yet common knowledge, however, was that the missiles had been built by hundreds of German scientists and technicians secretly recruited by Egypt. Under their guidance, three secret factories had been built: Plant 36, where an Egyptian jet plane was developed; Plant 135, where jet engines were manufactured; and most secret of all, Plant 333, for the production of operational medium-range missiles.

Israeli experts feared that Egypt would arm her missiles with non-conventional warheads: either nuclear bombs or materials banned under international law, such as gas, dangerous germ cultures, or radioactive wastes. At the same time, the Egyptian missiles had their Achilles heel, for the German scientists had yet to develop an effective guidance system.

Isser Harel, head of the Security Services, advised Ben-Gurion to approach Chancellor Adenauer without delay and demand that he take immediate action to put an end to the scientists' work. But Ben-Gurion refused. He preferred to have Shimon Peres intervene with the West

German defense minister, Franz Josef Strauss. A few days later, on 20 August, Golda Meir and Shimon Peres also approached President Kennedy. In December, when Golda Meir met with Kennedy in Florida, she brought up the subject of the Egyptian missiles, and asked for his intervention, but her appeal was of no avail.

Meanwhile, a man by the name of Dr Otto Joklik approached Israeli security agents in Europe, and told them that he had visited Cairo and learned that the Egyptians were developing warheads that would be filled with radioactive wastes. Upon landing in Israeli territory, the missiles would give off dangerous radiation that could contaminate the environment for months or even years. Joklik came to Israel and was questioned by Isser Harel and his men. He claimed that Egypt had tried to acquire weapons that give off radiation capable of destroying "all living tissue". The head of the Egyptian missile program was trying to get hold of large amounts of cobalt 60 – a radioactive isotope of cobalt to fill the missiles' warheads. Alarmed, Harel passed the information on to Ben-Gurion.

In retrospect, Isser Harel's reports on Egypt's non-conventional weapons appear highly exaggerated. But at the time, Israel's leaders were deeply perturbed by the activities of the German scientists and believed it was vital to put an end to their projects at the earliest possible moment.

At the end of 1962, terror struck the hearts of the German scientists in the wake of several bizarre events. On 11 September, an unknown man entered the Munich offices of the Intra Company (which purchased raw materials for the Egyptian missiles) and accompanied its director, Dr Krug, outside. Krug's white car was found a few days later, abandoned on the outskirts of a forest. Since then, no trace of him has been found.

On the morning of 26 November, a parcel exploded in the hands of the secretary to the head scientist at Plant 333 in Egypt. As a result of the explosion, she was blinded and lost her hearing. Another parcel exploded the following day in the managerial offices at 333, and five Egyptians were killed.

On 20 February 1963, an attempt was made on the life of Dr Kleinwachter, an electronics expert working on the development of a guidance system in his laboratory in Lorrach, Germany. Various guesses were raised about the identity of the assailants gunning for the German scientists.

Ben-Gurion did not take any active initiative in regard to the German scientists; nor did he wish to make them into a focal issue of Israeli-German relations. He preferred to employ other methods because of his policy toward Germany. After all, Ben-Gurion had coined the term "another Germany". He believed that the Federal Republic genuinely wished to atone for the sins of Hitler's Reich. The $500 million loan promised by Konrad Adenauer was on its way. Furthermore, Germany had initiated secret deliveries of the most modern arms – including tanks, planes, and helicopters – on astonishing terms: for some of the weapons, the Germans demanded no more than 10 per cent of their worth, while other, more expensive weapons systems were delivered to Israel free of charge. The prime minister was protective of these links. Precisely as Isser Harel was launching his campaign against the German scientists, negotiations were in progress with Germany for a large arms deal and the eventual establishment of diplomatic relations. It was imperative to deal with the question of German citizens in Egypt cautiously.

In contrast, Isser Harel was vigorously antagonistic toward Germany. Since his capture of Adolf Eichmann, his anti-German feelings had developed into unconcealed hatred. As Harel stepped up his clandestine activities, the German scientists in Egypt were subject to threatening letters, and phone calls. Their friends and relatives were urged to convince the scientists to leave Egypt and return to Germany, lest harm befall them. On 2 March 1963 a young woman by the name of Heidi Goerke met in Basel with Otto Joklik, who was now working for Israel, and Yosef Ben-Gal, an Israeli agent. Heidi was the daughter of Professor Goerke, the electronic expert of Plant 333. The two men attempted to persuade her to fly to Cairo and convince her father to stop his work for Nasser. That same night, Joklik and Ben-Gal were arrested by the Swiss police.

On Friday, 15 March, the U.P. reported the arrest of Ben-Gal and Joklik "on suspicion of attempting to coerce the daughter of a German missile scientist employed in Egypt". That same night, Isser Harel and Golda Meir, who held very similar views on the German question, held consultations concerning Israel's reaction. The following day, Harel set out for Tiberias, where Ben-Gurion was on holiday, and presented several of Golda's proposals to him. Ben-Gurion decided that there was to be no reaction at all on the official Swiss statement about the arrests. As for the press, the Old Man declared, "The missiles issue is not to be brought up, but the matter of the arrests must be explained."

Harel returned to Tel Aviv and summoned the editors of the daily papers for a briefing on the background to the Ben-Gal affair. He had not given sufficient consideration to the fact that Germany was a most sensitive subject in Israel. Whether or not he intended it, he set off a wave of charges – both true and imaginary – against Germany that spread panic in Israel.

Newspapers in Israel and abroad were inundated with sensational reports and headlines: former Nazis were developing chemical, biological, atomic, and radiological weapons for Nasser; they were manufacturing horrible gases, disease-bearing microbes, and death rays with which to arm Nasser's missiles, not to mention to the possibility of nuclear bombs or radioactive wastes. The newspaper campaign was accompanied by hints, and proof that the German government was not doing a thing to dissuade its citizens from their diabolical activities against the Jewish people. Within a few days, the campaign had plunged into generalizations and exaggerations, losing all sense of proportion. A bitter wave of criticism and scorn was unleashed at Ben-Gurion's term "another Germany".

In view of the public outrage, the Cabinet decided to make a political statement to the Knesset. Ben-Gurion was still in Tiberias, and the task devolved upon Golda Meir. Due to the grave danger stemming from the activities of the German scientists, all the parties represented in the Foreign Affairs and Defense Committee of the Knesset decided to submit a joint draft resolution, to demonstrate the unity of the people of Israel to the world. The draft proposal was approved by Ben-Gurion, and Golda Meir submitted it to the Knesset on 20 March.

Golda Meir spoke in a restrained manner, but the debate that followed her statement soon took on extreme, if not demagogical overtones. Most of the speakers launched angry attacks on Ben-Gurion's policy toward Germany, but they all were outdone by Menahem Begin, who accused the prime minister of providing "an alibi for Germany", and stated: "You send our Uzi [sub-machine-guns] to Germany, and the Germans provide our enemies with microbes." When she arose to wind up the debate, Golda Meir dissociated herself from Begin's charges, but she did not say a word in defense of Ben-Gurion's policy toward Germany. The Knesset had become the arena in which that policy was denounced, and not a single Mapai member took the prime minister's side.

In the wake of the Knesset debate, the campaign against Germany and the German scientists working for Egypt was stepped up. It was 24 March 1963, after a week of all but unprecedented turbulence in the press, before Ben-Gurion saw his error in not handling the German scientists issue personally the moment it erupted. One cannot overlook the strong resemblance between his behavior at the first outbreak of the Lavon Affair and his lethargic response at the beginning of the latest crisis. Once again he chose to withdraw into seclusion, engaging in reading and writing and taking rests and walks while the snowball began to roll. His responses were impulsive and feeble, and when he finally decided to intervene and regain control of the runaway wagon, it was already well down the slope.

Finally, the chief of staff asked military intelligence for an assessment of the Egyptian missile program. The examination did not provide any evidence that the German scientists in Egypt were engaged in developing chemical or bacteriological weapons. As for radiological and nuclear weapons, they, too, belonged more to the realm of fantasy than reality. Later on it was learned that the amounts of cobalt delivered to Egypt were tiny. While Joklik had reported orders for hundreds of thousands of curie – themselves insufficient to engender fatal radiation – the amount delivered to Egypt was no more than forty curie, a trivial quantity by any yardstick.

Ben-Gurion received the first reports of military intelligence's more moderate assessment on 24 March. He returned to Tel Aviv and summoned Isser Harel. The Old Man began by commenting that the press reports inspired by Harel were harmful and went on to criticize several points connected with Harel's activities in recent weeks. According to Harel, the two men parted late at night in "a correct atmosphere", but with "a certain tension". The real storm broke the following day.

On the morning of 25 March, Shimon Peres came to see Ben-Gurion, accompanied by the chief of staff and Meir Amit, the chief of military intelligence. Ben-Gurion subjected Amit to a full interrogation, and for the first time he received an evaluation totally unlike Harel's. Amit's report presented a clear picture: the men at work in Egypt were a group of mediocre scientists who had developed antiquated missiles. The panic that had overtaken the country's leadership – including the experts of the Defense Ministry and the General Staff – was highly exaggerated.

Immediately after his talk with Amit, Ben-Gurion again summoned Isser Harel and told him of the new assessment submitted by the chief of military intelligence. Incensed, Harel argued with the prime minister about the various points he had raised. "Your new assessments," he said, "are in complete contradiction to the evaluations and reports which I know to be authoritative and generally agreed upon." But the Old Man stuck to his view and told Harel that he intended to call a meeting of the Foreign Affairs and Defense Committee in order to prove to its members that the missile threat was not so fearsome. Harel objected, and the two men plunged into a sharp argument. A few hours later, Harel sent Ben-Gurion a brief letter, notifying him he had decided to resign. His resignation went into effect the following day. Forced to accept it, Ben-Gurion appointed military intelligence chief Meir Amit to head the Security Services in Harel's place.

Harel's impulsive resignation was a grave blow to Ben-Gurion's standing. In time, it would transpire that Ben-Gurion was right: the Egyptian missiles were no danger; their guidance systems did not function; nor were they fitted with nonconventional warheads. Discreet political action behind the scenes convinced the German government to lure some of the key scientists out of Egypt by offering them tempting salaries in Germany. In speeches and letters, Ben-Gurion denounced the campaign against the

German scientists as "noise . . . in part exaggerated, in part the fruit of demagogy" harmful to Israel.

From Ben-Gurion's point of view, the affair of the German scientists set off a threefold crisis: in his German policy; in his relations with close colleagues and aides, headed by Golda Meir and Isser Harel; and with the parliamentary opposition, particularly Begin's Herut. These three upheavals were to cause his final downfall ten weeks later. Harel's resignation marked the onset of the twilight of Ben-Gurion's rule, lasting into mid-June. During this period, one can observe a somber development in the Old Man's behavior. His judgment appears to have become impaired; his political vision was dimmed; and his thoughts and responses were impulsive and unbalanced.

Ben-Gurion's fear of Herut's accession to power became an obsession. Ever since his return from Tiberias, he had been searching for an opportunity to settle accounts with Begin for his speech in the Knesset. Such an opportunity arose in the Knesset on 13 May, and he launched a violent attack on Herut. A tremendous uproar broke out. Herut members erupted into shouts and disorder, and the session was recessed for three hours. When the session resumed, the speaker of the Knesset stated that the Herut faction had committed an infringement of Knesset regulations; but addressing Ben-Gurion, he asked him to withdraw his sharp attack. Pale and tense, Ben-Gurion obeyed. It had not escaped him that Mapai members had not, for the most part, risen to defend him against Herut's onslaught.

Ben-Gurion predicted that if Begin gained control of the state, "he will replace the army and police command with his ruffians and rule the way Hitler ruled Germany, using brute force to suppress the labor movement; and will destroy the state . . . I have no doubt that Begin hates Hitler, but that hatred does not prove that he is unlike [Hitler] . . ." These were strange words, lacking a sense of proportion and a harsh testimony against the man who wrote them.

On the eve of Independence Day, Ben-Gurion's last surviving close friend, Yitzhak Ben-Zvi, passed away. Ben-Gurion had entertained a great affection for him. "I had three comrades," he wrote.

We were friends rather than comrades. The first was Ben-Zvi; the second was S. Yavnieli, whom I met at Sejera . . . the third was Berl [Katznelson] . . . I have many colleagues and friends. But with those three, I had a profound spiritual communion, and now I feel orphaned and bereaved . . . But why should I mourn? After all, I too will follow them . . .

Ben-Gurion's mood was clearly depressed, but his final decision to resign was adopted at the height of a different crisis.

On 17 April 1963, Egypt, Syria, and Iraq decided to unite in what they called the Arab Federation. Ben-Gurion was deeply concerned by the danger stemming from such a union because of an article in its charter stating that the federation had come about "to implement the military union that will be capable of liberating the Arab homeland from the Zionist menace". In fact, this article was no more than a routine proclamation, resembling hundreds of similar statements issued by Arab leaders. But it evoked unprecedented forebodings in the Old Man. He regarded this federation, which had yet to arise, as the terrible menace to Israel's existence that he had feared ever since 1948. Very few shared his gloomy prediction. But his plunge into extremes, and the lost sense of proportion that characterized him at that time induced Ben-Gurion to launch a political campaign unprecedented in the annals of the state.

Ben-Gurion began to address dramatic letters to all the heads of state in the world, describing the threatening article in the charter of the Arab Federation and asking them "to urge the Arab states, at the forthcoming U.N. General Assembly, to respect United Nations principles and their commitment to achieving a permanent peace between them and Israel". In the course of five weeks, Ben-Gurion's secretaries typed out dozens of letters and sent them to all corners of the earth.

He proposed to President Kennedy that the president of the U.S. and the prime minister of the U.S.S.R. publish a declaration to the effect that they jointly guarantee the territorial integrity and security of every state in the Middle East . . . He went even further: "If you can spare an hour or two for a discussion with me on the situation and possible solutions, I am prepared to fly to Washington at your convenience and without any publicity."

His proposal to President de Gaulle was also dramatic: "In my eyes, the principal matter is to prevent war, and only a military alliance between France and Israel is capable of preventing war . . . Has not the time come to consolidate the existing loyal friendship between the two countries by a political treaty of military assistance in the event of an attack upon us on the part of Egypt and her allies?"

His reaction was extreme, and he erred all the way. The Arab Federation perished before it even arose. The Old Man's appeals to the heads of state were a complete failure, since all his requests were denied. Kennedy expressed "real reservations" about any joint declaration with Khrushchev. He also rejected Ben-Gurion's offer to come to Washington.

The Old Man was disappointed by this answer and five days later, he sent a further note to Kennedy. "Mr President, my people have the right to exist . . . and this existence is in danger." Ben-Gurion proposed the signature of a security treaty between Israel and the United States and its allies.

This note from Ben-Gurion also failed to extract an affirmative reply from Kennedy. Golda Meir knew of the abortive diplomatic offensive but stayed clear of it personally: "We knew about these approaches," she said later. "We treated David Ben-Gurion deferentially . . . We said nothing, even though we wondered."

The prime minister never finished dictating all the letters he had planned to send. On the afternoon of 15 June 1963, Golda Meir came to see him. She was profoundly upset, after learning of a German news agency report that Israeli soldiers were being trained in the use of new weapons in Germany. Recently, Golda had become increasingly aggressive in her disagreement with Ben-Gurion's policy toward Germany. She now urged him to order the military censor to delete the report about Israelis undergoing training at a German military base. Publication of the report, she said, would provoke "superfluous trouble". Ben-Gurion refused, explaining that he was not empowered to disallow any report. That lay solely within the jurisdiction of the military censor, who followed precise instructions. Golda left in a rage.

Upon learning of Golda's mood, Teddy Kollek decided to bring her back to the Old Man for a further meeting. About eleven o'clock that evening, he accompanied her to Ben-Gurion's house, where the three sat down in the kitchen and Ben-Gurion and Golda plunged into a sharp argument on the German question. Around midnight, Ben-Gurion and Golda took leave of one another "amidst disagreements".

There would be no more arguments over that question, for the following morning, Ben-Gurion entered his office and told his secretary, "I am going to submit my resignation." The news hit like a thunderbolt. Teddy Kollek and Yitzhak Navon tried to dissuade him, but the Old Man was adamant. He dictated laconic, single-sentence letters to the president and the speaker of the Knesset, notifying them of his resignation.

More than any of the other appeals to change his decision before the resignation became effective, he was profoundly affected by an unexpected visit from Generals Yitzhak Rabin and Meir Amit. Rabin was visibly upset. He told the Old Man that the army's commanders "were all astounded" by his resignation. One of the generals had described it as "a disaster". Rabin stressed that "the army does not intervene in politics, does not constitute a party, and must not exert pressure", but he "regarded this as a calamity". "What will happen to the army now?" he asked. Ben-Gurion tried to explain that he was forced to leave, for reasons unrelated to the army. "All the generals said that it's inconceivable," said Rabin. "They don't see how its possible [to manage] without Ben-Gurion." The Old Man was on the verge of tears. "His words touched me profoundly," he wrote in his diary, "and I scarcely managed to suppress my feelings and my tears."

Ben-Gurion refused to go into detail over the reasons for his resignation. The real key to unravelling his motives is to be found in his diary entry for that day, 16 June. His notes prove that the causes for his resignation had, in fact, been simmering within him over a prolonged period, but his act was impulsive.

In fact, I made the decision two and a half years ago, when "the hypocritical vulture" [Ben-Gurion's nickname for Pinhas Lavon] succeeded in mobilizing all the parties against us. But at the time, I feared that the party would be destroyed if I resigned. . . . "The leader" [Begin] sensed his power growing, his audacity increased, and violence began to gain control of the Knesset, as was proved in the foreign policy debate and the pandemonium [Herut] provoked . . . And only the blind . . . do not see [that this is] the beginning of "the leader's" takeover. . . . It is possible that "the officer-in-charge" [Harel] will stand up in the [Mapai] Central Committee and play the role "the hypocritical vulture" filled two years ago. And there is nothing that will bring on Fascist rule in Israel as much as this insanity.

This passage again highlights Ben-Gurion's strange, fears of Herut; his bitterness and anger against his own colleagues; and his indignation over the attack on his policy toward Germany. His resignation came about while he was under tremendous emotional strain, and his motives and urges were irrational. The previous evening's incident with Golda was no more than the last straw. The emotional state Ben-Gurion had been in for the past ten weeks made him unfit to rule the country.

Ben-Gurion did not think matters over rationally; he gave no consideration to the future. Sick and tired, he simply walked out. His unexpected decision was a heavy blow to his young supporters, and the war of succession, conducted under the cover of the Lavon Affair had now ended in total victory for the veteran leadership. Levi Eshkol was chosen to replace Ben-Gurion as premier. Eshkol would do everything he could to maintain the party's existing balance of power, but he would not follow Ben-Gurion's precedent of gradually replacing the veteran leadership with younger, more vigorous men. The Lavon Affair and its aftermath put paid to Ben-Gurion's rule, pushing his protégés aside and deflecting the party from the path he had blazed. More than any other event in the annals of the State of Israel, Ben-Gurion's resignation marked the end of an epoch. But it was not yet the end of his public career.

A day after he resigned, Ben-Gurion received journalist Haggai Eshed's work, *Who Gave the Order?* In response to a request Ben-Gurion addressed to him late in 1962, Eshed had sifted through all the material relating to the 1954 "mishap", as well as the proceedings of the 1960 seven-man minister-ial committee. He came to the conclusion that Lavon had, in fact, given the infamous order. Ben-Gurion decided to approach the Cabinet and request a renewed investigation into "the affair". In doing so, he broke a public promise made on the eve of the Knesset elections, when he had vowed not to concern himself with "the affair" any longer. But the actions of the Committee of Seven "gave him no rest". It was not the question "who gave the order?" that engaged Ben-Gurion's attention but "the miscarriage of justice perpetrated by the Committee of Seven". He was determined to denounce the ministers' behavior and have the "miscarriage of justice" investigated by a juridical forum.

It was only natural that Levi Eshkol – the moving spirit behind the Committee of Seven, had no interest in a renewed examination of the issue. Ben-Gurion invited Eshkol for a talk about "the affair" and told him: "There is one possibility. The premier could demand judicial procedings. This will save him from disgrace and enhance his dignity. If he does not do so, I shall do so. But I would not want the truth to be revealed by me." Eshkol asked for time to think the matter over. Eight days later, he told Ben-Gurion that he had "considered his proposal, and decided in the negative".

The Old Man decided to take action. On 27 April, he began to edit all the material having to do with "the affair" in his possession. He revealed the details of his plan to an old and trusted friend:

I shall submit all the material I know of to the attorney-general and the justice minister. It is quite clear to me that they will do nothing on their own initiative. They will bring the matter to the Cabinet, and the Cabinet will no doubt decide in the negative. I shall [then] publish the material about what happened in Egypt with the exception of classified material, and rid myself of the moral burden. I know that the papers . . . will denigrate me. Such denigration has been going on for four years, and I have given up caring about it long ago. But there are honest and intelligent people in this country, and they will defend truth and justice. I, at all events, will do my duty.

On 22 October, Ben-Gurion went to Jerusalem to present the material on the affair to justice minister, Dov Joseph. He scored his first victory when the attorney-general supported his principal charges against the Com-mittee of Seven. Joseph adopted his recommendations and advised the Cabinet to order a renewed inquiry. Up to the last moment, Eshkol tried to evade adoption of the justice minister's recommendations. But Ben-Gurion now felt himself on firm enough ground to address a strongly worded letter to Eshkol:

I feel that it is my comradely duty toward you even more so my duty towards the party, and above all my duty toward Israel to prevent a grave mishap – a personal mishap to you, the mishap of the party's disintegration, and a public mishap to the state – and tell you that you will be making a terrible mistake if you again attempt [to proclaim] a "full stop". There will be no "full stop" as long as some court does not express its opinion on whether the Committee of Seven was in order or committed an error. . . . There will be no "full stop" without a commission of inquiry of the finest judges in the country, in whom the people have confidence . . . Call up your courage and do the only thing that will conclude this matter honorably! Instruct the justice minister to fulfil the request I addressed to him.

But Eshkol refused to set up a commission of inquiry, in spite of the heavy pressure brought to bear upon him by wide sections of his party.

The final trial of strength between Ben-Gurion and Eshkol within the framework of Mapai took place at the party conference held in mid-February 1965. On one side was the veteran leadership, united behind Eshkol, together with most of the party apparatus. On the other, Ben-Gurion's young supporters and many representatives from development areas and new settlements believed that they could count on 800 of the 2,200 delegates. Even though it was not on the agenda, the Lavon Affair became the central issue of the convention. The terrible drama that had rocked Mapai now raged on a veritable stage – the wide platform of the Mann Auditorium in Tel Aviv. Behind the long table, sat the principal protagonists in the bitter confrontation, deploying for their final showdown before the delegates who packed the large hall and its gallery.

Ben-Gurion delivered an aggressive speech to the conference: "The truth . . . is what I am fighting for, have fought for, and will fight for all my life. It is desirable for our people that truth and justice shall reign in our country!"

The three principal speeches against Ben-Gurion were delivered by Moshe Sharett, Golda Meir, and Levi Eshkol. The first was Sharett, who spoke immediately after Ben-Gurion. There was something tragic about his address. He was brought to the conference in a wheelchair. For several months, his friends had known that his end was near; cancer was spreading throughout his body. But he still had strength enough to attack Ben-Gurion with unprecedented ferocity: "By what moral right does [Ben-Gurion] fling this matter at the party? What moral right does he have to make this the focal point of the party conference, and thereby overshadow and confuse the true issues standing on the horizon . . ." At the end of his speech, Golda Meir walked over to Sharett and demonstratively kissed him on the forehead.

She herself addressed the conference that evening. Dressed in black, she approached the speakers' rostrum and delivered one of the harshest speeches anyone had ever made against Ben-Gurion. "The first curse lying over the threshold of our home," she said, "occurred when people began to talk of 'favorites' and 'non-favorites'." They attacked Ben-Gurion's stance. "What does our comrade Ben-Gurion do? He accuses and he judges – from the outset. He says: 'half-truth'; 'miscarriage of justice', 'partiality'." Golda implied that Ben-Gurion had resigned because the Committee of Seven had adopted decisions that were not to his liking and flung harsh charges and bitter questions at him.

Ben-Gurion's face was flushed and a storm raged within him. That very same "dear and beloved Golda" who had been so close to him was now settling accounts with him in a cruel fashion. The sight of Golda speaking angrily, while Ben-Gurion sat dazed at the end of the table, was etched deeply into the memory of Ben-Gurion's friends, who referred to the event as "the night of the long knives". The Old Man was scheduled to reply after Golda's speech. Instead, he stood up and left the convention. "The ugliest thing at the conference," he wrote in his diary, "was Golda's venomous speech. I was sorry to hear her speaking in this manner, pouring out hatred and poison. Where did it come from? What is its source? Is it new or not?" It was a long time before he recovered from the harsh impact of her address. "Had I not heard it with my own ears," he wrote, "I would not have believed that she is capable of soaking up and pouring out such poison . . . I think she lives in a contaminated environment and drinks from muddy springs."

In the secret vote taken at the end of the conference, the proposal submitted by Ben-Gurion and his supporters, calling for "the 1954 affair" to be investigated by "state juridical bodies", received 841 votes, compared to 1,226 against – a 40 per cent minority. Ben-Gurion's enthusiastic supporters came to his home in the middle of the night to notify him of the outcome of the vote. Some of them actually sang and danced before his house, overjoyed at the high proportion of delegates who had voted for him. But Ben-Gurion did not join in their rejoicing. The results spoke for themselves. A majority of the party had rejected his demand.

In view of the conference's outcome, Ben-Gurion finally arrived at the conclusion that he must contest the forthcoming elections on an independent slate. He had long been dropping hints to that effect, but for weeks he put off an explicit declaration. During the final days of June, it became clear that a large group of Ben-Gurion's supporters – headed by Dayan and Peres – were not in favor of a schism. The "staff" they had established even decided that "the minority" was remaining inside Mapai. Shimon Peres drew up a draft resolution to that effect and had it readied for distribution to journalists when it was adopted. But on 29 June, when some forty-five people gathered at Ben-Gurion's home to discuss whether or not to split off from Mapai, the Old Man turned the tables, deciding the question on his own.

At first, Shimon Peres presented the various possibilities facing them and asked his companions to express their opinions. But Ben-Gurion immediately announced that the gathering was a meeting of people who wanted to set up an independent slate. In this fashion, he presented his followers with a *fait accompli*. All they could do was choose between identifying with him or leaving. The Old Man demanded that a statement immediately be issued to the press announcing the formation of the slate. Shimon Peres and a few of his friends tried to postpone the announcement in the hope of forestalling the split, but that was precisely why Ben-Gurion insisted on issuing it without delay. That same evening, the final news broadcast announced the establishment of an independent slate headed by Ben-Gurion. The schism had come about.

Ben-Gurion succeeded in his gamble. With a few exceptions, all the minority leaders joined the new slate. In effect, the Old Man had left them no choice. The moment he decided to go it alone, the faithful Shimon Peres, whose loyalty to Ben-Gurion was above challenge, was incapable of leaving him. On the contrary, Peres headed the new organization. The same went for Dayan.

Ben-Gurion did not wish to appear as the man who had caused the split in Mapai. The new body he had founded was called Rafi (the Israeli Workers' List), and he contended that it was still a part of Mapai. But Mapai's leaders were furious at this strange way of having the best of both worlds. Mapai's secretariat declared that the founders of Rafi had left the party, and when the Rafi leaders persisted in claiming that they were still members of Mapai, the party set up a "court" to try them. The trial aroused a public storm, its most prominent aspect being the ugly, crude terms employed by the prosecution. Particular prominence was achieved by the jurist Ya'akov Shimshon Shapira, who called Ben-Gurion "a coward" and referred to Rafi as "a neo-Fascist group".

Shapira's hysterical onslaught reflected the somber tone of the election campaign. It is doubtful whether at any time in Israeli history parties and leaders flung such sickening insults, and charges as were now bandied about by erstwhile comrades. Ben-Gurion hurled denigrations at Mapai and its leaders and was repaid in kind. Anyone with a grudge against the Old Man or who had been offended by him in the past was recruited for Eshkol's election campaign, and many of the principal Rafi leaders were harassed by the Mapai party apparatus, which took its vengeance by dismissing them from their jobs in the Histadrut and government bodies. It was not the slander or Mapai's vindictiveness that harmed Rafi, however. The new slate published an imposing platform, which featured calls for change in Israeli society and government. But neither the young leaders nor the progressive program could alter the image that had taken root in the Israeli public of a resentful, vindictive, ageing leader who had turned against his successor and wished to displace him.

Ben-Gurion justly characterized this as "the ugliest election campaign ever held in Israel". He was equally right in noting in his journal that the outcome of the election showed a victory for the Labor Alignment (Mapai's coalition with Ahdut ha-Avodah), while Rafi had "suffered a great defeat". The new list gained only ten Knesset seats, while the Alignment won forty-five. A group comprising several of Israel's most gifted leaders found itself in barren opposition. Ben-Gurion was an ageing lion whose strength was on the wane and whose roar was progressively fading. Beginning as the just fight of a courageous and honest leader, his battle had ended in a shameful defeat which heralded his final decline.

Epilogue

On 15 May 1967, while Israel was celebrating her Independence Day, large units of the Egyptian army crossed the Suez Canal, entered Sinai, and deployed in the vicinity of the Israeli border. Radio broadcasts and newspaper headlines throughout the Arab world heralded that the decisive battle between Israel and the Arabs was imminent. In response, Israel decided on a partial mobilization of its army on 19 May. This decision horrified David Ben-Gurion. He feared that the deterioration of the situation would lead to a new war.

As usual, he blamed Levi Eshkol for the tension that had arisen. Eighteen months had passed since the elections, and Ben-Gurion's bitter criticism of Eshkol had not diminished at all. He was scathing in his comments on the escalation in Israel's reactions to Syrian attacks in April 1967 (which had aroused the present crisis), and at a meeting with Rafi leaders on 21 May, he proposed that the party's Knesset faction demand Eshkol's resignation, "as was done to Prime Minister Chamberlain in 1940". But Moshe Dayan and Shimon Peres opposed him. Ben-Gurion also expressed his fear of the missiles in Egypt's possession and the danger to Israel's civilian population centers from Egyptian air attacks. He held that from a military and political viewpoint, this was not an opportune moment for Israel to become involved in a war, and it would be better to discharge the reserves and make efforts to reduce tension. In the course of the discussion, a note was delivered to him, and he reacted with considerable surprise: Chief of Staff Yitzhak Rabin wished to see him. Ben-Gurion consented immediately.

Rabin was under great pressure at the time. The unexpected Egyptian moves had caused confusion and indecision within the government leadership. Levi Eshkol was not a military man and was not built for tests of this nature. He failed to adopt a clear position against the Egyptian menace and wavered for days. Ever since Nasser initiated his threatening moves, Eshkol had been spending his time in meetings and consultations, leaving it to the chief of staff not only to advise and report, but essentially to carry out the tasks of a defense minister. This responsibility, coupled with the hesitation of the prime minister, placed a heavy burden on the shoulders of the chief of staff. He asked to see Ben-Gurion in order to hear his assessment of the situation.

But his encounter with Ben-Gurion was of little comfort to Rabin. "My talk with Ben-Gurion was a great shock," Rabin was to relate later. The Old Man used "sharp terms" and employed a sober, rational analysis to explain "why it is unthinkable that war should break out [now]". Ben-Gurion accused Rabin of "endangering the people of Israel", by mobilizing. He did not provide the chief of staff with the advice and encouragement he sought; on the contrary, their talk added to Rabin's gloom. "Yitzhak was depressed," Ben-Gurion noted after their conversation.

The truth is that in 1967 Ben-Gurion was no longer the audacious, far-sighted leader his admirers knew. His age, his remoteness from the centers of power, and memories of past lessons all had their impact on him. The legend which still lived on in men's hearts covered up the decline that had overtaken the eighty-one-year-old leader. "He is living in a world that has passed away," Dayan said ruefully on the eve of the Six Day War. "He admires de Gaulle, over-estimates Nasser's strength, and is unable to grasp the full power of the army." Ben-Gurion was sure that unlike the Sinai Campaign, Israel's next war would be long – several weeks, if not months – and the army would have to take on Syria and Jordan as well as Egypt. There could be thousands of casualties, with grave effects on the morale of the civilian population. The country would require massive and continuous deliveries of arms from the Western Powers and support in the international arena. Consequently, he believed that Israel must explain her viewpoint to the world and ensure the support of the Western powers, but refrain from attacking.

Even after he learned on 23 May that Nasser had decided to close the Tiran Straits to Israeli shipping, Ben-Gurion did not change his mind. Even after de Gaulle turned his back on Israel, and courted the Arabs, Ben-Gurion continued to believe in the genuineness of his friendship. The Old Man's views were in total contrast to his public image of decisiveness and daring. As the crisis worsened and public criticism of Eshkol grew because of his hesitation to go to war, there was a growing clamor for Ben-Gurion's return to power. Influential circles believed that he was capable of providing Israel with decisive leadership and leading her into the war that now seemed unavoidable. Few people knew that the truth was otherwise; that Ben-Gurion was adamantly opposed to any military action. On 24 May, the day after the closing of the straits, even Menahem Begin, previously Ben-Gurion's most outspoken rival, proposed to Levi Eshkol that Ben-Gurion be placed at the head of a government of national unity.

Eshkol rejected the proposition outright. "These two horses will not pull this cart," he stated.

Ben-Gurion's assessment of the situation was totally wrong, as subsequent events proved. At first his prestige, his former triumphs, and his clear powers of analysis provided substantial weight to his opinions at this time of confusion and indecision. But in the course of the tempestuous days of late May, as more and more leaders actually heard Ben-Gurion's views, they withdrew their demand for him to be coopted into the Cabinet. After a conversation with the Old Man, even Begin and his colleagues were convinced that their proposal to Eshkol was no longer practical. The clamor for Ben-Gurion's return gradually faded, and the Old Man stepped aside. In consultations among Rafi members, he proposed Moshe Dayan as prime minister and defense minister and offered to act as his adviser, if Dayan so wished.

In the meantime, the country was in uproar and there was a revolt within Mapai against Eshkol and Golda Meir, who were urged to entrust the defense portfolio to Moshe Dayan. Eshkol's indecision, his stammered radio broadcast, rumors of the chief of staff's collapse, and a sense of terror as the noose tightened about Israel all provoked a great outcry in public opinion, in the army, and in Mapai itself. On 1 June, Eshkol capitulated. That evening he invited Dayan to join a government of national unity as defense minister.

The Rafi Knesset faction convened and approved Dayan's appointment. By his support for Dayan, Ben-Gurion seemed to be supporting a policy that he had opposed completely. Yet he still hoped that he could convert Dayan over to his views and drew some encouragement from the fact that Dayan "laid down a condition that he be 'linked' to me, in other words, that he would consult me". But matters turned out otherwise. In effect, Dayan was determined not to consult Ben-Gurion. He acknowledged that "his political wisdom is greater than mine", but was convinced that Ben-Gurion had a distorted view of the situation. "For better or worse, this is the way matters have evolved," he wrote in a complacent tone. "In this war I will have to rely on my own wings." Dayan's appointment as defense minister, and the Cabinet's decision to go to war led to Ben-Gurion's final decline as a statesman.

That decline was not a gradual, unobserved process. On the contrary, it was sudden and dramatic. It lasted six days – just as long as the war. On the eve of its outbreak, the Old Man was still a leader of the first rank, a candidate for national and military leadership, projecting the image of a national savior to whom thousands turned their eyes. At the end of the war, he was a retired statesman, an old man whose time had passed. Israel's tempestuous battle for survival was directed by others with complete success.

Ben-Gurion had his first taste of frustrating helplessness during the evening of 4 June. Throughout the day, he had awaited the arrival of Moshe Dayan, who was to notify him of the Cabinet decision taken that morning. "At 10 in the evening, when I was lying in bed reading ... I heard a knock at the door below. I went down to open it, thinking that Dayan had arrived. I was surprised to see that it was Chaim [Yisraeli, head of the defense minister's bureau]." Yisraeli told the Old Man that Dayan was unable to come, as he had a meeting scheduled with Eshkol.

It has been decided to launch an operation tomorrow, seemingly in the air. But Moshe is prepared to come to me for five minutes. I told Chaim that it was not worth his while to trouble himself, because in five minutes, [I cannot] explain the situation to him ... I am not wholeheartedly in favor of tomorrow's operation, not knowing what has been discussed between us and the leaders of America and Britain ... I am anxious concerning the steps about to be taken. Moshe told me twice that he wishes to be "linked" to me. There is no use in being "linked" after the fateful deed has been done.

On 5 June, the Six Day War erupted. The first news of its outbreak angered Ben-Gurion. "I am sure that this is a grave error," he wrote in his diary. "They should have told Washington and London that we are about to start action if the straits are not reopened. This morning, Dayan sent a general to notify me that operations had begun. There was no need." But his mood began to improve somewhat with the first reports of the brilliant success of the air force's onslaught, which had destroyed the enemy planes on the ground.

On the second day of the fighting, Ben-Gurion asked Yisraeli about the situation on the northern front. "The Syrians are running wild," he replied, "but Moshe is leaving them alone for the moment, so that he can strike a proper blow at them some time later." Ben-Gurion replied: "There should be no delay, because the border settlements are suffering, and they must be protected. I told [Yisraeli] that I wished to go to [Dayan] whenever he can find the time." But Dayan did not find the time – not that day nor in the days to come. Ben-Gurion was forced to rest content with the reports brought him by Defense Ministry officials.

On the morning of 9 June, Ben-Gurion heard an announcement that Syria had agreed to a cease-fire and the war had therefore come to an end. A short time later, however, he learned that the battles with Syria were still in progress. This time, Ben-Gurion phoned Dayan directly. "Why not strike a fatal blow at the Syrians?" he asked. Dayan replied that "the Syrians are fighting bravely, and we have massed large forces to fight them".

"How was the cease-fire broken, and who did it?" the Old Man asked. Dayan did not answer. "That reply is also sufficient," the old man noted. He understood that it was Israel which had broken the cease-fire, and once again, he was furious. Up until then, he had badgered Dayan to attack the Golan Heights. But the moment a cease-fire was agreed upon, he changed his mind and opposed any further operations. That evening, an aide of Dayan came to his home and told him of the Syrians' consent to a cease-fire and Dayan's decision early in the morning to attack the heights. "That was a great mistake, not preserving the cease-fire with Syria," he grumbled. "We have no need of the heights, because we won't remain there. The principal error is that we disobeyed the Security Council's order needlessly. We will have to fight for more vital things, and it is not necessary that our enemies learn that we broke our word." Ben-Gurion overlooked the fact that he himself had acted similarly, both in the War of Independence and during the Sinai Campaign. The following day, the Old Man kept up his criticism of the army's operations in the Golan Heights. "I am afraid that we are forfeiting no small part of the sympathy and friendship that our armies' blows have gained throughout the world – at least in the democratic world. What for?" After the radio announced that the U.S.S.R. had severed diplomatic relations with Israel, he wrote. "This is the outcome of the needless continuation of the battles in Syria! It is impossible to deceive the whole world." That evening, the Golan Heights were occupied, and the Six Day War came to an end.

In the course of the Six Day War, Ben-Gurion grasped that his active involvement in Israeli politics was at an end. Being realistic and courageous, he bowed his head before the facts of life. After the war he began to withdraw from the political scene. He finally shelved his demand for a judicial inquiry into "the affair" and for the "miscarriage of justice" to be corrected; and he did not obstruct the negotiations initiated by his Rafi colleagues to reunite with Mapai, though as a man of integrity, he objected to the move and did not join the Labor Party that was formed as a result of the merger. In 1969 he still headed a small Knesset slate (the State List), but he avoided confrontations with his former colleagues, and a year later he finally resigned from the Knesset and withdrew from public life.

Ben-Gurion spoke little about foreign affairs and plunged into writing history. Although he devoted himself to composing his memoirs, his gaze rarely lingered on current realities. Instead he turned to the distant past, to the works of the early pioneers, to his thoughts and deeds while still a young man in the fields of Sejera, or a hard-working student at Constantinople, the brusque secretary of the Histadrut, and the man leading a reluctant labor movement in a powerful thrust to conquer the Zionist Organization.

Quietly, almost secretly, "the quarrelsome obstreperous man" laid down his arms. He extended his hand to former enemies, erased old hatreds, and healed gaping wounds. He was even on good terms with his old rival Menahem Begin and wrote to him, "My Paula was always an admirer of yours." He befriended Ya'akov Shimson Shapira, who had called him "a coward" and dubbed his supporters "neo-Fascists", and even made him executor of his will. After a number of stormy confrontations, he even made his peace with Golda Meir, though their mutually inflicted wounds had not completely healed. He bore no grudge towards Isser Harel, who, willingly or not, had influenced his resignation in 1963; on the contrary, he was Harel's colleague in the State List election slate and sat beside him in the Knesset during his final year in the legislature. The Old Man even showed moderation toward Lavon.

During his final years at Sdeh Boker, Ben-Gurion was no longer a lion in a cage, no angry prophet, no man of war. He became a genial old man, conciliatory, forgiving, quarreling with no one. He now became the "Father of the Nation", who watched his successors' deeds from his desert oasis, uttering words of encouragement and inspiration, instead of rebukes and criticism. Old age gradually overcame him. He fought it with all his strength, but it was a gloomy, painful, rear-guard action. He suffered repeated forgetfulness, which caused him to confuse names, dates, and events. His physical health began to deteriorate and he required frequent medical care and physiotherapy. During the seventies, he suffered from sharp pains in his right hand, which interfered with his writing and even prevented him from shaking hands. The inevitability of death occupied his thoughts, and he prepared a tomb for himself in front of the Sdeh Boker Academy building, on top of a rock facing the wilderness of Zin. But Paula preceded him. She passed away in January 1968. "I always thought I would die before her," he said sadly, "and suddenly, Paula is dead and gone."

Ben-Gurion's eighty-fifth birthday was celebrated by the whole nation. The Cabinet, headed by Golda Meir, came to Sdeh Boker to visit him, and the Knesset passed a special law to permit the Old Man to address it again. Knesset members from all factions gave a standing ovation to his speech about the future of the people of Israel in its own land. Many noted the frequent mention he made of religion and faith in his address. In the twilight of his days, he was wholeheartedly convinced of the existence of God.

That year, he undertook his last journey, to a conference in Brussels concerning the Jews of the Soviet Union. That year, he ceased his entries in his diary. That year, a fellow-member of Sdeh Boker was overcome by profound sorrow when Ben-Gurion turned to him on one of their daily marches, and said, quietly: "Let's go back." His strength declined, but he lived to experience – at the age of eighty-seven – the bitter events of the Yom Kippur war. Sitting alone in his home in Tel Aviv, his strength was seeping away, but his spirit and faith were as complete and fiery as ever.

Ben-Gurion collapsed a few weeks later with a cerebral haemorrhage, but he did not give in. He had been a man of war all his life, and now, too, he fought back valiantly, right up to his last moment. He lay in the hospital for two weeks, and for much of the time he was fully conscious. The stroke had caused partial paralysis, and he was incapable of speaking. But he would shake hands with his visitors and gaze at them with his wise eyes. There was no despair in his glance, nor helplessness. There was a kind of tranquility about him, but no suggestion or surrender. The whole nation made the analogy between the two entities fighting for their lives in those bitter November days of 1973 – Ben-Gurion and the State of Israel. One of the evening papers wrote:

Even if the people of Israel is overwhelmingly concerned with the Yom Kippur War, with its errors and triumphs, and there is much pain over the boys who have fallen, [the people] cannot overlook the great drama of Ben-Gurion's battle for life. It is hard to avoid the historical parallel between Ben-Gurion and the epoch linked to his name, both of them locked in an epic battle for survival.

Ben-Gurion died on 1 December 1973. He was buried next to his wife at Sdeh Boker. At his request, his funeral was marked by silence, which was more overwhelming than any eulogy. His grave overlooks the immortal landscape of the wilderness of Zin, where three millennia ago David Ben-Gurion's people first made their way out of the desert to Canaan and the struggle of the Jewish people for the Land of Israel first began.

Centenary

Ben-Gurion emerged at the helm of the Zionist movement in June 1942, at the height of the World War, when he convinced the 603 delegates of the American Zionist conference to adopt the Biltmore Program. The program, named after the New York hotel where the conference was held, defined the new goal of Zionism: the immediate establishment of a Jewish state in Palestine.

Officially, that was the first time that statehood was defined as the ultimate goal of the Zionist movement. Of course, there had been other leaders who had tried to hoist that same flag in the past, Chaim Arlosoroff, the great hope of the Labor movement in the thirties, Zeev Jabotinsky, the authoritatian leader of the dissident Revisionists. Chaim Weizmann, on the other hand, was inclined to wait another ten or fifteen years; that was why he mocked and ridiculed the Biltmore Program in letters and articles.

Ben-Gurion's decisive contribution to Israel's independence was primarily in his sense of timing. He was the only one to understand that the World War was a unique opportunity for the creation of a Jewish state. He felt that in times of peace, calm and routine there were only slight chances that the great powers would dare to unsettle the tricky balance in the Middle East by establishing a Jewish state. But in the dramatic reality of the World War, when the entire universe was in flames, when empires were crumbling down and other emerging in their stead, when boundaries were being erased from the maps and others drawn, it was the "now or never" moment for the Jewish people to stake its claim for its own state. "A statesman cannot create", Bismarck had said. "He has only got to lie in wait till he hears the echo of the steps of God; then he should leap and grab the fringe of His mantle." And Ben-Gurion, indeed, grabbed the fringe of God's mantle at that forgotten conference in the Biltmore Hotel, when he declared that a Jewish state should be created immediately after the war.

The establishment of the state of Israel was the foremost achievement of David Ben-Gurion. In the stormy aftermath of the World War he knew how to provide the Zionist movement with the leadership it needed. He was simultaneously the careful statesman, the cool-headed analyst, the charismatic leader and the war chief.

In spite of his attachment to the idea of a greater Eretz Israel, the statesman in Ben-Gurion accepted partition in 1946, understanding that this was the price to be paid for the support of the United States. A detached analysis of the situation in the Middle East made him reject the optimistic reports of the

Hagana experts, who predicted only a limited resistance of local Palestinian bands to the creation of a Jewish state; he foresaw the eruption of a full-scale war with the neighboring Arab states, and drew the conclusions. He took under his personal responsibility the security affairs, dispatched his envoys around the world to buy weapons, and transformed the underground Hagana into the nucleus of a regular army that would be able to repel the Arab invasion.

His charismatic leadership was affirmed during the most despairing months before the proclamation of the state, when many top figures of the Jewish community in Palestine, alarmed by the bloody Arab attacks, wavered in their resolution to proclaim Israel's independence. Inspired by a quasi-messianic faith, Ben-Gurion succeeded in convincing some, imposing his will upon others, and carrying through his decision to proclaim Israel's statehood. And finally he proved to be an outstanding war leader. A 62-year-old man, who had never fought in his life, he nevertheless grasped the strategic issues of the War of Independence much better that his generals, and succeeded in achieving both his goals in the war: check the attack of the Arab armies; and conquer a much larger part of Eretz Israel than that offered the Jews by the United Nations.

The creation of the state was for Ben-Gurion not an end but a beginning. Now, as prime minister, he had to shape the new republic according to his vision and his ideals. His first endeavor was to instill the principle of "Mamlakhtiut" – statehood – into his nation. A nation that had lost its independence two thousand years earlier had to be made to understand that the term " government" didn't mean foreign rule anymore, but her own; the voluntary organizations, as devoted and as efficient as they might be under British rule, had to be replaced by formal bodies controlled by the state. Therefore, while battles were still raging all over Eretz Israel, he disbanded the private armies – the Irgun Zvai Leumi and the Lehi (Stern); with the same reasoning, he dissolved the separate framework of the elite units of the Palmach. He promulgated a series of laws on matters of education, labor, and youth. These initiatives of Ben-Gurion were to make him quite a few enemies; many political leaders found it very difficult to part from the private organizations they or their parties had established, and hand over their domains to the the state.

But "statehood" was for Ben-Gurion only an instrument to fulfill his vision. And his vision was expressed in Ben-Gurions's dramatic, fiery style while the war was still going on. In 1948 he proclaimed the next national goal: double Israel's population in four years, and submerge the country in an unprecedented wave of immigration. He rejected the argument of some of his colleagues that the immigration should be "selective" and that only young and able immigrants should be allowed into the country. Driven by his characteristic sense of urgency, he opened wide the gates of Israel, although he expected that the massive immigration might produce tremendous economic and social difficulties. He didn't stop at that, and confronted the nation with a succession of challenges: the liberation of the homeland; the return of the Exiles; the teaching of the Hebrew language to young and old; the conquest of the desert; the transformation of the Jewish people into a nation of workers and farmers; the shaping of Israel as "a chosen people and light unto the nations."

From his idealistic vision of the State of Israel stemmed Ben Gurion's uncompromising attitude toward world Zionism. Now that the Jewish state has been created, he said, the Zionist movement should follow its own preaching, and every Zionist in the Diaspora should make aliya to Israel. That attitude embarrassed and irritated many Zionist leaders abroad; still, it was the only formula consistent with the principles of true Zionism.

The first years after the creation of the state were hectic and exhausting for Ben-Gurion. He had to lead his nation through the tremendous task of absorbing the new immigrants and building a modern economy; he had to create an army able to confront any Arab coalition; he had to face the world's wrath by establishing Jerusalem as the capital of Israel; he was to reopen many unhealed wounds when he decided to accept hundreds of millions of dollars from Germany as reparations for the plunder of Jewish property by the Nazis.

In foreign policy, Ben-Gurion strived in vain to conclude an alliance with a Western power, in order to counter the military build-up of the Arab states, and secure Israel's defense for the future. But the internal problems exasperated him – petty quarrels with his partners in the government coalition, bitter disagreements within his own party, frequent cabinet crises. Ben-Gurion was a leader for the great, dramatic moments, where his leadership and resolve were needed; he was unable to cope with the tedious day-to-day matters. In 1953 he decided to resign and settle in a new kibbutz in the Negev, Sde Boker. Thus he hoped to revive the golden memories of his youth, when he had been a farm laborer in the Galilee, and by working the land of Israel had fulfilled Zionism in its purest form. He also hoped to make Israel's youth follow him to the desert and settle it. He failed in that goal. His appeal wasn't heard and his call to the young generation to make the Negev bloom remained a voice lost in the desert.

Ben-Gurion was to resume power, first as defense minister and later as prime minister as well. He was to lead his country through the trying years of Arab terrosism and Israeli reprisals, Egyptian rearmament and the Sinai campaign in 1956; he rached the peak of his power during Israel's "golden era" that followed the Sinai campaign. But imperceptibly he was growing old and his iron grip on the affairs of the country was slackening; in matters like the Sinai campaign, the conclusion of secret alliances with France, and later with

Turkey, Iran and Ethiopia, the conception of the nucelar reactor in Dimona, and other enterprises, he delegated a great deal of power to his young aides – Dayan, Peres and others – and contented himself with approving their initiatives and shielding them from his opponents' criticism.

When in 1960 the Lavon affair erupted, Ben-Gurion's weakness was suddenly exposed. He didn't manage to cope with the crisis that shook his own party, and resigned in 1963. In his diary he predicted the ascension to power of Menahem Begin, who, he feared, "would destroy the state by his political adventures."

The twilight years of Ben-Gurion's reign and the last ten years of his life are the years of his decline. When we speak about Ben-Gurion we should bear in mind his "heroic era" that started in the early forties and ended in the mid-fifties. As a man, he set standards of national leadership and outstanding statesmanship. Yet, as he excelled in his great endeavors, he also knew bitter failures. He did not succeed in settling the Negev; he didn't complete shaping the Israeli society; he didn't reduce the bitter rivalry and hatred between different poitical currents.

Ben-Gurion was a tempestuous man, a war horse; the same energy and fervor that enabled him to confront the fateful problems of the nation would turn in his hands into destructive weapons with which he would smash rivals and enemies. He could be a formidable political foe, and left many wounds that never healed. Yet, he also was sensitive and humane; he couldn't bear the grief for the lives lost in the wars of Israel. He delved into matters of the mind and spirit, and was the only leader of Israel till today who firmly believed in establishing a permanent dialogue between the intellectual and political spheres. He often met with writers, philosophers, university dons, and asked their advice. He maintained a continuous correspondence with thinkers, religious leaders, historians from all over the world.

In this unquenchable quest for knowledge, he plunged into the treasures of the world's literature, studied foreign languages, religious concepts ad moral treaties. He seemed to emulate Plato's philosopher statesman. The note scribbled by John F. Kennedy, a few hours before his death in Dallas, could be inspired by Ben-Gurion: "Leadership and learning are indispensable to each other.".

That was David Ben-Gurion. His close friend Berl Katzenelson called him "the great gift of history to the Jewish people". These were true words; but Ben-Gurion himself was awarded history's greatest gift. More than any leader in the modern world, more than Washington, Ataturk, Bolivar, de Valera, and Gandhi, Ben Gurion lived to become the father of a nation. He took the children of Israel out of Egypt like Moses, conquered the Promised Land like Joshua, and like David built the Kingdom of Israel.

★ ★ ★

"Ben-Gurion", I asked him on the twenty-fifth anniversary of the state of Israel, a few months before his death. "Is this the state of Israel you dreamt about?"

He looked at me, his eyes grave, thoughtful.

"The state of Israel hasn't been created yet", he finally said. "All we've done till now is laying the foundations and establishing frameworks, rules, formal procedures. But the state itself will be shaped and formed only in ten, twenty years, perhaps more."

Thirteen years after he spoke those words, and a hundred years after Ben-Gurion's birth, it clearly appears that the state of Israel, in its present phase, is not the one Ben-Gurion envisioned and struggled for.

True, in the 38 years of its existence Israel has realized incredible achievements. Most of the inspiring challenges Ben-Gurion placed before the young nation have been successfully met. The creation of the Israeli army, the victory in the Independence War, the mass immigration and its absorption, the return to the land, the teaching of the Hebrew language, the free education, the industrialization of the country, the swift development of science and the academy – all those join together to project a dramatic image of the Jewish people's revival in its homeland. Israel's victories in her wars after Ben-Gurion's retirement and death, as well as the peace treaty with Egypt and the budding rapprochement with some moderate Arab states also suit the pattern of Ben-Gurion's vision.

All these achievements, however, aren't but the first step in the establishment of the state, as seen by Ben-Gurion. They belong to the stage he qualified as the laying of the foundations and the creation of the frameworks of the new nation. Most of Israel's achievements up to the present times guarantee her physical existence and her survival. The state of Israel, born in doubt and uncertainty, is here to stay. But the framework still waits to be filled with that unique contents of Jewish and universal moral values, that will make Israel "a light unto the nations", and a model society. That uniqueness was in Ben-Gurion's eyes the very condition for Israel's survival.

Israel has come into existence. But its existence hasn't been assured yet.

"The fate of Israel depends on two things", Ben-Gurion once said. "On her strength and on her righteousness".

Out of those two goals, Ben-Gurion concentrated mostly in achieving the first. He regarded as his most urgent and vital purpose the creation of a strong army that would guarantee Israel's security. During Israel's early years many doubted she would be able to match the combined strength of her hostile Arab neighbors. Ben-Gurion, too, shared these fears; that was why he launched a preventive war against Egypt in 1956, sought an alliance with a foreign power, and made tremendous efforts to equip Israel with non-conventional deterrent weapons.

The Old Man's efforts were fruitful. The danger of annihilation that threatened Israel in her first years is no more. Thanks to her strength Israel would survive, even if she were attacked by all the Arab states.

But would that be Israel that Ben-Gurion dreamt about?

The answer to that question depends on the achievement of the second goal that Ben-Gurion formulated, beside her strength: her "righteousness".

Israel, Ben-Gurion thought, would survive only if she succeeded to establish a just and moral society. He kept touring the country, preaching about the necessity for Israel to become "a chosen people and a light unto the nations". Most of his listeners dismissed his fiery discourses with a forgiving smile. The Old Man was again reciting his flowery cliches, they said.

They were wrong. The vision of "a chosen people and a light unto the nations" was a goal that Ben-Gurion had set up before his people after a lucid and candid analysis of his condition. The Promised Land where he had led his people was far from being a land of milk and honey. A faraway, desertic land it was, surrounded by enemies; nature had given it no bounty, no gold and mines and oil; its small, isolated society, the economic hardships, the constant security tensions, generated tremendous pressures on its inhabitants. The Jewish people, that centuries of humiliation and need had taught to frequently migrate and set sail for new horizons, could easily be tempted to abandon the harsh Israeli reality and depart toward the glittering, prosperous cities of America and Western Europe.

Ben-Gurion knew that Israel wouldn't be able to offer her citizens neither the standard of living nor the feeling of serenity and calm that prevailed in the West. There was a one and only means to attach the people to its land for good: the feeling that Israel is the only place in the world where the Jewish people could live a life based on superior humane and moral values. The life of a chosen people and a light unto the nations. A life based on the "righteousness" of the Israeli society,that together with its "strength" would guarantee the state's future.

According to the vision of Ben-Gurion, only a just society and a unique way of life could guarantee the long term survival of Israel. The intoxicating feeling of building a homeland, molding a better society instilled with Jewish values – that feeling was the only defense against the temptation of the fleshpots across the seas. That also was the only means to attract to Israel idealistic Jewish youths seeking new challenges, yearning to participate in an heroic enterprise of building a new country.

That was Ben-Gurion's dream. But it still is a dream.

Ben-Gurion showed the way and made the first steps. Not all his initiatives, however,were crowned with success. The essence of his Zionist faith was "aliya" – immigration to Israel. He dreamt of gathering in Israel the great majority of the Jewish people. But the Jews of the West deceived him, and most ot them preferred to remain in the Diaspora. Ben-Gurion predicted the exodus of Jews from the Soviet Union, but didn't expect that most of them would turn their backs to Israel and emigrate to America. The drying of the immigration is a cruel verdict for Israel: she is sentenced to remain a small nation forever.

Israel failed to reach some other goals, whose successful realization was vital to the achievement of the just society Ben-Gurion envisioned. The educational system, that was originally meant to infuse values of Zionism and pioneering into the young generation, turned to be a deception; the gap between children of Western and Oriental origin hasn't disappeared yet, and has become a cause of deep frustration for many Sephardic Jews. The young Israeli democracy is also in danger. The very establishment of a democratic regime in Israel was a miracle by itself, considering that half of the population has immigrated from Eastern Europe, which was always under totalitarian regime, and the other half came from the Arab and Muslim countries which were governed by absolute rulers. Nevertheless, Israel developed into the only democracy in the Middle East; but its ailing electoral system, based on proportional representation has broken its political leadership into a score of uneven fragments. The establishment of a coalition in Israel today becomes a Sisyphean task, involving despicable bargaining between political parties, cynical blackmail by politicians controlling a few coveted votes in the Knesset, and a permanent governmental instability. Those ugly political habits have tarnished the image of democracy in the eyes of a large section of the population and stirred it toward authoritarian, right-wing political parties, and in the extreme cases – toward the racist mobs of Rabbi Kahana.

The budding racism and intolerance toward the Arabs, together with the polarization in the Israeli society, point at a slackening of the common values and ideals that have held together the Israeli society in the past. Israel today is plagued by confrontations between liberals and conservatives, secular and pious Jews, annexionists and fanatics of peace at all costs; Israel isn't a pioneering society anymore, and the Lebanon War has proved that even in its most sacred domain – security – she isn't immune from tragic errors. The young Israelis are no more called to meet dramatic challenges, and their parents look back with nostalgia at the heroic years, when Ben-Gurion led the nation into an inspiring struggle for a unique Israel.

And so we're bound to reach the inevitable conclusion, that Ben-Gurion was his own worst enemy. He built a State in his own image, fitting his own measures; he established institutions, customs and a scale of values suiting his own vision and his strong, charismatic personality. But after he stepped down, his heirs were unable to maintain the same spirit of challenge and dedication that Ben-Gurion knew how to convey to his people. The major condition for the fullfillment of Ben-Gurion's vision was that a Ben-Gurion had to be at the helm. And when he was no more, the new leaders of Israel couldn't stand up to the challenge of steering the country through its turbulent adolescence.

Ben-Gurion was conscious of the tremendous importance of paving the way for a young generation of determined and inspired leaders. When he was in power, he often promoted young and talented men over the heads of his oldtime companions, whose force was waning. During the late fifties and the early sixties he selected a group of rising politicians, whom he regarded as his worthy successors: Moshe Dayan, Shimon Peres, Abba Eban, Itzhak Navon, Teddy Kollek and others. He treated Itzhak Rabin with genuine warmth and held Yigael Yadin and Igal Allon in high esteem.

Most of those young leaders were talented people indeed, and their qualifications had been tested in war and peace. But the long years they had spent in the shade of Ben-Gurion turned into a severe handicap for them. Life in the shade of a strong and charismatic man like Ben-Gurion has a devastating effect on the determination and self-confidence of a young leader. The younger man is free to conceive ideas, to plan operations, to execute them; but he isn't allowed to decide, for the decisions are always taken by the older, stronger man. The young men whom Ben-Gurion promoted grew up under his protection. Every decision they took had to be approved by him. When they were in their forties, even in their early fifties, they still stood before him like children, waiting for their father's approval. This reality badly damaged their decisiveness and their willingness to take unpopular steps, and confront the public opinion. They were unable to emulate Ben-Gurions's way of defying criticism and disregarding the current trends in the nation's mood. "I don't know what the nation wants", he once threw at his critics. "I know what the nation needs!"

This attitude was characteristic of Israel's founding fathers, but not of their successors. The present leaders of Israel lack the firm, confident stance of their predecessors, and seem reluctant to undertake the radical reforms without which Israel cannot become a better society. Israel will overcome its present crisis only when the present leadership hands the torch to a younger generation of Israelis. Not a generation that has emerged from the giant shadows of the founding fathers, but a new leadership that has blazed its trail by its own power and dedication. These are the young Israelis, who have grown up in this country, and are deeply rooted in its complex reality. Only when this new generation accedes to power, will Ben-Gurion's vision of "a chosen people and a light unto the nations" come back to life. Only then will Israel become a pole of attraction to young diaspora Jews sharing the dream that burned in the heart of young David Gruen at the dawn of this century, when he set to the Land of Israel, to found a state for his people.

Index